TOURISM IN THE GREEN ECONOMY

The concept of the green economy has now entered mainstream policy debates and been endorsed by a range of United Nations and other organizations. The Rio+20 UN conference specifically drew attention to the green economy approach in the context of sustainable development to move away from business-as-usual practices, act to end poverty, address environmental destruction and build a bridge to the sustainable future. It is increasingly recognized that the tourism sector can make a major contribution to the green economy through more sustainable practices, climate change mitigation and ecotourism. The role of the tourism sector will continue to be crucial in the post-2015 sustainable development agenda too. However, there are ambiguities about how tourism and allied industries can maximize their contribution to human well-being and ensure environmental sustainability, embracing issues of political economy, geography and business ethics.

In this context, this book provides consensus about what the green economy entails, what role tourism can play in a green economy, early responses from many countries, and ongoing and emerging research initiatives that will enable tourism's transition to a green economy. The chapters address three key themes: understanding the green economy concept and the role of tourism; responses and initiatives in greening tourism; and emerging techniques and research implications. A wide range of case studies from around the world and in different contexts is included to demonstrate the extent of the challenge and range of opportunities for the tourism industry.

Maharaj Vijay Reddy is the Deputy Head of Department for Marketing, Enterprise and Tourism within the Lord Ashcroft International Business School at Anglia Ruskin University, UK.

Keith Wilkes is the Executive Dean of the Faculty of Management, Bournemouth University, UK.

'This publication offers an objective assessment of the challenges faced by green economy and their application to the tourism sector, as well as opportunities for promoting a global and local sustainable tourism through resource efficiency, green jobs and sustainable consumption and production patterns. Tourism stakeholders will find inspiration in this book, from its multiple case studies, in defining and promoting methods and tools for implementing sustainable tourism while valuing local resources and educating the tourist community.'

Arab Hoballah, Chief of the Sustainable Consumption and Production Branch, UNEP

'We welcome this publication which covers the topic of tourism, and in particular the aspect of sustainable tourism, with the aim of providing useful insights on how tourism could adapt to green economy, and how to make tourism more sustainable.'

Francesca Tudini, Head of Tourism Policy Unit, European Commission

'This publication brings new insights into the need to green the rapidly growing tourism industry. The case studies show the challenges and opportunities common to both developed and developing countries, echoing UNESCO's efforts to build inclusive green societies and sustainable tourism through Biosphere Reserves, World Heritage (including marine) sites and Geoparks.'

Wendy Watson-Wright, Executive Secretary, Intergovernmental Oceanographic Commission and Assistant Director General a.i., Natural Sciences, UNESCO

TOURISM IN THE GREEN ECONOMY

Edited by Maharaj Vijay Reddy and Keith Wilkes

Routledge
Taylor & Francis Group

LONDON AND NEW YORK

earthscan
from Routledge

First published 2015
by Routledge
2 Park Square, Milton Park, Abingdon, Oxon OX14 4RN

and by Routledge
711 Third Avenue, New York, NY 10017

First issued in paperback 2017

Routledge is an imprint of the Taylor & Francis Group, an informa business

British Library Cataloguing-in-Publication Data
A catalogue record for this book is available from the British Library

Library of Congress Cataloging in Publication Data
Tourism in the green economy/edited by Maharaj Vijay Reddy and Keith Wilkes.
  pages cm
  Includes bibliographical references and index.
  1. Sustainable tourism. 2. Sustainable tourism – Economic aspects.
  I. Reddy, Maharaj Vijay, 1977– editor of compilation.
  II. Wilkes, Keith, 1951– editor of compilation.
  G156.5.S87T647 2015
  338.4'791 – dc23
  2014041825

ISBN 13: 978–1–138–09563–2 (pbk)
ISBN 13: 978–0–415–70921–7 (hbk)

Typeset in Bembo and Stone Sans
by Florence Production Ltd, Stoodleigh, Devon, UK

'The earth provides enough to satisfy every man's needs, but not for every man's greed.'

Mohandas Gandhi

CONTENTS

LIST OF CONTRIBUTORS

Sheela Agarwal is Professor in Tourism Management at the School of Tourism and Hospitality, Faculty of Business School, University of Plymouth in the UK. She is Deputy Head of the School of Tourism and Hospitality and Director of the Services and Enterprise Research Centre. She has written and co-authored numerous journal articles and book chapters and co-edited a book relating to various economic, social and environmental aspects of coastal/seaside resort tourism including the impact and consequences of globalization, economic restructuring, deprivation, social exclusion and climate change. Her research interests include discourses of globalization, sustainability and climate mitigation and adaptation strategies, economic restructuring, conceptualizations of place and space, local governance, disability, deprivation and social exclusion.

Dzintra Atstaja is Professor at the BA School of Business and Finance, Latvia. She is a scientific expert in Management Sciences of the Latvian Council of Science and an expert of the IFO Institute for Economic Research in Munich through regular Latvian macroeconomic expertise. Dzintra Atstaja is one of the founders of the Latvian Economic Association, a member of the social network SMART civil society organizations, Society Association of Latvian Professors, Green Economics Institute, and was a member of the European Society for the History of Economic Thought (2006–2011). Prof. Atstaja specializes in economics and sustainability, green entrepreneurship, business control systems and management, civil defence and work safety.

Rosemary Black teaches and undertakes research in sustainable tourism, tour guiding, heritage interpretation, sustainable behaviours and adventure tourism. Prior to joining Charles Sturt University, Australia, she worked in protected area management, adventure travel and community conservation. She has worked in academia for the past 17 years and published four books and more than thirty-five refereed publications. She has attracted $500,000 of research and consulting funding. Rosemary undertakes applied research with industry partners including protected area management and tourism agencies and community-based organizations.

Gilson Zehetmeyer Borda is Professor and Researcher at the Centre for Excellence in Tourism (CET) – University of Brasília, Brazil. He has a PhD in Economic Sociology, researches at the Laboratory for Tourism and Sustainability Studies (LETS) and is currently a postdoctoral researcher at the Centre for Sustainable Development (CDS) of the University of Brasilia. His research interests include the green economy, climate change, social sustainability, trust, planning and management of tourism destinations. He has led and participated in several Brazilian and international sustainable tourism development projects.

Jeremy Buultjens works in the Business School at Southern Cross University, Australia. He is also the Managing Editor of the *Journal of Economic and Social Policy*. He has taught in a number of units ranging from Economics and Industrial Relations through to Tourism Planning and Indigenous Tourism. Jeremy's research interests include indigenous entrepreneurship, regional development and tourism, and tourism in protected areas.

Corazon Catibog-Sinha completed her BS and MS degrees from the University of the Philippines and her PhD from Oklahoma State University, USA. Before joining the University of Western Sydney, Australia, as a Senior Lecturer in Sustainable Tourism Management, she served as the Director of the Protected Areas and Wildlife Bureau of the Philippine Department of the Environment and Natural Resources. She was on the Executive Committee of the Species Survival Commission of the International Union for the Conservation of Nature (IUCN) for 10 years (1996–2004). She is also a member of the IUCN World Commission for Protected Areas. She is currently a freelance consultant in the field of environmental management, sustainable tourism, and biodiversity conservation.

Jennifer Kim Lian Chan is Associate Professor and has a PhD in Tourism and Hospitality Management from the University of Strathclyde, Scotland, and is a tourism lecturer at the Faculty of Business, Economics and Accounting. She is also the Deputy Director for the Centre for Strategic and Academic Management of Universiti Malaysia Sabah, Malaysia and a national panel auditor appointed by the Malaysian Qualifications Agency. Her research interest areas include nature tourism management/ecotourism, consumer behaviour in tourism and hospitality, small and medium-sized accommodation. Her recent research work includes sustainable responsible tourism, developing sustainable tourism human resources, tourist behaviour in low-cost airlines, operating small and medium-sized accommodation, nature quality tourism in Sabah, and marketing and positioning Sabah as a tourist destination.

Jaeyeon Choe holds her PhD in Tourism Management (Cultural Anthropology) from Pennsylvania State University, USA, completing a dissertation in 2012 on Buddhist meditation as a stress-coping strategy among Americans. Her primary research areas are quality of life and tourism, and (secular) religious tourism and pilgrimage. She has published her research work in many journals and has presented her papers at several international conferences in the United States, Ireland, Italy, Spain and Malaysia.

Patrick Brandful Cobbinah is a PhD student with the School of Environmental Sciences, Charles Sturt University, Albury, Australia. He holds a BSc (honours) in Human Settlement Planning from the Kwame Nkrumah University of Science and Technology, Kumasi, Ghana. He is a member of the Institute for Land, Water and Society, Charles Sturt University, Australia. His research interests include tourism and poverty reduction, and sustainable urban and regional planning and policy. Cobbinah has published in many international and regional journals.

Colin Crawford is the Robert C. Cudd Professor of Environmental Law at Tulane University Law School in New Orleans, USA, where he also serves as Executive Director of the Payson Center for International Development. His work concentrates on comparative environmental and land use law and policy in the Americas, with a special focus on the social implications of environmental and land use choices.

Pavlo Doan is a postgraduate student at the Tourism Department within the Geography Faculty of the Taras Shevchenko National University of Kyiv, Ukraine. He currently also works as an assistant lecturer, and his teaching areas are Research Methods in Tourism and Tourism Management. His research interests include human geography, tourism and recreation, tourism politics, geoglobalistics, the green economy, green tourism and sustainable development. Pavlo Doan is the author and co-author of several published works, including textbooks. Besides his academic work, he is commercial director of a tourist company.

Athula Gnanapala is Senior Lecturer and HOD in the Department of Tourism Management, Sabaragamuwa University of Sri Lanka. His research interests include consumer behaviour in tourism including motivation and satisfaction, sustainable tourism planning and development, tourism and green marketing. Dr Athula Gnanapala has published scholarly papers and research reports on a variety of tourism issues. He completed his PhD in Tourism Management at the Xiamen University, People's Republic of China.

Amelia Green is currently a doctoral candidate in marketing in the Griffith Business School, Australia. Her research interests include fashion and sustainability, and fashion and city branding. She has a particular interest in the contribution of exhibitions such as the Great Exhibition (1851) and various Paris Expositions to city branding.

C. Michael Hall is Professor in the Department of Management, Marketing and Entrepreneurship, University of Canterbury, New Zealand; Docent, Department of Geography, University of Oulu, Finland; Visiting Professor, Linnaeus University, Kalmar, Sweden; and Senior Research Fellow, School of Tourism & Hospitality, University of Johannesburg. He is co-editor of *Current Issues in Tourism*, and has published widely on tourism, environmental history, environmental change and gastronomy. Current research includes second-home tourism in Morocco and Finland, green hotels and gastronomy in Freiburg, and the application of rebound theory to the analysis of tourism and mobility.

Andrew Holden is Professor of Environment and Tourism and also the Director for the Institute for Tourism Research (INTOUR) at the University of Bedfordshire, UK. He is a Fellow of the Royal Geographical Society in London. His research focuses on the interaction between human behaviour and the natural environment within the context of tourism. He has written several academic texts including *Environment and Tourism*, and *Tourism, Poverty and Development* published by Routledge.

Victoria Hurth is Lecturer in Marketing at Plymouth University, UK. Her research is in the areas of sustainable marketing, identity, philanthropy and behaviour change. Victoria has over 10 years of experience consulting in marketing and sustainability, having previously worked for Accenture and with companies such as Marks and Spencer, Cancer Research, and J. Sainsbury. Victoria has been engaged by organizations such as The British Council, British Standards Institute, the ISO and LEAD International and is also active locally, being a board member of the Plymouth Climate Change Commission and the Plymouth Social Enterprise Network.

Tazim Jamal is Associate Professor in the Department of Recreation, Park and Tourism Sciences, Texas A&M University, USA, and an Adjunct Associate Professor at the Institute for Tourism, Griffith University, Australia. Her primary research areas are in sustainable tourism development and management, collaborative tourism planning and cultural heritage management. She also examines climate change issues related to residents and visitors in tourism destinations. She has published extensively on these topics in various journals and edited books. She is the co-editor of *The SAGE Handbook of Tourism Studies* (2009), and is on the editorial board of several academic journals.

Fu Jia has been working as a consultant with the United Nations Division for Sustainable Development and is an independent researcher on subject matters of sustainable transport, electric mobility and tourism, with electronic publications available at the UNDSD website. Travel, tourism industry, cultures, design and communications are her lifelong interests. She obtained her MA in Applied Linguistics from Beijing Foreign Studies University, China. She is currently based in Beijing.

Viktoriya Kiptenko is a docent of the Taras Shevchenko National University of Kyiv, Ukraine, based at the Department of Tourism and Regional Geography, Faculty of Geography. She is Associate Professor and her main teaching areas are research methods in tourism, tourism management, tourism policy and spatial planning for tourism, theory of regional geography and geoglobalistics. Viktoriya is the author and co-author of over seventy published works, including textbooks. Before her academic positions, she used to work as a manager and tour guide at Intourbureau, Kyiv, Ukraine.

Adele Ladkin is Professor of Tourism Employment in the School of Tourism, Bournemouth University, UK. She was previously Associate Dean in the School of Hotel and Tourism Management, Hong Kong Polytechnic University. She gained her PhD at the University of Surrey, UK. Her research interests and publications are in tourism employment and education, human resources management and labour migration and mobility. She was joint Editor-in-Chief for the *International Journal of*

Tourism Research 2003–2009, and serves on the editorial boards of a number of journals, including *Annals of Tourism Research, Tourism Economics*, and *The International Journal of Contemporary Hospitality Management.*

Agita Livina is Associate Professor in the Faculty of Tourism and Hospitality Management at the Vidzeme University of Applied Sciences, and Director of the Economic, Social and Humanities Research Institute in Latvia. She is also a scientific expert in Management and Economics Sciences of the Latvian Council of Science. Agita Livina is a member of the Latvian Economic Association. Her research interests are tourism planning, protected areas, sustainable development, dark tourism and regional planning. She was a Fulbright scholar on research in 2012 at the University at Buffalo, The State University of New York. She has held a PhD in economics since 2005.

Lena-Marie Lun is a Researcher at the Institute for Regional Development and Location Management at the European Academy of Bozen–Bolzano (EURAC research), Italy. Her research interests include rural tourism development and sustainability in tourism.

Everson Cristiano de Abreu Meireles is a PhD student in Psychology (Psychological Evaluation) at the University of Saint Francis, São Paulo State, Brazil. She holds a Masters degree and Bachelors in Psychology from the University of Brasilia. She is also an Assistant Professor and Researcher of the Federal University of the South of Bahia (UFRB).

Bill Merrilees is currently Professor of Marketing in the Griffith Business School, Australia. His research interests encompass branding (including corporate rebranding and brand morphing) and innovation in various contexts including firms, cities, communities, retailing, and franchising. He has published papers on the green or sustainability mode, in the fields of business events and retailing. His research has been published internationally including in the *European Journal of Marketing, Journal of Business Research, Industrial Marketing Management* and *Journal of Strategic Marketing.*

Dale Miller is currently Senior Lecturer in Marketing in the Griffith Business School, Australia. Dr Miller's research spans various branding domains including corporate rebranding, corporate branding, cities, communities, retailing, and not-for-profit branding and sustainable business. As a Visiting Researcher in Canada, she has investigated green festivals and events. She has published widely, including in the *Journal of Business Research, European Journal of Marketing, Long Range Planning, Journal of Retailing and Consumer Services, Journal of Brand Management* and *Journal of Historical Research in Marketing.*

Elimar Pinheiro do Nascimento is a Sociologist, Political Scientist, Associate Professor and ex-Director of the Centre of Sustainable Development at the University of Brasilia, Brazil. He is a coordinator of research lines on sustainability and tourism, and economy, environment and business. He is the coordinator of the Laboratory for Tourism and Sustainability Studies (LETS). He has a degree in sociology from the Ecole Praticque des Hautes Etudes, a PhD in sociology from the Université of Paris V (René Descartes), and a postdoctoral qualification in social sciences from EHESS – the Ecole des Hautes

Etudes en Sciences Sociales of Paris. He was a professor at Maputo's Universities (Moçambique) and at the Federal Universities of Paraíba and Pernambuco, Brazil.

Adrian C. Newton is Professor in Conservation Science and Director of the Green Economy MSc at the Bournemouth University, UK. He has coordinated a number of international, collaborative research projects, principally in Latin America, but also in East and West Africa, Central and SE Asia, and in the UK. His recent research activities have included analysis of the impacts of ecological restoration on biodiversity and provision of ecosystem services, human impacts on forest biodiversity, and the effectiveness of protected areas in reducing biodiversity loss. Professor Newton has produced over 150 research publications on conservation science and management, including books on biodiversity loss and conservation, forest ecology and tropical forest resources. He has also supervised more than thirty PhD and MPhil students.

Michael O'Regan worked alongside the National Tourism Development Authority of Ireland before joining Gulliver after completing his Masters at the University of Limerick, Ireland. He then joined Wicklow County Tourism as Marketing Executive before starting a PhD programme at the School of Sport and Service Management, University of Brighton, UK, which he completed in 2011. He is now Assistant Professor at the Institute for Tourism Studies, Macao.

Harald Pechlaner holds a Chair in Tourism at the Catholic University of Eichstaett-Ingolstadt, Germany, and is scientific director of the Institute for Regional Development and Location Management at the European Academy of Bozen-Bolzano (EURAC research) (Italy). He earned a Doctorate in Social and Economic Sciences at the University of Innsbruck, Australia. He is a board member of the Association Internationale d'Experts Scientifiques du Tourisme (AIEST).

Bruce Prideaux holds the position of Professor of Marketing and Tourism Management at the Cairns campus of James Cook University, Australia. He is actively engaged in climatic change research with a particular interest in its impacts on coral reef systems and rainforests. Other active areas of research include tourism in agricultural areas, city tourism, military heritage, tourism transport, tourism aviation, crisis management, heritage and ecotourism. His current book project focuses on rainforest tourism from a global perspective. He has authored over 250 journal articles, book chapters and conference papers on a range of tourism related issues.

Iraj Ratnayake, PhD (Utara Malaysia) is currently attached to the Department of Tourism Management, Sabaragamuwa University of Sri Lanka, as a Senior Lecturer. He has served as the founder Head of the Department of Tourism Management. Dr Ratnayake has also contributed as a member of editorial boards and is active in reviewing manuscripts for a number of national and international journals. His research and literary presentations mainly encompass development and promotion of special interest tourism and tourism planning in developing countries. He also participates actively in training, and consultation projects include tourism information systems, site planning, visitor management, product marketing, and community tourism.

Maharaj Vijay Reddy is Principal Lecturer in Marketing and the Deputy Head of Department for Marketing, Enterprise and Tourism within the Lord Ashcroft International Business School at Anglia Ruskin University, UK. Previously, he worked as a Lecturer, Senior Lecturer and Principal Lecturer in the Faculty of Management at Bournemouth University, UK. His expertise areas are in the fields of sustainable consumption and production patterns, green strategy, biospheres, blue economy and tsunamis. Vijay gained a PhD from the University of Exeter, UK. He has completed projects commissioned by international and national agencies, for example, research exploring disaster impacts following the 2004 Asian and 2011 Japanese tsunamis. His consultancies for UNESCO resulted in the inscription of natural and cultural properties on the UNESCO List. He has been invited by policy organizations including UN Secretariat, UNEP, UNWTO and the Intergovernmental Oceanic Commission to comment on sustainability issues.

Hana Sakata is a PhD candidate at the University of Technology, Sydney, Australia, and is investigating project management of community-based ecotourism in developing countries. She has a degree in natural science and a Masters in tourism management. Her research interests are community-based tourism, community-based natural resource management and community development.

Gunjan Saxena holds a PhD from Staffordshire University, UK (2002) in tourism marketing and is currently a senior lecturer (marketing) at the University of Hull (Business School), where she has been working since 2004. She has previously published on integrated rural tourism in international refereed journals. She is now developing her research on the topic from a marketing perspective for her monograph (to be published by Edward Elgar) entitled *Marketing Rural Tourism: Experience and Enterprise.*

Susan L. Slocum is Assistant Professor at George Mason University, USA, in the Department of Tourism and Event Management. She has worked in the area of regional planning and development for 15 years with a primary focus on rural sustainable development and policy implementation, specifically working with small businesses and communities in less advantaged areas. She has specialized in building local development plans around food and tourism partnership in Great Britain, the United States and Tanzania.

Jared Sternberg is a Human Rights and Environmental Law Specialist, Photographer, Pioneer, and Founder of Gondwana Ecotours. In his work and travels he has researched in Ghana, Nicaragua, Spain, Brazil, Cuba, and Panama among many others, and has lived with indigenous communities in the Amazon Basin in Ecuador. Through Gondwana Ecotours (www.GondwanaEcotours.com) Jared is providing opportunities for travel that are both enriching and enjoyable for travellers while also supporting and respecting local environments and communities. Jared has a Juris Doctor from Tulane University Law School and a Bachelors in International Studies and Spanish Literature from UCSD.

Edith M. Szivas is Director of SeaStar Consultancy, United Arab Emirates. Prior to this she was Director of the PhD Programme and Programme Leader of Tourism MSc

Programmes at the University of Surrey, UK, and Director of Research and Consultancy at The Emirates Academy of Hospitality Management, Dubai. She gained her PhD at the University of Surrey, UK. She is a tourism development specialist with over 20 years of international experience in sustainable tourism development and planning, tourism labour market planning and tourism education development. She has worked with a number of clients globally including the UNWTO.

João Paulo Faria Tasso is a PhD researcher at the School of Community Resources and Development (SCRD – Arizona State University, USA) and holds a Masters degree in Sustainable Development from the Centre for Sustainable Development (CDS – University of Brasilia, Brazil). He has a Bachelors in Tourism (UNESP) and is a researcher at the Laboratory for Tourism and Sustainability Studies (LETS). He has experience in several tourism development projects.

Nisarat Thaithong holds an MBA in Hospitality Marketing from Les Roches School of Hotel Management, Switzerland (2008) and is Lecturer at the International School of Tourism, Surat Thani Rajabhat University, Thailand where she has been a faculty member since 2010. Currently, she is a PhD candidate at the University of Hull (Business School), UK focusing on (un)sustainable tourism practices in Samui Island, Thailand.

Michelle Thompson is a PhD candidate at James Cook University in Cairns, Queensland, investigating the development of agri-tourism in regional areas of Australia. Michelle's research interests are agri-tourism, and food and wine tourism. Michelle also works at James Cook University as a research assistant, and has been involved in a number of projects monitoring tourism trends in the Tropical North Queensland tourism region. Most recently, she has been involved in a federally funded research project through the National Environmental Research Program (NERP) investigating tourists' travel motivations and experiences, with an emphasis on the region's iconic reef and rainforest experiences.

Rik Thwaites is a Human Geographer in the School of Environmental Sciences at Charles Sturt University, Australia. He has taught across the fields of ecotourism, sustainable development and environmental management, community development, recreation and land use planning, and social research methods. His research interests focus largely around the nexus of community development and environmental management and conservation, as well as the implications of global environmental policies for local communities in less developed countries.

Dimitrios Tsagdis holds a PhD from Lincoln University, UK (2001) and is Senior Lecturer and Programme Leader for the BA in International Business at Hull University Business School, UK, where he has been a faculty member since 2003. He has held several visiting professorships, and his work is published in top international journals such as *Environment and Planning A*, *Regional Studies*, *Cambridge Journal of Economics*, *Entrepreneurship and Regional Development*, *Industrial Marketing Management*, and the *International Journal of Hospitality Management*. His research interests evolve around firm internationalization, clusters, policy and multi-level governance. He is keen to hear from PhDs in these areas.

Michael Volgger is a Researcher at the Institute for Regional Development and Location Management at the European Academy of Bozen-Bolzano (EURAC research), Italy, and a doctoral student at the Catholic University of Eichstaett-Ingolstadt (Germany). His main fields of research are destination governance, cooperation and innovation in tourism.

Ralph Wahnschafft is Independent Senior Advisor on Sustainability Policies associated with the Division for Sustainable Development, United Nations Department of Economic and Social Affairs (UNDESA), and the Global Forum on Human Settlements (GFHS), New York. He has worked with the United Nations for more than 25 years in various duty stations, including in Africa (Lesotho, South Africa), the Middle East (Baghdad, Iraq), South-east Asia (Bangkok, Thailand), and at the UN Headquarters in New York (2003–2013). Dr Wahnschafft has initiated a considerable number of technical cooperation and technical assistance projects in developing countries, in particular in Asia. He holds a Doctorate from the University of Goettingen, Germany. He was a leading team member in servicing the Rio+20 UN Conference.

Rachel Welton is Senior Lecturer in Tourism and International Marketing at Nottingham Trent University, UK. Rachel's early career in the hospitality and tourism industry led her into the education sector, teaching tourism, international business and hospitality in the HE sector. With an ongoing interest in environmental issues, the combination of climate change and tourism was a natural area of research, hence her PhD in Coastal Tourism. Specifically this researched the response of Indian Ocean island tourism destinations to climate change. Rachel has been involved in a number of research projects, including conducting research for the EU exploring the role and spatial effects of cultural heritage, and she has provided consultancy support to local organizations, particularly in the area of ecotourism.

Emma Whittlesea is Associate Lecturer and Researcher at Plymouth University, UK and is completing a PhD that investigates the challenges and opportunities for a low carbon tourism economy in the South West of England. Her research interests are in the field of sustainable tourism with a particular focus on the inter-relationships between tourism and climate change. Emma was the former Sustainability Strategist for South West Tourism and has over 14 years' experience working in environmental and sustainability roles for the public, private and voluntary sectors, nationally and internationally.

Keith Wilkes is Executive Dean of Bournemouth University's Faculty of Management, UK, one of the world's leading centres for tourism research and education. Keith was a UK Quality Assurance Agency (QAA) Subject Specialist Reviewer and a long-standing member of the Association for Tourism in Higher Education (ATHE) Executive Committee. His research focuses on sustainable tourism development, visitor attractions, heritage management and tourism education. He has played a significant role in developing tourism education in the UK.

FOREWORD

Tourism and the green economy are intrinsically linked. As one of the world's fastest-growing industries and an important source of foreign exchange and employment for many developing countries, tourism has the potential to significantly contribute to sustainable development at the national, regional and global levels. However, tourism is also a sector that depends on the natural environment, the health and viability of which is essential to sustain the foundation for tourism activities in the longer term.

The United Nations Conference on Sustainable Development (Rio+20), held in June 2012, emphasized in its outcome document, *The Future We Want*, that 'sustainable tourism, well managed and designed, can make significant contributions to sustainable development'. This includes the promotion of sustainable patterns of consumption and production, which is central to a post-2015 development agenda anchored in sustainability. Rio+20 further called for enhanced support for sustainable tourism activities and relevant capacity-building in developing countries in order to contribute to the achievement of sustainable development.

Building on the outcome of Rio+20, the United Nations Department of Economic and Social Affairs, through its Division for Sustainable Development, has been working closely with the UN system, in particular, the World Tourism Organization and United Nations Environment Programme to advance sustainable tourism in the context of sustainable development and more specifically in national planning processes.

In this regard, initiatives by the academic world to help policy-makers and practitioners develop a better understanding of the dynamic and concrete linkages between tourism and sustainable development are therefore of great importance.

This publication addresses the potential role that tourism could play towards a green economy. It also provides good practices and policy orientations as well as implications for future research in this area. The publication is therefore a timely and important input for tourism and sustainability stakeholders.

Nikhil Seth

Director, Division for Sustainable Development,
United Nations Department for Economic and Social Affairs

ACKNOWLEDGEMENTS

The editors express their gratitude to Ms Birgitte Bryld Alvarez-Rivero at the United Nations Division for Sustainable Development, United Nations Secretariat, New York; Ms Helena Rey de Assis and Ms Deirdre Shurland at UNEP DTIE Paris; Ms Ilona Lelonek Husting at the Tourism Policy Unit of the European Commission, Brussels; and Mr Luigi Cabrini, Chair of the Global Sustainable Tourism Council, for all their support and cooperation. Special thanks are due to Mrs Ashley Wright and Mr Tim Hardwick at Routledge, Abingdon, for their patience, efficiency and encouragement.

Disclaimer

The views and findings expressed in this book are the responsibility of the authors and contributors, and do not necessarily represent the views of organizations or the individuals who have kindly endorsed the book on a crucial topic.

PART 1

Understanding the concept of the green economy and the role of tourism

1

TOURISM IN THE GREEN ECONOMY

Rio to post-2015

Maharaj Vijay Reddy and Keith Wilkes

Introduction

The concept of the green economy has now entered mainstream policy debates and been endorsed by United Nations and many other organizations. The Rio+20 UN Conference specifically drew attention to the green economy approach in the context of sustainable development to move away from business-as-usual practices, act to end poverty, address environmental destruction and build a bridge to a sustainable future.

Tourism has been identified as a globally important industry in most international meetings and publications outlining the economic status of the world (e.g. 2012 *World Economic Situation and Prospects*). Together with the travel industry (i.e. including tourist transport, air travel but excluding commuter transport services), tourism contributed $7 trillion to the global economy in 2013, equalling 9.5 per cent of the world's GDP as a result of the direct, indirect and induced impact of this industry (WTTC, 2014). This quick recovery after the recent economic crisis has been noticed in many countries. The increasing importance of the travel and tourism industry in balancing and improving people's financial and social capital is realized in almost every country (Reddy, 2013). Equally, it is evident that the environmental impacts of tourism and travel continue to increase in countries across geographic regions. Therefore, it is extremely important to identify many methods and pursue appropriate strategies that will reduce the hurdles facing the carbon reduction targets of the tourism and travel sector to step up measures for transition to a green economy (Reddy and Wilkes, 2012). It is increasingly recognized that the tourism sector can play a pivotal role in a green economy through more sustainable business practices, climate change mitigation and adaptation techniques. However, there are ambiguities about how tourism and allied industries can maximize their contribution to human well-being and ensure environmental sustainability, embracing issues of political economy, geography and business ethics.

In this context, this book provides consensus about what the green economy entails, what role tourism can play in a green economy and ongoing and emerging research initiatives from many countries that will enable tourism's transition to a green economy. This chapter will review the origins of the green economics concept and how it evolved as a major paradigm in the sustainable development agenda from the First Rio Summit to the current post-2015 framework by assessing a range of international policies. The outcomes of the Rio+20 debates in relation to the post-2015 situation and the areas of focus to advance sustainable tourism are outlined, urging more international, industry and academic engagement. The lessons from Rio+20 and the need to encourage and shape tourism practices to benefit the global sustainable development agenda are discussed. It also addresses the potential role of and the challenges and opportunities that the tourism sector faces in developed and developing countries in line with the UNEP sustainable consumption and production initiative. Finally, the chapter reinstates a set of recommendations to foster green growth in the tourism sector by briefing the skeleton of the other chapters and the organization of the book.

Green economy origins and Rio 1992 outcome

The report to the UK Department of Environment by Pearce, Markandya and Barbier (1989) of the London Environmental Economic Centre called a *Blueprint for a Green Economy* first used the term 'green economy'. The authors discussed the meaning of sustainable development in relation to economic wealth and declining environment while addressing the monetary value of national environmental damage, the need for direct and indirect valuation of the environment and the monetary and physical approaches of environmental accounting. Sustainable development was debated as a bequest to the future and that future generations should be compensated for reductions in the endowments of resources brought about by the actions of present generations. Pearce *et al.* (1989, p. 3) discerned two ways in which the compensation should take place at the heart of the debate over sustainable development:

1   'Compensation for the future is best achieved by ensuring that current generations leave the succeeding generations with at least as much capital wealth as the current generation inherited';
2   'Compensation for the future should be focussed not only on man-made capital wealth, but should pay special attention to environmental wealth', meaning that 'the future generations must not inherit less environmental capital than the current generation inherited'.

They went on to suggest that it is important to understand how the economy and environment interact and that the economy is not separate from the environment we live in, referring to how the chlorofluorocarbons as a result of environmental damage affect the ozone layer that in turn affects human health and economic productivity. Following Pearce *et al.* (1989), several publications especially in the areas of environmental and ecological economics called for planners and policy-makers to focus on the green economy concept and advance awareness measures to make it one of the main paradigms for our sustainable future. For instance, Hutchinson, Mellor and Olsen (2002) widened the consideration of economics beyond the classical economists. Cato (2009) summed up the debates as the conventional (area of) economics considers environmental impact to be an externality, something outside its concern whereas the environmental economists were keen to bring these negative impacts back within the discipline.

In United Nations circles, the concept of green economics gained some attention in the run-up to the Earth Summit (United Nations Conference on Environment and Development) at Rio de Janeiro in 1992 as the Canadian Government's Green Plan was discussed (Meakin, 1992). Among the principles articulated at Rio 1992 were the recognition of the right of states to develop their forests to meet their socio-economic needs, promotion of the transfer of technology to developing countries to help them manage their forests sustainably, and the need for all countries to make efforts to 'green the world' through reforestation and forest development (UNEP, 2010).

The first Rio Summit was attended by the heads and representatives of 178 countries and attempted to reduce greenhouse gases and environmental damage to the earth's life support system. Three decisive agreements were adopted aimed at changing the traditional approach to development, namely: (i) Agenda 21 – a comprehensive programme of action for global action in all areas of sustainable development very much welcomed, utilized and applied by tourism stakeholders; (ii) the Rio Declaration on Environment and Development – a series of principles defining the rights and responsibilities of states; and (iii) the Statement of Forest Principles – a set of principles to underlie the sustainable management of forests worldwide (UN, 1997). Although these agreements that were signed were not explicitly to push the green economy paradigm they gave momentum and ways for the UN member states to work towards sustainable development. In addition to the above three agreements, two crucial legally binding conventions aimed at preventing global climate change and the eradication of the diversity of biological species emerged from Rio 1992.

First, the United Nations Framework Convention on Climate Change (UNFCCC) was set up, which came up with the treaty of the 1997 Kyoto Protocol. The Kyoto Protocol has been ratified by 192 of the UNFCCC parties with a commitment to setting internationally binding emission reduction targets placing heavier responsibilities on developed nations under the principle of 'common but differentiated responsibilities'. Article 11 of the Kyoto Protocol (UN, 1998) also entrusted the developed countries to provide new and additional financial resources to meet the agreed full costs incurred by developing country parties in advancing the implementation of existing commitments to reduce combined aggregate anthropogenic carbon dioxide equivalent emissions of greenhouse gases. This was in line with Pearce *et al.*'s (1989) green economics thinking of compensating for environmental damage. The Protocol also called on the developed countries to provide new financial resources, including for the transfer of technology and methodologies, needed by developing country parties to meet the agreed full 'incremental' costs of advancing the implementation of existing carbon reduction commitments. Under the Kyoto Protocol, countries must meet and monitor their carbon reduction targets primarily through national measures and also through additional market-based mechanisms such as the international emissions trading scheme.

Second, Rio 1992 led to the establishment of the Convention on Biological Diversity (CBD). The objectives of this Convention are the conservation of biological diversity, the sustainable use of its components and the fair and equitable sharing of the benefits arising out of the utilization of genetic resources, including by appropriate access to genetic resources and by appropriate transfer of relevant technologies, taking into account all rights over those resources and to technologies as well as by appropriate funding (UN, 1992). The ultimate objective of Kyoto and the CBD was to stabilize greenhouse gas concentrations in the atmosphere at a level that will prevent dangerous human interference with the climate system (UN, 1997). All these link with the principles of a green economy (i.e. significantly reducing environmental risks and ecological scarcities).

Rio 1992 also called on the General Assembly to establish the Commission under the Economic and Social Council (ECOSOC) as a means of supporting and encouraging action by governments, business, industry and other non-governmental groups to bring about the social and economic changes needed for sustainable development (UN, 1997). To implement the recommendations of this summit and to follow up the sustainable development programmes, the UN adopted three more agreements aimed at changing the traditional approach to development, including the formation of the UN Commission on Sustainable Development under the Department of Economic and Social Council (UNDESA), currently known as the Division for Sustainable Development. Besides these agreements, Rio 1992 also discussed financial mechanisms for worldwide sustainable development initiatives. It estimated that US$600 billion was required annually by developing countries to implement Agenda 21 (UN, 1997).

In the tourism discipline, Agenda 21 was discussed by several authors (e.g. Aronsson, 2000; Weaver, 2006). Reddy and Wilkes (2012) addressed the shifts in the focus of sustainable development based on global priorities from the 1972 Stockholm Conference to the 2002 Johannesburg Summit outlining the Millennium Development Goals, and the preparatory events for the Rio+20 Summit. With particular reference to the green economy, more clear recognition of the approach in relation to tourism started largely after the Millennium Ecosystem Assessment findings in 2005 listing recreation and ecotourism under the cultural ecosystem services (Reddy, 2013). Other publications by many tourism researchers have contributed to highlight the adaptive capacity of tourism, though there may be variations between subsectors of the industry to adapt to climate change implications (see Barr *et al.*, 2011; Cohen *et al.*, 2014; Dickinson and Lumsdon, 2010; Gossling and Hall, 2006; Peeters, 2007; Scott, 2006; Simpson *et al.*, 2008).

From 2007–08 the world witnessed the worst global economic crisis since the Great Depression of the 1930s and the launch of the 'New Deal' by then US President Franklin Roosevelt to provide employment and reform taxes and social security to stimulate the economy. Following the 2007–08 economic crisis, there were calls in the global policy arena for a UN response to tackle the contemporary multiple crises through a green economic action as a means of broad-based long-term recovery for countries around the world, which resulted in the 'Global Green New Deal' (GGND). The objectives of the GGND were to represent a common desire to restore a disrupted financial system and severe job losses by addressing the vulnerability of the poor; to ensure that our post-crisis economy follows a sustainable model and does not continue to add to the two most significant risks faced by society: ecological scarcity and climate instability (UNEP, 2009). There was no trade-off suggested because all human activity depends on the existence of a responsible framework for using environmental assets. This is especially true of the poorest populations as they depend disproportionately on the ecological commons both for livelihoods and for consumption (UNEP, 2009). In 2010, the UNEP Global Ministerial Environment Forum acknowledged in their declaration that the green economy concept can significantly address current challenges and deliver economic development opportunities and multiple benefits for all nations. The forum also acknowledged UNEP's leading role in further defining and promoting the green economy concept, and encouraged UNEP to contribute to this work through the preparatory process for the UN Conference on Sustainable Development in 2012 – known as Rio+20 (UN, 2012).

The UNEP (2011) Green Economy report released in the run-up to Rio+20 raised global awareness about the role tourism could play in a green economy. This report defined a green economy as 'one that results in improved human well-being and social equity, while significantly reducing environmental risks and ecological scarcities' (UNEP, 2011, p. 16). It also set the stage for a green economy transition by focusing on the eleven key sectors considered to be driving the defining trends of the transition to increase human well-being and social equity reducing environmental risks and ecological scarcities.

Lessons from Rio+20

At Rio+20, tourism was emphasized as a global industry benefiting many countries with the potential to contribute to global sustainable development by paying for environmental conservation, and to reduce poverty and social inequalities. The outcome document of the Rio+20 summit, *The Future We Want*, outlined how tourism can promote sustainable development while encouraging countries to enhance sustainable tourism practices to benefit local economies and the human and natural environment. 'We call for enhanced support for sustainable tourism activities and relevant capacity building in developing countries in order to contribute to the achievement of sustainable development' (UNDESA, 2012, p. 23). Following Rio+20, influential expert group meetings were organized by the UN Division of Sustainable Development to advance environmental protection and reduce poverty through sustainable tourism. Seth (2013, p. 2) states that 'international tourism can boost foreign exchange earnings while reducing domestic unemployment and lifting individual incomes. And by supporting traditional economic sectors such as textiles and local crafts, it can play a significant role in cultural preservation'. There were several other sustainable tourism capacity-building events, and stock-taking efforts were made to identify research priorities and funding mechanisms by the UN World Tourism Organization as well as by UNEP and the partners of the Global Partnership for Sustainable Tourism.

Conversely, in terms of the slow progress in meeting the overall global sustainability targets with reference to the Millennium Development Goals (MDGs) and slipping away from producing binding agreements like those in the past (e.g. Rio 1992), it was argued by a few authors that Rio+20 was a climate inaction summit. The world has failed to deliver on many of the promises it made 20 years ago at the Earth summit in Brazil (Tollefson and Gilbert, 2012).

Although nations have made some marginal advances, the three conventions (i.e. UNFCCC, CBD and United Nations Convention to Combat Desertification) have failed to achieve even a fraction of the promises. Overall, industrialized countries are on track to surpass the Kyoto goal with a reduction of some 7 per cent, but this is largely due to the demise of the Soviet Union and its inefficient factories, as well as to the industrial slump caused by the recent economic crisis, which is starting to reverse. The United States, the developed world's largest greenhouse-gas producer, never ratified the protocol and increased its greenhouse-gas output by 11 per cent between 1990 and 2010. In the meantime, developing countries more than doubled their emissions, increasing their share of the global total from 29 per cent to 54 per cent (Tollefson and Gilbert, 2012, p. 21).

While acknowledging the Rio+20 conference efforts in that it challenged the world community to take the green economy approach seriously, Barbier's (2012) article published in the aftermath outlined the audacious actions that should have been taken during the conference as well as the steps to take in the future as the ways forward (see Table 1.1) to make a paradigm shift in international policy.

Barbier argues that Rio+20 should have declared that it is an anachronism in the twenty-first century as the world cannot wait so long to determine whether the current push for green growth is successful. His main concern is that unceasing funding mechanisms are needed to foster green growth. For instance, 'the cost of funding for the UN Millennium Development Goals of reducing global poverty is estimated to require additional development assistance of $83 billion annually, but over the past 10 years, developing countries have received only $37 billion in total extra aid for this purpose' (*ibid.*, p. 888). Yet, there are a wide range of global funding sources for environment and development initiatives, including financial transaction taxes; international financing facilities; sovereign wealth funds; and taxes on global arms, tobacco, and the fuel trade (*ibid.*). Nevertheless, how effectively all these funds can be mobilized and directed to finance green growth transition, will be a challenge.

The other proposal by the European Union and African Union to upgrade and announce UNEP as a specialized agency for the environment named 'World Environment Organization (WEO)' or 'United Nations Environment Organization (UNEO)' was defeated by opponents that included the US, Canada, Japan and some members of the G77 including India. Kemp (2014) discusses the flaws, functions and reforms centred on the debate about upgrading UNEP, which suggested four pathways for change in UNEP based on critical issues, barriers and drivers, namely: (i) WEO form, (ii) UNEO form, (iii) formation of a World Sustainable Development Organization (WSDO) merging UNEP and the United Nations Development Programme (UNDP), and (iv) a change to the mandate, function and organizational structure of UNEP, but not its legal status. All these depend upon support from the US and the G77 member states. At present, UNESCO is the only UN agency with national commissions in many countries. This set-up helps UNESCO to initiate national programmes and actions focusing on the development of education, science and culture. If UNEP is transformed as a specialized agency, it will be expected to have more freedom to come up with useful multilateral agreements and to step up its actions in strengthening environmental conservation. But then, it will also lose the benefits that it has under the UN General Assembly and will become open to financial and political barriers.

Regardless of some criticism, Rio+20 did provide additional momentum for the ongoing green growth initiatives in many countries including the developing countries. The usual concerns of environmental conferences such as the exclusion of social aspects,

TABLE 1.1 Rio+20: Missed actions and steps for the future

Missed actions	Steps for future
Adapting the green economy theme for Rio+20 was laudable. However, an international conference every 10 or 20 years to review and promote progress on sustainable development is no longer helpful or relevant	The shortfall between international aid needs and commitments is growing. Therefore, the international community must establish urgently new financial mechanisms for long-term funding of sustainable development
The Rio+20 recommended sustainability reporting for capital markets and abolishing fossil fuel subsidies. However, these are only modest financial proposals. Environmental conferences such as the Rio+20 often propose targets for action and promise financial commitments without considering the mechanisms by which those funds will be raised	The richer and emerging economies such as the G20 should honour their promises from past summits to work together on further measures to build sustainable economies. Supporters of green growth among the G20, such as Australia, Denmark, the EU, Mexico, South Korea and the UK should collaborate to promote green economy initiatives
Global sustainable development issues need a permanent international champion. The EU proposed the transformation of UNEP into a fully-fledged specialized UN agency during the preparatory meetings and in the 'zero draft' of the Rio+20 outcome document, but this was defeated	UNEP should be converted into a specialized UN agency for the environment with a strengthened mandate and stable, adequate, and predictable financing which will be an onerous task in the current scenario

Source: Authors based on Barbier (2012)

economy recovery and poverty reduction aspects were carefully addressed at several of the preparatory conferences organized in the run-up to the Rio +20. The High-Level Political Forum's leadership in the development of a post-2015 agenda is commendable and the proposed Sustainable Development Goals (SDGs) are meant to incorporate the lessons learned and continue with the progress made in tackling the Millennium Development Goals in the post-2015 setting too.

Post-2015: sustainable development goals

The high-level plenary meeting of the General Assembly on MDGs asked the Secretary-General 'to report annually on progress in the implementation of the Millennium Development Goals until 2015 and to make recommendations in his annual reports, as appropriate, for further steps to advance the United Nations development agenda beyond 2015' (UN, 2010, p. 29). The Secretary-General made an initial recommendation for open and inclusive consultations on the development agenda in his report in August 2011. He then established the UN System Task Team to coordinate system-wide preparations for the post-2015 UN development agenda. Its terms of reference include: (i) assessing ongoing efforts within the UN system; (ii) consulting with external stakeholders, such as civil society, academia and the private sector; and (iii) defining a system–wide vision and road map to support the deliberations on a post-2015 agenda. So the Rio+20 conference also initiated an inclusive intergovernmental process to prepare a set of SDGs. There is broad agreement on the need for close linkages to arrive at one global development agenda for the post-2015 period, with sustainable development at its centre (ECOSOC, 2013).

There are many opinions on the characteristics of the SDGs. While cautioning that the earth ecosystem has entered into a new phase in which human actions are threatening the planet's life support systems and drawing down the planet's natural capital, Young *et al.* (2014) argue that it is essential for the SDGs to reconfirm the commitments of the MDGs and also the SDGs must address issues of earth system governance and the challenge of redirecting unsustainable practices of individuals, groups, and countries worldwide. Griggs *et al.* (2013, p. 305) argue that 'with the human population set to rise to 9 billion by 2050, definitions of sustainable development must be revised to include the security of people and the planet'. This reiterates the initial recommendations by Pearce *et al.* (1989) on green economy principles that the separation of economic

---

BOX 1.1 CHARACTERISTICS OF SDGS

- An integrated agenda:
  The social, economic and environmental dimensions of sustainable develop-ment are critically important. The post-2015 agenda needs to be balanced in terms of how much emphasis it places on each of these dimensions. It also needs to recognize that these dimensions can be treated in isolation or in silos. They are inextricably linked. The real challenge is how to operationalize an integrated agenda into a set of goals and targets.
- A universal agenda:
  Unlike the MDGs, if we are to eradicate extreme poverty by embracing a more sustainable pathway and if we are to truly tackle emerging global challenges, the next set of goals needs to be universal in nature. The goals will need to be applicable to all countries while still respecting the principles of common but differentiated responsibilities. We will need to move from a set of goals that is about North-South solidarity to a set of goals that is also about a shared destiny. Building the political will for a universal agenda will need a compelling vision and bold leadership – much of both in the coming years.
- A transformative agenda:
  Although we have made considerable advances in MDGs, we still have unacceptable levels of poverty and inequality in many places around the world. We are also not living within our planet's carrying capacity. To tackle all these challenges, we need a post-2015 agenda that is not about incremental change but that will lead to a more profound shift in the role of governance, in the economic growth model that we embrace and the power of citizens and civil societies.

Source: Bapna (2014)

development and environmental policies is artificial. Defining a unified set of SDGs is challenging, especially when there can be conflict between individual goals, such as energy provision and climate-change prevention. In light of these, Griggs *et al.* (2013) proposed a new definion for sustainable development in the 'anthropocene' that indicates the current geological age viewed as the period during which human activity has been the dominant influence on climate and the environment. Their new definition outlines sustainable development as 'development that meets the needs of the present while safeguarding earth's life-support system, on which the welfare of current and future generations depends' (p. 306).

Young *et al.* (2014) state that there are different ways to design the menu of targets and to achieve SDGs. In Approach I, regional, national and local authorities can design their own targets that connect within the global target defined in the SDGs process. In Approach II, these sub-global targets are nested within each other in a system where political decisions at one level shape progress at other levels. While there may be advantages and disadvantages to both approaches, they can both be deployed in the SDG system with Approach II being used in regions with strong regional authorities and Approach I being used in areas where local constituencies can mobilize around creating targets at a specific level. At the second meeting of the High-Level Political Forum on sustainable development at the UN secretariat, Bapna (2014) defined that the post-2015 agenda needed to have the characteristics outlined in Box 1.1, that were not fully incorporated or less visible in the MDGs. These characteristics need to be taken care of to transform the soft global goals into hard targets embedded in national policies.

Tourism in the green economy: post-2015 policy perspective

With specific reference to tourism and post-2015 SDGs, no international debate or academic engagement has yet been initiated. Timely consultation, debates, knowledge-sharing at international and national levels involving policy organizations, national agencies, industry and academia are needed at the earliest possible time, so that the progress made in sustainable tourism initiatives and practices at the international, regional, national and local levels to date are carried forward beyond 2015 without a pause. The ongoing international policy aspects and the themes through which sustainable tourism initiatives are to be improved and continued are detailed in the following sections of this chapter. These aspects need more deliberation and multi-stakeholder discussion through expert group meetings and capacity-building events to identify post-2015 tourism priorities for subsectors and reinforce plans.

For instance, greening the transport sector is one of the key priorities in the post-2015 scenario. The business-as-usual tourism-related travel (i.e., aviation, road, rail and water transport excluding commuter transportation) contributes considerably to global warming. Reddy (2013) argues that transport in particular is one of the less performing sectors challenging green transition, and larger investments and regulations are needed to cope with the change and alter future production and consumption patterns. The International Energy Agency's Global Transport Outlook to 2050 (IEA, 2014) advocates that 'building a sustainable transport system globally is cheaper than a conventional one and the financial flows shift from operating costs (fuels) to investment costs (infrastructure for mass transit, efficient vehicles)' is needed. To formulate and implement sustainable transport measures, the United Nations recently established an advisory group to work 'with governments, transport providers, businesses, financial institutions, civil society and other stakeholders to promote sustainable transport systems and their integration into development strategies and policies' (UNDESA, 2014a). Sustainable water use and safer water consumption are some of the other challenges the tourism industry faces in many destinations. For instance, TUI Travel (2013) stated that a tourist in Spain visiting a hotel with swimming pool and golf course can use up to 880 litres of water a day compared with 250 litres a day for a Spanish city dweller. The United Nations University Policy brief on water and education for the post-2015 development agenda outlines the need for people worldwide to acquire 'water literacy' and the importance of the water-education nexus for dealing with a variety of different sustainable development challenges including inequity in education, disaster recovery, and local mobilization. In the post-2015 agenda, the overall importance of sustainable tourism and the role it can play in aiding sustainable development globally has been broadly acknowledged. The outcome document of the Open Working Group on Sustainable Development Goals (UNDESA, 2014b) incorporated tourism priorities under three of the seventeen SDGs (see Table 1.2). But the specific ways to achieve these targets need to be worked out.

The UN World Tourism Organization, UNEP, UNESCO, UNCTAD, EU, ILO and the World Bank are some of the international organizations already working towards the targets of advancing the promotion of responsible, sustainable and universally accessible tourism contributing to inclusive economy and environmental conservation measures even though there may be variations in their focus. For instance, UNWTO

TABLE 1.2 SDGs – tourism targets

	Sustainable development goal	Tourism targets
Goal 8	Promote sustained, inclusive and sustainable economic growth, full and productive employment and decent work for all	By 2030 devise and implement policies to promote sustainable tourism that creates jobs, promotes local culture and products
Goal 12	Ensure sustainable consumption and production patterns	Develop and implement tools to monitor sustainable development impacts for sustainable tourism that creates jobs, promotes local culture and products
Goal 14	Conserve and sustainably use the oceans, seas and marine resources for sustainable development	By 2030 increase the economic benefits to SIDS (small island developing states) and LDCs (least developed countries) from the sustainable use of marine resources, including through sustainable management of fisheries, aquaculture and tourism

is the specialized agency of the UN for tourism. It promotes tourism as a driver of economic growth, inclusive development and environmental sustainability and offers leadership and support to the sector in advancing knowledge and tourism policies worldwide. UNWTO encourages the implementation of the Global Code of Ethics for Tourism, to maximize tourism's socio-economic contribution while minimizing its possible negative impacts, and is committed to promoting tourism as an instrument in achieving the MDGs, geared towards reducing poverty and fostering sustainable development (UNWTO, 2014). The World Bank promotes poverty reduction measures in Africa and other less developed countries. Chapter 8 in this book specifically addresses the ILO's green job initiatives.

Within the European Union, the European Destinations of Excellence (EDEN) initiative promotes sustainable tourism based on commitment to social, cultural and environmental sustainability in emerging and rural destinations. Over 100 destinations in Europe have received the award of 'destination of excellence' following national competitions (Lelonek-Husting, 2013). Since its launch in 2006, EDEN has helped to develop tourism, employment and regeneration in the relatively unknown destinations of the post-Soviet countries that joined the EU in 2004 (Grebliunaite-Reddy, 2014). As relatively new destinations are emerging in Europe, in order to meet the increasing tourism demand, reduce seasonality and minimize resource use, EDEN enables countries to raise awareness of sustainable practices across the EU, turn these places into year-round venues, decongest over-visited tourist destinations, and encourage dialogue among stakeholders. A platform called 'EDEN Network' has been established for the exchange of good practices at European level between awarded destinations but also with the aim of persuading other destinations to adopt sustainable tourism development practices (Lelonek-Husting, 2013). Future actions in line with the Europe 2020 strategy and its flagship initiatives include smart growth to promote innovation in the EU, sustainable growth to make the EU more resource-efficient, and inclusive growth to work on an agenda for new skills and jobs as a European platform against poverty (Lelonek-Husting, 2013).

UNESCO, through several of its programmes (e.g. World Heritage Sustainable Tourism, Man and Biosphere, and Global Geoparks) promotes dialogue and stakeholder cooperation where planning for tourism and tangible and intangible heritage management is integrated at a destination level, the natural and cultural assets are valued and protected, and appropriate tourism is developed. UNESCO's Education for Sustainable Development (ESD) programme aims to allow every human being to acquire the knowledge, skills, attitudes and values necessary to shape a sustainable future. ESD also means including key sustainable development issues in teaching and learning, for example, climate change, disaster risk reduction, biodiversity, poverty reduction, and sustainable consumption (see UNESCO, 2014). With specific reference to sustainable tourism, more academic and capacity-building initiatives are needed in less developed countries and Small Island Developing States (SIDS) to transform tourism practices to follow green economy principles. In relation to sustainable management of marine ecosystems, the UNESCO Intergovernmental Oceanic Commission, UN Office of the High Representative for the Least Developed Countries, Landlocked Developing Countries, and the SIDS, Oceans and Climate Branch within UNDESA are expected to step up important initiatives focusing on oceans, seas and marine areas in the post-2015 scenario.

Blue economy

In this context, the concept of the 'blue economy' has also gained attention recently, referring to a new market-oriented sustainable business model that Gunter Pauli and the Zero Emission Research Initiative of the United Nations University widely advocated during the Kyoto Protocol. Later this was used to address improving social capital and innovations by refining entrepreneurship, jobs and generally the patterns of business. The term was largely applied in relation to the sustainable management of oceans and seas when Ms Marlene Moses, Permanent Representative of the Mission of Nauru to the United Nations, used it to highlight the sustainability challenges of the small islands in the Pacific in the run-up to the Rio+20 conference: 'the sustainable development of our island countries relies on the health and vitality of the marine environment. For the Pacific SIDS, the "green economy" is in fact a "blue economy"'.

A joint report of the IOC/UNESCO, IMO, FAO and UNDP (2011, p. 8) underlines that

> ocean and coastal areas provide many benefits to sustainable development, including both human (social and economic) and environmental (ecosystem services). This includes benefits to economic sectors such as fisheries, energy, tourism, and transport/shipping, as well as 'non-market' benefits such as climate regulation, carbon sequestration, habitat and biodiversity, among many others.

The blue economy approach will particularly encompass the principles of green economy but pioneered for coastal countries that rely on marine resources facing sustainability challenges. Though the blue economy concept is advocated by small island nations, it actually recognizes and places renewed emphasis on the critical need for the international community to address effectively the sound management of resources in and beneath international waters by the further development and refinement of international law and ocean governance mechanisms, as stated at the 'Blue Economy Summit', held in Abu Dhabi, January 2014.

The position of sustainable tourism in a blue economy will also be crucial not only for the SIDS but also for the coastal areas of a number of countries for sustainable use of coastal ecosystems and to alleviate poverty and debt burdens, aiding developing economies. The Small Island Developing States Accelerated Modalities of Action, called the 'Samoa' Pathway, released after the third International Conference on Small Island Developing States in Apia (September 2014) urged establishing, and maintaining, the governance and management structures for sustainable tourism and human settlements that bring together responsibilities and expertise in the areas of tourism, environment, health, disaster risk reduction, culture, land and housing, transportation, security and immigration, planning and development, to enable a meaningful partnership approach among the public and private sectors and local communities in SIDS (UN, 2014).

Sustainable consumption and production

In the post-2015 scenario, sustainable tourism initiatives are expected to be accelerated by UNEP through its Sustainable Consumption and Production (SCP) branch. There have been arguments centred on unsustainable tourism consumption patterns for many years (e.g., de Kadt, 1979). Through the Agenda 21 principles, the First Rio Summit detailed proposals for action in social and economic areas such as combating poverty, 'changing patterns of production and consumption' and addressing demographic dynamics, and for conserving and managing the natural resources that are the basis for life – protecting the atmosphere, oceans and biodiversity; preventing deforestation; and promoting sustainable agriculture (UN, 1997). Ten years after the Rio Conference, the world leaders signed the Johannesburg Plan of Implementation (JPOI) explicitly called for 'changing unsustainable patterns of consumption and production' declaring that 'fundamental changes in the way societies produce and consume are indispensable for achieving global sustainable development. All countries should promote sustainable consumption and production patterns' (UNEP, 2010). The three main objectives of the SCP approach of the UNEP are presented in Box 1.2. Following the Johannesburg summit, UNEP was asked to set up a global framework of action, called the 10-Year Framework of Programmes (10YFP) to enhance international cooperation to accelerate the shift towards SCP patterns in both developed and developing countries. In 2003 the first International Expert Meeting on the 10YFP was convened in Marrakech, known as the Marrakech Process, coordinated by UNEP and UNDESA as a collective multi-stakeholder effort to develop the framework. The 10YFP framework supports capacity-building, and facilitates access to technical and financial assistance for developing countries for this shift.

BOX 1.2 MAIN OBJECTIVES OF SCP APPROACH

1   Decoupling environmental degradation from economic growth:
    This is about doing more and better with less, increasing net welfare gains from economic activities by reducing resource use, degradation and pollution along the whole lifecycle, while increasing quality of life. 'More' is delivered in terms of goods and services, with 'less' impact in terms of resource use, environmental degradation, waste and pollution.

2   Applying the lifecycle thinking:
    This is about increasing the sustainable management of resources and achieving resource efficiency along both production and consumption phases of the lifecycle, including resource extraction, the production of intermediate inputs, distribution, marketing, use, waste disposal and re-use of products and services.

3   Sizing opportunities for developing countries and 'leapfrogging':
    SCP contributes to poverty eradication and to the achievement of the MDGs. For developing countries, SCP offers opportunities such as the creation of new markets, green and decent jobs as well as more efficient, welfare generating natural resource management. It is an opportunity to 'leapfrog' to more resource-efficient, environmentally sound and competitive technologies, by-passing the inefficient, polluting, and ultimately costly phases of development followed by most developed countries.

Source: UNEP (2014)

The SCP approach is not only about decoupling environmental degradation and the 'life-cycle' of products and services but also focuses on issues such as poverty eradication and green and decent jobs. UNEP's GGND called for a reviving of the global economy with a holistic approach and boosting employment while simultaneously accelerating the fight against climate change, environmental degradation and poverty. In addition, the SCP approach guides countries to move forward in various forms depending on the resource bases of countries, overarching problems of management and governance. For instance, the circular economy adopted by the Government of China balances economic development with environmental and resource conservation by putting emphasis on environmental protection and the most efficient use of and recycling of resources (UNEP, 2010). In particular the 10YFP programme contributes to meeting the goals and principles of the response to national and regional needs, priorities and circumstances by encouraging the participation of governments, business, civil society and all relevant stakeholders. The 10YFP focuses initially on six programme areas, namely, (i) consumer information, (ii) sustainable lifestyles and education, (iii) sustainable public procurement, (iv) sustainable buildings and construction, (v) sustainable tourism, and vi) sustainable food systems.

In relation to sustainable tourism, the 10YFP continued through the establishment of the International Task Force on Sustainable Tourism Development (2006–2010) and with the Global Partnership for Sustainable Tourism (2011 to 2014) and it will now culminate with the 10YFP Sustainable Tourism programme (post-2015). The UNEP SCP Branch paid particular attention to the tourism sector and led the Global Partnership for Sustainable Tourism. It involved several multilateral partners including the World Tourism Organization, several government ministries, non-governmental organizations, private sector organizations and universities. The past decade has laid a solid foundation for the next 10 years under the 10YFP. The role of UNWTO, UNEP SCP, and UNDESA is expected to be vital to advance sustainable consumption and production patterns in the tourism sector. In the post-2015 scenario, the Global Partnership for Sustainable Tourism will be transitioned into the 10YFP Programme on Sustainable Tourism to scale up activities in the global tourism sector as required under the intergovernmental mandate of the 10YFP. This has been echoed in the recent draft of the SDGs put forward by the UN high level political forum with SDG# 12 aiming to promote sustainable consumption and production patterns (see Table 1.2). This particular goal proposes to develop and implement tools to monitor sustainable development impacts for sustainable tourism that creates jobs, and promotes local culture and products (UNDESA, 2014b).

Post-2015 sustainable tourism and travel: practices and challenges in developed vs developing countries

The transition of the tourism and travel sector to a green economy provides numerous opportunities as well as massive challenges. The direct and induced benefits of tourism in terms of employment, revenue, investments, transport, accommodation, food, events, leisure services, and linkages with allied industries including insurance, housing, clothing, and local produce are well known. The tourism industry is well-developed in developed countries, struggling in many less developed countries when impressive steps are taken by the fast developing countries to benefit more from tourism.

According to the World Travel and Tourism Council (WTTC, 2014), the total (direct and induced) contribution of travel and tourism to the global GDP was US$6,990.3 bn (9.5 per cent of the global GDP) in 2013, and the forecast was to rise by 4.3 per cent by the end of 2014, and expected to rise by 4.2 per cent p.a. to US$10,965.1 bn (10.3 per cent of the global GDP) in 2024. The economic growth of the travel and tourism sector is not only outpacing the wider economy, but also growing faster than other significant sectors such as financial and business services, transport and manufacturing. In 2013, the total contribution of travel and tourism to employment, including jobs indirectly supported by the industry, was 8.9 per cent of total employment (265,855,000 jobs). This was expected to rise by 2.5 per cent in 2014 to 272,417,000 jobs and rise by 2.4 per cent p.a. to 346,901,000 jobs in 2024 (10.2 per cent of the global total) (WTTC, 2014).

However, the contributions of tourism to countries in regions worldwide differ. The SIDS around the world have a high reliance on tourism. In terms of developed economies, in 2013 the total contribution of travel and tourism sector was high. For example, 15.5 per cent to Spain; Austria, 13.4 per cent; 10.5 per cent to the GDP of the UK; and 9.5 per cent to France. The developed countries envisage that their move to green growth will improve competitiveness, that smart growth will promote innovation, and more resource-efficient and inclusive growth will develop new skills and jobs as stated earlier with reference to the Europe 2020 strategy. There are several best practices and certification schemes working well in tourism sub-sectors in developed countries. For instance, in the city of Bonn, the transportation network company SWB is recycling some of the out-of-date trams as a cost-cutting measure to save over 1 million euros per tram, in comparison with manufacturing new ones, and to produce energy-efficient and stronger trams for the future (see Figures 1.1 and 1.2).

Correspondingly, another example from the accommodation sector of Bonn is the Kameha Grand hotel, a state-of-the-art largely emission-free hotel and one of the largest geothermal buildings in Europe. With the geothermal concept, this hotel is able to cover 70 per cent of the heating and cooling required. The geothermal power plant (Figures 1.3 and 1.4) in the basement of the hotel generates energy using the existing resources in a natural way. The CO_2 emissions are reduced by roughly 400 tons (Kameha Grand, 2014).

Many other examples can be drawn from destinations around the world. Tourism authorities continue to work towards embedding innovation for energy and resource efficiency to reduce the emission levels. Even though several leading travel and tourism companies are engaging in low-carbon business practices as well as encouraging their consumers to follow sustainable tourism ideals, the signs of 'greenwashing' are apparent when the overall effort of the industry is carefully observed. The majority of current legal and institutional frameworks regulating the travel and tourism industry inter-nationally, nationally and locally at the destination levels are dreadfully weak (Reddy, 2013).

In a number of developing countries, the benefits of tourism are not fully understood in the context of sustainable development. For instance, the total contribution of the travel and tourism sector to some of the less developed countries was only 2.2 per cent to Democratic Republic of Congo (DRC); and 3.2 per cent to Nigeria. Even though DRC has some unique rainforests and nature-based tourism (e.g. gorilla tourism)

FIGURE 1.1 Tram recycling in process
Source: Authors

FIGURE 1.2 Recycled tram in Bonn
Source: Authors

FIGURE 1.3 Geothermal plant at the Kameha Grand
Source: Authors

FIGURE 1.4 Geothermal plant at the Kameha Grand
Source: Authors

FIGURE 1.5 Low-emission Geothermal Hotel Kameha Grand in Bonn
Source: Kameha Grand Bonn

attractions, there are safety concerns for tourists as a result of conflicts, poor infrastructure and tourism services, which are very important for tourists. A slight increase in tourism revenue will hugely help less developed countries such as the DRC, Rwanda, Sudan, Djibouti and Burundi to step-up environmental protection and reduce unemployment and extreme poverty. The total travel and tourism rankings of world regions based on their GDPs (Table 1.3) in absolute and relative contributions show significant variations in terms of their travel and tourism sector dependency.

The European Union, ranked globally second in terms of absolute contribution with US$1512 billion has only 9 per cent of their GDP relying on travel and tourism

TABLE 1.3 Travel and tourism total contribution to GDP: regional rankings

Absolute contribution		*Relative contribution*	
Rank	*2013 US$ billion*	*Rank*	*2013 percentage share*
1 North America	1665.6	1 Caribbean	14.0
2 European Union	1512.4	2 South-east Asia	12.3
3 North-east Asia	1389.3	3 North Africa	12.1
4 Latin America	388.0	4 Oceania	10.8
5 Other Europe	362.1	5 European Union	9.0
6 South-east Asia	294.4	6 Latin America	8.9
7 Oceania	188.0	7 North-east Asia	8.6
8 Middle East	167.6	8 North America	8.4
9 South Asia	145.4	9 Other Europe	7.5
10 Sub-Saharan Africa	95.7	10 Sub-Saharan Africa	6.9
11 North Africa	75.0	11 Middle East	6.5
12 Caribbean	49.0	12 South Asia	6.4

Source: Authors, based on WTTC (2014)

in relative terms whereas the North African region which is ranked eleventh in terms of absolute contribution has the third highest share of tourism contribution to their regional economy. The challenge before the regions such as North Africa and Sub-Saharan Africa is how to maximize the contribution of tourism to achieve sustainable development by enhancing tourist safety and regional integration and reducing conflicts. Tourism can contribute to peace-building by strengthening the socio-economic foundations in post-conflict areas. The United Nations Economic Commission for Africa (UNECA, 2011) advocated the important role tourism can play in post-conflict areas in the Eastern African countries including Sudan, South Sudan and Rwanda to reduce poverty, and enhance cultural integration and biodiversity conservation. With reference to the post-conflict tourism situation in Burundi, Novelli *et al.* (2012) argue that around 60 per cent of the poorest countries in the world that have experienced civil conflict of varying intensity and duration usually erupt after a period of economic stagnation or collapse. Therefore, the economic situation and conflicts are very much linked. Stabilizing the socio-economic foundations of a country will reduce the fragility and result in building peace and an image that facilitates tourism.

The tourism situation is very different in the BRIC nations. Though the economic transformation in the BRIC countries is not mainly through tourism (but as a result of developing other industries, e.g. manufacturing, improved agricultural production and IT), the growing economic wealth of the population allows them to travel more these days for leisure purposes. For instance, the number of people who made more than a million dollars in India grew by 14 per cent – at a rate faster than in the USA or the UK (UNWTO, 2006). In recent years, the figure for domestic tourist arrivals in China in 2011 was 2.64 billion (National Bureau of Statistics, Beijing) whereas in India it was over 0.85 billion (Tourism Statistics, Ministry of Tourism, New Delhi) – both contributing to an immense domestic tourist total of around 3.5 billion visits in one year. In addition, international tourism arrivals to the fast-developing countries have grown as they have become more open to international markets. Vital interventions are needed to make tourism growth sustainable in BRIC countries.

Fast-developing countries such as India have not been able to fully harness tourism benefits. India has always had a rather uneasy and ambivalent relationship with tourism (Hannam and Diekmann, 2011). Tourism contradictions and the results of economic transformation in a few Indian states that are relying heavily on tourism (e.g. Kerala and Goa), have drawn the attention of several tourism researchers as a result of important social sustainability concerns. Several reported incidents portray the unethical practices of tourism resulting in crime, drug use and suicidal deaths among the tourism-dependent communities in a few Indian destinations that indicate the urgent need to investigate the consumption and production patterns of tourism. The tourism-dependent communities are predominantly from the low-income and middle-income categories, working for hotels, restaurants, taxis, auto-rickshaws, guides, travel agencies, petty shops, dance groups, massage parlours, health and ayurvedic clinics, and handicraft and souvenir shops. Value chain analysis and pro-poor tourism approaches proposed by researchers working on low-income countries such as Laos, Cambodia, Ethiopia and Tanzania (e.g. Mitchell and Ashley, 2009) give useful insights to understand and diagnose the pro-poor impacts in supply chains and identify best interventions to improve the role of tourism in poverty eradication. However, the tourism-induced social transformation and associated contradictions in fast-developing countries need investigation to understand the market transformation, improve environmental conservation, manage socio-cultural issues and reduce poverty by avoiding economic imbalance. For instance, the participation of women in SME hotels, health tourism, ayurvedic treatments and souvenir manufacture is considerable in India and there are still unequal gender-based classifications such as 'women's work' (Rao, 1997; Chaudhary and Gupta, 2010).

Tourism Departments of the Indian State Governments often lack the required expertise and technical knowhow to develop effective sustainable tourism indicator sets with theoretical underpinnings and practical applicability to capture the complex and rapidly changing tourism impacts in this fast-developing country. However, sustainability is heavily used as a buzz-word in most tourism meetings and future agendas. In the context of the widening gap between the poor and the rich, it is important to investigate the diversified tourism impacts; how well the demand and supply aspects cope with economic transformation and develop effective strategies to foster sustainable growth. If unchecked, tourism will cause more serious impacts in some of these destinations. Nevertheless, the BRIC countries are adding investments in the travel and tourism sector as their inbound and outbound tourism levels did not change much during the recent economic crisis. In 2013–2014, India announced the construction of sixty new airports across the country to meet the growing demand of travellers. Similarly, China is building 100 new airports. The current national regulations encourage carbon reduction measures in the BRIC countries. For example, the Rajiv Gandhi International Airport in Hyderabad is India's first, with Level 3 optimization accreditation that achieved energy saving of 3.97 million kWh (kilowatt hours) and reduced carbon footprint by about 3331 tons during 2009–2011 (see Figure 1.6). Nevertheless, the rapid infrastructure development raises environmental concerns in the fast-developing countries.

FIGURE 1.6 India's Hyderabad International Airport reducing CO_2
Source: Authors

While China and India continue to develop their domestic air connectivity, accommodation services, and other tourism infrastructure, a more serious shift towards green practices should be ensured (Reddy, 2013). To make the green technology approaches work for larger sections of the travel and tourism industry, larger investments are needed to cope with the change and there is a need for inclusive growth that will alter future production and consumption patterns. Next to the BRICs, the EAGLEs' Nest countries (Emerging and Growth-Leading Economies) or the Watch List with incremental GDP in the next decade (e.g. Thailand, Mexico and Nigeria) should also utilize their relatively fast economic growth to further develop their travel and tourism practices sustainably at destination levels. Therefore, this chapter reinstates the ten recommendations (see Box 1.3) that Reddy (2013) outlined for the tourism and travel industry to advance its measures for transition to a green economy.

In order to discuss some of the tourism challenges and opportunities for the post-2015 situation, the United Nations Division for Sustainable Development convened a high-level Expert Group Meeting in November 2013, which was attended by representatives of the UN system and other relevant international organizations, public sector, academic and non-governmental organizations. One of the recommendations of this meeting was to make a proposal to the United Nations to launch consultative processes towards the declaration of 2017 as the 'International Year of Sustainable Tourism for Development'. If this proposal goes ahead in 2017 or in future, global awareness of the role of tourism for sustainable development and efforts for greening the sector will widen.

In the interim, more cutting-edge research approaches and methods advancing green growth in tourism need to be intensified. Therefore the role of academia is expected to be crucial in the post-2015 setting. A few years previously, Cato (2009, p. 5) argued that 'green economics is not, as yet, an academic discipline with a major place in the universities', which is regrettably still pertinent. This gap can be reduced by implementing the Principles for Responsible Management Education (PRME), a worldwide initiative that was first launched in 2007 at the UN Global Compact Leaders' Summit in Geneva. This event was attended by more than 1000 leaders representing business, academic and civil society groups. During the closing ceremony, the Secretary-General, Ban Ki-moon, acknowledged the potential saying that 'the Principles for Responsible Management Education have the capacity to take the case for universal values and business into classrooms on every continent' (PRME, 2014). PRME has over 500 business schools around the world as members, and sustainable tourism management topics should also be widely incorporated in the curriculum globally. If the UN Sustainable Tourism Expert Group proposal to start consultation to declare the 'International Year of Sustainable Tourism for Development' goes ahead, it can create a strong enabling platform for greening tourism.

The following chapters are included to address three key themes: understanding the green economy concept and the role of tourism; responses and initiatives in greening tourism; and emerging techniques and research implications. A wide range of case studies from around the world and in different contexts are included, to demonstrate the extent of the challenge and range of opportunities available for greening the tourism industry.

BOX 1.3 TEN RECOMMENDATIONS FOR GREENING THE TOURISM AND TRAVEL SECTOR

1 Appreciation of community-based skills and ways to make more use of local and indigenous knowledge need to be explored and adopted. For example, carbon emissions could be reduced in less expensive ways in many tourism destinations through improved ecotourism practices, better use of ecosystem management and rainforest conservation measures (e.g. Reducing Emissions from Deforestation and Forest Degradation – REDD+).

2 Added focus on vulnerable groups such as the Small Island Developing States (and poor countries) to mitigate the impacts of climate change, allow investments for green practices and develop tourism-based economic revival frameworks with local stakeholder involvement to enhance community well-being and resilience.

3 Government funding, private sector investments and expertise need to be improved for the accommodation sector, other SMEs and tour and travel operators in destinations (not only in developing countries but also in developed economies) – to transform their business-as-usual practices to green approaches.

4 Improvement of aircraft design and engines, enhancing road, rail, and water transport to increase fuel efficiency and sustainable transport options as well as practising modal shift and slow travel forms.

5 Reducing the water usage in the accommodation sector and improving energy efficiency in products such as refrigerators, bulbs, and through meaningful building construction and renovation (e.g. more ventilation instead of air-conditioning).

6 Recycling and reducing waste in the hotel, events and cruise industries; mobilizing credit schemes; reducing huddles to favour renewable energy and improve enabling conditions.

7 Moving towards green jobs by training the current tourism and travel workforce as well as educating and developing the latest skills among new employees.

8 Increasing awareness among tourists; encouraging tourists to buy local produce; tourists and host communities to practise travel and tourism responsibly; behavioural change and marketing; respecting local practices and culture.

9 Efficient management and conservation of forests and other natural resources; quantifying the costs of ecosystem services; indicator assessments; monitoring and reporting.

10 Regulations and standard-setting in relation to emission trading schemes, air passenger duty, and the use of biofuel as well as carbon disclosure, bench-marking destinations to compare and reduce carbon.

Source: Reddy (2013)

Organization of the book

Part 1: Understanding the concept of the green economy and the role of tourism

In Chapter 2, Newton examines what the green economy is and the role tourism can play in the green economy. It analyses a variety of different perspectives, including those informed by environmental science, environmental activism, green politics and environmental economics. This chapter indicates that the concept of the green economy is contested: there is no universally agreed definition and there is even some scepticism about its value.

Arguing for a place for an ecological ethic in tourism's role in the green economy, Chapter 3 by Holden points out that significant challenges are faced in relation to mobility and patterns of resource usage. This chapter presents an argument that technological and economic solutions are unlikely to meet the totality of these challenges and that an ecological ethic in the consumer market is necessary to create a tourism system that can lay claim to greater environmental sustainability.

Application and implementation of the concept of the green economy can be a challenge to achieving sustainable tourism especially in developing countries. Catibog-Sinha's Chapter 4 explores the key initiatives in the Philippines that can contribute to a broader understanding and application of the green economy in the context of nature-based tourism, providing management recommendations to guide the tourism industry, relevant stakeholders including governments and non-government organizations.

With reference to nature-protected areas, Chapter 5 by Livina and Atstaja analyses strategic planning documents, institutional reports and interviews with different stakeholders in Latvia and the United States. The chapter illustrates the best experiences and achievements of separate cases in both countries while providing recommendations.

Focusing on the Achuar nation in the Ecuadorian Amazon, Crawford and Sternberg's Chapter 6 makes a normative case for vigorous ecotourism regulation in order to achieve truly sustainable tourism, informed by tourism models practised by traditional peoples. This example and others provide lineaments for an ecotourism regulation model that, with proper advocacy, can become the world standard to guide tourism and other industries in the shift to a green economy, demonstrating carbon-based energy and techniques.

In Chapter 7, O' Regan and Choe argue that since the demise of the Kyoto Protocol and coordinated global action, the role of governments and their commitment and investment in the greening of tourism has become central to the process of achieving low-carbon inclusive sustainable growth, improved human well-being and reduced inequalities while not exposing future generations to significant environmental risks and ecological scarcities. This chapter looks at the role of China, given its rapid growth (and accompanying rise in carbon emissions and resource consumption) as a world leader in tourism (becoming the top domestic, inbound and outbound market).

Part 2: Best practices for the greening of tourism and allied industries

This part highlights interesting case studies representing a range of tourism subsectors from countries around the world. Green jobs, by their nature, are immensely important to sustainability. Chapter 8 by Ladkin and Szivas explores three main areas related to green jobs and briefs the role of the International Labour Organization. They address the definitions and dimensions of green jobs, the benefits of green jobs for the wider economy and individuals and an exploration of green jobs and employment opportunities in the tourism industry and its related sectors. Case studies of green jobs and employment in tourism are used to illustrate the points made by the authors.

Buultjens, Ratnayake and Gnanapala's Chapter 9 assesses the capacity of the Sri Lankan tourism industry to achieve a green economy through an examination of government and academic publications, a selection of industry case studies as well as interviews with academics and government and non-government stakeholders. Their conclusion is that, despite the green initiatives, the industry still faces issues such as a weak knowledge of green technology and practices, inappropriate development, inadequate waste management, a lack of infrastructure and the exceeding of carrying capacity in many natural areas.

In relation to the national parks of Sabah, Malaysia, Chapter 10 by Chan presents a preliminary and ongoing research work in exploring and identifying the key motivations, directions and strategies from tour operators and park officers with regard to initiatives in green tourism. The chapter provides an insightful understanding of the extent of green tourism within the context of national parks, and identifies a set of criteria for green tourism initiatives. It subsequently proposes ways to move forward in practising green tourism in a holistic manner.

The emerging field of energy tourism can make an important contribution to a green economy. In Chapter 11, Lun, Volgger and Pechlaner present multiple case studies on Bolzano, South Tyrol and three theme parks in Germany and Austria, each focusing on the interconnection of climate, renewable energy production, soft mobility and energy-efficient building. They discuss the conditions and potential impacts of energy-based theme parks, analysing interviews and an extensive survey on the Italian and German markets.

Chapter 12 by Jia and Wahnschafft provides an overview of the hotel star-rating system in China, as well as a comparative analysis of voluntary eco-certification and eco-labelling programmes. This chapter also outlines the related policies, rules and regulations, analyses the perceptions of the different stakeholders, discusses the impacts of the programmes and submits policy options for potential improvements. It explains the Chinese government's commitment to carry forward the concept of a green economy.

Welton's Chapter 13 on the Seychelles addresses the importance of tourism, implications of economic recession and climate change impacts for Small Island Developing States. It argues that visitor arrivals are falling and the country is now under the guidance of the International Monetary Fund. This chapter provides an in-depth exploration of the sustainability challenges facing the Seychelles and examines whether the tourism initiatives adopted by the Seychelles will act as the catalyst to transform the current economic situation into an inclusive green economy.

The ongoing pathways and effects of greening tourism in Ukraine constitute the aim of the scoping study presented by Kiptenko and Doan in Chapter 14. The innovative activities have proved to be the litmus test of the transition to a green economy in business, social and educational aspects. The authors argue that current responses provide space for further implications of the green economy in tourism understanding and practice, in particular for tourism policy, which is a topical issue for modern Ukraine.

In Chapter 15, Cobbinah, Thwaites and Black examine the potential of ecotourism as a strategy for achieving a green economy in developing countries particularly around the Kakum Conservation Area in Ghana. Issues regarding the implementation of ecotourism in achieving a green economy, success and challenges constitute the pivot of the chapter. This chapter establishes a strong relationship between ecotourism and the green economy with recommendations to increase government commitment and awareness-creation at the local level as important factors in achieving a green economy in the developing countries.

On local food, Slocum explores the rising 'farm-to-fork' movement as a form of sustainable development and provides literature-based research to support the inclusion of local food in tourism value chains as a method to green the tourism industry. In Chapter 16, she addresses consumer preferences for local food and the advantages of utilizing local food networks for social inclusion, rural development, sustainable consumption, and industry benefits. The chapter reviews current green hospitality initiatives regarding locally sourced food, regional labelling, and the constraints.

Merrilees, Miller and Green's Chapter 17 reviews green events and argues that very limited progress has been made. Their chapter examines exemplar cases of green events including the Burlington Ribfest, at Burlington in Ontario, Canada, which is portrayed as Canada's largest ribfest but, more importantly, it is the greenest ribfest. The chapter explains how the lessons from exemplar events can be mainstreamed and thus ramp up the diffusion of green principles in the mainstream event industry.

Part 3: Research implications and emerging issues

Chapter 18 by Jamal, Prideaux, Sakata and Thompson reviews the sustainable management initiatives at a globally significant World Heritage Site, the Great Barrier Reef in Australia. It looks at collaborative relationships between protected area managers, tour operators and visitors in addressing this challenging issue. The chapter presents research findings, examines certification initiatives related to reef users, and forwards some critical thoughts for further discussion towards a green economy in natural area destinations such as the Great Barrier Reef.

Saxena, Thaithong and Tsagdis investigate the case of Samui Island to illustrate the difficulties that are inherent in attempts to adopt green practices, and in Chapter 19 they address the serious environmental impacts resulting from mass tourism. They review the complex roles and relationships between human and non-human entities to provide green economy strategists with innovative pathways to develop sustainable tourism practices in Samui Island that will be useful for other less developed small islands.

Leadership and innovation will be required to drive a paradigmatic change to reduced fossil-fuel dependency when low emissions and sustainable economic systems become paramount. Whittlesea, Hurth and Agarwal's Chapter 20 explores the role and contribution of marketing as a strategic 'leadership' tool in the drive to green the economy, through an analysis of consumption patterns and impacts of different market segments. The implications for tourist behaviour, product innovation and the use of marketing are highlighted and the opportunities and challenges discussed.

Brazil's steps towards a green economy are addressed by Borda, Nascimento, Tasso and Meireles in Chapter 21. They analyse the contributive factors for socio-economic insertion of surrounding populations based in protected areas of Brazil. Their methodology is based on questionnaires and interviews conducted in three different regions of the country. The results show factors as diverse as trust, tourism training, previous job experience, and participation in cooperative associations, with suggestions to improve local low-carbon socially inclusive sustainable growth.

Finally, to conclude with a comprehensive view of the green economy approach, the economic greenwash and immense challenges facing tourism and green growth are addressed in Chapter 22 by Hall. The chapter provides a critical analysis of tourism and green growth ideas by pointing out that not only do they not serve to conserve rapidly declining natural capital but they also fail to appreciate the role of rebound effects. It concludes that efficiency and market-based approaches are only a small component of what is required with respect to reducing tourism's environmental impacts and instead posits the need for degrowth and sufficiency-based approaches.

References

Aronsson, L. (2000) *The development of sustainable tourism*. Continuum: London.

Bapna, M. (2014) HLPF 2 – Moderated Dialogue 'From Rio+20 to post-2015: towards an integrated and universal sustainable development agenda' (dated 30 June 2014). UN Secretariat, New York. Accessed via UN web TV on 7 July 2014.

Barbier, E.B. (2012) The green economy post Rio+20. *Science*, vol. 338, no. 6109, pp. 887–8.

Barr, S., Shaw, G. and Coles, T. (2011) Sustainable lifestyles: Sites, practices, and policy. *Environment and Planning A*, vol. 43, no. 12, pp. 3011–29.

Cato, M.S. (2009) *Green economics: An introduction to theory, policy and practice*. Earthscan: London.

Chaudhary, M. and Gupta, M. (2010) Gender equality in Indian hotel industry - a study of perception of male and female employees. *International Journal of Hospitality and Tourism Systems*, vol. 3, no. 1.

Cohen, S.A., Higham, J.E.S., Peeters, P. and Gossling, S. (2014) *Understanding and governing sustainable tourism mobility: Psychological and behavioural approaches*. Routledge: London.

de Kadt, E. (1979) *Tourism: Passport to development?* Oxford University Press (for the World Bank and UNESCO): New York.

Dickinson, J. and Lumsdon, L. (2010) *Slow travel and tourism*. Earthscan: London:

ECOSOC (2013) Millennium development goals and post-2015 development agenda. www.un.org/en/ecosoc/about/mdg.shtml (Accessed 22 June 2014).

Gossling, S. and Hall, C.M. (2006) (eds) *Tourism and global environmental change: Ecological, social, economic and political interrelationships*. Routledge: London.

Grebliunaite-Reddy, I. (2014) The European Union and tourism issues. Guest Lecture delivered on 20 March 2014 to Masters students at the Bournemouth University, UK.

Griggs, D., Stafford-Smith, M., Gaffney, O., Rockström, J., Öhman, M.C., Shyamsundar, P., Steffen, W., Glaser, G., Kanie, N. and Noble, I. (2013) Sustainable development goals for people and planet. *Nature*, vol. 495, pp. 305–07.

Hannam, K. and Diekmann, A. (2011) *Tourism and India: A critical introduction*. Routledge: London.

Hutchinson, F., Mellor, M. and Olsen, W. (2002) *The politics of money: Towards sustainability and economic democracy*. Pluto: London.

IEA (2014) Global transport outlook to 2050: Costs of the transport sector under low carbon scenarios. Presentation delivered at the Consultation on Sustainable Transport in the Post-2015 Development Agenda at the UN New York on 26 September. http://sustainabledevelopment. un.org/content/documents/23490411Globaltransport.pdf (Accessed 30 October 2014).

IOC/UNESCO, IMO, FAO and UNDP (2011) *A blueprint for ocean and coastal sustainability.* IOC/UNESCO: Paris

Kameha Grand (2014) Ecological responsibility. www.kamehagrand.com/en/ecology (Accessed 26 August 2014).

Kemp, L. (2014) Realpolitik and reform at Rio+20: The politics of reforming the United Nations Environment Programme (UNEP). Paper to be presented at the 2014 Earth System Governance Norwich Conference, 1–3 July. http://norwich2014.earthsystemgovernance.org/ wp-content/uploads/2014/06/2014-Kemp-Realpolitik-and-Reform-at-Rio-ESG-Con ference-Paper.pdf (Accessed 10 September 2014).

Lelonek-Husting, I. (2013) Challenges and opportunities for sustainable tourism development: The European Commission's actions to enhance sustainable tourism. UN Expert Group meeting on Sustainable Tourism, 29–30 October, UN Secretariat, New York. http://sustainabledevelop ment.un.org/content/documents/4119I.LELONEK_HUSTING_UN (Accessed 7 October 2014).

Meakin, S. (1992) The Rio Earth Summit: Summary of the United Nations Conference on Environment and Development. http://publications.gc.ca/Collection-R/LoPBdP/BP/bp317-e.htm#C (Accessed 20 July 2014).

Mitchell, J. and Ashley, C. (2009) Value chain analysis and poverty reduction at scale: Evidence from tourism is shifting mindsets. Briefing Paper – 49. Overseas Development Institute: London.

Novelli, M., Morgan, N. and Nibigira. C. (2012) Tourism in a post conflict situation of fragility. *Annals of Tourism Research*, vol. 39, no. 3, pp. 1446–69.

Pearce, D., Markandya, A. and Barbier, E.B. (1989) *Blueprint for a green economy*. Earthscan: London.

Peeters, P. (2007) (ed.) *Tourism and climate change mitigation: Methods, greenhouse gas reductions and policies*. Stichting NHTV: Breda.

PRME (2014) *Principles for responsible management education: The six principles*. PRME Secretariat: New York. www.unprme.org/about-prme/the-six-principles.php (accessed 10 October 2014).

Rao, N. (1997) 'Women and tourism' for the workshop on women and tourism, 21–23 July, in Cochin, organized by the Institute of Management in Government, Thiruvananthapuram, India.

Reddy, M.V. (2013) Global tourism and travel industry: Performance during the double-dip recession and recommendations for transition to a green economy. *The World Financial Review*, Jan–Feb edition (pp. 26–31) (www.worldfinancialreview.com/?p=977) (Accessed 13 October 2014).

Reddy, M.V. and Wilkes, K. (2012) (eds) *Tourism, climate change and sustainability*. Routledge: London.

Scott, D. (2006) Climate change and sustainable tourism in the 21st century. In Cukier, J. (ed.) *Tourism research: Policy, planning and prospects*. University of Waterloo: Waterloo, ON, pp. 175–248.

Seth, N. (2013) Opening remarks by Mr Nikhil Seth, Director, Division for Sustainable Development. Expert Group Meeting on Sustainable Tourism: Ecotourism, poverty reduction and environmental protection. 29–30 October, United Nations Division for Sustainable Development: New York.

Simpson, M.C., Gossling, S., Scott, D., Hall, C.M. and Gladin, E. (2008) *Climate change adaptation and mitigation in the tourism sector: Frameworks, tools and practices.* UNEP, Oxford University, UNWTO and WMO: Paris.

Tollefson, J. and Gilbert, N. (2012) Rio report card. *Nature*, vol. 486, pp. 20–24.

TUI Travel (2013) What TUI Travel PLC is doing to become a more sustainable business. Guest lecture delivered in October to the Tourism students at the Bournemouth University, UK.

UN (1992) Convention on Biological Diversity. United Nations: Montreal. www.cbd.int/doc/legal/cbd-en.pdf (Accessed 9 October 2014).

UN (1997) Earth Summit. UN Department of Public Information: New York. www.un.org/geninfo/bp/envirp2.html (Accessed 17 June 2014).

UN (1998) Kyoto Protocol to the United Nations Framework Convention on Climate Change. UNFCCC: Bonn.

UN (2010) Resolution adopted by the General Assembly 65th Session: Keeping the promise: united to achieve the Millennium Development Goals, pp. 1–29. UN: New York.

UN (2012) A guidebook to the green economy: Issue 1: Green economy, green growth, and low-carbon development – History, definitions and a guide to recent publications. UNDESA Division for Sustainable Development: New York.

UN (2014) Draft outcome document of the third International Conference on small island developing states, Apia, 1–4 September 2014. www.sids2014.org/content/documents/358A-CONF-223–5 %20ENGLISH.pdf (Accessed 12 October 2014).

UNDESA (2012) *The future we want.* UNDESA Division of Sustainable Development: New York.

UNDESA (2014a) Press release: Secretary General appoints 12 members to High-Level Advisory Group on Sustainable Transport. UNDESA: New York. http://sustainabledevelopment.un.org/content/documents/4718PressRelease_TransportAdvisoryGroup.pdf (Accessed 30 September 2014).

UNDESA (2014b) Outcome document – Open Working Group on Sustainable Development Goals. UNDESA Division of Sustainable Development: New York. http://sustainabledevelop ment.un.org/content/documents/4518SDGs_FINAL_Proposal (Accessed 20 July 2014).

UNECA (2011) *Towards a sustainable tourism industry in Eastern Africa.* United Nations Economic Commission for Africa, Eastern Africa Sub-region Office: Kigali. (pp. 1–130).

UNEP (2009) *Global green new deal: policy brief – March 2009.* UNEP Green Economy Initiative: Geneva.

UNEP (2010) *ABC of SCP clarifying concepts on sustainable consumption and production.* UNEP Division of Technology, Industry and Economics: Paris.

UNEP (2011) *Towards a green economy: Pathways to sustainable development and poverty eradication.* UNEP: Nairobi.

UNEP (2014) What is SCP? www.unep.org/10yfp/About/WhatisSCP/tabid/106246/Default.aspx (Accessed 24 September 2014).

UNESCO (2014) *EFA Global Monitoring Report 2013/4: Teaching and Learning: Achieving quality for all.* UNESCO: Paris.

UNWTO (2006) *India: The Asia and the Pacific intra-regional outbound series.* World Tourism Organization: Madrid.

UNWTO (2014) World Tourism Organization: Who we are. www2.unwto.org/content/who-we-are-0 (Accessed 24 September 2014).

Weaver, D. (2006) *Sustainable tourism: Theory and practice.* Butterworth-Heinemann: Oxford.

WTTC (2014) *Travel & tourism: Economic impact 2014 – World.* WTTC: London.

Young, O.R., Underdal, A., Kanie, N., Andresen, S., Bernstein, S., Biermann, F., Gupta, J., Haas, P.M., Iguchi, M., Kok, M., Levy, M., Nilsson, M., Pintér, L. and Stevens, C. (2014) *Earth system challenges and a multi-layered approach for the sustainable development goals.* POST2015/ UNU-IAS Policy Brief #1, United Nations University Institute for the Advanced Study of Sustainability: Tokyo.

2

DEFINING THE GREEN ECONOMY AND THE POTENTIAL ROLE OF GREEN TOURISM

Adrian C. Newton

Introduction

In recent years, the green economy has become the focus of widespread interest and dialogue, illustrated by its inclusion within policy at national and international scales. At the same time, it has attracted extensive media coverage, while being widely heralded as providing new opportunities for business (Makower, 2009; Esty and Winston, 2006; Croston, 2008; Kane, 2010; Weybrecht, 2010). This interest has been stimulated by the coincidence of multiple global crises, notably the financial crisis of 2008, a rapid increase in food prices, and the environmental issues of anthropogenic climate change and biodiversity loss. The green economy has been identified as a 'win–win' solution to these problems, offering a potential way of supporting economic development while at the same time addressing environmental degradation and issues of socio-economic inequality (Jones, 2009).

Yet what is meant by the term 'green economy'? And what is the potential role of tourism within it? This chapter will examine these questions, by first tracing the development of the concept, and then exploring different perspectives regarding its definitions and underlying principles. The specific case of green tourism will then be considered, based on recent developments at the international scale.

A brief history of the green economy

The term 'green economy' was first used by Pearce *et al.* (1989) in the title of their book *Blueprint for a green economy*. The report was commissioned to advise the UK Government regarding definition of the term 'sustainable development', and the implications of this concept for the measurement of economic progress (Allen and Clouth, 2012). The book presented a perspective drawn from ecological economics, and focused on the benefits of proper valuation of the natural environment to ensure its sustainable use and conservation. The book can be seen as a response to the Brundtland report, *Our common future* (WCED, 1987), which essentially launched the principle of sustainable development in international policy. Interestingly, however, the green economy is not explicitly defined or referred to in the book itself, but only in the title (Pearce *et al.*, 1989).

The term 'green economy' only became widely used following the global financial crisis of 2008, which helped drive it to the top of the political agenda. At the international scale, it was proposed as a tool to address this crisis, and as a means for strengthening international cooperation and support for sustainable development (Allen and Clouth, 2012). Most significantly, the green economy was included as one of two principal themes for the 2012 UN Conference on Sustainable Development (Rio+20), which led to the production of a large number of position papers, background reports and other resources to support the international dialogue at the conference. A useful overview of these publications is provided by Allen and Clouth (2012).

Arguably the most significant contribution to this dialogue was the flagship report produced by UNEP (2011), entitled *Towards a green economy*. This aimed to provide guidance to policy-makers on what reforms they need to introduce, to support the development of a green economy. The report profiles a number of different economic sectors, and includes an explicit section on tourism, as examined further below. Other key publications supported by UNEP included *A global green new deal* (Barbier, 2009, 2010). This again identified the potential opportunity provided by current crises, by supporting economic recovery while addressing other global challenges such as reducing carbon dependency, protecting ecosystems and alleviating poverty. The green economy was identified as the only way of revitalizing the global economy on a more sustained basis (Barbier, 2009).

Inclusion of the green economy as a core theme of Rio+20 stimulated a great deal of debate about the concept, including an extensive critique of how the issue was considered and promoted by the UN. This is considered further below. However, it is important to note that the green economy is not solely a subject debated by intergovernmental policy processes. One of its striking features is the degree of interest that it has generated within the business community, who have identified many emerging opportunities for business development and growth (Makower, 2009; Esty and Winston, 2006; Croston, 2008; Jones, 2009; Kane, 2010; Weybrecht, 2010). These include the development of new technologies for production of renewable energy, increasing energy efficiency and reducing carbon emissions.

At the same time, the green economy can be considered as a social movement, with many civil society organizations encouraging grass-roots innovation (Newton and Cantarello, 2014). These include initiatives to encourage changes in behaviour, such as reducing consumption, increasing recycling and the purchase of green products and services. The green economy also has a political dimension, being related to the interests of Green political parties and the associated discipline of green economics (Cato, 2009). This broad constituency provides a wide range of different perspectives regarding how the green economy should be defined, and how it might be implemented in practice.

Today, the green economy is growing rapidly through the development of environ-mentally enhancing goods and services, including cleaner and more efficient technology, renewable energy, ecosystem- and biodiversity-based products and services, chemical and waste management, and the construction or retrofitting of ecologically friendly buildings (UNEP, 2011). Green tourism is part of these developments. Understanding the potential role of tourism, however, first requires consideration of how the green economy should be defined.

Definition of the green economy

At the outset of its use, the term 'green economy' was treated as synonymous with the concept of sustainable development, as noted above (Pearce *et al.*, 1989; Jacobs, 1991). More recently, a variety of other definitions have been proposed, some of which are listed below (Newton and Cantarello, 2014):

- UNEP (2011) defines a green economy as one that results in 'improved human well-being and social equity, while significantly reducing environmental risks and ecological scarcities'. Put another way, a green economy is 'low-carbon, resource efficient, and socially inclusive'. Furthermore, 'growth in income and employment are driven by public and private investments that reduce carbon emissions and pollution, enhance energy and resource efficiency, and prevent the loss of biodiversity and ecosystem services' (UNEP, 2011).
- The Green Economy Coalition (2012), which is a large multi-stakeholder alliance, defines the green economy as 'one that generates a better quality of life for all within the ecological limits of the planet'. These authors highlight the need for green economies to improve human well-being, while also improving natural capital and systems.
- UNCTAD (2010) defines a green economy as 'an economy that results in improved human well-being and reduced inequalities, while not exposing future generations to significant environmental risks and ecological scarcities. It seeks to bring long-term societal benefits to short-term activities aimed at mitigating environmental risks'.
- The International Chamber of Commerce (2011) defines the green economy from a business perspective, as 'an economy in which economic growth and environmental responsibility work together in a mutually reinforcing fashion while supporting progress on social development'.
- The Danish 92 Group (2012) defines the green economy as 'not a state but a process of transformation and a constant dynamic progression. The green economy does away with the systemic distortions and disfunctionalities of the current mainstream economy and results in human well-being and equitable access to opportunity for all people, while safeguarding environmental and economic integrity in order to remain within the planet's finite carrying capacity. The economy cannot be green without being equitable'.
- UNU-IHDP (2012) defines a green economy as 'one that focuses on enabling people around the world to pursue and achieve lives that are meaningful to them, while minimizing humanity's negative impacts on the environment. It is an economy that is measured against the yardsticks of human well-being and its productive base. It is an economy that is anchored by a passion for equity and a celebration of ingenuity'.
- Chapple (2008) defines the green economy as 'the clean energy economy, consisting primarily of four sectors: renewable energy (e.g. solar, wind, geothermal);

green building and energy efficiency technology; energy-efficient infrastructure and transportation; and recycling and waste-to-energy. The green economy is not just about the ability to produce clean energy, but also technologies that allow cleaner production processes, as well as the growing market for products which consume less energy. Thus, it might include products, processes, and services that reduce environmental impact or improve natural resource use'.

These different definitions highlight the lack of consensus about precisely what the green economy entails. Rather, this is an area of active debate. For many commentators, particularly those in the business community, the green economy is synonymous with the 'clean energy' economy, as described by Chapple (2008). Many of the definitions listed above, however, also refer to the goals of improving human well-being and social equity. Some also explicitly mention the environment, by referring to the concept of environmental limits or carrying capacity. As noted by Peters and Britez (2010), the existence of various definitions indicates that the term 'green economy' is ambiguous and can contain multiple meanings. It could also be described as contested (Newton and Cantarello, 2014).

Other related concepts have also been widely used, including the 'low-carbon economy' and 'green growth'. The concept of low-carbon development originates in the United Nations Framework Convention on Climate Change (UNFCCC) adopted in 1992. This is based on the approach of amending economic development planning to ensure reduced emission of greenhouse gases (GHGs), which are associated with anthropogenic climate change. Many individual countries have produced low-carbon growth plans, supported by international organizations such as UNDP, UNEP, and the World Bank (Allen and Clouth, 2012). The low-carbon economy can therefore be considered as an element of the green economy.

Green growth overlaps substantially with concepts of the green economy, including a shared focus on environmental protection, resource efficiency, ecological sustainability, human well-being and equity (Allen and Clouth, 2012). However, the issue of whether economic growth is consistent with the green economy is an area of particular contention. Much of the dialogue surrounding the green economy at Rio+20 was based on the assumption that it could contribute to economic growth and recovery. This is reflected in a number of the definitions that have been proposed (Allen and Clouth, 2012). However, for some commentators, a green economy should be a zero-growth economy (Cato, 2009; Daly and Farley, 2011; Jackson, 2009). This is based on the idea that there are environmental limits or boundaries to economic activity, which should not be crossed if catastrophic environmental change is to be avoided (Rockström et al., 2009). It can therefore be argued that a green economy should be a 'steady state economy', in which human population and stocks of capital remain constant over time (Daly and Farley, 2011). Conversely, according to Davidson (2000), biological or physical limits are seldom actually limiting to economic growth. If economic growth were to continue indefinitely, it would likely lead to continuous environmental degradation without clear limit points, rather than ecological collapse (Davidson, 2000). This highlights the degree of scientific uncertainty that surrounds the relationship between the global economy and the environment.

The various definitions of low-carbon development, green growth and green economy can therefore be seen to cover a spectrum of different 'shades of green', from narrow concerns about climate change at one end of the spectrum to more extensive critiques of the environmental sustainability of modern capitalism at the other (Allen and Clouth, 2012).

Principles of the green economy

One way of supporting future development of the green economy is to identify a set of principles, to help guide future decision-making. A variety of different organizations have developed sets of principles, which were reviewed by UNDESA (2012). The most commonly identified principles were that the green economy (UNDESA, 2012):

- is a means for achieving sustainable development;
- should create decent work and green jobs;
- is resource and energy efficient;
- respects planetary boundaries or ecological limits or scarcity;
- uses integrated decision-making;
- measures progress beyond GDP using appropriate indicators/metrics;
- is equitable, fair and just – between and within countries and between generations;
- protects biodiversity and ecosystems;
- delivers poverty reduction, well-being, livelihoods, social protection and access to essential services;
- improves governance and the rule of law; and it is inclusive, democratic, participatory, accountable, transparent and stable;
- internalizes externalities (referring to a situation where the costs of environmental damage are borne by producers or consumers).

Interestingly, while these green economy principles encompass the social, economic and environmental aspects of sustainable development, the most common emphasis is on the social dimension. This illustrates how various organizations and stakeholders are currently interpreting the green economy (UNDESA, 2012). It is also interesting to compare these principles, which were produced in the run-up to Rio+20, with those that were recognized in the Rio+20 outcome document (UNCSD, 2012). The latter included explicit reference to economic growth, but no mention of planetary boundaries or ecological limits (see Rockström et al., 2009).

A very different set of principles is presented by Cato (2011), adapted from Milani (2000), which originate from a 'deeper green' perspective:

- The primacy of use-value, intrinsic value and quality: the primary objective as the meeting of need rather than the generation of profit.
- Following natural flows and working with the grain of nature, rather than engaging in a battle for domination of nature.
- Waste equals food: the by-product from one production process should become an input to another production process.

- Elegance and multifunctionality: the search for energy-efficient design and synergies in all economic processes.
- Appropriate scale: rejecting the quest for economies of scale in favour of a size that is sustainable and just.
- Diversity: seeking a range of forms of organization in place of the uniformity of the global marketplace.
- Self-reliance, self-organization and self-design.
- Participation and direct democracy.
- Valuing and encouraging human creativity and development.
- The strategic role of the built environment, the landscape and spatial design.

These contrasting principles again highlight the fact that the green economy is currently a contested concept, with differing perspectives on what it entails (Newton and Cantarello, 2014). This is further illustrated by the critique of the concept that resulted from the dialogue associated with Rio+20, as explored further below.

The green economy post-Rio+20

The principal outcome document of Rio+20 was entitled *The future we want*. This recognized the green economy as an important tool for achieving sustainable development, which 'should contribute to eradicating poverty as well as sustained economic growth, enhancing social inclusion, improving human welfare and creating opportunities for employment and decent work for all, while maintaining the healthy functioning of the earth's ecosystems' (UNCSD, 2012). The document also encouraged countries to develop green economy policies, and provided some guidance for development of such policies.

Some commentators have criticized the outcome of Rio+20 for lacking firm commitments from countries, and lacking detail on how to implement the green economy in practice (Barbier, 2012; Borel-Saladin and Turok, 2013; Morrow, 2012). However, many countries have subsequently begun to develop national strategies and plans for green economic development. These efforts are being supported by a range of international organizations, such as the OECD and the World Bank, as well as other UN agencies. At the European scale, the EU 2020 strategy aims to develop a 'smart, green and inclusive economy' (EC, 2010). At the national scale, green economic plans are under development in countries such as Indonesia, Brazil, Mexico, Ethiopia, Cambodia, Guyana, Kazakhstan, Mongolia, Papua New Guinea and the Philippines (Benson and Greenfield, 2012). Other countries that have developed national strategies or plans for the green economy include Barbados, Canada, Grenada, Jordan, South Africa, France and the UK (Allen and Clouth, 2012). Some countries have already made significant progress towards development of such strategies. For example, South Korea has incorporated green growth into its national development strategy, and has dedicated 80 per cent of its fiscal stimulus plan to green growth projects. In China, some US$140 billion is targeted at green investments, and its Twelfth 5-Year Plan (2011–15) dedicates an entire section to green development (Benson and Greenfield, 2012).

Morrow (2012) highlights the debate surrounding the concept of the green economy, as developed by UNEP and other UN agencies associated with Rio+20. Some developing countries expressed scepticism about the green economy as a creative 'fix' for flaws in the global economic system, noting that the financial crisis was largely Western in origin. Concerns about the potential negative impacts of 'green' technologies were also raised, together with the risks of 'greenwashing', or misleading claims being made about green credentials. A number of developing countries, including Bolivia, Paraguay and Ecuador, pressed for major changes in the relationship between humanity and nature, which were more radical than the concept of the green economy promoted by the UN (Morrow, 2012).

Borel-Saladin and Turok (2013) and Lander (2011) similarly highlight concerns that some conceptions of the green economy may not represent a significant enough departure from the current economic system to be effective. Other issues relate to the monetization of nature, or the financial valuation of ecosystem goods and services, which is widely perceived as an element of the green economy (Lander, 2011; Spash, 2008). A further area of concern relates to international trade, including the possibility of trade protectionism, potential attempts by some countries to gain enhanced market access for their products, and the potential role of transnational corporations. This relates to the issue of power, the grabbing of land and natural resources, and ultimately who controls the green economy (ETC Group, 2011). In addition, much of the recent dialogue surrounding the green economy has failed to consider the potential ecological limits to economic growth (Borel-Saladin and Turok, 2013).

The green economy vs sustainable development

The focus on the green economy at Rio+20 can be viewed in terms of an attempt to apply new thinking or new impetus to the concept of sustainable development, specifically by linking it to the concept of green growth (Morrow, 2012). This therefore raises the question – what is the relationship between the green economy and sustainable development?

Sustainable development is often defined as development that 'meets the needs of the present without compromising the ability of future generations to meet their needs' (WCED, 1987). The main components of sustainable development are generally agreed to be economic, environmental and social, which are often represented by three pillars or three interlocking circles (Dresner, 2008; Kates et al., 2005). Sustainable development has spread rapidly as a concept, and can now be considered as a global movement that is central to the mission of many international organizations, national institutions, corporate enterprises and locales (Kates et al., 2005). This is despite the fact that the standard definition is highly ambiguous, resulting in a substantial and ongoing debate about what it really means in practice (Dresner, 2008; Kates et al., 2005).

As sustainable development continues to be the overarching policy goal of the international community, the green economy is widely seen as a means of supporting its achievement (Allen and Clouth, 2012), or as an enabling component of it (UNCTAD, 2010). Allen and Clouth (2012) highlight the widely held view that the green economy should not compete with or displace sustainable development, nor focus on environmental and economic dimensions to the detriment of the social element.

However, as noted by IUCN (2010), the concept of the green economy often carries a more distinctive meaning, which focuses specifically on the fundamental changes that are required to ensure that economic systems are made more sustainable. Similarly, for the Green Economy Coalition (2012), the green economy is about a different way of doing things. Cato (2011) suggests that a key difference between sustainable development and the green economy is that under the latter concept, the environment is viewed as underpinning the global economy, rather than simply comprising an element of it. Similarly, Dawe and Ryan (2002) note that the standard definition of sustainable development implies that a compromise can be reached between our economic needs, human well-being and the environment. However, humanity can have neither an economy nor social well-being without the environment. The environment should therefore be viewed as the foundation of the economy (Dawe and Ryan, 2002).

At the very least, development of the green economy concept has stimulated debate into how the global economy might be improved in future, to help achieve sustainable development. Allen and Clouth (2012) suggest that this debate has stimulated global efforts to transform the current economic system, including development of operational principles and measures that can be adopted by national governments to shift to a more sustainable economic framework. A further key point is that the green economy is a concept that has engaged the business community, and arguably civil society more generally, in a way that sustainable development never has (Newton and Cantarello, 2014). How, then, does it relate to the specific business sector of tourism?

Tourism in the green economy

Tourism is one of the world's largest industries, representing 5 per cent of world GDP (UNEP, 2011). It is also an industry that is growing steadily in size and importance. However, while tourism is a vital source of income for many countries, it can also result in pollution, environmental degradation, deforestation, inefficient energy use and cultural exploitation (UNEP, 2011). In response, new policies are being developed to encourage sustainable practices in tourism (GSTC Partnership, 2008).

Key points relating to green tourism are presented by UNEP (2011):

- *Tourism has significant potential as a driver for growth for the world economy*. International tourism ranks fourth (after fuels, chemicals and automotive products) in global exports, with an industry value of US$1 trillion a year. It is the main source of foreign exchange for one-third of developing countries.
- *The development of tourism is accompanied by significant challenges*. The sector contributes 5 per cent of global GHG emissions. Other challenges include excessive water consumption, the generation of waste, damage to biodiversity, and threats to the survival of local cultures, built heritage and traditions.
- *Green tourism has the potential to create new jobs and reduce poverty*. Travel and tourism are human-resource intensive, employing 8 per cent of the global workforce. The greening of tourism, which involves efficiency improvements in energy, water, and waste systems, is expected to reinforce the employment potential of the sector.
- *Investing in the greening of tourism can reduce the costs of energy, water and waste, and enhance the value of biodiversity, ecosystems and cultural heritage*. Investments can

usefully be made in increasing energy efficiency, improving waste management, in cultural heritage and in the conservation and restoration of ecosystems.

- *Tourists are increasingly demanding the greening of tourism.* More than a third of travellers are found to favour environmentally friendly tourism and be willing to pay between 2–40 per cent more for this experience. Ecotourism, nature, heritage, cultural and 'soft adventure' tourism are predicted to grow rapidly over the next two decades.
- *The private sector, especially small firms, need to be mobilized to support green tourism.* The awareness of green tourism currently exists mainly in a selection of larger-scale firms. Much of the economic potential for green tourism is found in small and medium-sized enterprises (SMEs), which need better access to financing for investing in green tourism. Specific mechanisms and tools are also needed to educate SMEs.
- *Destination planning and development strategies are the first step towards the greening of tourism.* In developing tourism strategies, local governments, communities and businesses need to establish mechanisms for coordinating with ministries responsible for the environment, energy, labour, agriculture, transport, health, finance, security and other relevant areas.
- *Government investments and policies can leverage private sector actions on green tourism.* Government spending on public goods such as protected areas; cultural assets, waste management and renewable energy infrastructure can reduce the cost of green investments by the private sector in green tourism. Governments can also use tax concessions and subsidies to encourage private investment in green tourism.

Such issues highlight both the contribution that tourism could potentially make to the global green economy, but also the challenges that need to be overcome. Particular challenges include (UNEP, 2011): (1) energy and GHG emissions; (2) water consumption; (3) waste management; (4) loss of biodiversity; and (5) effective management of cultural heritage.

UNEP (2011) points out that green tourism is not a special form of tourism. Rather, all types of tourism could become greener through various means, for example by becoming more energy-efficient, using less water, generating less waste, conserving biodiversity, supporting culture and traditions, and improving local livelihoods by providing income. This implies significant improvements in the performance of conventional tourism, as well as growth and improvements in smaller, niche areas centred on natural, cultural and community resources (UNEP, 2011).

Efforts to develop tourism as an element of the green economy link directly with previous efforts to increase the sustainability of tourism. Specifically, there have been a series of international meetings designed to promote the environmental, socio-cultural and economic sustainability of tourism. Examples include:

- The World Ecotourism Summit, organized by the United Nations World Tourism Organization (UNWTO) and UNEP, held in 2002. The Quebec declaration that emerged as a result of this meeting provides a template for policy-makers to formulate an official policy on ecotourism.

- The Cape Town Conference in 2002, which was organized by the Responsible Tourism Partnership as an event preceding the WSSD (World Summit on Sustainable Development) in Johannesburg, and produced a declaration that later fed in to the WSSD (ICRT, 2002).
- More recently, the Global Sustainable Tourism Criteria (GSTC) were launched at the World Conservation Congress in 2008. The criteria mainly address issues of poverty alleviation and environmental sustainability, providing guidance in these areas for the tourism industry (GSTC Partnership, 2008).

Although none of the recommendations of these initiatives are binding, they nonetheless provide an indication of the direction in which the tourism industry needs to move in order to become greener.

A further key approach is offered by accreditation and certification schemes. Such accreditation is important because it sets quality standards for both industry and markets, and adds credibility and validity to the different certification schemes. There are now many tourism certification schemes around the world, including (following Jarvis *et al.*, 2010):

- Green Globe 21, a global benchmarking and certification programme for travel and tourism;
- Green Key, an international eco-label for leisure that operates in more than sixteen countries;
- The Certificate for Sustainable Tourism, a programme to encourage environmental practice in hotels in Costa Rica; and
- STEP, the Sustainable Tourism Eco-certification Standard.

At present, there is no formal global regulation of the certification process for global tourism (Jarvis *et al.*, 2010), although the GSTC criteria provide a potential approach by which global standards might be identified.

Conclusions

Development of the green economy as a concept received enormous impetus from Rio+20, and the international dialogue that it stimulated. However, this dialogue featured some dissenting voices, and some doubts were expressed about the vision of the green economy promoted by the United Nations. For some, the green economy offers a potential 'win–win' solution to the current financial, socio-economic and environmental crises, whereas, for others, the prevailing rhetoric does not go far enough in advocating sufficient change in the current economic system to successfully avert these crises.

Given the nature of the debate surrounding Rio+20 and its limited political impact, doubts could legitimately be expressed about the value and potential longevity of the green economy as a concept. However, this would ignore the significant traction that the green economy has already gained as an element of national and international policy, as illustrated by its widespread inclusion in strategies for economic development. It has also generated significant interest in the business community, and in civil society more generally, to a degree that the related concept of sustainable development has arguably failed to achieve. The substantial investments now being made in renewable energy throughout the world provide evidence that the green economy will continue to develop rapidly, whatever its place in intergovernmental dialogue.

Interest in the green economy from politicians lies in its potential to support economic growth and development, as well as supporting employment and job creation. Similarly, many businesses are keen to capitalize on the many opportunities that are emerging in the green economy, supported by developments in green technology. These include both the development of new goods and services, and the greening of existing business practices, which can deliver benefits in terms of increased efficiency and enhanced brand image.

Such opportunities are also available to the tourism sector, and there is clearly enormous potential to develop tourism as an element of the green economy. To achieve this goal, a number of significant challenges will need to be overcome, particularly relating to the consumption of energy and associated GHG emissions, the consumption of water and other resources, waste management and impacts on both cultural and natural heritage.

Development of green tourism will require clarity regarding how it is defined and the principles on which it is based. As profiled here, development of the green economy as a concept has been informed by a wide variety of different perspectives, around which there is still substantial debate. A central issue that remains contentious is whether or not the green economy is compatible with economic growth, or whether a global economic structure is required that will ensure environmental boundaries are not transgressed. Other key issues that have attracted debate include social justice, the economic valuation of nature, inequities in global trade and the risks of 'greenwashing'. These are issues that green tourism could usefully consider as it develops, for example through the development of criteria for accreditation of green tourism operations.

Despite the lack of consensus about what the green economy entails, there is widespread agreement that it can potentially make a positive contribution to sustainable development. As one of the world's largest industries, tourism can potentially make a major contribution to this process. Realization of this potential will require Government intervention, to provide appropriate investments and policies and to support appropriate planning and development strategies. However, the private sector, especially small firms, will need to play a leading role. Their incentive to do so will lie in the anticipated growth in consumer demand for green tourism products and services.

What kind of tourism might prevail in a future world where the green economy has developed successfully? One potential trend is for much greater emphasis on tourism at the local scale. It is already recognized that tourism is an important and effective driver of local economic development (UNEP, 2011). Making tourism greener could involve creating stronger linkages with the local economy, and embedding it within local natural and cultural heritage. A potential model for this lies in the bioregional approach, which has been proposed as a central element of the green economy (Cato, 2013). This focuses on the process of localization, which has long been a feature of green economic thinking (Cato, 2013). Examples would include increasing purchasing directly from local businesses, recruiting and training local staff, entering into neighbourhood partnerships to make the local social environment a better place to live, work and visit, and improvement of the local natural and cultural environment (Ashley *et al.*, 2006; Hall and Coles, 2008). More radically, it might focus on encouraging tourists to visit places near where they live and work, rather than travelling to long-haul destinations, thereby reducing GHG emissions. Given the current high rates of global environmental and socio-economic change, there is likely to be an increasing need for such radical re-imaginings of how tourism should develop in the future.

References

Allen, C. and Clouth, S. (2012) *A guidebook to the green economy. Issue 1: Green economy, green growth and low carbon development – history, definitions and a guide to recent publications.* UN Division for Sustainable Development, Department of Economic and Social Affairs (UN-DESA): New York.

Ashley, C., Goodwin, H., McNab, D., Scott, M. and Chaves, L. (2006) *Making tourism count for the local economy in the Caribbean. Guidelines for good practice.* Pro-Poor Tourism Partnership and the Caribbean Tourism Organization.

Barbier, E.B. (2009) *Rethinking the economic recovery: A global green new deal.* UNEP: Geneva.

Barbier, E.B. (2010) *A global green new deal: Rethinking the economic recovery.* Cambridge University Press: Cambridge.

Barbier, E.B. (2012) The green economy post Rio+20. *Science*, vol. 338, pp. 887–8.

Benson, E. and Greenfield, O. (2012) *Surveying the 'green economy' and 'green growth' landscape.* Green Economy Coalition, IIED: London.

Borel-Saladin, J.M. and Turok, I.N. (2013) The green economy: incremental change or transformation? *Environmental Policy and Governance*, vol. 23, pp. 209–20.

Cato, M.S. (2009) *Green economics. An introduction to theory, policy and practice.* Earthscan: London.

Cato, M.S. (2011) *Environment and economy.* Routledge: Abingdon, UK.

Cato, M.S. (2013) *The bioregional economy: Land, liberty and the pursuit of happiness.* Routledge: Abingdon, UK.

Chapple, K. (2008). *Defining the green economy: A primer on green economic development.* Center for Community Innovation, University of California: Berkeley, CA.

Croston, G. (2008) *75 green businesses you can start to make money and make a difference.* Entrepreneur Press: Irvine, CA.

Daly, H.E and Farley, J. (2011) *Ecological economics: Principles and applications.* Island Press: Washington, DC.

Danish 92 Group (2012) *Building an equitable green economy.* The Danish 92 Group Forum for Sustainable Development: Copenhagen, Denmark.

Davidson, C. (2000) Economic growth and the environment: Alternatives to the Limits Paradigm. *BioScience*, vol. 50, no. 5, pp. 433–40.

Dawe, N.K. and Ryan, K.L. (2002) The faulty three-legged-stool model of sustainable development. *Conservation Biology*, vol. 17, no. 5, pp. 1458–60.

Dresner, S. (2008) *The principles of sustainability.* Earthscan: London.

EC (2010) *Europe 2020. A strategy for smart, sustainable and inclusive growth. COM(2010) 2020 final.* European Commission: Brussels.

Esty, D.C. and Winston, A.S. (2006) *Green to gold: How smart companies use environmental strategy to innovate, create value, and build competitive advantage.* John Wiley & Sons: Hoboken, NJ.

ETC Group (2011) *Who will control the green economy?* IIED: London.

Green Economy Coalition (2012) *The green economy pocket book.* The Green Economy Coalition, IIED: London.

GSTC Partnership (2008) *Global sustainable tourism criteria.* United Nations Foundation: Washington, DC.

Hall, C.M. and Coles, T. (2008) Introduction: Tourism and international business. In Coles, T. and Hall, C.M. (eds), *International Business and Tourism: Global Issues, Contemporary Interactions.* (pp. 1–25). Routledge: London.

ICRT (International Centre for Responsible Tourism) (2002) *Cape Town Declaration.* ICRT: Cape Town, South Africa.

International Chamber of Commerce (2011) *The ICC task force on green economy.* International Chamber of Commerce: Paris.

IUCN (2010) *A guidebook for IUCN's thematic programme area on greening the world economy (TPA5).* IUCN: Gland, Switzerland.

Jackson, T. (2009)*Prosperity without growth.* Earthscan: London.

Jacobs, M. (1991) *The green economy: Environment, sustainable development and the politics of the future.* Pluto Press: London.

Jarvis, N., Weeden, C. and Simcock, N. (2010) The benefits and challenges of sustainable tourism certification: A case study of the Green Tourism Business Scheme in the West of England. *Journal of Hospitality and Tourism Management,* vol. 17, pp. 83–93.

Jones, V. (2009) *The green collar economy: How one solution can fix our two biggest problems.* Harper Collins: New York.

Kane, G. (2010) *The three secrets of green business: Unlocking competitive advantage in a low carbon economy.* Earthscan: London.

Kates, R.W., Parris, T.M. and Leiserowitz, A.A. (2005). What is sustainable development? Goals, indicators, values and practice. *Environment,* vol. 47, no. 3, pp. 9–21.

Lander, E. (2011) *The green economy: the wolf in sheep's clothing.* Transnational Institute: Amsterdam, The Netherlands.

Makower, J. (2009) *Strategies for the green economy: Opportunities and challenges in the new world of business.* McGraw Hill: New York.

Milani, B. (2000) *Designing the green economy: The post-industrial alternative to corporate globalisation.* Rowman & Littlefield: New York.

Morrow, K. (2012) Rio+20, the green economy and re-orienting sustainable development. *Environmental Law Review,* vol. 14, pp. 279–97.

Newton, A.C. and Cantarello, E. (2014) *An introduction to the green economy: Science, systems and sustainability.* Routledge: London.

Pearce, D.W., Markandya, A. and Barbier, E. (1989) *Blueprint for a green economy.* Earthscan: London.

Peters, M.A. and Britez, R. (2010) Ecopolitics of 'green economy', environmentalism and education. *Journal of Academic Research in Economics,* vol. 2, no. 1, pp. 20–35.

Rockström, J., Steffen, W., Noone, K., Persson, A., Chapin, F.S., Lambin, E.F., Lenton, T.M., Scheffer, M., Folke, C., Schellnhuber, H. J., Nykvist, B., de Wit, C.A., Hughes, T., van der Leeuw, S., Rodhe, H., Sorlin, S., Snyder, P.K., Costanza, R., Svedin, U., Falkenmark, M., Karlberg, L., Corell, R.W., Fabry, V.J., Hansen, J., Walker, B., Liverman, D., Richardson, K., Crutzen, P. and Foley, J.A. (2009) A safe operating space for humanity. *Nature,* vol. 461, pp. 472–5.

Spash, C. L. (2008) How much is that ecosystem in the window? The one with the bio-diverse tail. *Environmental Values,* vol. 17, pp. 259–84.

UNCSD (2012) *Report of the United Nations Conference on Sustainable Development.* A/CONF. 216/16. United Nations: New York. www.uncsd2012.org/content/documents/814UNCSD. Accessed 9 April 2015.

UNCTAD (2010) *The green economy: trade and sustainable development implications.* Background note prepared by the UNCTAD Secretariat. United Nations: New York. http://unctad.org/en/ Docs/ditcted20102_en.pdf. Accessed 9 April 2015.

UNDESA (2012) *A guidebook to the green economy. Issue 2: exploring green economy principles.* UNDESA: New York. http://sustainabledevelopment.un.org/. Accessed 9 April 2015.

UNEP (2011) *Towards a green economy: Pathways to sustainable development and poverty eradication.* UNEP: Geneva. www.unep.org/greeneconomy. Accessed 9 April 2015.

UNU-IHDP. (2012) *Green economy and sustainability: A societal transformation process.* Summary for Decision-Makers. Secretariat of the International Human Dimensions Programme on Global Environmental Change (UNU-IHDP): Bonn, Germany.

WCED (1987) *Our common future.* Oxford University Press: Oxford.

Weybrecht, G. (2010) The *sustainable MBA: The manager's guide to green business.* John Wiley & Sons: Chichester, England.

3

ENVIRONMENTAL ETHICS AND CHALLENGES TO TOURISM'S PLACE IN THE GREEN ECONOMY

Andrew Holden

Introduction

This chapter assimilates two relatively recent concepts, environmental ethics and the paradigm shift to the green economy. Both are representative of an evolution in human reasoning about our interaction with the surrounding environment and about how development should and should not take place in the future. They can also be seen as intersecting conceptual frameworks with an environmental ethic, being understood as representing a force of individual and collective agency merging with a global policy shift to a green economy. While tourism is recognized by UNEP (2011) as being one of the key economic sectors of the green economy, several challenges that threaten a positive relationship between tourism and environmental sustainability have also been identified. The subsequent aim of this chapter is to evaluate the relevance of an environmental ethic to tourism's place in the green economy.

An evolving environmental ethic

While expressions of doubt over anthropocentric-driven climate change still exist, typically residing in parties with a vested interest in retaining the benefits of a carbon-based political economy, the environmental debate has become a mainstream one in society. This dialogue encapsulates the responsibilities of stakeholders, including international organizations such as the United Nations and World Bank, national governments, the private sector, non-governmental organizations (NGOs), local communities and individual citizens, to produce cohesive responses of how to adapt to and mitigate environmental challenges. It consequently involves a re-evaluation of how we should live in the future to maximize well-being and ensure environmentally sustainable development, embracing issues of political economy, geography and ethics.

A part of this evaluation involves a consideration of the duties and responsibilities towards nature. The origins of contemporary environmental concern can be traced to the advent of the Industrial Revolution in the late eighteenth century and concerns about the effects of scientific and industrial advancement resulting in changes in landscape and the loss of wilderness. At the same time there was a re-awakened interest in the spiritual and aesthetic values of wilderness, encapsulated in the poetry, music and writings of the broadly labelled Romantic movement, a part of which engaged in a creative dialogue with the power of nature and scenery, in a mix of awe and adoration. A notable example of this was the publication of *La nouvelle Héloise* by Jean-Jacques Rousseau, which publicized the appeal of the European Alps for tourism in the eighteenth century (Blanning, 2010). Concern about the effects of the Industrial Revolution on wilderness led to the evolution of the national parks movement during the nineteenth century in the United States of America led by John Muir, and the foundation of the Sierra movement. This movement was influenced by the earlier philosophical writings of Henry Thoreau who was damning in his criticism of the material values transgressing society in an urbanizing America that, in his view, detracted from the spiritual enrichment and health lent to humankind by wilderness and nature. The theme of a human reconnection with nature was an inherent part of the founding of the national parks in America, with an emphasis on 're-creating' in wilderness areas for reasons of physiological and psychological well-being, allied with the goal to conserve nature and biodiversity from the processes of economic development.

The mantle of environmental concern was furthered by Aldo Leopold (1949) linking our behaviour directly to nature in his concept of the 'land ethic'. The land ethic represents a direct challenge to the previously widely accepted Western paradigmatic construction of humans as the dominant species of the planet, a tenet of Roman Christian thinking embedded in Descartes' philosophy and the subsequent Cartesian dominance of thought that permitted an instrumental use of nature for human benefit. This emphasis on the centrality of humans in the universe was reinforced through the philosophy of Humanism in the mid-seventeenth century that challenged the role of the divine, stressing deontology or 'rights'-based ethics that recognized the rights and duties of human beings but did not extend them to the non-human world. A consideration of rights and duties in the context of our relationship with the non-human environment thus represents a significant shift in the boundaries of recognizable ethical debate. For Nash (1989) this extension of ethical and moral reasoning to non-human species is as profound as the ideals of human rights that evolved in the eighteenth century, which can be understood as being rooted in our capacity to extend sentiments of empathy and sympathy to others, ultimately leading to the abolition of the slave trade.

The sentiments of empathy and sympathy are emphasized by Wenz (2001) as being the core ones for human cooperation which historically has been predominantly confined to the geographical boundaries of family and immediate community. While the strength of bonds of sympathy and empathy may be eroded and weakened with distance, global charitable responses to contemporary natural disasters including the Asian tsunami, the Haitian earthquake and famines in several African countries, suggest a conceptualization of 'community' that has progressively become more geographically extensive and culturally diverse. Contributing to this trend are heightened levels of mobility, including migration and tourism, combined with the spatial diffusion of information technology and other forces of globalization. Alongside the sentiments of sympathy and empathy and the notion of 'community', what one feels to be connected and belonging to, brings accompanying responsibilities and duties. The resonance of such reasoning to environmental ethics is axiomatic in Leopold's (1949) land ethic that places 'us', humankind, within and as a member of an ecological community rather than the conqueror of it. It subsequently challenges the notion of a human dominance of nature and the accompanying rationale of its value being solely limited to its usefulness for human benefit. Instead it emphasizes the requirement for an acknowledgement of humans as members of the ecological community rather than conquerors of it (Leopold, 1949).

While Thoreau, Muir and Leopold are seminal to the evolution of environmental philosophy, it is particularly in the latter half of the twentieth century that a widening acceptance of environmentalism and the relevance of an environmental ethic to inform the actions of society can be traced. The combination of observable and scientifically measured impacts in the environmental sciences and ecology, has led to a profound questioning of how anthropocentric activities are affecting natural rhythms, processes and cycles, including a questioning of what is indeed still 'natural'. This evidence challenged pre-existing assumptions of what had previously been held as environmentally benign economic activity and practice. For example, Rachel Carson's (1962) *Silent spring*, the classic analysis of how the industrialization of farming was destroying the ecosystems of the American countryside, was a seminal point in the realization that even those commonly viewed as custodians or stewards of the environment were not immune from industrial advancement and subsequent negative impacts of their activities upon nature.

Since the 1960s the environmental effects of economic and industrial activity have become ever more apparent, with the accompanying knowledge that environmental problems frequently transgress national geographical boundaries and subsequently require coherent political responses between governments. Ozone depletion, acid rain and global warming are examples of environmental problems that have necessitated political cooperation and action. It is particularly this latter challenge of global warming that has created anxiety about a global economy that is reliant upon carbon-derived energy, leading to unprecedented levels of media coverage about how anthropocentric actions may negatively impact upon our surroundings and the ecosystems and species that constitute it. This concern extends not only to the survival of species or ecosystems but also derives from the realization that by damaging the range of ecosystem services and climatic stability we rely upon, there is a reciprocal effect upon our own economic, physiological and psychological well-being.

The evolution of an environmental awareness by the 1970s was recognized by Naess (1973) in a seminal thesis based upon a continuum of environmental philosophy and ideology ranging from 'deep ecology' to 'shallow ecology'. While having contrasting political ideologies of how to deal with the 'environmental crisis', both positions represent a recognition of the need to mitigate the anthropocentric causal factors of environmental problems. They nevertheless differ in their environmental philosophies, with deep ecology rejecting the Cartesian dualism of humans and nature, instead emphasizing the human and environment relationship as a holistic entity. It also recognizes an intrinsic value to nature, a 'right to be', independent of human decree or value, emphasizing a change in individual consciousness to promote values, attitudes and lifestyles that are compatible with nature (Pepper, 1996). By contrast, shallow ecology can be understood as being synonymous with 'environmentalism' according to Dobson's (2000, p. 3) definition: '*environmentalism* [Dobson's emphasis] argues for a managerial approach to environmental problems, secure in a belief that they can be solved without fundamental changes in present values or patterns of production and consumption'.

The significance of Naess's (1973) work is that even though a common goal of mitigating environmental problems may be shared, the approaches of how to achieve this may vary substantially according to environmental philosophy and the types of value accorded to nature beyond the economic. Such values would include nature's life-support value; re-creational value; scientific value; aesthetic value; genetic-diversity value; and historical value (Rolston III, 1988). How we prioritize these, and the weighting of importance we lend them has significant implications for how we construct and recognize environmental problems and the subsequent responses we view as being adequate to deal with them. Yet all of these values are derived from an anthropocentric stance, i.e. they are ones bestowed on nature by humans. The extension into a deeper environmental philosophy akin to deep ecology would embrace recognition of nature to have an intrinsic 'right to be', independent of the value bestowed upon it by humans. The relevance of types of environmental values is emphasized by Curry (2011) who states that they are critical within a normative ethical framework for deciding what is good or bad; and which practices are right or wrong.

How the environment is 'used' also incorporates dimensions of ethical decision-making related to the rights of other humans as a consequence of the externalized effects of individual action. Issues of the negative economic externalities of lifestyles enjoyed by the majority of peoples in developed countries being pushed onto the poor of the developing world; contestation between developed and developing countries over greenhouse gas (GHG) emission limits for reason of denying economic opportunities to peoples of the least developed countries and a potential threat to the longevity of humans as a species on the planet; are all examples of challenges that relate to our interaction with nature and raise ethical debate of rights and wrongs.

Accepting empathy and sympathy as conditional sentiments for the construction of ethical frameworks, the growth in membership and support of environmental non-government organizations (ENGOs), including the World Wide Fund for Nature and Greenpeace, reflect an increasing connection and empathy with nature. The loss of habitats or species may result in sorrow especially when the strength of association with the natural environment has a strong personal empathy. Such sentiment is aptly captured in the following homage to a statue of a pigeon by Leopold (1949, p. 108):

> We have erected a monument to commemorate the funeral of species. It symbolizes our sorrow. We grieve because no living man will see again the onrushing phalanx of victorious birds. . . . There will always be pigeons in books and in museums, but these are effigies and images, dead to all hardships and to all delights.

This passage expresses a sadness of loss over a species, implying an extension of empathy and sympathy beyond the human realm to another living entity, recognizing an 'intrinsic value to another species being' and its right to existence, conveying an extension of an emotional connection to the wider non-human community.

Closely related to Naess's (1973) typology of 'deep ecology' is the ethic of 'libertarian extension', which recognizes all sentient and non-sentient beings' rights to an existence, independent of any value bestowed on them by humankind. This recognition of an intrinsic value to nature, a value independent of human use or transference, focuses on a non-human species' right to evolve and develop to achieve its end goal or *telos*. This deep ecocentric ethic raises subsequent questions about the 'rights' of nature, the basis of deciding these rights, and how non-anthropocentric concern can be justified. Alongside feelings of empathy and sympathy, Callicott (1993) observes that in Western philosophy there is almost unanimity of opinion that the origin of ethics is based upon human reason and experience, i.e. that morality comes from rationality. Subsequently, it can be argued that there is a rationale for nature having rights, on the basis that the human species is a relative newcomer to earth, evolving on a planet that has been the home of other species for hundreds of millions of years. On a combined basis of empathy, sympathy and rationality it could thus be interpreted that we have a duty to other species to respect their existence and habitat, a position akin to Sagoff's (1993) concept of a 'moral community' whose members respect each other's rights and treat their interests with equal respect and concern.

An extreme enforcement of a deep ecology ethic to the non-human environment would pose a major challenge to our own existence, raising issues of our rights to use nature in any way for our own benefit, including for food. There are, however, various continuums and degrees of the recognition of the intrinsic rights of nature in religious practice and secular society that represent a worldview that is akin to a deep ecology ethic. For example Jainism, vegetarianism and veganism all embody an approach to nature that embodies an environmental ethic that recognizes an intrinsic value of nature, that seek to minimize harm, suffering and a negative impact on nature. These worldviews are recognition of being part of a wider community than purely a human one, necessitating a consideration of our actions towards the non-human world and a subsequent modification of behaviour. As Rolston III (1993) observes, the ultimate test for environmental ethics is its ability to conserve life on earth, based upon a respect of the values held by nature. It can thus be argued that the conservation of species and ecosystems may in reality be a more realistic goal of the influence of an environmental ethic upon lifestyle rather than the conservation of one particular animal or plant, an objective which is unrealistic to maintain in the context of our own survival.

Given the difficulty of establishing commonly agreed principles to define the rights and values of nature this means that decisions on its use typically fall into 'situation ethics', where each situation is judged upon its own merits. As the guiding contemporary ethic to our interaction with nature, Vardy and Grosch (1999) hold that the conservation ethic is the diktat of society's moral reasoning about nature; being central to much of environmental policy, as exemplified in the Brundtland Report (WCED, 1987). However, the moral basis of the conservation ethic is not always evident, as it may have either an anthropocentric or non-anthropocentric orientation (i.e. the conservation of nature for humans' benefit or conservation based on the recognition of the right to exist of non-human species and ecosystems). Even from a purely anthropocentric perspective, the application of a conservation ethic has a strong rationale, as our own well-being is dependent upon the ecological soundness of plant and animal communities.

The environmental ethic in the green economy

The presence of a conservation ethic is evident in the call for a green economy that is characterized by being low-carbon resource-efficient and socially inclusive (UNEP, 2011). It also embraces an implicit ethical dimension both of care for our surroundings and the welfare of the non-human environment combined with a duty and obligation to fellow members of the human race to ensure their well-being. As an integral sector of the green economy, tourism has been recognized as a key economic player in the shift from a brown economy. Yet key challenges relating to the character of its consumption have been identified by UNEP (2011) that threaten tourism's role in the green economy: mobility and patterns of resource usage, including a consumer trend to travel further for shortening durations of time; a preference for energy-intensive transportation based upon non-renewable fuel usage with an accompanying growth in GHG emissions; excessive water consumption; damage to marine and terrestrial biodiversity; and threats to local cultural traditions and built heritage. While the last of these lies outside the domain of environmental ethics, although it has a strong ethical component, it is evident from this list that individual choices and actions are an important catalyst to the acceleration of de-acceleration of these environmental challenges.

A shallow ecology approach centred on economic solutions to ensure market correction and incorporate environmental costs as advocated by international agencies including the United Nations, World Bank and International Monetary Fund may offer a partial solution to these environmental problems. However, as Jamieson (2008) emphasizes, it is market economics and technology that have been two of the key drivers of the environmental crisis, and to subsequently expect them to produce the solutions could be deemed as being highly optimistic. The transition of economic theory into practice also typically involves a significant time delay. For example Butcher (2006) draws attention to the concept of 'natural capital' in ecological economics that emphasizes biophysical and geophysical processes and their outcomes, for example, fish in the sea, oil in the ground, in the context of their relationship to human needs over time (Butcher, 2006). Yet, two decades later, difficulties still exist in translating the worth of natural capital into market values (Butcher, 2006). Similarly, theoretical concepts such as the 'polluter pays principle' have been established in environmental economics since at least the 1980s but have to date had little practical application. Environmentally benign technological advancement also has lengthy time-lead dimensions, and its adaptation and financial feasibility is dependent upon the ability of market mechanisms to reflect full environmental costs. Thus it is argued that progress towards meeting the challenges of tourism's place in the green economy rests upon the actions and behaviour of consumers as tourists alongside progress in market reforms and environmentally benign technologies.

As a component of mass consumption, tourism may be understood as an outcome of the Industrial Revolution, technological advancement, increased levels of wealth and disposable income, heightened motilities, combining with an innate desire to travel to new environments, facilitated by an increasingly sophisticated service sector. As part of consumerism it is thus rational to expect tourism to reflect changing paradigms and fashions of societal and environmental concern. To an extent this is exemplified through the plethora of market labels that have emerged to prefix tourism, including eco, nature, sustainable, responsible and fair-trade, indicating at the least a valorization of social and environmental consciousness. Yet the extent that the emergence of these new typologies of tourism is underpinned by environmental ethics is difficult to determine, not least because of the sporadic character of research into the environmental ethics of the tourism market.

While UNEP (2011) views consumer preference and behaviour as the catalyst for the environmentally sustainable tourism that is integral to the green economy, stating that: 'tourists are demanding the greening of tourism' (UNEP, 2011, p. 419), the universal application of this maxim is unsure. The relationship between environmental challenges and consumerism is not one that may be necessarily construed by the individual. For example, in a survey of 27,000 respondents conducted across twenty-seven Member States of the European Union, virtually all the respondents (96 per cent) stated that environmental problems were very or fairly important to them. A high level of understanding of the relationship between a high quality environment and the well-being of society was also revealed, with 78 per cent of respondents agreeing that environmental problems have a direct effect on their daily lives and that its protection is important. However, while the highest ranked environmental concerns, those of climate change, water pollution, and air pollution were understood to be primarily anthropocentric in their origins, seemingly little association was made between these problems and consumption. Specifically, while 57 per cent of the respondents cited climate change as the most environmentally challenging problem facing society, when asked about its causes only 12 per cent of the respondents linked it to transport choices and just 11 per cent to consumption.

The linking of causal factors to environmental problems is also significant for the perception of who has responsibility for their mitigation. A total of 90 per cent of the sample agreed that the big polluters, i.e. corporations and industry should be mainly responsible for environmental protection. While individual action was also stressed as a means of environmental protection by 86 per cent of the respondents, a type of cognitive dissonance exists between possessing a positive attitude towards environmental protection, a stated willingness to engage in behaviour to achieve this, and the actual taking of action. Concerning their consumer behaviour, while 75 per cent of respondents agreed they were willing to buy environmental products even if more expensive than normal ones, only 17 per cent stated they had done so in the month before the survey. A similar reluctance to pay a premium for environmental protection was also unearthed in a study carried out for the Association of British Travel Agents (ABTA, 2012). Although one in three holidaymakers believe that holidays should carry an environmental rating, only 19 per cent of the sample stated that they were prepared to pay more for a holiday with a company that had a strong environmental record.

Reluctance for a behavioural change in tourism consumption to benefit the environment was also identified in a household survey in the United Kingdom. Despite over 80 per cent of the households agreeing that climate change was already evident, only 22 per cent expressed a willingness to 'fly less' as defined by flying to only one holiday destination per annum (Energy Saving Trust, 2007). Based upon their willingness to forego personal benefits for the sake of the environment, flying less was the second most undesirable statement out of five choices presented to the interviewees, the most unpopular being a willingness not to purchase a plasma television. The other statements related to people's willingness to: 'Stop leaving the tap running when brushing teeth'; 'Give up driving when able to walk'; and 'Cook more local produce'. A reluctance to relinquish the right to fly for the sake of environmental protection was also found by Becken (2007) in her research with tourists in New Zealand, which found a demonstrable reluctance by tourists to take voluntary initiatives to be proactive in reducing the global impact of air travel. She found that a low level of awareness of air travel's contribution to global warming and climate change existed, and that responsibility for the mitigation of probable environmentally negative impacts resulting from climate change was viewed to be that of governments and business. The demonstration of an unwillingness to fly less unearthed by Becken (2007) and the Energy Saving Trust (2007) lends credence to the view of Attenborough (2007) that in the absence of a stronger environmental ethic in society it will be very difficult to impose controls on behaviour designed for environmental protection and conservation when they dictate against pleasure maximization.

The theme of contrasting attitudes over stakeholder responsibility for addressing the negative impacts of flying was also unearthed in research by Asthana and McKie (2005) who suggest that there are a growing number of concerned individuals who are relinquishing their right to fly, as a consequence of global warming. However, the comments of interviewees indicate uncertainty and confusion over the division of responsibility between stakeholders to reduce the demand for flying. While government was cited as having the responsibility to legislate to restrict the choice for people to fly, it was also recognized that they want to expand aviation to facilitate economic growth. There was a subsequent realization that individual action to fly less would be critical to reducing demand but that this choice would be difficult given the price attractiveness of flying.

Discordance in resource-use behaviour at home vis-à-vis when on vacation was found by Chesshyre (2005) when researching the motivations of women for participating in 'responsible tourism'. The results reveal a level of culpability about flying as being a type of behaviour that is discordant with the respondents' usually environmentally conscious lifestyles. The reluctance to forego the pleasure of travel for environmental protection is emphasized in the statement of one respondent who commented: 'The only way to preserve things is not to go there at all. But you have to draw the line between complete restraint and enjoying something. It should be about having a minimal impact'. While concord among tourism stakeholders that includes governments, private sector, non-governmental organizations, communities and pressure groups as to what constitutes a 'minimal impact' has a propensity for disagreement, a reduction in impacts related to the travel element of tourism is achievable. Using less environmentally damaging modes of transport where feasible, carbon off-setting, and flying to fewer destinations but staying longer, are examples of ways of reducing resource usage and GHG emissions.

Conclusion

There exists a prima facie case for the recognition of tourism as a key economic sector in the transition to a green economy given its reliance on high quality natural resources and climatic stability. If adequately environmentally planned and managed, it offers an economic sustainability for future generations that has an axiomatic correlation with environmental sustainability. Yet the spatial dimensions and complexity of the tourism system suggest that while this may be achievable at a destination level, the heavy reliability upon carbon-based fuels for the mobility and transportation of tourists threatens the long-term stability of the industry, as recognized by UNEP (2011). While the challenges of mobility and patterns of resource usage, travelling further for shorter durations of time, and a preference for energy-intensive transportation based upon carbon-based fuel may be mitigated to an extent through market correction and advancements in environmentally benign technologies, the practical difficulties of achieving this suggest it to be a long-term solution.

As a means of realizing environmental sustainability UNEP (2011) view the consumers as the catalyst to greening tourism but existing research evidence points to an inability of individuals to establish a relationship between environmental problems and their own individual consumption. This is perhaps even more so when the forgoing of consumption is viewed as detrimental to pleasure maximization. As an exemplar that constitutes many of the challenges to tourism's place in the green economy, the issue of 'casual flying' is one that poses a serious threat to the longevity of tourism by contributing to the destabilization of the climatic and environmental sustainability on which it depends. While technocentric solutions, i.e. those focused upon market price corrections and technological advancements in environmentally benign technologies have evident appeal, not least because they mean a minimum of interference to our lifestyles and consumption patterns, placing faith in two of the key drivers of the environmental crisis to provide the solutions is evidently problematical. Nor is there any evidence at present to suggest that the majority of consumers would accept either paying an environmental premium or government coercion to persuade them to fly less. Indeed the evidence suggests the contrary, that there is a demonstrable reluctance to pay a premium for environmental protection and a stated unwillingness to fly less.

Certain voluntary actions have been identified that emphasize individual action as a way to minimize the impacts of flying, including flying to fewer destinations but staying longer, taking more environmentally sustainable transport options where feasible, and utilizing carbon off-setting schemes. For these actions to have a significant effect there is reliance upon their adoption by the majority and not the minority of consumers, which will necessitate a paradigm shift in the consumer behaviour of tourists. Integral to this shift will be a change in individual consciousness built upon a stronger environmental ethic that extends the notion of community and emotions of empathy and sympathy beyond purely human boundaries, encouraging values, attitudes and lifestyles that are compatible with nature. There is a subsequent need for a much stronger identification between one's actions and the welfare of the environment, including a greater understanding of the effects of resource-use behaviour in tourism destinations alongside the home environment. To achieve this, radical measures may be needed to raise levels of awareness, for example flight advertisements carrying warnings similar to those on cigarette packets but relating to the quantity of GHG emissions generated on a trip compared with resource behaviour at home (e.g. a flight from Paris to San Francisco contributes as much to climate change as heating your home for one and a half years).

While education and raising levels of awareness have a key role in the rationale for the use of environmental ethics, there is also a requirement to understand the range of values embedded in nature, to establish a closer empathetic relationship between humans and ecology, tourists and environmental surroundings, and to help determine the rights and wrongs of our use of the earth's ecology and natural resources. Convincing people to change behaviour for environmental protection and conservation requires them to perceive themselves as a part of nature and not separate from ecological systems, akin to Leopold's (1949) concept of the land ethic. It is thus argued that for a considered response to the five challenges that have been identified by UNEP (2011) to tourism's place in the green economy, such a paradigm shift is essential to producing successful adaptive strategies and mitigating negative environmental impacts.

References

ABTA (2012) ABTA travel trends report 2012. Available at http://abta.com/news-and-views/press-zone/abta-publishes-2012-travel-trends-report. (Accessed 8 April 2014.)

Asthana, A. and McKie, R. (2005) Rising number of greens ditch cheap air travel. *The Observer*, London, 1 May 2005, p. 6.

Attenborough, R. (2007) A change in the moral climate. *The Guardian*, 2 June 2007, p. 6.

Becken, S. (2007) Tourists' perception of international air travel's impact on the global climate and potential climate change policies. *Journal of Sustainable Tourism*, vol. 15, pp. 351–68.

Blanning, T. (2010) *The romantic revolution*. Weidenfeld & Nicolson: London.

Butcher, J. (2006) Natural capital and the advocacy of ecotourism as sustainable development. *Journal of Sustainable Tourism*, vol. 14, pp. 529–44.

Callicott, J.B. (1993) Holistic environmental ethics and the problem of ecofascism. In Zimmerman, M.E., Callicott, J.B., Sessions, G., Warren, K.J. & Clark, J. (eds) *Environmental Philosophy: From Animal Rights to Ecology*. Prentice Hall: Upper Saddle River, NJ, pp. 110–34.

Carson, R. (1962) *Silent spring*. Houghton Mifflin: New York.

Chesshyre, T. (2005) Lean, keen and green. *The Times Travel Supplement*, 27 August 2005, pp. 4–5.

Curry, P. (2011) *Ecological ethics: An introduction* (2nd edn). Polity Press: Cambridge.

Dobson, A. (2000) *Green political thought* (3rd edn). Routledge: London.

Energy Saving Trust (2007) *Green barometer: Measuring environmental attitudes*. Energy Saving Trust: London.

Jamieson, D. (2008) *Ethics and the environment: An introduction*. Cambridge University Press: Cambridge.

Leopold, A. (1949) *A sand county almanac and sketches here and there*. Oxford University Press: Oxford.

Naess, A. (1973) The shallow and the deep, long-range ecology movement: a summary. *Inquiry*, vol. 16, pp. 95–100.

Nash, R.F. (1989) *The rights of nature: A history of environmental ethics*. The University of Wisconsin Press: Wisconsin, WI.

Pepper, D. (1996) *Modern environmentalism: An introduction*. Routledge: London.

Rolston III, H. (1988) *Environmental ethics: Duties to and values in the natural world*. Temple Press: Philadelphia, PA.

Rolston III, H. (1993) Challenges in environmental ethics. In Zimmerman, M.E., Callicott, J.B., Sessions, G., Warren, K.J. and Clark, J. (eds) *Environmental philosophy: From animal rights to ecology*. Prentice Hall: Upper Saddle River, NJ, pp. 135–57.

Sagoff, M. (1993) Animal liberation and environmental ethics. In Zimmerman, M.E., Callicott, J.B., Sessions, G., Warren, K.J. and Clark, J. (eds) *Environmental philosophy: From animal rights to ecology*. Prentice Hall: Upper Saddle River, NJ, pp. 84–94.

UNEP (2011) *Green economy: Pathways to sustainable development and poverty eradication: A synthesis for policy makers*. Nairobi, Kenya.

Vardy, P. and Grosch, P. (1999) *The puzzle of ethics*. HarperCollins: London.

WCED (1987) *Our common future*. Oxford University Press: Oxford.

Wenz, P.Z. (2001) *Environmental ethics today*. Oxford University Press: Oxford.

4

THE ROLE OF NATURE-BASED TOURISM IN THE GREEN ECONOMY

A broader perspective for conservation and sustainability in the Philippines

Corazon Catibog-Sinha

Introduction

The economic contribution of tourism to the national and local economy is significant; but to remain viable and sustainable, the tourism industry should ensure that tourism development leads to 'improved human well-being and social equity, while significantly reducing environmental risks and ecological scarcities' (UNEP, 2011a, p. 9). The UN Green Economy Report (UNEP, 2011a, p. 14) further states that the 'green economy is a new economic paradigm – one in which material wealth is not delivered perforce at the expense of growing environmental risks, ecological scarcities and social disparities.' Thus, the notion of the green economy is consistent with that of sustainable tourism, which aims to integrate the ecological, social, and economic aspects of development without causing irreparable damage to the bio-physical environment of the tourist destination and the socio-cultural fabric of the host community (UNEP-WTO, 2012).

Protected areas, the last refuge of threatened species, are popular tourist destinations. The Convention on Biological Diversity (CBD) underscores the role of the tourism industry in protected area management (WSSD, 2002; CBD, 2012). The green economy, which is informed by the core principles of sustainable tourism, can contribute to meeting the CBD's Aichi Target by 2020, particularly in conserving biodiversity at natural destinations while enriching the tourist experience and sustaining the tourism industry (Catibog-Sinha and Plantilla, 2012). Maintaining the biodiversity assets of protected areas enhances the recreational experience of tourists, which leads to repeat and longer visitation, a high quality tourist experience, and better support for biodiversity conservation (UNWTO, 2010).

The green economy complements the payment for ecosystem services, thus, greening tourism is actually investing in the benefits that tourists derive from nature-based recreational experiences. Given that the protection of natural areas is closely connected to the tourism industry, the Millennium Ecosystem Assessment (MEA) Report (MEA,

2005a, p. 470) recommends that tourism management in protected areas should be able to link sustainable use and conservation and to recognize the important financial aspects of sustainable tourism for these areas. A market-based approach to the management of ecosystem services with 'external costs' (e.g. recreation and aesthetic enjoyment) through the application of ecotourism user fees was specifically recommended (MEA, 2005b, p. 21).

Recognizing the social and ecological costs associated with increased tourism, the payment of user fees in nature-based tourism, for example, can be a means to internalize the costs associated with the use of protected areas for recreational purposes as well as to attract additional funding for sustainability (Pagiola, 2007). Paying for the ecosystem services provided by protected areas supports not only human economies and societies but also the sound management of tourist attractions including biodiversity conservation. Incentives for nature-based tourism, as one of the benefits from conserving biodiversity, through payment for such services can generate a better and broader appreciation for sound management of natural attractions in the Philippines.

The green economic gains from utilizing protected areas, although essential for tourism development, have to be ploughed back for local livelihoods, mainstream employment, and local investments. Furthermore, tourism development and visitor impact should not compromise the integrity of the social and ecological environments, by ensuring that the occurrence of pollution, inefficient energy use, wasteful consumption of natural resources, and loss of biodiversity and ecosystem services are minimized or eliminated.

While the current discourse on the green economy after Rio+20 has been focusing on cross-sectoral issues, such as carbon footprints, green jobs, energy efficiency, and waste management, only little is known about ways by which nature-based tourism, especially within protected areas in developing countries, can contribute to the green economy. UNWTO (2009) in *Roadmap for recovery – tourism and travel: A preliminary vehicle for job creation and economic recovery*, however, states that tourism could play a significant role in the transition to a green economy by developing green jobs and skills, responding effectively to climate change, integrating tourism in all green economy strategies, encouraging green tourism infrastructure investment, and promoting a green tourism culture in suppliers, consumers, and communities.

Developing countries with rich biodiversity are well positioned in the transition to a green economy through enabling policies, investment incentives, and government support (UNEP, UNCTAD and UN-OHRLLS, 2011). In the Philippines, the transition of nature-based tourism towards more sustainable practices is envisioned as a positive step toward achieving biodiversity conservation and poverty alleviation, especially among the rural poor who are dependent on natural resources for their daily subsistence (Catibog-Sinha, 2010, 2012a). The United Nations Environment Programme (UNEP, 2011a) in its report *Towards a green economy* affirms that the benefits derived from the use of natural resources should be shared with the local communities as a means of alleviating poverty and better conservation of the 'ecological commons'. In the context of tourism, market-based benefits when not shared with the local community can trigger further exploitation of the natural resources upon which they depend for survival.

Broadening the concept of the 'green economy' is a challenging approach to achieving sustainable tourism especially in developing countries with a high level of biodiversity and species endemism (Huberman, 2010). The broader notion of the green economy should be able to embrace the need to sustain destinations not only as tourist attractions but also as areas for the conservation of biodiversity.

Regulatory reforms are essential in moving forward to greening development including tourism. Enabling policy and institutional frameworks aimed at reducing or reversing environmental decline can integrate payments for environmental services. In the Philippines, the relevant policy and regulatory frameworks which support the greening of tourism have been formulated, although their implementation is far from desirable. This chapter explores the key initiatives in the Philippines that can contribute to a broader understanding and practice of a green economy in the context of nature-based tourism. The chapter argues that nature-based tourism, when sustainably managed, can play a significant role in a greening tourism economy especially in the conservation of biodiversity, protection of wildlife and their habitats, and management of protected areas.

The chapter is based on primary and secondary data including the results of face-to-face interviews with relevant officials as well as a comprehensive review of government reports and academic literature. The issues and challenges learned from various scenarios in the Philippines will be discussed in the context of tourism towards a broader understanding and implementation of a green economy.

The Philippines: a biodiversity-rich country in peril

The Philippines, an archipelago of more than 7,000 islands, is one of the most diverse countries in the world (see Figure 4.1). It is home to at least 38,000 animal species, of which some 35,000 are invertebrates and 3,000 are vertebrates (NRMC-UP, 1986; DENR/UNEP, 1997; PBCPP, 2002). The estimated number of Philippine plant species ranges from about 14,000 to more than 15,000 representing about 5 per cent of all species globally described so far. The terrestrial and aquatic vertebrate fauna of the Philippines represents about 5 per cent of the total number of vertebrates known globally (57,739 species) – about five times as many as would be expected on the basis of the size of the country (Catibog-Sinha and Heaney, 2006).

The Philippine government has set aside more than 1.5 million hectares of land as watershed forest reserves. The protected areas in the Philippines, under the National Integrated Protected Areas System (NIPAS), represent about 10–12 per cent of the total area of the Philippines. However, even these areas are at risk as some portions of the reserves are denuded by logging and occupied by settlers. Studies have predicted that the rapid loss of forest vegetation in the Philippines will lead to massive extinction of endemic species if it continues (Brooks *et al.*, 1997; Dinerstein and Wikramanayake, 1993).

Philippine tourism

Tourism contributes an average of 6.2 per cent to the gross domestic product of the Philippines, making it a major contributor to the country's economic growth. The Philippines hosted 15–20 million visitors per year from 2005 to 2007; inbound tourists comprised 5–8 per cent of the total number of visitors per year. In 2007, the direct employment in tourism totalled 3.25 million, representing a 9.7 per cent share of the

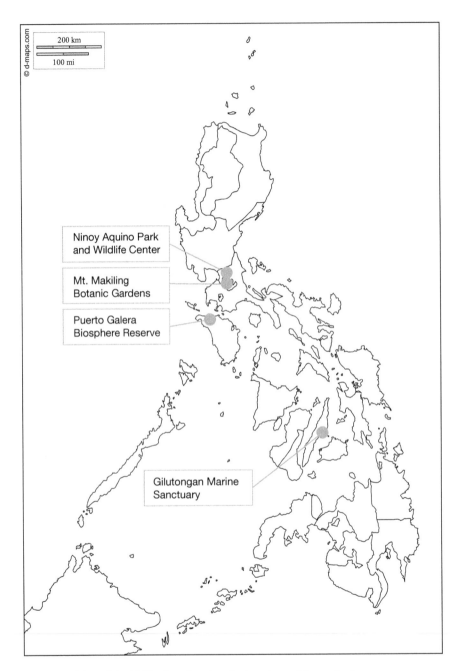

FIGURE 4.1 Map of the Philippines showing the locations of the study sites

Source: d-maps.com http://d-maps.com/carte.php?num_car=26011&lang=en; embellished by D. Cocal and S.C. Sinha

country's total employment (DOT, 2009). In 2011, nearly 4 million overseas visitors arrived in the country; however, the records do not specify if protected areas or natural destinations were the major destinations (DOT, 2013). Nonetheless, Seo *et al.* (2009) state that the diverse cultural and natural attractions as well as the attractive foreign exchange rate have pulled in many foreign visitors, in particular South Korean, to the Philippines.

The rich biodiversity of the country is a major tourist attraction. As in many archipelagic countries, the islands and coastal areas of the Philippines are the most popular tourist destinations. Unfortunately, the socio-economic and natural systems of islands are quite vulnerable to external risks from both human and natural activities (Conlin and Baum, 1995; D'Ayala, 1992).

Since the notion and practice of ecotourism in the Philippines is relatively young, there is a considerable gap between policy development and field implementation. After the Earth Summit of 1992, the Philippine government took serious, although small, steps to incorporate the notion of sustainable development in tourism policy and planning. For example, the Philippine Agenda 21 (Tourism sector) affirms that ecotourism can be implemented through sustainable use of natural and cultural resources while protecting the environment and providing employment opportunities. The National Ecosystem Strategy (NES) was initiated in 2001 by virtue of Executive Order 111. The Strategy provides the framework for the development of ecotourism in the country. The sustainable development principles embodied in NES are 'the management of the natural and cultural resources, environmental education and conservation awareness, empowerment of the local communities, and development of tourism products that satisfy visitor needs and promote the Philippines as a globally competitive destination' (DOT-DENR, 2002, p. 3).

The green economy in nature-based tourism

The Philippines has initiated some environmental programmes that mark the early beginnings of the green economy. These initiatives can transition into the greening of tourism for biodiversity conservation and wildlife protection. They can also help broaden one's understanding of how a green economy can be implemented in the context of nature-based tourism. None of these initiatives is a silver bullet that can solve all environmental issues, but they can be useful tools in addressing site-specific problems especially in natural destinations where ecosystem benefits are either undermined or abused, leading to mismanagement and over-exploitation.

1 Integrated Protected Areas Fund

As a signatory to the Convention on Biological Diversity (UNEP, 1992), the Philippines has a legal obligation to develop measures to link biodiversity and tourism development. The Department of Environment and Natural Resources pursued the enactment of the National Integrated Protected Areas Law (RA Act 7586 of 1992), which recognizes the need to establish and manage protected areas in a holistic manner and underscores the value of tourism as a new source of funding for the management of protected areas in the country.

Nature-based tourism is permitted in all categories of protected areas except in Strict Nature Reserves. However, the management is inadequate because of insufficient and unreliable government funds for operational needs and capital. Hence, a funding mechanism, known as the Integrated Protected Areas Fund (IPAF) has been established by virtue of the National Integrated Protected Areas Law. The Law requires that an IPAF has to be set up for each protected area, and the income generated from its use should accrue to site management (75 per cent); the rest (25 per cent) to be used to support the management needs of other protected areas.

As of 2012, 62 per cent (149 out of 240) of protected areas had formally established their respective IPAF systems to augment the national budget for protected area management. However, only 63 per cent of the established IPAFs had a functional collection and disbursement process. As of December 2012, a total of PHP 244 million (USD 5.6 million) had been generated, but only 64 per cent of this amount (USD 3.6 million) had been disbursed and utilized (PAWB, 2012). The slow rate of fund utilization for protected area management is partly due to the slow and bureaucratic process within the national treasury system.

2 Environmental User Fee System

For some other protected areas (mostly small marine reserves and sanctuaries, and urban parks) a localized and relatively independent variant of IPAF, the Environmental User Fee System (EUF), has been established. Each government municipality in the Philippines that directly administers marine reserves has the authority and discretion, by virtue of the Local Government Code of 1991 (Republic Act 7160), to design an EUF system applicable to the site and socio-political situation.

The user-fee concept is based on the tenet that users, such as tourists, have to pay for the recreation services provided by the natural/ecological system within destination areas. The user-fee system is meant to raise funds to offset the environmental damage caused by tourism and to increase public awareness about environmental protection and biodiversity conservation (IUCN, 2000). User fees are economically desirable because they can help resource managers allocate resources and services for better tourist satisfaction. User fees can also boost the income of the local economy and supplement the livelihoods of the local communities.

In the Philippines, many divers are willing to pay more for a diving experience in marine reserves. For example, Arin (1997 in White and Vogt, 2000) reports that scuba divers are willing to pay an entrance fee of US$5.00 per person and an additional donation of US$5.00 for buoy maintenance. The same observation was reported by Thur (2010) who states that nature-based tourists supportive of environment-friendly tourism in Bonaire National Marine Park (Netherlands, Antilles) are willing to pay more for a memorable tourist experience. A study in Jamaica also shows that tourists are more willing to pay for an 'environmental tax' than a general 'tourism development tax' as a sustainable funding mechanism for ocean and coastal management (Edwards, 2009).

To ensure that the environmental user fee system is consistent with green economy principles, its design should take into account equity, justice, and legitimacy (Turner and Daily, 2008) as well as the socio-economic benefits that accrue to local communities directly affected by tourism development (Greiner and Stanley, 2013). A good tourism marketing strategy that will justify payment of Environmental User Fees by tourists is through honest public disclosure of funds that are earmarked and invested for such purposes. The use of conservation or user fees in tourism in several protected areas in the Philippines has proved to be helpful in promoting biodiversity conservation and public awareness at tourist destinations (M. Lim, personal communication, 9 July 2013).

The EUF systems in the following examples are tailored to local conditions and needs with some degree of administrative flexibility. The EUF scheme supports local employment and livelihood benefits, although much has yet to be done to make the sharing of tourism benefits more equitable and transparent.

(a) The Ninoy Aquino Park and Wildlife Center (NAPWC) (14° 39' 2" N 121° 2' 34"E) (Figure 4.1) is an urban park in Metro Manila visited by more than 300,000 guests every year. It is managed by the Department of Environment and Natural Resources – Biodiversity Management Bureau. The recreational facilities at NAPWC include a small zoo, flower gardens, picnic facilities, a man-made lagoon, walking/running and cycling trails, and a visitor centre for educational and interpretation purposes. It earns an average yearly income amounting to some PHP 3–4 million (US$70,000–93,000) from entrance and other user fees (rental, parking and donations). The income contributes substantially to the management of the Park, which includes wages, garden and facility maintenance, infrastructure development, tourism services, and public awareness and conservation programmes (N. Castillo, personal communication, 9 July 2013). The application of a market-based approach towards the payment of recreational services in urban green parks contributes to the greening of tourism economy that supports the national goal in pursuing ecological and social sustainability within an urban setting (Catibog-Sinha, 2012b).

b) The Makiling Botanic Gardens (14°9'23"N 121°14'2"E), (Figure 4.1), one of the major peri-urban attractions within the Mount Makiling Forest Reserve, generates an average of nearly PHP 1 million (US$23,000) (Roslin et al., 2009). The user fees, in addition to the donations from private companies and other organizations, are used for park management and refurbishment. The green economy, as in this case, is not a panacea for sustainable forest conservation because tourism income is not adequate to sustain the protection of the Reserve from illegal settlement and resource exploitation (R. Cereno, personal communication, 5 February 2012). As echoed by UNEP (2011b, p. 8),

> transitioning towards a green economy requires mobilizing increased public and private investments in forests. Thus, the University of the Philippines, who has been given the task to manage the Botanic Garden as well as the entire Forest Reserve, should endeavor to provide better opportunities for green investments, both from public and private sources, towards the protection of the natural resources for ecotourism, environmental education, and conservation.

(c) The marine-based destination in Puerto Galera (13.5000° N, 120.9542° E), (Figure 4.1), within a UNESCO-MAB reserve has been implementing the

Environmental User Fee system since late 2007. During the period November 2007 to November 2008, the local government collected more than PHP 10 million (US$228,000) from the Environmental User Fee scheme from at least 3 million visitors over the year. The municipal government announced that it would use the collected fees to finance the establishment of sewage treatment facilities and the protection of marine resources (Catibog-Sinha, 2012c). Although the investment in improving waste management can save money for businesses, create jobs, and enhance coastal tourism (UNEP et al., 2012), the local government should ensure that regular public funds are available and they do not totally depend on the EUF to maintain the sewage treatment facilities.

The application of user fees in promoting a green tourism economy is appropriate in the management of marine protected areas, however, it is not the only solution for reducing marine biodiversity loss. As a UNESCO-MAB reserve, Puerto Galera has to also consider the following elements in its transition to a green economy: (a) education – as a weapon to fight poverty and inequality and foster environment-friendly attitudes and behaviour; (b) science, technology and innovation – as drivers for equity and sustainable development, (c) culture – as a key component that should be integrated into developmental activities, and (d) information – as the message by which the media can convey better policies and public awareness about the environment (UNESCO, 2011).

(d) Gilutongan Marine Sanctuary (10°12'6"N 123°59'11"E) (Figure 4.1) is a 14.89-ha marine reserve under the administrative jurisdiction of the municipal government. The yearly average income during the period 2000 to 2012 was about PHP 2.4 million (US$50,000), ranging from PHP300,000+ (US$6,000) to PHP 5.9 million (US$140,000) gross total (MCC, 2011). It was estimated by White et al. (2000, cited in Ross et al., 2000) that in addition to the tourism income and 'off-site' indirect benefits, the potential annual economic net revenue of the Marine Sanctuary could be as much as US$200,000.

The establishment of the EUF system at the Marine Sanctuary was stipulated in the local ordinance (Municipal Ordinance No. 004–2008). The EUF system spells out the fee schedule, the revenue-sharing scheme, and the creation of a Protected Area Management Board to decide on budget disbursements. The distribution scheme of the EUF at the Gilutongan Marine Sanctuary is as follows: 60 per cent – Municipality; 30 per cent – Barangay (Village) Gilutongan; 5 per cent – Livelihood projects of Accredited Umbrella Fisherfolks Organization; and 5 per cent – United Municipal Employees of Cordova. The Planning Unit of the municipal government (L. Ator, personal communication, 6 July 2012) states that the municipality's share is earmarked for major expenses such as the construction and maintenance of the guardhouse/Visitor Centre, payment of salaries/wages, coral reef monitoring, and the purchase of boats. The Barangay's share is used to support livelihood programmes, honoraria, refuse collection, and law enforcement.

As shown in this example, the application of a green economy in small marine sanctuaries, where tourism is a major ecosystem service and the main local revenue source, can only be sustained if the distribution of economic and social benefits accruing from tourism is transparent, democratic, and equitable.

3 Environmental Guarantee Fund

The Philippine Environmental Guarantee Fund (EGF) is a financial security mechanism which aims to ensure that a liable party (e.g. tour operator) provides compensation for any environmental damage on a nature-based tourist destination. The EGF mechanism was established pursuant to the Philippines Environmental Impact Statement System (EIS) law (Presidential Decree No. 1586) and its implementing order (DAO No. 21/1992).

Proposed tourism projects that are located in critical habitats (e.g., protected areas) are required by law to set up an EGF. For example, the tour operator within a diving site at Gilitungan Marine Sanctuary in Central Philippines has been required to set aside a mandatory payment of EGF of not less than 1.25 per cent of the contracted yearly rental fee to the Local Government Treasury; it remains as a trust and may be refunded at the end of the contract (Catibog-Sinha et al., 2013).

Through the legal imposition of the EGF, the liability of the company can be secured in case the operator declares bankruptcy or undercapitalization. The funds are kept in trust to be released to finance the restoration and rehabilitation of the environment damaged by the industry. It may also be used for financing environmental quality monitoring and environmental enhancement.

The EGF scheme complements the 'polluter pays principle', which plays an important role in the tourism industry – an inherently uncertain and vulnerable enterprise especially when established on islands. With a policy framework in place, it is mandatory that any damage caused will be more or less compensated. The EGF shall be made readily available for the immediate rehabilitation of a damaged site resulting from the project's operation or abandonment. It shall likewise be used to compensate communities that have been affected by the negative impacts of the project, and to finance community-based projects including information and education and emergency preparedness programmes.

Thus the EGF, as set by Philippine Law, comprises three components. The first component is a multi-sectoral fund allocated for environmental monitoring; the second is a trust fund set aside to compensate aggrieved parties and to finance the restoration and rehabilitation of damaged sites caused by project operations; and the third is a cash fund to be used in implementing environmental enhancement measures. The EGF is managed by a multi-sectoral group (Administrative Order No. 30–03; Aruelo, 2010).

4 Green purchasing of tourism products and services

Increasingly, green purchasing is being considered an effective tool to mitigate the environmental impacts of consumption and to promote the development of clean production technology (Chen, 2005; UNEP and UNWTO, 2012). One way to address environmental problems in the supply chain of tourism products is by greening the purchasing aspect (through waste minimization), which is at the early stage of the supply chain (Rao, 2005).

The Philippine government is recognizing its role in protecting the environment and preserving the country's natural resources. Consequently, the government has initiated activities towards the development of new and environmentally sound avenues for trade in goods and services with the objective of promoting green purchasing practices among government agencies. Given that government bodies and entities constitute one of the largest consumers of products and services in the Philippines, a Presidential Executive Order (EO No. 301) was issued requiring all government departments, offices and agencies in the Philippines (including the Department of Tourism) to establish their respective Green Procurement Programmes and promote within the government system the culture of making environmentally informed decisions regarding the purchase and use of different products.

The rationale behind the Green Procurement Programme was to make consumption and production patterns more sustainable by reducing the energy and materials used per unit of production, minimizing the generation of waste, and making consumers aware of environmentally sound purchasing. Thus, the Programme ensures that the environmental criteria in public tenders of products or services are incorporated by setting environment-friendly product specifications and purchase requirements. In addition, the Programme offers an incentive to suppliers so that they will only manufacture and sell environmentally sound products and services.

Studies have shown that environmentally responsible purchasing behaviour is closely linked to environmental consciousness (Schlegelmilch *et al.*, 1996). By extension, green purchasing will create 'green jobs' and 'green services' that contribute to improved environmental quality including the conservation of natural resources from which raw materials are extracted (UNEP and ILO, 2011). Furthermore, businesses can accelerate the transition to a green economy by aligning their investments with climate change adaption opportunities.

The Philippine Department of Tourism has developed a green purchasing programme in conjunction with its accreditation programme whereby hotels and resorts are required to have fixtures and supplies that are energy-efficient and environment-friendly. A set of eco-labelling criteria was also officially adapted in May 2013, to promote green purchasing for the food services providers in the Philippines. To facilitate the implementation of the Green Purchasing Programme, a group of stakeholders (i.e., private businesses from the tourism industry and trade, government agencies and non-government organizations) established the Green Purchasing Alliance Movement with the assistance of the Philippine Centre for Environmental Protection and Sustainable Development, Incorporated. These organizations have been promoting green purchasing by patronizing green products and services and holding relevant workshop and training sessions to ecotour operators and hotel/resort owners (R.Velazco-Catibog, 25 November 2013).

Conclusion

The notion of the green economy is consistent with that of sustainable tourism, which aims to integrate the ecological, social and economic aspects of development without causing irreparable damage to the bio-physical environment of the tourist destination and the socio-cultural fabric of the host community (UNEP and UNWTO, 2012). The green economic gains from utilizing protected areas, although essential for tourism development, have to be ploughed back for local livelihoods, mainstream employment and local investments. A green economy, informed by the core principles of sustainable tourism, can contribute to meeting the Convention on Biological Diversity Aichi Target by 2020 (Catibog-Sinha and Plantilla, 2012; UNWTO, 2010).

Broadening the concept of the 'green economy' is a challenging approach to achieving sustainable tourism especially in developing countries with rich biodiversity. These countries are well positioned in the transition to a green economy through enabling policies, investment incentives, and government support (UNEP, UNCTAD and UN-OHRLLS, 2011).

The key initiatives of the Philippines can contribute to a broader understanding and application of the green economy in the context of nature-based tourism. These initiatives are supportive of several United Nation reports that focus on the green economy. For example, the MEA (2005a) reiterates that ecosystem services in the form of aesthetic enjoyment and nature-based recreation should be accorded economic value through the implementation of a user fee system, such as the Integrated Protected Area Fund or the Environmental User Fee System. A green economy may also be applied under the tenet of the 'polluter pays principle' by requiring an Environmental Guarantee Fund to address any potential risk from proposed tourism development in natural areas. The UN Green Economy Report (UNEP, 2011a, p. 14) states that the 'green economy is a new economic paradigm – one in which material wealth is not delivered perforce at the expense of growing environmental risks, ecological scarcities and social disparities'. Furthermore, the UNWTO (2009) in *Roadmap for recovery – tourism and travel* mentions that reducing tourism impacts while increasing tourism benefits can be achieved by developing green jobs and skills, responding to climate change, integrating tourism in all green economy strategies, encouraging green tourism infrastructure investment, and promoting a green tourism culture in suppliers, consumers, and communities.

While none of these initiatives is a silver bullet that can solve all environmental issues in the Philippines, they can be useful tools in addressing site-specific problems in nature-based destinations. Developing a coherent government-private-civil society partnership is essential in promoting a green economy in nature-based tourism. It is a challenge for the government and the tourism industry to develop appropriate social and legal mechanisms to encourage sustainable consumption/use and a green economy and to promote investments that minimize environmental impacts on nature-based destinations and uplift the quality of life of the host communities.

References

Aruelo, L. (2010). Financial security: The example of the Philippine environmental guarantee fund. Third Meeting of the Group of the Friends of the Co-Chairs on Liability and Redress in the Context of the Cartagena Protocol on Biosafety. Kuala Lumpur, 15–19 June.

Brooks, T.M., Pimm, S.L. and Collar, N.J. (1997) Deforestation predicts the number of threatened birds in insular Southeast Asia. *Conservation Biology*, vol. 11, pp. 382–94.

Catibog-Sinha, C.S. (2010) Biodiversity conservation and sustainable tourism: Philippine initiatives. *Journal of Heritage Tourism*, vol. 5, no. 4, pp. 297–308.

Catibog-Sinha, C.S. (2012a) Philippine tourism initiatives: Issues and challenges. In Sloan, P., Simons-Kaufman, C. and Legrand, W. (eds). *Sustainable hospitality and tourism as motors for development – Case studies from developing regions of the world* (pp. 359–76). Routledge: London and New York.

Catibog-Sinha, C.S. (2012b) Urban green parks: Sustainable tourism, biodiversity, and quality of life. In Sloan, P., Simons-Kaufman, C. and Legrand, W. (eds). *Sustainable hospitality and tourism as motors for development – Case studies from developing regions of the world* (pp. 343–58). Routledge: London and New York.

Catibog-Sinha, C.S. (2012c) *Sustainable tourism: Concepts and case studies – Caring for nature, culture and people*. Haribon Foundation: Manila.

Catibog-Sinha, C.S., Guzman, R., Meniado, A. and Guzman, M. (2013) Enabling conditions for sustainability: Community tourism in marine reserves in the Philippines. *Proceedings of the 19th Asia Pacific Tourism Association Annual Conference*, Bangkok, 1–4 July.

Catibog-Sinha, C.S. and Heaney, L. (2006) *Philippine biodiversity: Principles and practice*. Haribon Foundation: Manila.

Catibog-Sinha, C.S. and Plantilla, A. (2012) Nature-based tourism and biodiversity conservation in protected areas: Philippine context. *Proceedings of the 10th Asia Pacific CHRIE Conference-Building bridges- creating opportunities*, Manila, 5–8 June.

CBD (2012) *Aichi biodiversity targets*. Retrieved on 20 February 2013, from www.cbd.int/sp/targets/

Chen, C.C. (2005) Incorporating green purchasing into the frame of ISO 14000. *Journal of Cleaner Production*, vol. 13, no. 9, pp. 927–33.

Conlin, M.V. and Baum, T. (1995) *Island tourism: Management principles and practice*. John Wiley and Sons: New York.

D'Ayala, P.G. (1992) Islands at a glance. *Environmental Management*, vol. 16, no. 5, pp. 565–8.

DENR/UNEP (1997) *Philippine biodiversity: An assessment and action plan*. Bookmark: Manila.

Dinerstein, E. and Wikramanayake, E.D. (1993) Beyond 'hotspots': How to prioritize investments to conserve biodiversity in the Indo-Pacific Region. In Samson, F.B. and Knopk, F.L. (eds) *Ecosystem management–selected readings* (pp. 32–45). Springer-Verlag: New York.

DOT (2009) *Philippine tourism: Stable amidst a global tourism downturn* [Brochure]. DOT: Manila.

DOT (2013) *National tourism development plan 2011–2016*. DOT: Manila.

DOT-DENR (2002) *National ecotourism strategy*. DOT, DENR, & New Zealand Agency for International Development: Quezon City, Philippines.

Edwards, P. (2009) Sustainable financing for ocean and coastal management in Jamaica: The potential for revenues from tourist user fees. *Marine Policy*, vol. 33, no. 2, pp. 376–85.

Greiner, R. and Stanley, O. (2013) More than money for conservation: Exploring social co-benefits from PES schemes. *Land Use Policy*, vol. 31, pp. 4–10.

Huberman, D. (2010) *A guidebook for IUCN's thematic programme area on greening the world economy*. IUCN: Gland, Switzerland.

IUCN (2000) *Financing protected areas*. IUCN: Gland, Switzerland and Cambridge, UK.

MCC (2011) *Gilitongan Marine Sanctuary management plan (2011–2016)*. Cebu: Municipality of Cordova, Philippines.

MEA (2005a) *Ecosystems and human well-being: Current state and trends*, Volume 1, Chapter 17- Cultural and amenity services. Retrieved 9 January 2014, from www.unep.org/maweb/documents/document.286.aspx.pdf

MEA (2005b) *Ecosystems and human well_being. Synthesis Report*. Retrieved on 10 January 2014, from www.millenniumassessment.org/en/index.aspx

NRMC/UP (1986) *Guide to Philippine flora and fauna*, vols. 1–12. NRMC-UP: Manila.

Pagiola, S. (2007) *Guidelines for 'pro-poor' payments for environmental services*. World Bank: Washington, DC.

PAWB (2012) *Establishing and managing protected areas*. Retrieved on 17 December 2013, from www.pawb.gov.ph/index.php?option=com_content&view=article&id=120:establishing-and-managing-protected-areas&catid=58:protected-area-management.

PBCPP (2002) *Philippine biodiversity conservation priorities: A second iteration of the national biodiversity strategy and action plan-* Final report (Edited by P. S. Ong, L. E. Afuang and R. G. Rosell-Ambal). PAWB-Department of Environment and Natural Resources, Conservation International-Philippines, BCP-University of the Philippines, Foundation for Philippine Environment: Quezon City, Philippines.

Rao, P. (2005) The greening of suppliers in the South East Asian context. *Journal of Cleaner Production*, vol. 13, pp. 935–45.

Roslin, A.Y., Maga, J., Rosales, A., Cereno, R. and Tapay, N. (2009) Social impact of ecotourism on the behavior of students on educational field trips to Makiling Botanic Gardens in the University of the Philippines Los Baños. *University of Southern Mindanao Research & Development Journal*, vol. 17, no. 1, pp. 71–80.

Ross, M., White, A., Sitoy, A. and Menguito, T. (2000) Experience from improving management of 'urban' marine protected areas: Gilutongan Marine Sanctuary, Philippines. *Proceedings of the 9th International Coral Reef Symposium*, Bali, Indonesia 23–27 October.

Schlegelmilch, B., Bohlen, G. and Diamantopoulos, A. (1996) The link between green purchasing decisions and measures of environmental consciousness. *European Journal of Marketing*, vol. 30, no. 5, pp. 35–55.

Seo, J.H., Park, S.Y. and Yu, L. (2009) The analysis of the relationships of Korean outbound tourism demand: Jeju Island and three international estimations. *Tourism Management*, vol. 30, pp. 530–54.

Thur, S. (2010) User fees a sustainable financing mechanism for marine protected areas: An application to the Bonaire National Marine Park. *Marine Policy*, vol. 34, pp. 63–9.

Turner, R. and Daily, G. (2008) The ecosystem services framework and natural capital conservation. *Environmental and Resource Economics*, vol. 39, pp. 25–35.

UNEP (2011a) *Towards a green economy: Pathways to sustainable development and poverty eradication*. Retrieved on 15 February 2013, from www.unep.org/greeneconomy.

UNEP (2011b) *Forests in a green economy – Synthesis report*. United Nations Environment Programme: Nairobi.

UNEP (1992) *Convention on biological diversity*. United Nations Environment Programme: Nairobi.

UNEP, FAO, IMO, UNDP, UNDESA, IUCN, WorldFish Center, GRID-Arendal (2012) *Green economy in a blue world – Synthesis report*, UNEP. Retrieved on 13 February 2013, from www.unep.org/pdf/green_economy_blue.pdf.

UNEP and ILO (2011) *Green jobs: Towards decent work in a sustainable, low-carbon world*. United Nations Environment Programme: Nairobi.

UNEP, UNCTAD, and UN-OHRLLS (2011) *Why a green economy matters for least developed countries*, Retrieved on 14 February 2013, from www.unep.org/greeneconomy/Portals/88/documents/research_products/

UNEP and UNWTO (2012) *Tourism in the green economy – Background report*. UNWTO: Madrid.

UNESCO (2011) *From green economies to green societies. UNESCO's commitment to sustainable development*. Retrieved on 14 March 2013 http://unesdoc.unesco.org/images/0021/002133/213311e.pdf.

UNWTO (2010) *Tourism and biodiversity – Achieving common goals towards sustainability*. WTO: Madrid, Spain.

UNWTO (2009) *Roadmap for recovery – Tourism and travel: A preliminary vehicle for job creation and ec onomic recovery*. Retrieved on 10 March 2013, from www.unwto.org/conferences/ga/en/pdf/18_08.pdf.

White, A.T. and Vogt, H.P. (2000) Philippine coral reefs under threat: Lessons learned after 25 years of community-based reef conservation. *Marine Pollution Bulletin*, vol. 40, no. 6, pp. 537–50.

WSSD (2002) *Report of the world summit on sustainable development* Johannesburg, South Africa, 26 August–4 September 2002. Retrieved on 24 May 2012, from www.world-tourism.org/sustainable/wssd/final-report.pdf.

5

UNDERSTANDING THE PHILOSOPHY AND PERFORMANCE OF TOURISM AND LEISURE IN PROTECTED AREAS FOR TRANSITION TO A GREEN ECONOMY

Agita Livina and Dzintra Atstaja

Introduction

The travel and tourism industry is possibly the most important industry in the world. During the twentieth century many studies around the world were conducted to evaluate the economic effect of tourism within regions and protected areas (PA), instead of studying the social effect and its environmental influence. The environment plays an important role in the development of tourism (Dambe and Atstaja, 2013).

Tourism is already an important economic sector for many countries and regions around the world. In terms of resources, many countries have little more than an attractive, currently unpolluted environment to market internationally to sustain the increasing demands of their growing population. It is vital that such destinations understand the ways in which modern tourism can be utilized to serve their needs without damaging the assets upon which prosperity depends (Middleton, 1998).

Nowadays, the volume of business of tourism equals or even surpasses the volume of oil exports, food products or automobiles. Tourism has become one of the major players in international commerce and at the same time represents one of the main income sources for many developing countries. This growth goes hand in hand with an increasing diversification and competition among destinations. This global spread of tourism in industrialized and developed countries has given economic and employment benefits in many related sectors – from construction to agriculture or telecommunications. The contribution of tourism to economic well-being depends on the quality and revenues of the offers of tourism. The United Nations World Tourism Organization (UNWTO) assists destinations in their sustainable positioning within ever more complex national and international markets. As the United Nations agency is dedicated to tourism, UNWTO points out that the developing countries particularly stand to benefit from sustainable tourism, and therefore acts to help to make this a reality (UNWTO, 2011).

The diversity of protected areas

PAs are internationally recognized regions that are set aside primarily for the conservation of nature and biodiversity and are a major tool in managing species and ecosystems which provide a range of goods and services essential to the sustainable use of natural resources. 'A protected area is a clearly defined geographical space, recognised, dedicated and managed, through legal or other effective means, to achieve the long term conservation of nature with associated ecosystem services and cultural values' (Dudley, 2008).

The International Union for Conservation of Nature (IUCN) divides PAs into six categories: strict nature reserve, wilderness area, national park, natural monument or feature, habitat/species management area, protected landscape/seascape and protected area with sustainable use of natural resources (Dudley, 2008). In general there are more than 131,000 different PAs in the world according to the categories set by the IUCN (WDPA, 2013). The total number of PAs includes well-known specific protected areas such as World Heritage Sites (981), Man and Biosphere Reserves (621) initiated by UNESCO, Ramsar Sites of Wetlands (2,131) established according the Convention on Wetlands of International Importance and Natura 2000 network (26,444) in the European Union 27 (UNESCO, 2013; Ramsar, 2013; European Commission, 2013b). At the same time there exist specific PA categories in different countries, for example, in the United States there are around twenty, and in Latvia eight. Each category of PAs has specific goals and functions for sustainable development, and Dudley (2008) has analysed differences between PAs.

The goal of PAs is to enable people to enjoy nature and to conserve delicate ecosystems for future generations. The arrival of international tourists has seen a steady growth from 25 million in 1950 to 1,035 million in 2012 and it is predicted to reach 1.8 billion by 2030 according to the newly released long-term forecast, *Tourism towards 2030*, by the UNWTO. The fact that 52 per cent of total trips in 2012 were for leisure, recreation and holidays, indicates the continuing importance of proper management of recreational areas, especially wilderness and parks. This is a challenge for society, managers and other stakeholders as to how to balance the conservation of ecosystems and visitations to PAs. How to connect PAs with tourism and leisure activities as well as with sustainable development in the context of the development of green tourism.

The Millennium Ecosystem Assessment (2005/6) provided challenges and recommendations for ecotourism opportunities and better utilization of ecosystem services in PAs. Changes in ecosystems have tended to increase the accessibility that people have to the ecosystems for recreation and ecotourism. People often choose where to spend their leisure time based partly on the characteristics of the natural or cultivated landscapes in the particular area. There are clear examples of declining ecosystem services disrupting social relations or resulting in conflicts. The demand for recreational use of landscapes is increasing, and areas are increasingly being managed to cater for this use, to reflect the changing cultural values and perceptions. However, many naturally occurring features of the landscape (e.g., coral reefs) have been degraded as resources for recreation.

The UNWTO has set out Tourism and Millennium Development Goals which will promote the development of responsible, sustainable and universally accessible tourism. What is being done to get closer to sustainable, responsible and accessible tourism?

The UNWTO created the Sustainable Tourism Eliminating Poverty (ST-EP) initiative, launched in 2002 (UNWTO, 2010). One of the supported activities of the ST-EP is training of local guides and hotel employees. The trained local guides are especially important for sustainable tourism development in PAs for comprehension of nature conservation and tourists' behaviour and their wishes. One of the supported projects is 'Canopy Walkway and Zip line: a new tourism attraction at Dong Hua Sao National Park' in Lao People's Democratic Republic.

The main attractions for visitors to PAs are the beauty of nature, water areas, mountains, culture and the opportunity to enjoy it with different activities. PAs provide preconditions for the development of tourism based on the resources of nature; moreover, these are secure and facilitated places and in some cases can be considered as tourism destinations. Local municipalities are supporting tourism and leisure business activities in PAs as one of the most important business activities in areas with limited economic and industrial activities. The area of distribution of tourism activities is dependent on the restrictions in the particular PA, for example, the type of ecosystem and its approachability. In cases of uninhabited PAs, gateway territories with tourism infrastructure for PAs are often created.

The environment plays an essential role in the development of tourism. From the economic viewpoint, those are the measures that help to improve the environment as a whole and guarantee that green tourism brings the environment to an optimum state of harmony. However, it is undeniable that all sectors of the tourism industry are increasingly responding to ecotourism problems or establishing environment-friendly tourism, which can be sustained while the number of tourists continues to increase. Tourism and the environment are constantly interacting. Tourism influences the environment and the quality of the environment influences tourism (Atstaja *et al.*, 2000), which is the background to the way to a green economy.

Tourism is an interdisciplinary industry which consists of five subsectors: accommodation, attractions, transport, travel organizers and destination organizers (Middleton, 1994). In recent decades the importance of tourism destinations has been increased by diversity and unique attractions. The uniqueness of tourism is characterized by the specific character of the service, how the service at the same time is created and used, and also by the fact that it is irregular and is influenced by a number of conditions, in particular the instability of natural conditions, including seasons and guides and locals.

Any form of industrial development will have an impact on the physical environment in which it takes place. In view of the fact that tourists have to visit the place of production in order to consume the output, it is inevitable that tourism activity will be associated with environmental impacts. The identification of the need to follow an environmentally compatible pattern of tourism development is now well into its second decade but little has been achieved in ensuring that future developments are environmentally compatible (Cooper *et al.*, 1998).

The significance of tourism and leisure for the green economy

The document *The future we want* adopted by Rio+20 stresses the holistic and integrated approach to sustainable development (UN, 2012). We completely agree, particularly in terms of a tourism policy and the management of PAs, that it must be integrated and a holistic approach to tourism development should be used. The other important point in the document is the necessity to generate decent jobs and incomes that decrease the disparities of living as well as promoting the sustainable use of nature resources and ecosystems (UN, 2012). One of the Rio+20 decisions was to strengthen the United Nations Environment Programme (UNEP). UNEP and EDO (Environmental Defenders Office) developed *Community protocols for environmental sustainability: A guide for policy makers* (2013). There is a specific paragraph on protocols for protected areas management. The main essence of this is to work together with stakeholders and to find commitment for future activities in a sustainable way (UNEP and EDO NSW, 2013).

The globalization of the markets has opened up new opportunities; tourists from new markets are able to afford vacations of high value. Attracting them to Europe would enhance the development potential of the European tourism industry and support the creation of growth and jobs in the EU. The Commission works together with the Member States and other tourism stakeholders on projects such as the European Tourist Destinations Portal and the preparatory action on European Destinations of Excellence and, at the same time, promotes synergies with all stakeholders in order to improve the visibility of tourism (European Union, 2013).

The green economy and green growth have been defined and understood in different ways. Concerning the green economy, this notion varies from a comprehensive, environmentally and socially sound economy in all its possible forms to some of its aspects being highlighted as key areas of the green economy. In this research we tend to agree that each country must have a broad understanding of the major theoretical and practical issues of green growth, impacts that traditional economic developments leave on society as a whole, processes that affect economic well-being, benefits and losses, and ultimately how all those developments affect the everyday life of each individual (Atstaja *et al.*, 2012). The aim of green economics is to create a new discipline which works for the benefit of all people around the world, the planet, the biosphere, non-human species, nature, and other life forms. Green economics integrates ideas and theories which also are designed to help to end the systemic and institutional causes of inequity and poverty. Green economics means understanding that the economy is dependent on the natural world and could not exist without it. Green economics needs to consider interaction between economic activity and the natural world (Anderson, 2006). We must be aware that the environment is the precondition for economic activity. If resources are depleted and ecosystems destroyed, society is not able to perform any economic activity. Since society cannot exist without various ecosystem services, there is no need for an economy at all (Hawken *et al.*, 1999).

The majority of green jobs combine existing skills sets with additional skills relating to green technologies, applications or processes. There will be a need for invention, innovation and moulding of some radically new professional expertise. The greening of tourism, which involves efficiency improvements in energy, water and waste systems, is expected to reinforce the employment potential of the sector with increased local hiring and sourcing and significant opportunities in tourism, oriented toward local culture and the natural environment (UN, 2012).

The green economy includes different sectors and operations. Figure 5.1 demonstrates the various sectors which include subsidies, tax discounts and other support tools

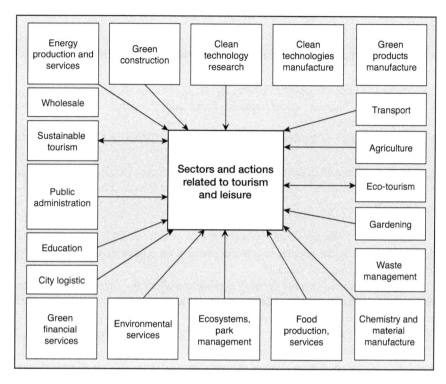

| Energy production and services | Green construction | Clean technology research | Clean technologies manufacture | Green products manufacture |

Wholesale

Sustainable tourism

Public administration

Education

City logistic

Sectors and actions related to tourism and leisure

Transport

Agriculture

Eco-tourism

Gardening

Waste management

| Green financial services | Environmental services | Ecosystems, park management | Food production, services | Chemistry and material manufacture |

FIGURE 5.1 Aspects of the green economy including different sectors and operations
Source: Authors

for the development of the green economy. We would like to stress the sectors that have interaction with the tourism industry, including PAs.

One of the best results on the way to green tourism has been achieved in ecotourism by implementing the certification of ecotourism services in various countries, such as Romania, Latvia, Japan and Australia (International Ecotourism Society, 2013) and in education, meaning accredited study programmes for tour guides from college to bachelor degree level, lifelong learning opportunities, student and staff mobility visits, in ecosystems, park management (through the regulations of the Environment Impact Assessment, UNDP, UNEP, OECD reports, etc.) and in public administration by ISO and EMAS (eco-management and audit scheme) certification in such fields as tourism and leisure to ensure service. The primary sectors which move forward to the green economy faster are primarily connected with a knowledge of humans and an understanding of the green economy, therefore they can be considered as the main sectors in the green economy.

A green tourism policy focuses on three main areas:

- mainstreaming measures affecting tourism;
- promoting tourism sustainability;
- enhancing understanding and visibility of tourism.

Public and NGO institutions elaborated the first global documents on green tourism in PAs such as:

- European Charter for Sustainable Tourism in Protected Areas (Europarc Federation, 2010);
- Towards a Green Economy (UNEP, 2011);
- Sustainable Tourism in Enterprises, Parks and Protected Areas (Europarc Federation, 2011);
- The Economics of Ecosystems and Biodiversity for Water and Wetlands (Russi et al., 2013);
- Nature and its role in the transition to a Green Economy (ten Brink et al., 2012);
- Green Infrastructure – Enhancing Europe's Natural Capital (European Commission, 2013a).

The UNWTO's *Sustainable development of tourism* e-bulletin (2011) on the first pages describes tourism in the context of green economics via sustainable tourism from the perspectives of supply and demand.

These reports provide more detailed explanations about the tourism sector in the context of the green economy as other recent studies and books have focused on tourism and low-carbon initiatives. In the autumn of 2012 we conducted face-to-face interviews with top-level managers in nature conservation or tourism development or academics in the environment field in the United States (2), Canada (4), India (2), Sri Lanka (1) and Latvia (4) on tourism as a green economy in PAs. The aim was to identify the understanding of professionals about tourism in a green economy.

All respondents from the twelve, apart from one, had heard the term 'green economy' and a third of respondents were familiar with the meaning of the green economy concept. Respondents were asked to provide their own description of green economy; most explanations included such keywords as sustainable use of natural resources, contribution in ecologically friendly and sustainable business, and five respondents mentioned social responsibility and local development issues as important in a green economy. We propose one of the explanations fully as it was written:

> Showcasing unique environments to individuals and groups while educating them for the future. Utilizing natural and local assets to assist with the business plan. Reconstruction of lost lands should be long-term goal. In order to be sustainable the green economy must profit!

No one mentioned carbon reduction or greenhouse gas emissions in their definitions. This explains the complex and deep understanding of employees of nature and tourism institutions about the green economy. In our comprehension, carbon reduction is only one of the components of green economy issues that need to be solved. All respondents saw opportunities for tourism enterprises that act as green economy companies in PAs.

Almost all respondents said they supported foreign tourism enterprises entering and acting in PAs if they met all the legislation rules. There is no specific support for local businesses; on the one hand, this ensures similar conditions in free market competition, on the other hand, it does not stimulate local economic development in limited diversified economic conditions as in PAs.

Regarding the statement that the development of tourism in PAs was too fast, there were two respondents in agreement, four respondents partly agreed and six disagreed. This confirms the recognized view of tourism in PAs as being primarily acceptable with the visitation capacity if it is well managed.

Responses to the statement that recreational and tourism infrastructure in PAs is used by visitors and local inhabitants equally demonstrates the necessity for a deeper analysis into the involvement of locals and visitors in PA visits. Five respondents partly agreed with this statement, two disagreed and five agreed. There are various examples of visitor segments in different PAs in the world. Shenandoah National Park in the US has 11 per cent foreign visitors from abroad per centin the summer and 4 per cent in the autumn (Manni *et al.*, 2011); in 2010 a survey conducted in four national parks in Latvia found that 84 per cent of respondents were locals and 16 per cent foreigners (Berzina, 2012). Why is this a very crucial issue in green tourism? There are several arguments as to why it is important to raise the number of visitations by locals. It helps with understanding the significance of their living place and being proud of the resources. A number of times during our research site visits to PAs, we heard questions such as – why are you coming? What would you like to see? This confirms that this is considered as a unique place and at the same time it provides local job opportunities in service delivery and provides such benefits as learning new cultures and languages. This issue is also connected with the driving distance to the destinations and the time spent on such visits. The National Park Service in the US provides entrance tickets valid for 7 days in national parks. How many of the visitors are using this opportunity to spend holidays in one national park, which offers hundreds of kilometres of hiking trails and other activities? For example, international tourist groups are stopping inside the park in a few of the most popular and known (marked) places for an hour; in this case it is difficult to call it green tourism. Green tourism requires an understanding of the concept of slow enjoyment, which gives an input into the local and regional development, an awareness of nature and the local culture, and communication with local professionals as guides. It is an opportunity to reduce the driving distances between attractions and sightseeing objects, the service infrastructure, but to popularize such healthy and recreational activities as walking, biking, canoeing, rafting, horse-riding, watching and discovering the surrounding nature. Another example is Iceland with four national parks and a UNESCO Heritage Site (2004) inside Thingvellir National Park (1930). Opportunities for the planning of trips depend on many factors, but in the context of green tourism factors such as comprehension of sustainability and a deeper introduction to the destination, as well as the creation of day-to-day relationships at the location must be taken into consideration.

Two respondents disagreed with statement 'I think tourism can create negative effect in the future for the natural habitats of the PAs', but ten respondents agreed. All respondents agreed with the proposed definition of the author: 'Tourism in the view of green economy is the reduction of use of resources and waste, and the preservation of natural diversity, cultural heritage and ecosystems, using local resources for tourism product as well as strengthening local economy and welfare.'

TABLE 5.1 Influence drivers of green tourism and driver input in green tourism

Influence drivers of tourism as green tourism in NPAs	Driver input in green tourism
Education about nature and natural resources in the context of consumption	Loyal visitor who takes responsibility according to the rules for being in PAs
The capacity of the place, people and infrastructure	Preserved nature
Maintenance of infrastructure	Saving of financial, human, nature and operational resources
Intercultural communication, self-enrichment of visitors	Changed experience, language skills Innovations for tourism and leisure
Promoting health and recreation	Productive work and development of new ideas and concepts
Use of modern information and communication technology tools in providing services	Cooperation on a global scale. Saving of resources The analysis of cost benefit for future investments
Increase in the length of stay per visitor in PAs	Reduction of carbon emission Growth of economy on the local scale Social responsibility at the destination

Source: Authors

What are the sustainability drivers in the field of recreation and tourism in nature protected areas?

Carbon reduction (greenhouse gas) is subject to considerably more detailed study and analysis than any other significant sustainability drivers of green tourism. Table 5.1 illustrates the main drivers of green tourism in PAs.

The *Green Infrastructure* strategy (2013) of the EU predicts the implementation of a green infrastructure in the area of ecotourism by decreasing the costs of investments and using the resources of natural ecosystems (European Commission, 2013a).

Best practices of offers in tourism and leisure as green economy in PAs

Long Point Eco-Adventures Company in Ontario Canada

The company has been operating since 2009, and in 2012 it was selected as one of forty-eight 'Signature Experiences Collections' by the Canadian Tourism Commission.

The mission of the company is to protect and conserve the abundance of nature and the human spirit. The company is located by the side of Long Point World Biosphere Reserve and less than 2 hours' drive from Toronto. A derivation of Long Point Biosphere Reserve is used in the title of the company to attract visitors, to better market it and to give the experience of the joy of being in nature. The company cooperates with Big Creek National Wildlife Area for paddling tours. A discussion (October, 2012) with the General Manager, Steve Martin, revealed his enthusiasm to create and develop Long Point Eco-Adventures as one of the top tourism eco-companies in Canada known globally. Martin is a member of the board of directors of the Southwest Ontario Tourism Corporation which has been the provincially mandated Regional Tourism Organization for Ontario's Southwest from 2011.

Environmentally friendly activities carried out by the company are waste recycling bins, information printed on brochures made from recycled paper, and the use of solar energy. The company is developing new green tourism innovations on a regular basis.

An attractive offering is the wilderness suites designed in tents with private flush toilet, outdoor shower with hot and cold running water, hardwood floors, sliding glass locking door, electrical outlets, private deck and atmosphere, providing the feeling that you are in wildlife (see Figure 5.2).

Specific activities and services offered are: zip line adventures, mountain biking, kayak adventures, astronomical viewing in the observatory, mushroom picking, five hiking trails. The company collaborates with Burning Kiln Winery which is located on the opposite side from Long Point Eco-Adventures. Overall services offered by the company or in cooperation with partners are examples of green tourism sustainability in practice.

FIGURE 5.2 Long Point Eco-Adventures wilderness suites
Photo: A. Livina, 2012

Bruce Peninsula and Point Pelee National Parks in Ontario, Canada

Both of these national parks demonstrate good practice of visitor management particularly during the off-peak season by using diverse self-registration forms. There are options to pay an entrance fee in a self-registration machine using a bank card or cash at Point Pelee National Park, and at Bruce Peninsula National Park there is the option to pay by cash in paper envelopes or using a bank card and then put in the collecting box (see Figure 5.3).

The positive side of such a solution is that the park is open for visitors all year particularly with the cuts to the financial resources.

Cuyahoga Valley National Park in Ohio, USA

Cuyahoga Valley National Park is unique in the context of the development of the green industry. The Cuyahoga River has been polluted thirteen times by industrial pollution between 1950 and the 1970s. Nowadays this region is still industrial, with factories and high chimneys, but a lot has been done in terms of sanitary measures for the environment and improvements in the technological processes in the factories has been made. The US congress in 1974 designated the Cuyahoga Valley National Recreation Area as an urban park, but in 2000 the recreation area became a National Park. The average number of visitors per year is 2.5 million, and there is no entrance fee for this park. Deputy Superintendent Paul J. Stoehr explained about new challenges in the park management regarding the attraction of visitors to the park from large cities

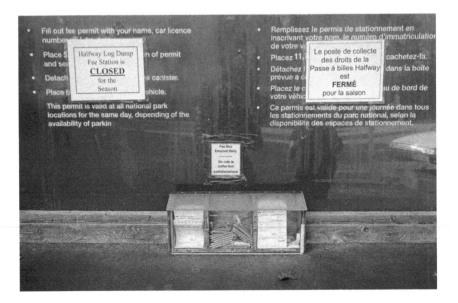

FIGURE 5.3 Self-paying box at Bruce Peninsula National Park

Photo: A. Livina, 2012

such as Cleveland which includes transport planning and organization, cross-cultural work for the awareness of the nature and education field with explanations about traditions and opportunities of how to spend free time in the park.

A Green Team has been created in this park who work with park and partner staff to meet the goals established in the park's Environmental Management Systems plan. The Green Team develops operational procedures to reduce the environmental footprint and promotes green practices among employees, partners and visitors. The park has set a goal to convert 15 per cent of all fluorescent lighting in the park to LED or higher efficiency systems annually (Sprague-Falk, 2012).

Luoyang Longtan Valley, member of Global Geoparks Network, China

Situated in north Xin'an County, about 60 kilometres from Luoyang in China's Henan province, the u-shaped valley that stretches 12 kilometres was formed by a stripe of purplish red quartz sandstone under the impact of flowing water. The valley is shrouded with rosy clouds and covered with splashing torrents. Green plants against the backdrop of red rocks, steep cliffs, and water-cut valleys formed over time, and wave-mark cliffs formed by gigantic collapsed blocks offer a wonderful visual feast.

Longtan Valley is the core tourist attraction of Daimei Mountain World Geopark, which has been awarded various titles including 'National Geopark', 'Scenic Spot with the Biggest Potential for Development in China', 'China's Outstanding Tourist Destination' and 'World Geopark' etc. It also enjoys titles such as 'The No. 1 Valley of Narrow Gorges in China', 'Natural Museum of Paleooceanography', 'Superb Landscape of Gorges' and 'Art Gallery of the Yellow River Landscape'.

There are six natural mysteries, seven ponds and eight natural wonders in the scenic spot. Tourists often marvel at these attractions and are unwilling to leave when they find themselves in the unique natural landscape gallery of red rock cliffs, splashing springs, ponds, narrow gorges, deep valleys, rare stones and shady trees. The scenic spot of Longtan Valley welcomes tourists with its beautiful environment, complete facilities, standardized management and excellent service.

Situation in Latvia

The development of the local tourism market is an essential part of the Latvian tourism sector and one of the goals of the marketing strategy of Latvian tourism. Nowadays priority is given to such aspects as quality, innovations and product compliance with the current market trends and requirements, namely, demographic changes and changes in consumer behaviour, safety, authentic offers, green solutions, sustainability and environment protection.

The nature of Latvia is still surprisingly rich and diverse, in spite of the rapid economic development in the twentieth century. Many do not realize how rich they are, if compared with the average indicators of Europe or around the world. The importance of environmental protection has reached the spotlight of global attention. Humans, society and nature have mutually interacted since the dawn of civilization, and it is now evident that economic concerns should never prevail over environmental protection (Stanka, 2004).

Kemeri National Park, Latvia

Kemeri National Park is situated in the central part of Latvia, bordering the Baltic Sea coastline for about 20 kilometres. The National Park is located just 40 kilometres from Riga. Kemeri National Park was established in 1997 with a view to preserving nature, cultural and historical values, and the resources of the health resort of the territory, as well as promoting education related to nature. The total area of the national park is 38.165 ha, including the sea area of 1.954 ha2.

Kemeri National Park is of great geological interest with rows of inland dunes and lagoon lakes along the coast that mark the border of the ancient Littorina Sea (see Figure 5.4).

It is one of most diverse wetland areas in Latvia. Large Kemeri Moorland is particularly outstanding. The bogs have a crucial role in the formation of numerous springs of sulphurous mineral water, which is the basis of the development of Kemeri as a resort. Lagoon lakes and bogs are nesting sites for lots of different waterfowl and a resting site for thousands of migratory geese and cranes.

The Kemeri National Park has became the first specially protected nature area in the territory of Latvia, to earn the European Sustainable Tourism Charter (Europarc Federation) in 2012. 'The Forest House' is the administrative centre of Kemeri National Park. An interesting tourism site, the Dumbraja (the Swamp Forest) footbridge, is located here. It is recommended to visit this rather short nature path in spring together with a guide – an ornithologist or botanist. The building was built in 1933, strictly abiding

FIGURE 5.4 Nature trail in bog, Kemeri National Park
Photo: Dz. Atstaja, 2013

by the national construction traditions; it is one of the most striking buildings of national Romanticism in Latvia (architect F. Skujins). After World War II the building had a sanatorium for children 'The Forest House'; children from all over the Soviet Union came here for treatment.

The restaurant 'Merry Mosquitoes', with a wide open-air terrace and a fireplace hall with luxurious woodcarvings, offered delicious food. The place was popular not only among the resort guests, but also with many celebrities at that time. The mosquitoes were not the only ones who enjoyed themselves – prosperous and well-known gentlemen came to visit this remote restaurant, and they were welcomed by cheerful ladies.Kemeri National Park is designated as a 'Natura 2000' area.

Gauja National Park, Latvia

Gauja National Park is the oldest national park in Latvia, being established in 1973. Since 2004, Gauja National Park (NP) has been a part of the Natura 2000 PA. The main part of the national park and the dominant is the old valley of the Gauja River. This valley is protected and can be used for nature tourism and cultural history, as well as recreation. There is a long tradition of tourism history in the Gauja NP (GNP, 2013).

The first visitors went hiking in the area in nineteenth century and it was also a top tourism destination in the Soviet period for domestic and foreign tourists. Nowadays it is one of the most marketable tourism places in Latvia. Gauja NP has good connections with the capital city, Riga. It is located approximately 1 hour away by train, bus or car. In 2012 the Gauja National Park established a long-term cooperation tourism cluster, which involves the owners of tourist sites and tourism service providers such as private, public and educational/research institutions. The aim of the Gauja NP tourism cluster is to turn Gauja NP into a tourist destination with a well-known brand 'Come to Gauja' and to be innovative in offering tourism services for specific target groups. The tourism cluster focuses on strengthening the national park's name through marketing campaigns to attract visitors to the tourist attractions and services inside and close to the national park. The challenge for the Gauja NP tourism cluster is to find a way to develop new green tourism services without negatively impacting nature, and how to effectively use Gauja NP's resources and value to increase the quality of the visitor experience and build awareness of sustainability. Green tourism means keeping undeveloped nature territories as they are, but the tourism companies want to earn profit from the visitors which means attracting more visitors up to the maximum capacity, to achieve the highest occupation rate. In Gauja NP the ski companies started to implement an innovation by offering a single entrance ticket for six companies. What will be the benefits for the skiers and the businesses from this innovation? The companies assume that it will attract clients particularly to these places because the skiers will have a variety of different offers, but the ski service owners do not need to form new slopes, cut down trees or change the landscape.

The above-mentioned cases (Long Point Eco-Adventures and Gauja National Park) demonstrate an insight into nature conservation, and the knowledge and skills of how to apply the value of nature-protected areas as advantages for customers in the supply of tourism services and products. Cuyahoga Valley National Park with its history of dramatic pollution in 1960 provides us with a deeper understanding of the necessary volumes of everyday consumption of different goods produced by industries, and their social responsibility.

Solutions and conclusions

The PAs of different countries are unique and play a significant role in the economy. Tourism can have both a positive and negative impact on sustainable development and the green economy. The cases mentioned above demonstrate that our designated drivers of tourism in the PAs are implemented in practice, for example, the driver of education about nature and natural resources (Thingvellir National Park, Kemeri National Park); the capacity of the place, people and infrastructure (Gauja National Park tourism cluster); maintenance of infrastructure (Bruce Peninsula and Point Pelee National Parks); intercultural communication, self-enrichment of visitors (Cuyahoga Valley National Park); promoting health and recreation (Luoyang Longtan Valley Geopark); IT in providing services (Bruce Peninsula and Point Pelee National Parks, Gauja National Park); and increasing the length of stay per visitor (Long Point Eco-Adventures).

The interviews conducted with the stakeholders of PAs testify that movements of non-governmental organizations are crucial in the development processes of PAs. The Long Point Biosphere Reserve Foundation joined together local nature enthusiasts who developed a tunnel under the Causeway road to reduce wildlife mortality. During the summer this road is swamped with visitors. Another example is the Gauja National Park tourism cluster which brings together almost sixty stakeholders (private business companies, self-governments, Nature Conservation Board of Latvia). The aim of this non-governmental cluster is to enlarge sustainable tourism by increasing the length of stay in the national park.

The majority of green jobs unite the existing skill sets with additional skills related to green technologies, applications or processes. Developing competences such as environmental awareness, system thinking and creativity will need as much attention as the delivery of specific skills such as intercultural communication. Promotion of the competences of learners need to have an integral part in the entire education system, from early childhood to life learning education. On the road to a green economy, it is necessary for society to conceptually change its attitudes and thinking, with new competences, specialists and experts being required.

A great number of private and public stakeholders at global, European, national, regional and local levels are involved in the development of green tourism. Given the complexity of tourism which is not easy to separate from other economic sectors, the stakeholders must develop partnerships if they want to stay ahead of their competitors. Therefore, the success of the renewed European Union policy depends on active involvement of all stakeholders in tourism.

References

Anderson, V. (2006) Turning economics inside out. *International Journal of Green Economics*, vol. 1, no. 1/2, pp. 11–22.

Atstaja, D., Kozlovs, V. and Kozlova, S. (2000) Hypertext technology in the models of work safety and environment protection economics. *International Conference Proceedings 'Integration of practice, education and research in tourism: experience and analysis*' Riga, School of Business and Administration Turiba, 30 March 2000, pp. 22–5, 255.

Atstaja, D., Dimante, D. and Livina, A. (2012) Public activities in developing green economy: Case studies in Latvia. *Proceedings of the 2012 International Conference 'Economic Science for Rural Development'*, Jelgava.

Berzina, I. (2012) Assessment of tourism economic significance in the regions of national parks of Latvia. PhD thesis - Latvia Agriculture University, Jelgava.

Cooper, C., Fletcher, J., Gilbert, D. and Wanhill, S. (1998) *Tourism: Principles and practice* (2nd edn). Longman.

Dambe, G. and Atstaja D. (2013) *Knowledge, skills and attitude in tourism industry: case study of Latvia. No: 7 European Integration Studies.* Kaunas University of Technology: Kaunas. pp. 177–84

Dudley, N. (ed.)(2008) *Guidelines for applying protected area management categories.* IUCN: Gland, Switzerland.

Europarc Federation (2010) *European charter for sustainable tourism in protected areas.* Europarc Federation: Regensburg, Germany.

Europarc Federation (2011) *Sustainable tourism in enterprises, parks and protected areas.* Europarc Federation: Regensburg, Germany.

European Commission (2013a) *Green infrastructure – enhancing Europe's natural capital.* European Commission: Brussels.

European Commission (2013b) *Natura 2000 Barometer.* Nature and biodiversity newsletter. No. 34, July 2013.

European Union (2013) Tourism EU policy. Available at: http://ec.europa.eu/enterprise/sectors/tourism/promoting-eu-tourism/tourism-policy/index_en.htm (accessed 9 January 2014).

GNP (2013) Tourism information – Guaja National Park. Available at: www.gnp.lv/en/gauja-national-park (accessed 3 January 2015).

Hawken, P., Lovins, A. and Lovins, L.H. (1999) *Natural capitalism: Creating the next industrial revolution.* Little, Brown and Company: New York.

International Ecotourism Society (2013) Industry news. Available at: www.ecotourism.org/news/industry-news (accessed 11 July 2013).

Manni, M.F., Morse, W., Le, Y. and Hollenhorst, S.J. (2011) *Shenandoah National Park visitor study Summer and Fall 2011.* University of Idaho: Moscow.

Middleton, V.T.C. (1994) *Marketing in travel and tourism* (2nd edn). Butterworth-Heinemann: Oxford.

Middleton, V.T.C. (1998) *Sustainable tourism: A marketing perspective.* Butterworth-Heinemann: Oxford.

Ramsar (2013) The Ramsar list of wetlands of international importance. Available at: www.ramsar.org/cda/en/ramsar-documents-list/main/ramsar/ (accessed 8 July 2013).

Russi, D., ten Brink, P., Farmer, A., Badura, T., Coates, D., Förster, J., Kumar, R. and Davidson, N. (2013) *The economics of ecosystems and biodiversity for water and wetlands.* IEEP: London and Brussels/Ramsar Secretariat: Gland:

Sprague-Falk, L. (2012) Cuyahoga Valley National Park responds to director's call with a progressive schedule. National Park Service. Available at: www.nps.gov/resources/2016.htm?id=EF44 2071-155D-4519-3E196EA8F1DFDA35 (accessed 15 January 2014).

Stanka, A. (2002) Risk management in rural tourism of Latvia. Proceedings of the Latvia University of Agriculture, (no. 11). pp. 49–53.

ten Brink P., Mazza L., Badura T., Kettunen M. and Withana S. (2012) *Nature and its role in the transition to a green economy.* TEEB, UNEP. Available at: www.teebweb.org/wp-content/uploads/2012/10/Green-Economy-Report.pdf.

UN (2012) *Report of the United Nations Conference on Sustainable Development*. UN: New York.

UNEP (2011) *Towards a green economy: Pathways to sustainable development and poverty eradication*. UNEP: Nairobi.

UNEP and EDO NSW (2013) *Community protocols for environmental sustainability: a guide for policy makers*. UNEP: Nairobi and EDO NSW: Sydney.

UNESCO (2013) Ecological sciences, man and biosphere reserve programme. Available at: www.unesco.org/new/en/natural-sciences/environment/ecological-sciences/man-and-biosphere-programme/ (accessed 8 July 2013).

UNWTO (2010) Tourism and the millennium development goals. Sustainable, competitive, responsible. Available at: www.unwto.org/tourism&mdgsezine/ (accessed 4 January 2014).

UNWTO (2011) *Sustainable Development of Tourism Bulletin*. No. 19, February 2011.

UNWTO (2012) *Tourism towards 2030*. UNWTO.

WDPA (2013) Discover the world`s protected areas. Available at: http://protectedplanet.net/about (accessed 8 July 2013).

6

ECOTOURISM REGULATION AND THE MOVE TO A GREEN ECONOMY

Colin Crawford and Jared Sternberg

This chapter makes a normative case for vigorous ecotourism regulation in order to achieve truly *sustainable* tourism. In this context, sustainable tourism is understood to mean tourism that promotes a low-carbon economic model. In particular, the chapter maintains that such a model can usefully be articulated and informed by tourism models practised by traditional peoples. To this end, the chapter focuses critically on the Achuar nation in the Ecuadorian Amazon. The Achuar example provides a model for ecotourism regulation that, with proper advocacy and deliberate regulation, can become a world standard. Such a model would guide tourism and other industries in the shift to a green economy, demonstrating techniques for drastically reduced use of carbon-based energy and techniques for thoughtful resource use and regeneration. Importantly, then, a secondary aim of this chapter is to argue that examples such as the Achuar must be used to define model laws and regulations for a low-carbon ecotourism model that can be adopted by governments and nation states to promote the important role of ecotourism in leading the way towards a low-carbon economy. The eventual availability of model laws and rules is especially important for economically and legally undeveloped countries that are among the most desirable sites for sun-and-sand tourism. Without such laws and regulations, this paper contends, the possibility for carbon-intensive and environmentally destructive tourism is high.

The dilemma: defining a sustainable tourism model

Tourism is a highly profitable industry. According to the United Nations World Tourism Organization (UNWTO) for example, 'international tourism (travel and passenger transport) accounts for 30 per cent of the world's exports of services and 6 per cent of overall exports of goods and services'. In 2012 alone, the UNWTO reports that, despite challenging economic conditions in much of the world, international tourism receipts grew by 4 per cent, to a staggering US$1,075 million (UNWTO, 2013). The figures continue to astound. According to the World Travel and Tourism Council, tourism and its related economic activities generated 9 per cent of global gross domestic product

(GDP) in 2012 and employed over 260 million people, one in 11 of the world's total jobs. These figures are predicted to continue expanding into 2023 (WTTC, 2013). Tourism also represents one of the top five exports for 150 countries and is the number one export for sixty (UNEP, 2013). Simply put, tourism is one of the largest, perhaps the largest, industry on the planet. Yet despite the magnitude of this activity, tourism is one of the world's least regulated industries. Research by the World Bank and PricewaterhouseCoopers that compares corporate responsibility practices across industry sectors shows that tourism is lagging behind – which has serious implications for ecosystems, communities and cultures around the world (Ashley *et al.*, 2007). Leaving such a large industry relatively unchecked produces health repercussions, environmental repercussions such as wasteful use of natural resources and biodiversity loss, and negative social consequences, including impacts on locals and local cultures (UNEP, 2013).

Curiously, however, in light of its economic importance as an activity and industry, tourism remains largely unregulated in formal, legal terms. (Crawford, 2006–7). There are no widely recognized and legally accepted model codes defining different forms of tourism, for example, or agreed upon sets of rules setting baseline performance standards by which the multinational tourism giants, whether hotel and cruise ship operators or discount package retailers and resort operators must operate. This is of particular concern where tourism takes hold in places where the non-local providers and vendors of services have a disproportionate degree of economic power as opposed to the populations they encounter. Furthermore, the practice of much global tourism is heavy in terms of resource expenditure, suggesting that the mostly foreign developers and operators of tourism projects have little interest in using their investments as opportunities to move to a lower-carbon or 'green' economy.

The concern that prompts this chapter is driven, therefore, by two observations. First, for many economically less-developed countries, tourism represents an important possible revenue source; its significance cannot thus be underestimated, making it essential to identify means for tourism to expand and develop in a truly sustainable manner. Second, the search for tourist-driven revenues in such economically less-developed countries is fraught with possible environmental hazards. In the medium- to long-term, these promise to prevent significant swaths of the less-developed world from transitioning to or becoming part of the green economy as they become ever more dependent on a fossil fuel-dependent development pattern. For these reasons, once again, it is therefore essential not only to identify best practices such as the Achuar example discussed below but also to use those examples to codify the best practices in guidelines, laws and rules that create incentives for following such practices and penalties for failing to do so.

Consider the importance of doing so, for example, in the example of the small and resource-poor island nation of the Dominican Republic. The island nation of just over 10 million people is both overwhelmingly dependent on fossil fuel imports for its energy needs (Worldwatch Institute, 2011) and a place where the government reports that nearly 50 per cent of the national population live below the national poverty line (World Bank, 2011). Like many countries similarly placed – resource-poor but blessed with natural attractions such as sun, sea and sand – it is small wonder that tourism has taken hold in the island nation. Although the government does not produce an integrated measure of tourist sector growth, it does track changes in flight arrivals as a measure of the sector's growth. For the period 1978–2013, air passenger arrivals have increased in a super-majority of quarters for the period, often by double digits. Of course, not all of this can be credited to tourism alone – although the government does use it as a proxy indicator for this sector's rise (Central Bank of Dominican Republic, 2013).

What merits note here is the mix of factors: dependence on imported fossil fuels in a poor country whose greatest commercial growth is occurring in an industry in which a disproportionate amount of the economic resources are held by foreign economic interests. An issue that should be of concern here is that there is no mechanism to help build local capacity for a green economy. There are contradictory forces at work in such a situation. First, it is reasonable to assume that human beings are most concerned to protect the health and sustainable development of those nearest to them physically, culturally and socially. That is, foreign investors invest to improve their own social, economic and environmental situation, and not – at least not in the first instance – that of the places where they invest. Second, and correspondingly, foreign economic interests are naturally likely to favour a form of investment that delivers their financial return at the lowest possible cost. In combination, these factors militate against long-term thinking that is concerned in the first instance with careful resource stewardship, the kind of stewardship that would promote the development of a low-carbon economy. Therefore, this sort of trend presents serious concerns and cause for reflection. In brief, the situation sketched above raises concern with an activity that is industrial in its dimensions in that, like the all-inclusive tourism that grows ever more rapidly in scope, a significant portion of tourism activities are not well integrated, if integrated at all, into the local community. Instead, much of today's mega-tourism imposes a heavy socio-environmental footprint – including (often imported) fossil fuel dependence, careless water use, and disruptive cultural and social practices. Many mega-tourism projects – especially in less-economically developed countries – are implemented without careful planning, and, in tropical countries, damage forest resources and biodiversity (Third World Network, 2013). To the extent that a green economic future can be understood as one in which energy, economic and environmental choices are integrated and coordinated, this booming industry's growth does not serve the green economic agenda, at least as most large-scale tourism is practised today.

The Achuar example

The Kapawi Ecolodge and Reserve (henceforth the 'Kapawi Ecolodge'), owned and operated by the Achuar, provides lineaments for model ecotourism regulation that can become the world standard. The Achuar model demonstrates techniques for drastically reduced use of carbon-based energy and techniques for thoughtful resource use and regeneration that can guide tourism and other industries in the shift to a green economy.

Background

Until the end of the nineteenth century, the region of the Amazon Basin, which is today occupied by the Achuar of Ecuador and Peru, was only occasionally visited by small numbers of missionaries and naturalist explorers (Kapawi, 2014). The latter half

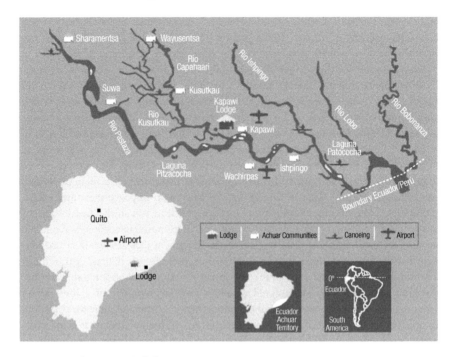

FIGURE 6.1 *The Kapawi Ecolodge*
Source: Courtesy of the Kapawi Ecolodge Reserve

of the nineteenth century saw the growth of the rubber industry in the Amazon Basin, but because of the remote location and inaccessibility of the Achuar, the Achuar's territory was only marginally affected (Kapawi, 2014). In 1941, war broke out between Ecuador and Peru, and the Achuar, whose territory spanned both countries, found themselves divided into two 'nationalities'. The Achuar continued to live in extreme isolation despite this divide and their territory was considered 'terra incognita' until the late 1960s, when Roman Catholics and Evangelicals began to enter their territory. Although the missionaries met limited success in their quest for converts, they did initiate a process of increasing intercultural contact that shaped the future of the Achuar nation (Kapawi, 2014).

To be sure, much of the contact in ensuing years was not positive. Approximately 600,000 square kilometres of the Amazon Rainforest have either been deforested or contaminated as a result of non-sustainable extraction and farming activities (Trujillo *et al.*, 2008, p. 17). According to a little-circulated study written in English and supported by the Achuar's non-indigenous partner in the Kapawi Ecolodge, this directly impacts the Achuar today, a population of approximately 6,000 indigenous people living in over sixty-four communities scattered over 1,700,000 acres of Amazonian rainforest in Ecuador and Peru (Trujillo *et al.*, 2008, p. 18). Achuar communities are largely self-dependent (meaning they receive little state support). As a result, their territories have not been completely free from the economic appeal of resource extraction and farming activities to help sustain them (Trujillo *et al.*, 2008, p. 17). These activities, providing short-term economic and sustenance benefits, can thus constitute very real threats to communities that may not realize the damage they will cause to their environment (Trujillo et al., 2008, p. 68).

Tourism represents 12 per cent of Ecuador's economic 'productive activities', although tourism in the Ecuadorian Amazon still represents only 10 per cent of this 12 per cent total (Reyes, 2010). Tourism in the Ecuadorian Amazon began in the 1970s. Improvements in the highway system led to an expansion of tourism in the 1980s, and by the end of the 1990s, a new tourism model with a focus on greater environmental responsibility and social awareness gained momentum (Reyes, 2010). Around the same time, several indigenous populations of Amazonia initiated protests, in defence of their forests and against oil and timber exploitation, which had produced countless social and environmental impacts and little to no improvements to local economies (Reyes, 2010).

Encouragingly, however, a successful ecotourism project in Achuar territory provides a promising example of an economic alternative that is far less resource-intensive and, thus, truly sustainable. With respect to the move to a low-carbon economy, two aspects of this story are of special interest. First, the Achuar example demonstrates that traditional communities can rarely develop and continue such projects without strong outside partners, if partners who respect their community interests and vision. Second, in the process of such collaborative developments, indigenous communities such as the Achuar can validate their cultural practices and values – practices and values that in fact promote low-carbon economic values.

Kapawi Ecolodge

The first stage of the Achuar's collaborative effort on the Kapawi Ecolodge spanned a period of 15 years. Specifically, in 1993, the Achuar Indigenous Nation in the Ecuadorian Amazon made an agreement with an Ecuadorian ecotourism company, Canodros S.A., to create an ecolodge within Achuar territory (Canodros, 2011). The process that led to this partnership could hardly have been predicted a generation earlier. In the 1960s, the Achuar people had barely made contact with society outside Achuar territory. It was around this time that they began to transition from a nomadic existence to one where Achuar lived in villages. It was only in 1993 that these new, small communities united to form the Organization of the Achuar Nationality of Ecuador ('OINAE' in its Spanish-language acronym). The OINAE President, Luis Vargas, was at that time contacted by non-Achuar outsiders, including a group talking about the possibilities of tourism as a route to self-sustainability. Vargas and other Achuar leaders reported that they saw in the ecotourism project proposal an opportunity to offer their people a better future that had the potential to provide income while at the same time retaining territory, preserving their environment, culture, and ethnic identity, and also as a bulwark to protect them from the encroachment of other industries that have the tendency to expel Amazonian communities from their ancestral lands and destroy their traditional habitats (Trujillo et al., 2008, p. 15). Although the Achuar leaders say they were convinced that ecotourism was a better alternative for them, introducing this concept to the various communities and convincing them of their leaders' view took a serious effort. The leaders and Canodros spoke to the communities in long assemblies in which they worked to dismantle myths and break down cultural barriers and fears. In the end, they acquired the approval of all the Achuar communities constituting the Achuar Nation. The approval was given in 1993, and the construction phase of the Kapawi Ecolodge started shortly thereafter (Trujillo *et al.*, 2008, p. 31). In 1996, the construction phase was complete and the lodge became operational (Trujillo *et al.*, 2008, p. 36).

In terms of the transition to a low-carbon economy, the importance of this decision cannot be underemphasized. In many instances, the principal alternative to tourism in traditional communities (which would include indigenous communities) is some form of extractive industry that lacks any value-added activity or local training. Whether this means extraction of petroleum-based products or other mineral extraction, the low-carbon economic alternative loses out either way. The combustion of petroleum-based products is of course carbon-intensive. Other mineral extraction, moreover, if not resulting directly in combustion, nevertheless typically results in deforestation of fragile tropical environments, losing the carbon sink function and benefits that such forests provide.

In the Achuar example, furthermore, the success of the indigenous project was made possible through a cooperative effort with outside promoters and developers who eventually ceded total control to the Achuar. Indeed, the Achuar's Kapawi Ecolodge is unusual because in January 2008, complete ownership of the enterprise was handed over from Canodros, which had been running it for the last 12 years, to the Achuar people (Trujillo *et al.*, 2008, p. 17). The project is now operated by the Achuar through an entity known as CEKSA – the Spanish language acronym for the entity (Complejo Ecoturistico Kapawi Sociedad Anonima, or Kapawi Ecotourist Complex, Inc.). CEKSA is a legal structure categorized as an Ecuadorian tour operator, in full charge of the ownership, operation, and management of the lodge.

However, although the Achuar are now the sole owners of the lodge, they do not operate in complete isolation. That is, cooperative strategies with outside interests continue to play an important role. As such, the Achuar receive help from a few local and international non-profit organizations that advocate politically and legally for them as well as help teach them the necessary skills (such as marketing and English) to run the lodge (Almendariz, 2011).

The Kapawi Ecolodge has helped preserve the environment in the Achuar territory and improve the lives of the Achuar communities. Due to a unified position against resource extraction, the Achuar in Ecuador have maintained their territory free of highways, oil, timber, and mining companies (Almendariz, 2011), in part because they have been able to develop a separate revenue source in the form of the Kapawi Ecolodge. The Achuar have been able to do this first because of their collective insistence that the forest should be maintained as both their 'supermarket' and their 'highway'; Achuar leaders report that their instincts have told them not to trust external parties that seek to exploit their natural resources (Freire, 2011). As a result, they have been open to ecotourism opportunities that they can control and they assert that the Kapawi Ecolodge continues to grow and help support the local communities (Freire, 2011).

Furthermore, since its inception, the Kapawi Ecolodge has helped shape the way the Achuar interact both with the Ecuadorian central government and with outsiders from Ecuador and beyond (S. Antik, 2011). Specifically, the positive attention the Achuar have received nationally and internationally for the Kapawi Ecolodge has increased their leverage to receive government benefits. These benefits have come both in the form of individual benefit transfers and as funds to help expand and sustain their activities. On the individual level, they have received increased funding for schools in their communities and greater access to healthcare, including free flights to visit cities with better health care services when necessary (S. Antik, 2011). On a collective basis, both government and international non-profit financial support since the commencement of the Kapawi Ecolodge helps support them as they work to preserve their forests and their way of life (R. Antik, 2011). In this way, according to the current Achuar Administrator of the Kapawi Ecolodge, Angel Etsaa: 'ecotourism has provided the Achuar the consciousness and capacity to identify with their own culture, conserve the local environment, and teach their children their own habits, customs, and traditions that other cultures lost a long time ago' (Etsaa, 2013).

Moreover, and most importantly for purposes of the argument advanced in this chapter, the Kapawi Ecolodge is a model for a low-carbon, 'green' business. The low-carbon processes and keen ethic of community social responsibility developed by the Achuar in collaboration with their outside partners over the life of the project development featured multiple low-carbon practices. These included intelligent construction, green energy systems (and specifically solar panels), low-impact waste management systems, small-scale, local sewage treatment (such as artificial marshes and sand bio-filters), and the use of efficient engines. Outside observers have therefore celebrated the Kapawi Ecolodge's systems and practices. The lodge is equipped with 'appropriate systems for minimizing environmental impacts, including solar energy, sewage treatment, and low emission motors' (USAID, 2008). Additionally, the Achuar have an ozonification water purification system that provides guests and employees with clean, local water that requires minimal energy to deliver (Etsaa, 2013). This system results in water with less than 0.05 per cent contamination, meaning that after the ozonification process the water is cleaner than in its natural state, which has a 0.06 per cent contamination average (Etsaa, 2013).

Ecotourism and the low-carbon economy

It is important to note here as well that the Kapawi Ecolodge was conceived as an ecotourism project from the start. That is, the Achuar model demonstrates the importance of deliberate planning to establish a low-carbon, green business model. The Kapawi Ecolodge master plan thus defines ecotourism as 'an activity inspired by the natural history of an area, including its indigenous cultures, whose areas have been adapted for this activity in a spirit of appreciation, participation and responsiveness'. The construction of the resort therefore emphasized the use of local materials and traditional Achuar building construction techniques. Where local materials and techniques were not judged sufficient to create an environment that would satisfy the comfort levels desired by non-Achuar tourists, the Achuar planners, in collaboration with their outside partners, focused on the selection and adoption of environmentally friendly technologies (Trujillo *et al.*, 2008, p. 73).

This is to point out that at no time did the Achuar seek to provide a wholly traditional (that is to say, technology-free) tourist experience. Instead, the goal of the Kapawi

Ecolodge's planners, both the Achuar and their outside collaborators, was to use local workers employing traditional techniques that could be adapted to include comforts desired by outside tourists (Trujillo *et al.*, 2008, p. 33). As a result, local materials were used and the Kapawi Ecolodge was built largely according to the traditional elliptical construction techniques of the Achuar, which allowed the resort to be constructed in order to stay cool in the tropical heat (Etsaa, 2013). However, the design did not slavishly adhere to traditional methods. Instead, a variety of techniques were employed, for example combining traditional Achuar elliptical architecture and durable palm thatch roofing to construct buildings that would require little in the way of cooling systems. This design was then complemented with the use of low-carbon technologies for lighting and waste disposal, including construction with solar panels and environmentally compatible sanitary waste treatment (Trujillo *et al.*, 2008, p. 36). The Kapawi Ecolodge uses thermal water bags, installed on the lodge rooftops to make hot water possible for showers. Satellite dishes also installed on the rooftop of the main lodge make internet connections possible.

That is, though a traditional people, the Achuar's model is very much located in the modern world. Theirs is a low-carbon model, not a no-carbon one. The Kapawi Ecolodge, for instance, has operated a hybrid power system since its inception. Power is generated by a photovoltaic solar power system of sixty-eight panels (Trujillo *et al.*, 2008, p. 74). In early 2013, the Achuar reported that this solar system provided more than 65 per cent of the electrical energy necessary for the entire Kapawi Ecolodge, including refrigerators, freezers, and current for the cabins and service areas. However, on days with high rainfall and no sunshine, the system depends on two diesel generators, which contribute approximately 35 per cent of the resort's remaining energy needs (Etsaa, 2013). By the end of 2013, the Achuar planned to replace the older batteries used within the solar power system for newer, more efficient solar power batteries (Etsaa, 2013). The old batteries would be transported out of the jungle to a facility where they could be properly disposed of and recycled when possible (Etsaa, 2013). And although the resort is not yet no-carbon in its energy use, the Achuar maintain such aspirations. According to an Achuar spokesperson, the Achuar have plans to increase their solar energy dependence to 100 per cent in the coming years (Etsaa, 2013).

Deliberate advance planning also resulted in waste management practices at the Kapawi Ecolodge that stand as a model for the transition to a low-carbon economy. Solid wastes are classified into three groups by the Achuar and are independently disposed of in a manner designed to reduce transportation and promote efficiency. First, non-organic wastes, namely glass, metals and plastics, are transported by air to a nearby town to receive proper treatment and recycling whenever possible. Second, organic wastes, including most kitchen wastes, are crushed, discarded on site and composted. Third, paper wastes are burned in a specific area designated for such purpose (Etsaa, 2013). During their stay at the hotel, tourists receive clear and specific instructions on waste management and are encouraged to collaborate in classification and carry any batteries home with them (Etsaa, 2013). In this way, the Achuar example nicely illustrates how low-carbon waste management practices can be taught, learned and implemented where they did not exist before.

Sewage treatment also received careful advance planning and implementation and demonstrates the possibilities for small-scale, low-carbon sewage treatment options.

Wastewater is treated at an on-site processing plant where it receives biological treatment via a system of constructed, artificial marshes and sand bio-filters (Trujillo *et al.*, 2008, p. 74). The treatment facility is in the jungle adjacent to the hotel and while it cost approximately US$40,000 to install (and thus a high-value item for the Achuar), the Achuar celebrate the fact that it effectively and efficiently treats wastewater to this day (Etsaa, 2013).

Transportation also follows a hybrid, low-carbon model. The Achuar themselves use wooden canoes; the majority of community members continue to use these handmade canoes without engines. Tourist visitors, however, are mostly transported in the handmade canoes with engines. The Achuar assert that all engines operating passenger canoes use the most recently available, efficient engines, designed to guarantee a minimum level of noise and emissions (Etsaa, 2013).

As a result of all of these designs, the Kapawi Ecolodge project has been recognized internationally as one of the most pioneering ecotourism projects in the world (Trujillo *et al.*, 2008, p. 77). Global organizations such as Conservation International have acknowledged the contribution of this project to the preservation of the environment. In addition, the Kapawi Ecolodge has received many rewards, not only from Conservation International, but also from Tourism for Tomorrow, Travel & Leisure Magazine, the International Association of Travel and Tourism Professional, Ministry of Tourism, Sustainable Tourism Award for Conservation, among others (Trujillo *et al.*, 2008, p. 74).

Normative lessons of the Achuar example

What, then, can be learned from the Achuar's Kapawi Ecolodge example? First, the Achuar case displays the potential of indigenous-led ecotourism enterprises to function as a viable form of green, low-carbon development for economically less-developed peoples and communities. Between 1996 and 2005 the Kapawi Ecolodge operation generated US$1,225,724 in direct contributions to the local communities and individual members of the Achuar of Ecuador Nationality (Nacionalidad Achuar del Ecuador in Spanish or NAE in its Spanish-language acronym, an indigenous grassroots organization whose object is to defend and value the Achuar culture and territory) (USAID, 2008). This economic contribution came from rental paid for the lodge, payment of entrance fees for visits to the Achuar communities, payments to Achuar personnel who work in the lodge, flights to and from the community, purchases of local products (food), donations and other expenditure. According to a report from the United States Agency for International Development, 'This alliance between an indigenous organization has produced significant outcomes through the implementation of an economic activity as a mechanism for sound natural resource management and for the financial sustainability of the organization' (USAID, 2008, p. 33). The direct income transfers to communities and their members because the tourism may be low in absolute terms. However, Achuar representatives say that these income transfers have been and continue to constitute important sources of support for their family finances and personal well-being.

Second, the Achuar example demonstrates that outside entities can be valued partners in the search for a sustainable tourism model that also protects traditional values. The example shows that tourism enterprises, whether private or public, can play a fundamental role in the success of indigenous-based ecotourism in many ways. For example, marketing is important in any business, not least in ecotourism, where the field is flooded with all manner of operators using the ecotourism label with little precision as to the meaning. In ecotourism projects, however fundamental marketing may be to success, it is too often neglected in community-based projects, likely because nature-conservation NGOs that support them are often unfamiliar with the rigours of business development. The Kapawi Ecolodge example is often cited as a success, largely because of Canodros SA, the private company engaged in the development of nature and cultural tourism that provided capital to the Achuar community to build the lodge, support technical services, management operations, and marketing of the destination (Coria and Calfucura, 2011, p. 15). As noted, the partnership between the private business and the indigenous community functioned for more than 15 years until the lodge was transferred to the Achuar in 2008 (Grench, 2009).

Third, and as documented in the preceding section, the Achuar example shows that, with careful planning, businesses can successfully implement an integrated, low-energy, low-carbon model. Importantly, too, it is a model that has traction beyond the confines of a single ecotourist resort. Consider the example of the Achuar people themselves. The lower-carbon systems set up from the start of the development of the Kapawi Ecolodge project are still in use – not only at the Kapawi Ecolodge itself but also in Achuar communities. For example, inspired by the Kapawi Ecolodge model and with the support of a private foundation, the Sharamentsa Achuar community implemented its own system of solar energy to supply its energy needs (Trujillo *et al.*, 2008, p. 73). This example demonstrates how environmentally sensitive tourism planning can provide not merely a model for that industry, but also a low-carbon option for economically developing communities that might otherwise have no option but to follow a petroleum-intensive or other carbon-intensive path.

Fourth, the Achuar example provides the elements to outline an effective definition of ecotourism. As noted at the outset, there is no generally agreed and internationally sanctioned such definition and even major hotel chains now trumpet their ecotourist initiatives, sometimes used as a shorthand merely for adventure or exotic 'nature' tourism, but with no insistence on sustainable design. The above Achuar example suggests that ecotourism occurs when, at a minimum, it contains the following elements: (1) in seeking to have the lowest possible carbon footprint, the project privileges non-carbon based energy use to the greatest extent possible and seeks constantly to reduce carbon-based energy consumption; (2) promotes resource conservation and recycles and reuses resources whenever and wherever possible; (3) locates itself and is constructed according to principles and practices successfully observed traditionally by local communities (e.g. the Achuar building practices adapted to produce structures acceptable for habitation by non-Achuar outside tourists but with a low physical impact on the surrounding environment); and (4) respects local community needs and consensus decisions.

To be sure, the picture of the Achuar's ecotourism example is not an entirely positive and rosy one. Despite all the benefits the project has brought, it has been far from easy or perfect. The biggest problem may in fact derive from the high expectations generated by conservationists and NGOs (Stronza and Gordillo, 2008), who have placed hopes that such enterprises can provide a magic answer to the long-term survival of traditional communities. In fact, the Achuar example at the Kapawi Ecolodge is but one part of a larger challenge to protect traditional communities in such a way as also to promote a low-carbon, alternative economic model. It is true that employment at the Kapawi Ecolodge does help a number of families in the nearby Achuar communities; that much is clear. But the pay is low and the number of jobs is limited (R. Antik, 2011). Most people in the communities still drink unfiltered water from the river and must travel great distances to seek medical care (R. Antik, 2011). That is, much remains to be done to improve the social and economic health of these communities. Successful ecotourism can help show a means to develop positively according to a low-carbon model, but this is only part of the answer for communities facing a wide array of challenges.

Nonetheless, overall the Kapawi Ecolodge project has been a positive resource for the Achuar, who have used it as a means for raising awareness about the value and potential of sustainable, low-carbon tourist development, both within the communities themselves as well as among a wider national and international audience.

Regulation informed by low-carbon ecotourism in traditional communities

In conclusion, the Achuar example provides an ideal point of departure for thinking about and redefining the role of indigenous tourist enterprises in the support of low-carbon, truly sustainable tourism and its role in the move to a low-carbon economy generally. The four definitional elements in the previous section provide normative guidance that could be used by international and regional governance entities (from those in the United Nations system and the World Bank to entities such as the regional development banks) to establish a widely accepted definition of the meaning of ecotourism, opening the way to adopt a uniform, internationally recognized set of criteria to be followed by those who seek to enter into the sustainable ecotourism market. Such a definition and/or criteria must emphasize the key role of traditional community choice and practice in project design. Second, the collaboration between the Achuar and Canodros SA, the Ecuadorian private partner, demonstrates a viable model that will be attractive to ecotourism actors with differing but overlapping interests. That is, private and public bodies have expertise and skills to share with indigenous and traditional communities seeking an alternative economic path via tourism and, as Canodros's participation shows, can make an economic return in such efforts. At the same time, however, indigenous and traditional communities equally have an important, key role in such partnerships. The Achuar example discussed above demonstrates that traditional investors need to be made to understand the potential for successful collaborations with traditional communities through active recruitment and education. To this end, the Achuar example underlines the importance of preparing a package of incentives (e.g. tax and business development measures) to enter into such arrangements, with the fundamental understanding that they must be guided above all by the desires and choices of local, traditional partners. In addition to financial incentives, finally, effective public education campaigns are needed. Public education campaigns about traditional communities and ecotourism can help make such entities understand that everyone shares an interest in such efforts because they not only reduce carbon use but also help preserve forest and water resources (and thus aid in climate change adaptation) as well preserve other environmental resources that may have unexploited economic value, such as biodiversity. These positive values are often lost in the din of exploration for yet more carbon-based energy resources. The Achuar example shows, however, that through carefully planned ecotourism the move to a low-carbon economy is possible – and in a beautiful natural environment at that.

In short, the example of traditional communities provides an important model not only for defining and identifying what is meant by 'ecotourism' but also for emphasizing the values at stake in the move to a low-carbon economy. Specifically, and first, the example of a traditional community like the Achuar demonstrates that moving to a low-carbon economy, while it may mean a sacrifice of some past patterns and practices, also comes with benefits in rethought forms of social organization and collaboration. Moreover, the example demonstrates that significant advances are available when stakeholders with little experience of one another work together to find mutually beneficial solutions. Third, the example demonstrates that such efforts will not only implement and lead to the observance of and respect for more sustainable energy uses but also to higher levels of protection and care of the physical and built environments. Fourth and finally, it merits noting that none of these aspects of the Achuar experience are so culturally curious or distinctive that the basic features of the experience cannot be repeated and copied in many other places and contexts. Indeed, it is the modest aim of this chapter to suggest that they should and can be.

References

Almendariz, P. (2011) Interview on Kapawi Ecolodge and Reserve Project. Interviewed by Jared Sternberg [in person] Quito, Ecuador, August.

Antik, R. (2011) Interview on Kapawi Ecolodge and Reserve Project. Interviewed by Jared Sternberg [in person] Kosutkau, Ecuador, August.

Antik, S. (2011) Interview on Kapawi Ecolodge and Reserve Project. Interviewed by Jared Sternberg [in person] Kosutkau, Ecuador, August.

Ashley, C., Debrine, P., Lehr, A. and Wilde, H. (2007) *The role of the tourism sector in expanding economic opportunity*. Economic Opportunity Series, Harvard University: Cambridge, MA.

Canodros (2011) Kapawi: Amazon Rainforest Ecuador. Available at: www.canodros.com/amazon/kapawi_pages-en/compromiso.html (accessed 5 August 2013).

Central Bank of the Dominican Republic (2013) Total of Non Resident Passengers [sic] Arrival By Air 1978–2013. Available at: www.bancentral.gov.do/estadisticas_economicas/turismo (accessed 9 April 2015).

Coria, J. and Calfucura, E. (2011) *Ecotourism and the development of indigenous communities: the good, the bad, and the ugly*. Abstract: Working Papers in Economics: University of Gothenburg, 489 pp. 1–28.

Crawford, C. (2006–7) Protecting environmentally-sensitive areas and promoting tourism in 'The back patio of the United States': Thoughts about shared responsibilities in ecosystem and biodiversity protection. *UCLA Journal of Environmental Law and Policy*, vol. 25, p. 41.

Etsaa, A. (2013) Interview with Administrator of Kapawi Ecolodge. Interviewed by Jared Sternberg [in person] Kapawi Ecolodge, April.

Freire, G. (2011) Interview with the President of the Achuar Nation. Interviewed by Jared Sternberg [in person] Kosutkau, Ecuador, August.

Grench, E. (2009) *Globalization and indigenous empowerment in Amazonian Ecuador.* The Ohio State University: Columbus, OH.

Kapawi Ecolodge (2014) The Achuar Community of Ecuador's recent history. http://kapawi. com/historia-reciente/ (accessed 15 January 2014).

Reyes, M. (2010) Tourism strategies for 'advantaging' the Amazon rainforest region: The Ecuador model. *Worldwide Hospitality and Tourism Themes*, vol. 2, no. 2, pp. 163–72.

Stronza, A. and Gordillo, J. (2008) Community views of ecotourism. *Annals of Tourism Research*, vol. 35, no. 2, pp. 448–68.

Third World Network (2013) Does tourism benefit the Third World. Available at: www.twnside. org.sg/title2/resurgence/207-208/cover1.doc (accessed 26 August 2013).

Trujillo, E., Maldonado, A., Rodriguez, P. and Lurdes De Montalvo, M. (2008) *A deep vision: Memories of Kapawi Ecolodge and Reserve Project.* (2nd edn). Canodros S.A., pp. 3–98.

UNEP (2013) *Climate change mitigation/tourism.* United Nations Environmental Programme. Available at: www.unep.org/climatechange/mitigation/Tourism/tabid/104347/Default.aspx (accessed 16 January 2014).

UNWTO (2013) International tourism receipts grew by 4% in 2012. Available at: http://media. unwto.org/en/press-release/2013-05-15/international-tourism-receipts-grew-4-2012 (accessed 28 August 2013).

USAID (2008) Tourism, protected areas and communities: Case studies and lessons learned from the Parks in Peril Program 2002–2007. [report] South America Conservation Region External Affairs Technical Publication No. 1.

World Bank (2011) Dominican Republic data. Available at: http://data.worldbank.org/country/ dominican-republic (accessed 28 August 2013).

Worldwatch Institute (2011) Transitioning to renewable energy creates jobs in Dominican Republic. Available at: http://blogs.worldwatch.org/revolt/how-transitioning-to-renewable-energy-can-create-jobs-in-the-dominican-republic/ (accessed 28 August 2013).

WTTC (2013) *The economic impact of travel & tourism 2013.* World Travel & Tourism Council. Available at: www.wttc.org/site_media/uploads/downloads/world2013_1.pdf (accessed 16 January 2013).

7

CHINA'S TOURISM'S MARCH FORWARD

Towards a green transition or unsustainable tourism

Michael O'Regan and Jaeyeon Choe

Introduction

Since the United Nations' Earth Summit in Rio de Janeiro forged landmark agreements on climate change and biodiversity in 1992, global carbon dioxide emissions have risen by nearly 50 per cent (Rogers and Harvey, 2012). In the intervening period, global cooperation has become harder to secure. The demise of the Kyoto Protocol and the non-binding document, The Future We Want, that emerged from the UN Conference on Sustainable Development (Rio+20) in 2012 has illustrated the halting coordinated action on climate change. Given that Rio+20 ended with merely the promise to launch a process to develop Sustainable Development Goals (SDGs) without environmental goals, targets and deadlines, the unilateral actions of individual countries such as the United States and China (along with Brazil and India) have become more vital to the transition towards a greener world, given their growing economies and a middle class ready to consume.

China's extraordinary economic growth, while pulling millions out of poverty, has come at an enormous environmental cost over the 20 years since the 1992 summit. The 'externalities' of economic growth from industrialization and urbanization long ignored, has in more recent years become an issue for the general public and policy-makers. After the Yangtze floods in 1998 caused death, displacement and financial cost, which were partly the fault of extreme logging, erosion of land cleared for farming; China could no longer ignore the cost of destroying its natural resources by prioritizing economic interests (Lang, 2002). While growth remains the priority for the local-regional-central government, the multiple crises in recent years – in climate, biodiversity, energy, as well as water shortages, even though all sectors of the economy have expanded, mean that environmental issues now receive increased attention in the media and in policy circles. Speaking to reporters at the end of the 2013 National People's Congress, the Chinese premier, Li Keqiang, told reporters that China should not pursue economic growth at the expense of the environment and spoke of building a 'beautiful' China (Kaiman, 2013). This and other policy pronouncements in relation to transport, infrastructure and new energies indicate that the national government has sought to address the externalities of economic growth.

However, China has largely done so alone, and has rejected environmental rules imposed by other countries. This has brought on criticism that China is not committed to coordinated global action on climate change (Lynas, 2009; Kirby, 2011). For example, Chinese state airlines, with the support of the government, face the prospect of fines and exclusion from airports in the European Union for refusing to comply with rules aimed at regulating resource and energy use. Top Chinese political adviser Yu Zhengsheng, chairman of the National Committee of the Chinese People's Political Consultative Conference, made a speech at the annual conference of the World Cultural Forum in 2013 to say that there is no 'one-size-fits-all' model for ecological civilization because of the principle of 'common but differentiated responsibilities' (Zhao, 2013). As China seeks to reduce the externalities of economic growth in the environment and other areas, so as to match the resources efficiency of Western nations (Ma and Shi, 2013), the government seems willing to seek a sustainable growth roadmap, or what the United Nations Environment Programme (UNEP, 2011) calls a 'green economy'. As many analysts argue that China has the ability to combine environmental and economic interests, with World Bank economist Carter Brandon noting how 'China can go green and continue to grow economically' (cited in Reardon, 2012), this chapter asks whether China's embrace of the green economy, without, can influence and/or be influenced by a greening of tourism.

A green economy

The 2012 United Nations Conference on Sustainable Development (Rio+20), and the Green Economy Report compiled by UNEP's Green Economy Initiative in 2011 demonstrates that the greening of economies is not generally a drag on growth but rather a potential new engine of growth (net generator of jobs, increased growth, economic development and/or diversification), and therefore can lead to a reduction in levels of persistent poverty. The UNEP-led Green Economy Initiative (GEI), launched in late 2008, aims to put forward strong and convincing evidence in support of the transition to a green economy – one that is dominated by investment in and consumption of environmentally enhancing goods and services. Among the main GEI activities, the Green Economy Report uses macroeconomic analysis to demonstrate that greening the economy across a range of sectors, such as tourism, can drive economic growth and job creation, while tackling social inequalities and environmental challenges.

A green economy is one that is low-carbon, resource-efficient and socially inclusive, with UNEP (2010) defining a green economy as one that results in 'improved human well-being and social equity, while significantly reducing environmental risks and ecological scarcities'. A green transition, according to UNEP (2011) requires green public and private investments, catalysed and supported by targeted public expenditure, policy reforms and regulation changes so as to reduce carbon emissions, pollution and enhance energy and resource efficiency. The UNEP Green Economy Report identifies ten economic sectors best able to kick-start the transition to a sustainable and inclusive green economy. While many of the identified sectors such as agriculture, fisheries, water, forests, transport and cities are inextricably linked to tourism, through forms and types of tourism such as nature tourism, urban tourism and coastal tourism; the report, in recognizing tourism as a key sector of the economy and a contributor to carbon emissions and environmental degradation, also identifies it as a significant driver for growth for the world economy and as one of the ten sectors that must be at the forefront of the transformation to a green economy. According to the UN Green Economy Report, the greening of tourism, which involves significant investment in efficiency improvements in energy, water and waste systems, would stimulate job creation, especially in poorer communities, with increased local hiring and sourcing, with a positive spillover effect on other areas of the economy.

In conjunction with the UNWTO, the UNEP (2011, p. 416) report describes the challenges and opportunities for tourism in a green economy, which it defines as tourism activities 'that can be maintained, or sustained, indefinitely in their social, economic, cultural and environmental contexts'. While it demonstrates the benefits for investing in the greening of tourism (greater spending, employment, local economic development, poverty reduction, environmental benefits), it also identifies the significant challenges (excessive water consumption, energy-intensive transportation). Its greening, the report suggests, under a scenario of green investments and adequate policies would make an increased contribution to GDP, with significant environmental benefits including reductions in water consumption (18 per cent), energy use (44 per cent) and CO_2 emissions (52 per cent), which if accomplished would reduce the cost of energy, water and waste and enhance the value of biodiversity, ecosystems and cultural heritage and reinforce the employment potential of the sector (UNEP, 2011). An investment of 0.2 per cent of global GDP per year until 2050 in the greening of tourism, can, according to UNEP (2011), allow the tourism sector to continue to grow steadily. 'Making tourism businesses more sustainable will foster the industry's growth, create more and better jobs, consolidate higher investment returns, benefit local development and contribute to poverty reduction, while raising awareness and support for the sustainable use of natural resources' (UNEP, 2011, p. 438).

Greening China

Information disclosure online, a more open media and non-governmental organizations (NGOs) have transformed environmental degradation into public issues in China. Reports, such as those that estimate that China sees 350,000–400,000 premature deaths due to outdoor air pollution each year (World Bank, 2007), and had 1.2 million premature deaths in 2010 (Wong, 2013b),[1] as well as hourly readings of the Air Quality Index (AQI) being reported by the United States Embassy in Beijing, have all fed into pressure and momentum for government action to improve air, water and soil quality in China (Bradsher, 2013). Even though the economic cost of environmental degradation arising from pollution and damage to the ecosystem is notoriously difficult to measure in China, many senior politicians within China now recognize the basic environmental problem, its costs, the path towards sustainability and the environmental legislation required to mitigate environmental degradation.

A 2007 World Bank and the State Environmental Protection Administration of China (SEPA) report estimated the cost of (water and air) pollution in 2003 was 2.68 per cent or 5.78 per cent of GDP depending on whether a Chinese or Western method of calculation was used. The first China Green National Accounting Study Report (Jing, 2006) issued by the SEPA and the National Bureau of Statistics of China (NBS) in 2006 showed that economic loss caused by environmental pollution accounted for 3.05 per cent of national GDP in 2004. According to the Environment and Planning Institute of China's Ministry of Environmental Protection[2] (MEP), the environmental cost was $248 billion in 2010, or 3.5 per cent of the gross domestic product (Wong, 2013c). Greenpeace (2012a) pegged the cost of pollution in Beijing at around US$328 million, based on levels measured in 2010. In Shanghai, the cost was even higher, at US$420 million. There are issues with how these figures were compiled, and their underlying accuracy, given that data related to chronic illness, lost productivity and environmental degradation are so difficult to measure. An analysis of the green accounting system by Li and Lang (2010) found that the cost of resource depletion, hard-to-quantify items such as the impact of pollution on public health and workforce productivity and loss of arable farmland (and agricultural productivity) as a result of soil erosion were largely omitted, with Ma and Shi (2013) noting the costs of environmental damage and ecocide could amount to 12 per cent of China's GDP.[3]

Even in the face of these statistics, the proponents of China's 'economic growth comes first' approach to development have considerable influence in local-regional-central government and special interest groups. While the environmental cost reports are now regularly published and the concept of 'ecological modernization' increasingly accepted by Chinese academia, Li and Lang (2010, p. 58) note that many officials are bound to the 'treadmill of production'. They argue that 'it is clear that economic development, the mainstay of the regime's political legitimacy' outweighs 'environmental protection whenever it appears that the two goals are in direct conflict' (Li and Lang, 2010). Statistics and hard data are often not used by central-regional-local governments to re-examine current models of development and the economic and social case for investing in sectors of the economy in order to shift development and unleash public-private capital flows onto a low-carbon, resource-efficient path development. While state environmental agencies, NGOs and the media are increasingly accepting the concepts of sustainability, given that pollution has had little effect on economic growth and given China's dependence on physical capital expansion and increased energy consumption, there is evidence that various state actors are often resistant to change. Many state actors and agencies in regional and local governments, apparently allied to proponents of economic growth within the central government are tied to the concept of economic growth (Xia, 2012). Given the past emphasis on economic growth based on heavy industries, Greenpeace (2012b) note that few cities in China have sought to implement 'green' action plans and targets. Cities often refuse to disclose basic environmental data such as pollution discharges or refuse to implement national directives, even though China's Air Pollution Prevention and Control Law (2011) stipulates that cities with substandard air quality must have a legally binding plan to gradually improve air quality. The Institute of Public and Environmental Affairs (IPE) and the Natural Resources Defence Council (NRDC),[4] who have carried out an annual evaluation of the state of pollution source information disclosure in 113 cities across China, note that disclosure has slowed.

However, there are exceptions. The Beijing municipal government has put the environment at the top of its work agenda, launching a 2013 campaign to tackle pollution by improving sewage disposal, garbage treatment and air quality, as well as curbing illegal construction. Beijing has sought (as has Shanghai) to introduce policies to control the increasing number of vehicles and require cleaner petrol (gasoline) and diesel (Greenpeace, 2012b). While some of these city-led initiatives have been adopted nationwide, Chinese state-owned enterprises in the oil, transport, and power industries have often sought to block efforts by pro-environment government officials to impose policies that would alleviate pollution (Wong, 2013a). In 2013, the government released a timetable, mandating that new fuel quality standards for diesel and gasoline be issued by the end of 2013. The policy was resisted by state companies such the China Electricity Company, just as a diesel standard endorsed by the State Council[5] in 2009 was undermined by the Ministry of Finance (Wong, 2013a). However, given the lack of coordination, national green initiatives often have unintended consequences. For example, a national scrappage programme that ran from June 2009 to May 2010, and sought to incentivize people to exchange old cars for new, lacked funding. Beijing, howeve, along with Hong Kong, had its own better-funded scrappage programme aimed at getting rid of half a million older vehicles by the end of 2015,[6] but many of these vehicles just get transferred to other parts of China. Meanwhile, the number of passenger cars is on track to hit 400 million by 2030, up from 90 million in 2013 (Wong, 2013a). Beijing's attempt to reduce air pollution has also been undermined by the consumption of heavily polluting coal in the nearby city of Tianjin and adjacent Hebei Province[7] (Jin, 2013a). The dependence on manufacturing and heavy industries in China mean that the 'treadmill of production' (Li and Lang, 2010) will ensure a continuing steep decline in the environment for the next decade. China is predicted to continue to grow using energy-inefficient and polluting industries, which will increase pollution unless environmental protection is increased and drastic action is taken (Xia, 2012) on energy, automobiles, the environment and public transport.

The costs of mitigation with regard to energy, automobiles, the environment and public transport will be considerable; the economics of an environmental clean-up with regard to reducing energy and GHG emissions; water consumption and waste management, are unclear. Replacing urban coal consumption with clean alternative energy sources, capping regional coal consumption, De-NOx retrofitting existing coal-fired power plants, shutting down inefficient coal-fired industrial boilers, improving environmental policies (i.e. penalties), lowering expectations for future growth, limiting the sales of passenger vehicles and increasing investment in public transportation may lead to China maintaining a lower economic growth rate. Changing policy measures would demand a shift in the types of industry that drive the country's economy, but would create new investment opportunities for Chinese companies, the preference being for environmental measures that can be combined with an economic stimulus or alleviated through tax breaks (Ma and Shi, 2013). While this recipe could cause some industries to suffer, others (energy conservation, pollution treatment, ecological protection and recycling) have new market opportunities.

The government hopes that the greening of the economy over the period of the new Twelfth 5-Year Plan (Chen, 2013) will provide investment opportunities for a developing energy-saving sector. This is expected to provide more than $315 billion in investment opportunities over the plan's 5 years (Lan, 2012). This follows the success of the Chinese government's 'ecocompensation' scheme, in which $100 billion was transferred to millions of farmers, which added 1.6 per cent to its forest cover each year from 2000 to 2010 and will restore 40 million hectares of forest by 2020 (Reardon, 2012), providing a means to more evenly distribute the benefits of economic growth.[8] However, the definition of energy-saving and environmental protection industries are still ambiguous in China, which according to Lan (2012) could lead to difficulties in evaluating their performance. Many analysts point to the glut of overcapacity in the solar panel industry which the government says it plans to develop further (Du, 2013).

While the government's approach is personified by the President, Xi Jinping's (The Economist, 2013) vision of a 'better environment', the issue is not the developing legislative measures, but the gap between words and action on the ground (penalties, convictions, attitudes, corruption). Despite popular support for environmental protection,[9] the authorities are still fighting against transparency. The country's soil pollution levels are classified as a state secret (Kaiman, 2013), a Greenpeace (2013) report[10] that criticized a state-owned company was recently censored, while the Green GDP[11] project in early 2007 was abolished due to widespread resistance from regional and local governments (Sun, 2007).

Greening tourism

A shift from energy-intensive manufacturing towards an increase in the high-technology and service industries, while leading to significant economic costs could be partially offset by an increase in more environmentally friendly jobs, such as tourism. Tourism is one of the most promising drivers of growth in China, which has grasped tourism's potential to create new jobs, and support the economy. However, the tourism industry faces a multitude of significant sustainability-related challenges to overcome barriers towards a green transition as well as a lack of enabling conditions. Although a vital sector of the economy in China, tourism does not have a central role in driving a response to environmental degradation. Air, soil and water pollution is driving a response by the government, but the explosive growth of inbound, domestic and internal tourism has not been linked to progress on adopting clean energy and new technologies, while reducing its carbon outputs and energy consumption. Statistics from the country's tourism authorities show that domestic tourists totalled nearly 3 billion in 2012,[12] and while the figure for the inbound tourist population according to the China Tourism Academy[13] is estimated to be 133 million 'person-trips' (Wen, 2013), various promotions, laws and legislation have focused on growth rather than sustainability. The Chairman of China's National Tourism Administration (CNTA), Shao Qiwei, affirmed that China's actions to counter the financial crisis would help global tourism. 'Policies from both central government and local governments to boost consumption will sustain domestic and outbound tourism'.[14] This has been reaffirmed in the Outline for National Tourism and Leisure (2013–20)[15] (UNWTO, 2013) plan issued by the government which speaks[16] about increasing consumption, with sustainability a secondary concern. Issued by the State Council (2013) of China, it speaks of promoting the taking of paid annual leave days and boosting the development of the tourism sector in China.

While there have been many research initiatives by Chinese academia and NGOs such as Greenpeace that focus on greening the economy, few have mentioned or sought to pressurize the government to create the conditions that might enable tourism's transition to a more sustainable path. Few reports address tourism as a key sector driving the economy, seek to address how explosive growth in tourism may be transitioned or how greening may impact other sectors such as transport or energy, or how the other nine key economic sectors might influence the tourism sector. A positive development was China's decision to issue revised administrative regulations by the end of 2013 that made it easier for domestic and overseas NGOs to set up in China (Dan, 2013), which should deliver a more empowered civil society that focuses on the tourism sector. While public pressure has in recent years blocked coal-fired power plants in Guangdong and Hainan, a copper smelter in Shifang, a town in Sichuan Province and chemical plants in Dalian, Tianjin and Xiamen[17] (Bradsher, 2012a, 2012b), zero tolerance of environmental harm has yet to coalesce into public protest or organization that focuses on the tourism sector. However, NGOs such as the Society of Entrepreneurs & Ecology, Professional Association for China's Environment, Friends of Nature and the Nature University may be a driving force for a more sustainable tourism sector in the coming years by pushing businesses and government to take a more proactive stance. While green and sustainable tourism has become one of the most vivid and promising businesses within the travel industry, building a detailed picture of just how unsustainable the tourism sector is, and the impacts it is having, may be a critical step for those trying to amass the momentum required to push for change. However, there is little evidence as to how China's legislature and state council will respond to hard data and research that concerns sustainability within the tourism sector.

In many ways, the government, in seeking to promote green tourism will face many of the same problems faced with greening other sectors in overcoming opposition from special interest groups, as well as mobilizing private sector actions on green tourism, even though the economic potential for green tourism is to be increasingly found. Since many of these regional and local governments are judged on economic growth, due to a lack of central funding they must bear greening effort costs through land sales, inappropriate development in ecologically sensitive areas, and increased entry prices to tourist attractions. This has made the investment in conservation, restoration, protection and diversification difficult. Comprising mainly small and medium-sized enterprises (SMEs), the private sector has little access to bank financing for green investments,[18] and little in-kind support such as technical, marketing or business administration assistance. Combined with a lack of central funding, destination planning, tourism strategies and commitment by regional-local governments, the private sector, especially small firms, is yet to be mobilized to support the greening of tourism. The sector lacks information and often does not recognize the opportunities in smaller, niche tourism areas centring on natural, cultural and community resources.[19] Tourism businesses have not sought to incorporate recognized standards for sustainable tourism, such as the Global Sustainable Tourism Criteria (GSTC).[20] At a national level, China has not created any collaborative platforms inside or outside government to support a greening of tourism. There are no national tourism industry stakeholder consultation groups, joint collaborative efforts among or between government ministries, or any national initiatives.

Investment and policies supportive of a transition are piecemeal, and do not focus on areas which might support greening within tourism. There are no mechanisms by which industry groups can coordinate with ministries responsible for the environment, energy, labour, transport, finance and other relevant areas, with the government not making the cross-sectoral linkages between tourism and other economically important sectors.

Public policies and support such as subsidies, concessions and direct funding could encourage investment in green tourism and provide the conditions for the further development of green tourism. Government spending on protected areas, cultural assets, water conservation, waste management, sanitation, public transport and renewable energy infrastructure could also reduce the cost of green investments by the private sector and encourage further private investment. Clear requirements in such areas as zoning, protected areas, environmental rules and regulations, labour rules, agricultural standards and health requirements particularly related to energy, emissions, water, waste and sanitation would also provide some foundation. Following the poorly implemented seven-point strategy as a basic framework for sustainable tourism development that sought to balance the rational use of resources for positive economic impact along with environmental protection (UN, 2001), legislation should ensure to get the balance between growth and sustainability right. The new tourism law[21] approved by the Standing Committee of the National People's Congress (NPC) which took effect in October 2013 was designed to regulate the tourism market, safeguard tourists' rights and interests, ensure reasonable use of resources, and foster the industry's sustainable and healthy growth. In theory, it was designed to balance industry and tourists' interests and but like the Outline for National Tourism and Leisure (2013–20), it does not offer any detail as to how it will spread the economic, socio-cultural and environmental benefits of tourism. It largely reflects public concerns over entry price increases, overcrowding at tourist attractions and forced goods purchases, but without defining what are 'reasonable prices' or the 'sustainable' limits to growth.

While it is difficult to imagine the sheer size of the tourism sector in China, and its unsustainable practices that affect China and the rest of the world, it is imperative that China succeeds in greening its tourism sector. As poor air quality, acid rain, toxic spills, worsening air quality, water pollution, overcrowding and price rises (Yang and Wang, 2013) that restrict its people's access to its natural and cultural heritage continue, China is already losing its attractiveness to domestic and overseas tourists (Jin, 2013b), with environmental pollution even threatening its neighbours' tourism industries (Fackler, 2013). There is also the increasing worry that water and soil pollution will create fear in the hospitality industry by way of polluted water river smells emanating from the showerhead, and worries that pollution in the country's agricultural centres will affect the food chain, and consequently tourist trust in domestic food products[22] (Ma and Adams, 2013). Given tourism's contribution to small and medium-sized enterprises and the creation of jobs in a tightening market (Bradsher and Wong, 2013), the lack of a clear path to the greening of tourism is sending a negative message to tourists, businesses and the international community. While there is hope that China's leadership is listening,[23] environmental and economic interests remain on a collision course in China.

Conclusions

This chapter sought to look at China, and ask whether the country, through policy and investment is transitioning to a green economy and a more sustainable path in tourism. Since the 1992 United Nations' Earth Summit in Rio de Janeiro, the 'growth first' doctrine in China has led to great environmental costs to China and the world. The 2012 Conference on Sustainable Development, dubbed Rio+20, in advancing the sustainable agenda, also renewed focus on China and its efforts to achieve sustainability. Recent strategies, new methods and national policy pronouncements seem to offer some mitigating processes to environmental degradation, and offer enabling conditions for a transition to a green economy. While often innovative and progressive, their implementation[24] and enforcement have been poor and although the tourism industry is growing in China along with the economy, the tourism sector is not a lead change agent in the transformation to the green economy in China. A driver of growth in China, the sustainability-related challenges accompanying tourism's sustainable development in China have not received the attention of policy-makers, NGOs or the public at large, even though it could hasten the transition towards a green economy and reduce the cost of energy, water and waste and enhance the value of biodiversity, ecosystems and cultural heritage. There is little recognition of the role that tourism could play in the green economy transition with few best practices, methods, strategies or investments related directly to the tourism sector. Without destination planning and specific development strategies, the first steps to create the enabling conditions for increased investments in a transition to a green economy have yet to be taken. While small changes towards greening could have significant impacts, few public actors have sought to instil the concept of sustainable development into the tourism sector. In the short-to-medium term, the greening of tourism may come from the increasing number of NGOs with an environmental bent, the demand of international tourists for green and ecological tourism products, greener financing mechanism options, and hard evidence and statistics. Given that tourism development is influenced by, and in turn influences society, both in China and globally, the world needs China's tourism sector to begin taking a more sustainable path. Whatever China does next will have global repercussions.

Notes

1 The summary of analysis of scientific data was first published by *The Lancet* (www.thelancet.com/themed/global-burden-of-disease), a British medical journal.

2 The MEP is a cabinet-level ministry in the executive branch of the Chinese Government. It replaced the SEPA during the March 2008 National People's Congress sessions in Beijing.

3 There are no numbers on how much money would be saved by protecting natural resources rather than exploiting them with unsustainable practices (Reardon, 2012).

4 See www.ipe.org.cn/Upload/file/Notices/Reports/From-Bottleneck-to-Breakthrough-PITI-Evaluation-Results-Press-Release-March-28–2013-EN.pdf.

5 The State Council can be considered China's cabinet.

6 See www.knowledgeatwharton.com.cn/index.cfm?fa=article&articleid=2763.

7 While individual provinces have established trans-provincial environmental compensation, there is no state-level trans-provincial compensation mechanism.

8 See http://chinawaterrisk.org/opinions/watershed-services-in-china/.

9 A 2013 Report of the Online Public Opinion published by Wuhan University, their environmental 'zero tolerance' for environmental pollution.

10 See www.greenpeace.org/international/en/news/blogs/makingwaves/chinese-medua-censorship-shenhua/blog/46033/.

11 The Green GDP Project was not reinstated until the MEP became a full ministry in 2008.

12 The number of domestic travellers in China was noted by Dai Bin, president of the China Tourism Academy (see www.globaltimes.cn/content/753565.shtml).

13 The China Tourism Academy (CTA) was set up in 2008 in accordance with Document No. [2007] 98 of the State Commission Office for Public Sector Reform and the Party Committee of China National Tourism Administration (CNTA). It was set up as a specialized research institute directly under CNTA.

14 See http://news.xinhuanet.com/english/2009-04/19/content_11215776.htm.

15 See http://dtxtq4w60xqpw.cloudfront.net/sites/all/files/pdf/the_outline_for_national_tourism_and_leisure_2013-2020.pdf.

16 The outline does note that

> We will be committed to putting the people and their safety first, improving people's livelihood, encouraging green consumption, promoting healthy, civilized and environment-friendly ways in tourism and leisure, and improving and expanding national tourism and leisure for social harmony and better quality of life.

17 Concerns about protests over environmental disputes led the government to require a 'social risk assessment' (Bradsher, 2013) before allowing major industrial projects to proceed.

18 While loans for clean energy, energy saving and other environmentally friendly projects are increasing (Chen, 2013), such loans usually go to the state sector and remain tied to the development policies of local government. Few banks implement a green credit policy (Nan, 2013).

19 To tempt tourists from heavily polluted Beijing to visit Fujian in the nation's southeast, the tourism bureau ran a clean-air tourism campaign in 2013, with TV ads that concluded 'Fresh Fujian, take a deep breath' (MacLeod, 2013).

20 The Global Sustainable Tourism Council (GSTC) serves as the international body for fostering increased knowledge and understanding of sustainable tourism practices, Its Global Sustainable Tourism Criteria and the development of the GSTC Criteria for Destinations are the guiding principles that tourism business or destination can aspire to (www.gstcouncil.org/).

21 See www.gov.cn/flfg/2013-04/25/content_2390945.htm.

22 One-sixth of China's arable land suffers from soil pollution, according to the Ministry of Environmental Protection (Wong, 2013d).

23 Chinese Vice Premier Zhang Gaoli's address at the 2013 Fortune Global Forum (FGF) in Chengdu, focused on the protection of resources, the environment and ecological systems 'as part of our effort to build a beautiful homeland with a blue sky, green land and clean water' (Mu, 2013).

24 China adopted its first environmental law in 1979 and has enacted over thirty such laws to date. See Wang (2007) for further detail on environmental law in China.

References

Bradsher, K. (2012a) Bolder protests against pollution win project's defeat in China', www.nytimes.com/2012/07/05/world/asia/chinese-officials-cancel-plant-project-amid-protests.html, (accessed 5 July 2012).

Bradsher, K. (2012b) 'Social risk' test ordered by China for big projects, www.nytimes.com/2012/11/13/world/asia/china-mandates-social-risk-reviews-for-big-projects.html (accessed 18 July 2012).

Bradsher, K. (2013) China sets new rules aimed at curbing air pollution. *New York Times*, 15 June 2013, p. A15.

Bradsher, K. and Wong, S. (2013) Faltering economy in China dims job prospects for graduates. www.nytimes.com/2013/06/17/business/global/faltering-economy-in-china-dims-job-prospects-for-graduates.html (accessed 10 July 2013).

Chen, D. (2013) Green growth. www.globaltimes.cn/content/799154.shtml#.UfhHZtI3v8k (accessed 12 July 2013).

Dan, H. (2013) New rules for NGOs to improve operations, *China Daily*, 17 April 2013, p. 1.

Du, J. (2013) Nation to maintain cap on energy consumption, *China Daily*, 25 January 2013, p. 16.

Economist (2013) Chasing the Chinese dream. www.economist.com/news/briefing/21577063-chinas-new-leader-has-been-quick-consolidate-his-power-what-does-he-now-want-his (accessed 20 July 2013).

Fackler, M. (2013) Scientist says pollution from China is killing a Japanese island's trees, www.nytimes.com/2013/04/25/world/asia/japanese-scientist-blames-china-for-yakushimas-dying-trees.html (accessed 9 April 2015).

Greenpeace (2012a) Dangerous breathing, www.greenpeace.org/eastasia/Global/eastasia/publications/reports/climate-energy/2012/Briefing (accessed 21 June 2013).

Greenpeace (2012b) Ranking Eastern Chinese cities by their 'clean air' actions. www.greenpeace.org/eastasia/publications/reports/climate-energy/2012/ranking-cities-air-action (accessed 20 June 2013).

Greenpeace (2013) Thirsty coal 2, www.greenpeace.org/eastasia/publications/reports/climate-energy/2013/thirsty-coal-two-china (accessed 23 July 2013).

Jin, H. (2013a) Beijing targets capital's suburban smog, www.chinadaily.com.cn/china/2013-03/29/content_16355357.htm (accessed 3 July 2013).

Jin, H. (2013b) Beijing sees decline in tourists, *China Daily*, 30 July 2013, http://usa.chinadaily.com.cn/china/2013-07/30/content_16854194.htm (accessed 30 July 2013).

Jing, D. (2006) Green GDP accounting study report 2004 issued, www.gov.cn/english/2006-09/11/content_384596.htm (accessed 30 June 2013).

Kaiman, J. (2013) Activists voice doubts over politicians' vow to 'build a beautiful China', www.guardian.co.uk/world/2013/mar/18/campaigners-sceptical-china-environment-changes (accessed 11 July 2013).

Kirby, D. (2011) Made in China: our toxic, imported air pollution, http://discovermagazine.com/2011/apr/18-made-in-china-our-toxic-imported-air-pollution#.UfjC2NJ0S2U (accessed 20 July 2013).

Lan, L. (2012) Green economy drive to deliver $315b in energy saving investment, www.chinadaily.com.cn/cndy/2012-07/05/content_15550031.htm (accessed 28 June 2013).

Lang, G. (2002) Forests, floods, and the environmental state in China. *Organization & Environment*, vol. 15, no. 2, pp. 109–30.

Li, V. and Lang, G. (2010) China's 'Green GDP' experiment and the struggle for ecological modernisation, *Journal of Contemporary Asia*, vol. 40, no. 1, pp. 44–62.

Lynas, M. (2009) How do I know China wrecked the Copenhagen deal? I was in the room, www.theguardian.com/environment/2009/dec/22/copenhagen-climate-change-mark-lynas (accessed 23 July 2013).

Ma, D. and Adams, W. (2013) If you think China's air is bad . . . *The International New York Times*. www.nytimes.com/2013/11/08/opinion/if-you-think-chinas-air-is-bad.html (accessed 10 December 2013).

Ma, J. and Shi, A. (2013) *Big bang measures to fight air pollution*, Deutsche Bank China Strategy, 28 February 2013.

MacLeod, C. (2013) In China, air pollution report brings despair, humor. www.usatoday.com/story/news/world/2013/07/09/china-air-pollution-study-fujian/2503319/ (accessed 9 April 2015).

Mu, X. (2013) Full text of Chinese Vice Premier Zhang Gaoli's address at opening dinner of 2013 Fortune Global Forum, http://news.xinhuanet.com/english/china/2013-06/07/c_124824012.htm (accessed 10 July 2013).

Nan, X. (2013) Chinese banks under 'almost negligible' pressure to protect the environment www.chinadialogue.net/article/show/single/en/5812-Chinese-banks-under-almost-negligible-pressure-to-protect-the-environment (accessed 30 July 2013).

Reardon, S. (2012) China leads the march for the green economy. *New Scientist*, June edition, pp. 8–9.

Rogers, S. and Harvey, F. (2012) Global carbon emissions rise is far bigger than previous estimates. www.guardian.co.uk/environment/2012/jun/21/global-carbon-emissions-record (accessed 3 July 2013).

State Council (2013) Notice on the Publication of The Outline for National Tourism and Leisure (2013–2020). http://dtxtq4w60xqpw.cloudfront.net/sites/all/files/pdf/the_outline_for_national_tourism_and_leisure_2013-2020.pdf (accessed 28 July 2013).

Sun, X. (2007) Green GDP shown the red signal. *China Daily*, 23 March 2007, p. 1.

UN (2001) *Plan of actions for sustainable tourism development in Asian and Pacific region (1999–2005): a progress report*, United Nations: Bangkok..

UNEP (2010) *Are you a green leader? Business and biodiversity: making the case for a lasting solution*, United Nations Environment Programme: Paris..

UNEP (2011) Towards a green economy: Pathways to sustainable development and poverty eradication. www.unep.org/greeneconomy (accessed 15 July 2013).

UNWTO (2013) China's new national tourism strategy set to increase outbound tourism. http://media.unwto.org/en/press-release/2013-03-25/china-s-new-national-tourism-strategy-set-increase-outbound-tourism (accessed 12 July 2013).

Wang, A. L. (2007) The role of law in environmental protection in China: recent developments. *Vermont Journal of Environmental Law*, vol. 8, pp. 195–223.

Wen, W. (2013) China lags behind in inbound tourism. www.chinadaily.com.cn/cndy/2013-07/27/content_16839649.htm (accessed 28 July 2013).

Wong, E. (2013a) As pollution worsens in China, solutions succumb to infighting. *New York Times*, 2 March 2013, p. A8.

Wong, E. (2013b) Air pollution linked to 1.2 million premature deaths in China. www.nytimes.com/2013/04/02/world/asia/air-pollution-linked-to-1-2-million-deaths-in-china.html (accessed 9 April 2015).

Wong, E. (2013c) Cost of environmental damage in China growing rapidly amid industrialization. *New York Times*, 30 March 2013, p.A4. www.nytimes.com/2013/03/30/world/asia/cost-of-environmental-degradation-in-china-is-growing.html (accessed 27 June 2013).

Wong, E. (2013d) With pollution rising, Chinese fear for their soil and food. *New York Times*, 31 December 2013, p. A6.

World Bank (2007) Cost of pollution in China: economic estimates of physical damages. The World Bank: Washington, DC: www-wds.worldbank.org/external/default/WDSContent Server/WDSP/IB/2007/03/30/000090341_20070330141612/Rendered/PDF/392360CHA0 Cost1of1Pollution01PUBLIC1.pdf (accessed 20 July 2013).

Xia, Y. (2012) An empirical research on the interactions of China's energy consumption, pollution emissions and economic growth. *International Journal of Global Energy Issues*, vol. 35, no. 5, pp. 411–25.

Yang, Y. and Wang, Q. (2013) Paying the price to travel. *China Daily*, 30 April 2013. http:// usa.chinadaily.com.cn/china/2013-04/30/content_16464556.htm (accessed 9 April 2015).

Zhao, S. (2013) China calls for international green efforts www.chinadaily.com.cn/china/2013-05/19/content_16509835.htm (accessed 25 July 2013).

PART 2

Best practices for the greening of tourism and allied industries

8

GREEN JOBS AND EMPLOYMENT IN TOURISM

Adele Ladkin and Edith Szivas

Introduction

Worldwide International tourist arrivals exceeded the 1 billion mark for the first time at the end of 2012 at 1,035 million, an increase from 995 million in 2011 (UNWTO, 2013). International tourism receipts reached US$1,075 billion worldwide in 2012 increasing from US$1,042 billion in 2011 (UNWTO, 2013). Although arrivals and receipts have regional and national variations, in overall terms the outlook for tourism demand has remained positive. This in turn provides opportunities for employment creation. The World Travel and Tourism Council estimated that in 2011 nearly 260 million jobs worldwide were supported by travel and tourism, either directly in the industry or in related sectors (World Travel & Tourism Council, 2011). By 2020, it is anticipated this figure, including direct and indirect jobs, will rise to 328 million jobs, or one in every ten jobs worldwide (World Travel & Tourism Council, 2012).

Set against this background of tourism growth and increased employment opportunities, one consideration is to what extent tourism can contribute to the green economy. Importantly, the question to ask is, does tourism have the potential to generate opportunities for green jobs? This chapter explores this question. It is important to state at the outset that the focus of this chapter is on conceptually exploring the opportunity for green jobs in tourism, rather than quantitative measures of employment generation. As a consequence, the assumption is made that green jobs are a reality and an important aspect of the green economy. The measurement of green jobs is problematic, and the subject of much debate (ILO, 2011a; ILO, 2011b) as is whether indeed the jobs can be described as such at all (Lesser, 2010; Furchtgott-Roth, 2012).

The chapter is organized in the following way. First, an overview of the nature of tourism employment is provided to set the context for the potential for green jobs. The discussion then turns to green jobs. In this section, definitions, the need for green jobs and its effects on employment and the skills required for green jobs are considered. The third area focuses on green jobs in tourism, and argues that the potential for green jobs can be considered in three areas. Finally, some conclusions are drawn.

Tourism employment

Employment generation is widely considered to be the most direct and beneficial impact of tourism development to the host population (Liu and Wall, 2005). Tourism employment has the potential to deliver long-term economic and social benefits to destinations (UNWTO, 2011). Tourist activities create direct, indirect and induced employment opportunities, fully described elsewhere (Weaver and Oppermann, 2002; Wall and Mathieson, 2006; Mason, 2008; Fletcher et al., 2013). Direct employment refers to employment in tourist sectors such as transport, hotels, tour operators, travel agencies etc. Indirect employment refers to jobs created by people working in activities that are partially dependent on tourism, for example, construction, financial services, care hire, etc. Induced employment is the additional employment resulting from the effects of the tourism multiplier as residents spend money on activities earned from tourism (Wall and Matthieson, 2006). The wide multiplier effect of tourism is at the heart of its appeal as a development option.

The characteristics of tourism employment are well documented (Duncan et al., 2013; Janta et al., 2011). However, there are a number of characteristics of tourism employment that are relevant in the context of the potential for green jobs. These are:

- Tourism employment contains a variety of opportunities, ranging from unskilled jobs to highly skilled and professional occupations. This broad spectrum allows for green jobs to be considered at a range of different skill levels.
- Tourism employment displays features of the dual labour market. The dual labour market (Doeringer and Piore, 1972) identifies the way in which labour markets become separated into primary and secondary sectors. Jobs in the primary sector generally have high status, recognized career paths, job security and higher education or skill requirements. Secondary sector jobs are poorly paid, have little or no job security, poor working conditions and few training opportunities. It is in this secondary market that considerations of 'Decent Work' (ILO, 2009b) can be considered.
- Many tourism jobs have low barriers to entry, especially for the low/semi-skilled positions. This creates opportunities for new entrants to the labour market in groups prone to unemployment such as, for example, younger people, economic migrants, women and those with minimal education or formal qualifications (UNWTO, 2009). Tourism employment offers part-time and shift work that may help people with families or household responsibilities
- Tourism development has opportunities for enterprise development in the form of SMEs. It can create employment opportunities for local communities who can provide products and services for the tourism industry, for example food products, handicrafts, tour guiding and accommodation etc.

The above characteristics have relevance for opportunities for green jobs, and will be returned to later in the chapter.

Green jobs

Definitions

Defining a green job is problematic, with significant challenges (ILO, 2011b; Furchtgott-Roth, 2012). At the outset, there is a lack of a commonly accepted definition of what is 'green', and defining the boundaries of renewable energy, energy efficient, clean technology, sustainable transport, and organic agriculture is a challenging task (UNEP *et al.*, 2008, p. 43). Defining a green job is surrounded by debate, controversy, technical deficiencies and different agendas. As previously mentioned, attempts to measure the actual number of jobs that can be classified as green is problematic. The United Nations Environment Programme (UNEP), International Labour Organization (ILO), International Organization of Employers (IOE) and the International Trade Union Confederation (ITUC) identify that while conventional industries are well captured in government and other statistics, when it comes to what can be characterized as green economic activities, employment data is scant. Where it is available, it may be only for certain segments or industries, and they tend to be estimates and snapshots rather than time series (UNEP *et al.*, 2008).

However, conceptually at least, there is general agreement that green jobs are ones that in some way are concerned with environmental protection, sustainability and have a positive effect on reducing carbon emissions and climate change. Furthermore, the green job concept has social as well as environmental aspects (ILO, 2011b). Green jobs also need to be 'good' jobs that meet long-standing demands and goals of the labour movement, e.g. safe working conditions, workers' rights, adequate wages and the right to organize labour unions (UNEP *et al.*, 2008, p. 4). Given the many different interpretations of green jobs, this chapter primarily draws on those that are used for policy development and have been determined by UN agencies. While recognizing the limitation of this, UN definitions do provide a global perspective and thus avoid international variations.

The UNEP/ILO concept of green jobs states:

> Green jobs can be generically defined as the direct employment created in different sectors of the economy and through related activities, which reduces the environmental impact of those sectors and activities, and ultimately brings it down to sustainable levels. This includes "decent" jobs that help to reduce consumption of energy and raw material, de-carbonize the economy, protect and restore ecosystems and biodiversity and minimize the production of waste and pollution.
> (ILO, 2011b, p. 10)

Given the above definition, examples of those sectors that hold the promise of green jobs for the future are identified by ILO (2011b, p. 11) as:

- delivering improvements in energy and resource efficiency, particularly in the building sector (new and existing built stock) and also industry and transport;
- renewable energy (including biofuels and renewable technologies);
- sustainable mobility (i.e. mass transportation);

- waste management and recycling of raw materials;
- eco-industries related to pollution control (air, water, waste, site decontamination, noise); and
- 'eco-friendly' services (conservation, ecotourism, etc.).

In developing economies other sectors may be at least as important, in particular:

- those involving the sustainable use of natural resources, including agriculture, forestry and fisheries; and
- activities relating to adaptation to climate change.

The Center for American Progress (2009) encourages a broad view of green jobs, stating that they

> represent new demand for labour that results from investments in transitioning our economy away from carbon-intensive energy, minimizing degradation of our natural resources, maximizing the efficient use of our natural capital, and protecting humans and the planet from pollution and waste.
>
> (Center for American Progress, 2009, p. 3)

They argue that the term 'green jobs' describes the work involved in undertaking a set of activities rather than specific occupations. Most green jobs are familiar jobs repurposed and expanded through new investments in a low-carbon economy, and green jobs are frequently more local and therefore more difficult to outsource (Center for American Progress, 2009, p. 3). What these and other definitions show are the broad areas that are considered important in the consideration of green jobs.

The need for green jobs

Attempts to identify and create green jobs have arisen out of growing calls for developing a green economy. The priorities for a green economy are to combat climate change and environmental degradation and remove negative environmental, economic and social impacts (ILO, 2011a, p. 15). In recent years, there has been increased interest in the relationship between the environment and employment (UNEP *et al.*, 2008). Furthermore, there is evidence to suggest that societal trends are impacting on employment issues. As well as the well-documented business cases for sustainability, positive environment impacts of jobs and the green credentials of a company are one way to attract people to a job or organization (Grolleau *et al.*, 2012), and green credentials can contribute to increased employee satisfaction and productivity (Walsh and Sulkowski, 2010) and competitiveness (Holcombe *et al.*, 2007. The rise of corporate social responsibility (CSR) implies that businesses should green their operations in order to minimize their environmental impact (Bohdanowicz *et al.*, 2011). The importance of environmental issues in relation to employment can be found on numerous websites, for example GreenJobs, SustainableBusiness, Greenjobshiring and GreenBiz.

According to UNEP, ILO, IOE and ITUC (2008) climate change and environmental degradation are jeopardizing the sustainability of many kinds of economic activity on a global scale. At the same time, moving towards a greener economy is creating opportunities for new technologies, investment and jobs. The Green Jobs report (UNEP *et al.*, 2008) estimates that attempts to address climate change could result in the creation of millions of new 'green jobs' in the coming decades. This group of four UN agencies has been leading the way in making an assessment of the potential and value of green jobs. The Green Jobs Initiative is a joint effort launched by the International Labour Organization, the United Nations Environmental Programme, the International Organization of Employers and the International Trade Union Confederation to help governments and social partners turn this potential for decent work into reality by aligning environment and employment objectives (ILO, 2011a).

To date, work under the Green Jobs Initiative has focused on gathering examples and evidence of green job creation, and importantly has stimulated debate on defining, understanding and quantifying green jobs. Crucially it has highlighted the differences in methodologies, definitions and estimates between countries that make it very challenging to compare the links between the environment, the economy and jobs worldwide (ILO, 2011b, p. 4).

Effects on employment and skills

The moves towards greater sustainability and a green economy will have a number of effects on employment. The Green Jobs Report (UNEP *et al.*, 2008) identifies that employment will be affected in four ways as the economy is oriented towards greater sustainability:

- Additional jobs will be created in some cases – as in the manufacturing of pollution control devices added to existing production equipment.
- Some employment will be substituted – as in shifting from fossil fuels to renewables, or from truck manufacturing to rail-car manufacturing, or from landfilling and waste incineration to recycling.
- Certain jobs may be eliminated without direct replacement – as when packaging materials are discouraged or banned and their production is discontinued.
- Many existing jobs (especially such as plumbers, electricians, metal workers and construction workers) will simply be redefined, as day-to-day skillsets, work methods, and profiles are greened.

(UNEP *et al.*, 2008, p. 43)

What these and other changes might mean for future skills requirements has been explored by the ILO (2011a). From an examination of country reports, they summarize the main core skills needed for green jobs as:

- strategic and leadership skills to enable policy-makers and business executives to set the right incentives and create conditions conducive to cleaner production, cleaner transportation etc.;
- adaptability and transferability skills to enable workers to learn and apply the new technologies and processes required to green their jobs;

- environmental awareness and willingness to learn about sustainable development;
- coordination, management and business skills to facilitate holistic and interdisciplinary approaches incorporating economic, social and ecological objectives;
- systems and risk analysis skills to assess, interpret and understand both the need for change and the measures required;
- entrepreneurial skills to seize the opportunities of low-carbon technologies;
- innovation skills to identify opportunities and create new strategies to respond to green challenges;
- communication and negotiation skills to discuss conflicting interests in complex contexts;
- marketing skills to promote greener products and services;
- consulting skills to advise consumers about green solutions and to spread the use of green technologies; and
- networking, IT and language skills to perform in global markets.

(ILO, 2011a, p. 107)

Many of these apply in the context of tourism, specifically in relation to 'soft' skills such as communication.

Green jobs in tourism

The greening of the economy and the conceptual definitions of green jobs provide the background for an assessment of the potential for developing green jobs in tourism. The case presented here argues that the potential for green jobs can be considered in three areas; those jobs that contribute to energy and waste reduction; those aimed at preserving or restoring the environment; and employment considerations within the Decent Work Agenda. The division into three areas implies that these are distinct categories, however this is not the case as there is overlap between the different areas.

Energy and waste reduction

Tourist activities, in common with other industries use non-renewable energy sources and create waste. The international and domestic movement of people for business and leisure purposes has a clear impact on energy consumption and waste. In tourism, the two sectors where this can be easily identified are transport and accommodation.

Transport creates jobs in tourism in terms of travel both to and within a destination and can be categorized as air, road and sea. In terms of transportation, air transport is often singled out for its carbon dioxide emissions and impact on climate change. Road transportation is also a major consumer of fossil fuels, again with likely contributions to climate change. UNEP *et al.* (2008) estimate that road transport is responsible for 23 per cent of energy-related greenhouse gas emissions, with the fastest rising carbon emissions of any economic sector. Railways are viewed as more environment-friendly, however this sector is not often given strategic priority, largely due to huge investment and infrastructure requirements. Green jobs associated with the above are those concerned with improved fuel efficiency and exploration into the use of renewable energy sources such as biofuels.

The accommodation sector also creates jobs in tourism both directly, in the form of employment in hotels or other accommodation providers, and indirectly, in terms of construction and its associated areas. Employment is a consideration in terms of buildings (for example employment in construction, lighting, heating, electronics, appliances, etc.) and in terms of energy efficiency, waste management and recycling. Energy-efficient lighting, insulation, solar heating, water efficiency, and the use of eco-products in cleaning and paper recycling all have a role to play in the green economy. A related area is the construction and buildings associated with administrative activities for tourism business.

Examples of how airlines and hotels are attempting to reduce their environmental impacts are abundant in the tourism literature. What is important here is the employment created in these areas by tourism activities and how they are viewed as 'green jobs'.

Preserving or restoring the environment

There is ample evidence to suggest that preserving the environment creates economic benefits and jobs. For example, coastal, marine and riverine habitats in 2010 supplied 58 per cent of the GDP and 66 million jobs in US coastal communities (NOAA, 2011). In a recent study of coastal habitat restoration projects in the United States, Edwards *et al.* (2013) demonstrate that coastal habitat restoration is an effective way to stimulate job creation, benefiting coastal economies in both the short and long term.

Central to this preservation perspective in tourism is an understanding of the relationship between tourism and the environment. The complexity of this relationship has been discussed in detail elsewhere (Holden, 2009). Over the years, tourism has been blamed for some of the most harmful impacts on the environment, as well as praised for its contribution towards environmental protection, and many variants in between. However, there is broad agreement that there is a symbiotic relationship between tourism and the environment and, as a consequence, the environment is of vital importance to the tourist industry.

Tourism and its relationship with the environment began to take centre stage with the emergence of the concept of sustainable development. The Brundtland Report, Our Common Future in 1987 defined sustainable development as 'development that meets the needs of the present without compromising the ability of future generations to meet their own needs' (WCED, 1987, p. 43).

Sustainable tourism development encompassed this, largely as a result of questions being raised as to the long-term sustainability of mass tourism development. Sustainability requires consideration to be given to the long-term economic, environmental, social-cultural and political well-being of all stakeholders (Fletcher *et al.*, 2013). As articulated by Sebele (2010) in broader terms, sustainable development as defined by the Brundtland Report (World Commission on Environment and Development, 1987) calls for environmental protection, improving the quality of life for communities influenced by tourism development and promoting community development (Milne and Ewing, 2004). Social equity and quality of life also play a part (Roseland, 2005).

Since then, primarily conceived as an alternative to mass tourism, 'alternative' types of tourism have been considered (Weaver and Oppermann, 2002). Important debates on the validity of sustainable and alternative tourism notwithstanding (Wheeller, 2003), some of these might be considered as 'Green Tourism', the principles of which are to minimize the overall impact on the environment, to benefit the local community and environment and to be sustainable. Examples of the types of tourism that fit within these broad parameters are ecotourism, nature-based tourism and community-based tourism. Although there is considerable debate about the definitions, ecotourism can be characterized as being small-scale, indigenous and low key, having preservation of the natural environment at its core, along with a desire to appreciate or learn about its intrinsic qualities (Weaver, 2004). Nature-based tourism is arguably broader than ecotourism (Arnegger *et al.*, 2010) and is ecologically sustainable tourism with a primary focus on experiencing natural areas (EAA, 2000). Viewed by some (Reynolds and Braithwaite, 2001) as a subset of ecotourism and nature-based tourism, wildlife tourism has been argued to have positive effects on both wildlife species and their habitats as a result of financial contributions (Tisdell and Wilson, 2002; Walpole and Leader-Williams, 2002; Pennisi *et al.*, 2004) and socio-economic incentives and education (Orams, 1995; Higginbottom *et al.*, 2001) and positive human experiences (Curtin, 2009). Community-based tourism seeks to achieve sustainable development to enable communities to improve their living conditions without irreversibly damaging the environment (Ruiz-Ballesteros, 2011). Empowerment and ownership, conservation of natural and cultural resources, and social and economic development are at the heart of community-based tourism (Hiwasaki, 2006). Community-based ecotourism, in addition to environmental conservation, aims to empower communities by allowing them to take control over tourism projects and their impacts (Fiorello and Bo, 2012). These three examples serve to illustrate the types of tourism that fit within the principles of green activities, and, as such, employment in these types of tourism could be catagorized as green jobs. Ecotourism in particular is singled out by the ILO (2011b) under the banner of 'eco-friendly services' of which conservation and ecotourism are part. Direct tourism green jobs in these areas could be tour guides, and park rangers and local small-scale accommodation providers, with indirect jobs created through associated services. Examples of the above are widely available in the tourism literature (Page and Dowling, 2002; Hall and Boyd, 2005; Russell, 2005; Fennell, 2007).

As outlined by Job and Paesler (2013) tourism is capable of slowing down the loss of biodiversity through improved planning and management of protected areas and encouraging local participation (McCool, 2006).

The Decent Work Agenda and tourism

Opportunities for tourism to create green jobs further lies in working to implement the Decent Work Agenda, as defined by the ILO (2009b). In the context of tourism, commitment to this ILO initiative has been given by the UNWTO through collaborative effort.

The Decent Work Agenda provides a unified framework for the key areas of ILO work, highlighting the relationships between its four strategic objectives; fundamental principles and rights at work and international labour standards; employment and income opportunities; social protection and social security; and social dialogue and tripartism. Decent work reflects the concerns of governments, workers and employers who together provide the ILO with its unique tripartite identity (ILO, 2009a). The framework of Decent Work covers the following dimensions:

- employment opportunities
- adequate earnings and productive work
- decent hours
- combining work, family and personal life
- work that should be abolished
- stability and security of work
- equal opportunities and treatment in employment
- safe work environment
- social security
- social dialogue, workers' and employers' representation.

(ILO, 2009a, p. 21)

An examination of the working conditions in the unskilled and low-skilled sections of the tourism workforce gives an indication of the application of the Decent Work Agenda. As previously stated, working conditions in tourism and hospitality have been outlined in detail elsewhere (Janta *et al.*, 2011). Low-skilled jobs have often been discussed in negative terms, relating to their status and working conditions (Walmsley, 2004; Baum, 2006) and have been criticized as being detrimental to a healthy work-life balance (Karatepe and Uludag, 2007; Wong and Ko, 2009). Low pay is also a much discussed feature (Lucas, 2004). Hospitality employment in particular contains a number of features associated with the secondary sector of segmented labour markets (Janta *et al.*, 2011) and is often seen as attracting vulnerable groups (MacKenzie and Forde, 2009). Certainly migrant workers form a significant part of the hospitality and tourism workforce (Williams and Hal, 2000; Baum, 2006; Duncan *et al.*, 2013). Young people and female workers are also often dominant in the unskilled jobs (UNWTO, 2010).

However, when looking at the characteristics of tourism work, tourism has opportunities for creating decent work. Returning to the characteristics of tourism employment that were outlined earlier in the chapter, tourism jobs with their low barriers to entry are open to many, and give opportunities for high unemployment groups such as younger people, economic migrants, women and those with minimal education or formal qualifications. As many of these jobs exist within the secondary labour market, there are opportunities for improving conditions here in line with the Decent Work Agenda. Community-based tourism and small business enterprise development has further potential for creating jobs through tourism development.

The ILO is working with countries in many developing regions to embed sustainability and green jobs in tourism in policy development. One example of this is in Indonesia through the creation of a Strategic Plan for Sustainable Tourism and Green Jobs (ILO, 2012). This plan explores how tourism can play a role in enhancing livelihoods and improving quality of life for people in Indonesia. This includes commitment to poverty reduction in localized destination areas and a commitment to supporting workers and employers towards a low-carbon, climate-change decelerating, socially and environmentally responsible development in Indonesia. In terms of employment, a strategic consideration has been given to younger people as a potential workforce to meet the demand for dynamic labour to cater for the growing demands of alternative tourism, at the same time addressing socio-cultural and socio-political issues. The achievement of Decent Work is an important part of sustainable tourism and the pro-poor and pro-employment agenda (ILO, 2012).

If tourism employment embraces the Decent Work Agenda, then it can be argued that it contributes to the development of green jobs. This is particularly significant when you consider that tourism activities taken as a whole are accounting for the growing share of economic activity in many countries and this upward trend is likely to continue (Chernyshev, 2009).

Conclusion

Green jobs have a fundamental part to play in the greening of the economy. As stated by UNEP *et al.* (2008), in a Utopian world a green economy is one that does not generate pollution or waste and is hyper-efficient in its use of energy, water and materials. In these terms, it means that currently there are few green jobs (UNEP *et al.*, 2008). If the focus becomes more process-oriented, green jobs are those that contribute appreciably to maintaining or restoring environmental quality and avoid future damage to the Earth's ecosystems.

Attempting to assess green jobs in tourism is currently a challenging task. There are two main reasons for this difficulty. The first relates to the problems associated with the definition of green jobs in the wider economy and, given these definitional challenges, the difficult task of any type of quantitative measurement either of their current or potential status. Second, measuring employment in tourism is equally troublesome due to the problems in defining the industry from both the demand and the supply side. Imperfections exist both in types of definitions and also with the use of tourism multipliers. Accurate tourism employment statistics in their entirety are not always available or reliable, therefore to be able to determine what proportion of these are green jobs is currently a near impossibility. However, as improvements to both of the above are made, this situation will change. Furthermore, there currently are many examples of areas in which tourism activity has responded to environmental and social challenges, either in ways that reduce the negative impacts on the environment and communities, or in ways that actively contribute to environmental protection and employment opportunities. Given the likelihood of increased employment in tourism in the coming years, keeping the green economy and potential for green tourism jobs in the discussion and debate seems to be a worthwhile challenge.

References

Argegger, J., Woltering, M. and Job, H. (2010) Toward a product-based typology for nature-based tourism: A conceptual framework. *Journal of Sustainable Tourism*, vol. 18, no. 7, pp. 915–28.

Baum, T. (2006) *Human resource management for tourism, hospitality and leisure: An international perspective*. Thomson Learning: London.

Bohdanowicz, P., Zientara, P. and Novotna, E. (2011) International hotels chains and environmental protection: An analysis of Hilton's 'we care!' programme. *Journal of Sustainable Tourism*, vol. 19, no. 7, pp. 797–816.

Center for American Progress (2009) Seven questions about green jobs. Available at www.americaprogress.org/wp-content/uploads/issues/2009/04/pdf/green_jobs_questions.pdf (Accessed 27 June 2013).

Chernyshev, I. (2009) *Employment in the Tourism Industries: Measurement issues and case studies.* Conference Paper, Fifth UNWTO International Conference on Tourism Statistics. Bali, Indonesia, 30 March, 2 April 2009.

Curtin, S. (2009) Wildlife tourism: The intangible, psychological benefits of human-wildlife encounters. *Current Issues in Tourism*, vol. 12, no. 5/6, pp. 451–74.

Doeringer, P.and Piore, M.J. (1972) *Internal labor markets and manpower analysis.* Heath: Lexington, MA.

Duncan, T., Scott, D. G. and Baum, T. (2013) The mobilities of hospitality work: An exploration of issues and debates. *Annals of Tourism Research*, vol. 41, no. 1, pp. 1–19.

EAA (2000) *NEAP application document.* Ecotourism Association of Australia: Brisbane.

Edwards, P.E.T., Sutton-Grier, A.E. and Coyle, G.E. (2013) Investing in nature: Restoring coastal habitat blue infrastructure and green job creation. *Marine Policy*, vol. 38, pp. 65–71.

Fennell, D.A. (2007) *Ecotourism.* (3rd edn). Routledge: London.

Fiorello, A. and Bo, D. (2012) Community based ecotourism to meet the new tourists expectations: An exploratory study. *Journal of Hospitality Marketing and Management*, vol. 21, pp. 758–78.

Fletcher, J., Fyall, A., Gilbert, D. and Wanhill, S. (2013) *Tourism Principles & Practice* (5th edn). Pearson Education: Harlow, UK.

Furchtgott-Roth, D. (2012) The elusive and expensive green job. *Energy Economics*, vol. 34, pp. S43–S52.

Grolleau, G., Mzoughi, N. and Pekovic, S. (2012) Green not (only) for profits: An empirical examination of the effect of environmental-related standards on employees recruitment. *Resource and Energy Economics*, vol. 34, no. 1, pp. 74–92.

Hall, C.M. and Boyd, S. (eds) (2005) *Nature based tourism in peripheral areas: Development or disaster?* Channel View Publications: Clevedon, UK.

Higginbottom, K., Northrope, C. and Green, R. (2001) *Positive effects of wildlife tourism on wildlife.* CRC for Sustainable Tourism: Griffith University, Australia.

Hiwasaki, L. (2006) Community-based tourism: A pathway to sustainability for Japan's protected areas. *Society and Natural Resources*, vol. 19, no. 8, pp. 675–92.

Holcombe, J.L., Upchurch, R.S. and Okumus, F. (2007) Corporate social responsibility: What are top hotel companies reporting? *International Journal of Contemporary Hospitality Management*, vol. 19, no. 6, pp. 461–75.

Holden, A. (2009) The environment-tourism nexus. *Annals of Tourism Research*, vol. 3, no. 3, pp. 373–89.

ILO (2009a) *ILO/UNWTO Joint Project on employment in the tourism industries: Statistical Component.* Fifth UNWRTO International Conference on Tourism Statistics. Tourism: An engine for employment creation. Bali, Indonesia 30 March–2 April 2009.

ILO (2009b) *Guide to communicating decent work.* International Labour Office: Geneva. Available at www.ilo.org/intranet/libdoc/announcements/guide.english.pdf (Accessed 2 June 2013).

ILO (2011a) *Skills for green jobs: a global view: synthesis report based on 21 country studies.* International Labour Office, Skills and Employability Department, Job Creation and Enterprise Development Department. ILO: Geneva.

ILO (2011b) *Assessing green jobs potential in developing countries: A practitioner's guide*. ILO: Geneva.

ILO (2012) *Strategic plan: sustainable tourism and green jobs for Indonesia*. ILO: Geneva.

Janta, H., Ladkin, A., Brown, L. and Lugosi, P. (2011) Employment experiences of Polish migrant workers in the UK hospitality industry. *Tourism Management*, vol. 32, no. 5, pp. 1006–19.

Job, H. and Paesler, F. (2013) Links between nature-based tourism, protected areas, poverty alleviation and crisis: The example of Wasini Island (Kenya). *Journal of Outdoor Recreation and Tourism*, vol. 1–2, pp. 18–28.

Karatepe, O.M. and Uludag, O. (2007) Conflict, exhaustion, and motivation: A study of frontline employees in Northern Cyprus hotels. *Hospitality Management*, vol. 26, pp. 645–65.

Lesser, J.A. (2010) Renewable energy and the fallacy of 'green' jobs. *The Electricity Journal*, vol. 23, no. 7, pp. 45–53.

Liu, A. and Wall, G. (2005) Human resources development in China. *Annals of Tourism Research*, vol. 32, no. 3, pp. 689–710.

Lucas, R. (2004) *Employment relations in the hospitality and tourism industries*. Routledge: London.

McCool, S.F. (2006) Managing for visitor experiences in protected areas: Promising opportunities and fundamental challenges. *Parks*, vol. 16, no. 2, pp. 3–9.

MacKenzie, R. and Forde, C. (2009) The rhetoric of the 'good worker' versus the realities of employers' use and the experiences of migrant workers. *Work, Employment and Society*, vol. 23, no. 1, pp. 142–59.

Mason, P. (2008) *Tourism impacts, planning and management* (2nd edn). Butterworth-Heinemann: Oxford.

Milne, S. and Ewing, G. (2004) Community participation in Caribbean tourism: problems and prospects. In Duval, D.T. (ed.) *Tourism in the Caribbean*. Routledge: London.

NOAA (2011) *State Coasts Report*. National Oceanic and Atmospheric Administration.

Orams, M.B. (1995) Towards a more desirable form of ecotourism. In Ryan, C. and Page, S.J. (eds) *Tourism Management: towards the new millennium*. (pp. 315–23). Pergamon: Oxford.

Page, S.J. and Dowling, R.K. (2002) *Ecotourism*. Prentice Hall: Harlow, UK.

Pennisi, L.A., Holland, S.M. and Stein, T.V. (2004) Achieving bat conservation through tourism. *Journal of Ecotourism*, vol. 3, no. 3, pp. 195–207.

Reynolds, P.C. and Braithwaite, D. (2001) Towards a conceptual framework for wildlife tourism. *Tourism Management*, vol. 22, pp. 31–42.

Roseland, M. (2005) *Towards sustainable communities: Resources for citizens and their governments*. New Society: Gabriola Island.

Ruiz-Ballesteros, E. (2011) Social-ecological resilience and community-based tourism. An approach from Agua Blanca, Ecuador. *Tourism Management*, vol. 32, pp. 655–66.

Russell, P. (2005) Community based tourism. *Travel and Tourism Analyst*, vol. 5, pp. 89–116.

Sebele, L.S. (2010) Community-based tourism ventures, benefits and challenges: Khama Rhino Sanctuary Trust, Central District, Botswana. *Tourism Management*, vol. 31, pp. 136–46.

Tisdell, C. and Wilson, C. (2002) Ecotourism for the survival of sea turtles and other wildlife. *Biodiversity and Conservation*, vol. 11, pp. 1521–38.

UNEP, ILO, IOE and ITUC (2008) Green jobs: Towards decent work in a sustainable, low-carbon world. Geneva. Available at: www.ilo.org/wcmsp5/groups/public/--dgreports/--dcomm/documents/publication/wcms_098504.pdf (Accessed 3 June 2013)

UNWTO (2009) *The tourism labour market in the Asia Pacific Region*. UNWTO: Madrid.

UNWTO (2010) *Global report on women in tourism 2012 strategic plan: sustainable tourism and green jobs for Indonesia*. UNWTO: Madrid.

UNWTO (2011) *The tourism labour markets in the Middle East and North Africa Region*. UNWTO: Madrid.

UNWTO (2013) *UNWTO Tourism Highlights*. UNWTO: Madrid.

Wall, G. and Mathieson, A. (2006) *Tourism: Changes, impacts and opportunities*. Pearson: Harlow, UK.

Walmsley, A. (2004) Assessing staff turnover: A view from the English Riviera. *International Journal of Tourism Research*, vol. 6, no. 4, pp. 275–88.

Walpole, M.J. and Leader-Williams, N. (2002) Tourism and flagship species in conservation. *Biodiversity and Conservation*, vol. 11, pp. 543–7.

Walsh, C. and Sulkowski, A.J. (2010) A greener company makes for happier employees more so than does a more valuable one: a regression analysis of employee satisfaction, perceived environmental performance and firm financial value. *Interdisciplinary Environmental Review*, vol. 11, no. 4, pp. 274–82.

Weaver, D.B. (2004) Manifestations of ecotourism. In Duval, D.T. (ed.) *Tourism in the Caribbean*. pp. 172–86. Routledge: London.

Weaver, D.B. and Oppermann, M. (2002) *Tourism Management*. John Wiley & Sons Australia: Sydney.

Wheeller, B. (2003) Alternative tourism – a deceptive ploy. In Cooper, C. (ed.) *Classic Reviews in Tourism*. (pp. 227–34). Channel View Publications: Clevedon, UK.

Williams, A. and Hall, C.M. (2000) Tourism and migration: New relationships between production and consumption. *Tourism Geographies*, vol. 2, no. 1, pp. 5–27.

Wong, S.C. and Ko, A. (2009) Exploratory study of understanding hotel employees' perception on worklife balance issues. *International Journal of Hospitality Management*, vol. 28, no. 2, pp. 195–203.

World Commission on Environment and Development (1987) *Our common future*. Oxford University Press: Oxford.

World Travel & Tourism Council (2011) *Travel and Tourism 2011*. World Travel & Tourism Council: London. Available at: www.wttc.org/site_media/uploads/downloads/traveltourism 2011.pdf (Accessed 27 May 2013).

World Travel & Tourism Council (2012) *Travel and Tourism: Economic Impact 2012*. World Travel & Tourism Council: London. Available at: www.wttc.org/site_media/uploads/downloads/ world2012.pdf (Accessed 27 May 2013).

9

SRI LANKA AND TOURISM

The need for a green economy approach

*Jeremy Buultjens, Iraj Ratnayake and
Athula Chammika Gnanapala*

Introduction

In 2012 it was estimated that 1 billion international tourists and over 4 billion domestic tourists generated more than US$1 trillion in international tourism receipts. The sector contributed 9.3 per cent of global GDP, 1 in 11 jobs, 5 per cent of investment and 5 per cent of exports (World Travel and Tourism Council, n.d.). The real and perceived benefits from tourism have encouraged governments in both developed and developing countries, including Sri Lanka, to pursue the expansion of the industry as a facilitator of future economic development.

The tourism industry in Sri Lanka had, until 2009, been stifled by the long-running civil war between the government and the Liberation Tigers of Tamil Eelam (LTTE). The tsunami that struck the country in December 2004 also had a substantial negative impact on the industry. Since the relatively successful recovery from the tsunami and the ending of the war in 2009, the tourism industry has expanded rapidly. This rapid expansion is clearly illustrated through the country's international visitation figures. Prior to 2009 the figures had remained relatively stagnant, however visitation increased rapidly from 447,890 in 2009 to over 1 million in 2012, with the government planning for 2.5 million visitors by 2016 (Sri Lanka Tourism, n.d.). Concomitantly, domestic tourism is expected to increase as local incomes rise due to the increased economic growth being experienced in the post–conflict period.

The growth in tourism is expected to deliver substantial economic benefits including increased foreign currency earnings and increased employment opportunities. However, the challenge for the government and the industry is to ensure that its expansion does not result in adverse environmental, social and economic impacts. The adoption of a green economy approach to tourism will allow the benefits from industry to flow to the government and its people while possible negative outcomes will be avoided or minimized. In order to achieve green or sustainable tourism there is a need for government, the private sector, and civil society to collaborate to create and implement sustainable policy (Ringbeck *et al.*, 2010). This chapter presents an examination of the tourism industry in Sri Lanka and the factors that are likely to impact upon its ability to adopt a green economy approach. It begins with a brief discussion of the green tourism economy concept followed by the methods section. In the next section an overview of the Sri Lankan tourism industry is provided followed by an examination of some sustainability issues in Sri Lanka. The sixth section provides an outline of the government and private sector's approach to achieving a green economy and the initiatives applied in the tourism industry. The chapter concludes with an evaluation of the green tourism initiatives and a conclusion.

Tourism in a green economy

The damaging aspects of tourism development resulting in the loss of environmental and cultural assets have been discussed extensively in the academic literature. The damage to these assets will also, in turn, negatively impact on the industry due to its reliance on these assets to maintain and/or improve competitiveness. Continued environmental and cultural damage is also likely to reduce community support for the industry, resulting in negative outcomes (see Byrd et al., 2008). The recognized importance of conserving environmental and cultural assets has encouraged government and industry to become increasingly committed to adopting and implementing sustainable (green) policies and practices (Reddy and Wilkes, 2013; Furqan et al., 2010).

Despite the acknowledged importance of a sustainable/green tourism industry there is no accepted and/or consistent definitions of these terms (Furqan et al., 2010). One definition provided by the United Nations Environment Programme (UNEP) (2011, p. 420) is that tourism in a green economy consists of 'tourism activities that can be maintained, or sustained, indefinitely in their social, economic, cultural and environmental contexts: "sustainable tourism"'. They go on to suggest that sustainable tourism 'describes policies, practices and programmes that take into account not only the expectations of tourists regarding responsible natural resource management (demand), but also the needs of communities that support or are affected by tourism projects and the environment (supply)'.

Dodds and Joppe (2001) suggest that there are four major components of green tourism. The first component, environmental responsibility, requires energy-efficient and climate-sound practices. It also involves the reduced consumption of water, the minimization of waste and the conservation of biodiversity. The next component is the need for local economic vitality. Local economic vitality occurs through the generation of local income and the integration of local communities thus improving livelihoods and reducing poverty. Preserving cultural diversity is the third component of green tourism whereby cultural heritage and traditional values are maintained and there is support for intercultural understanding and tolerance. The final component, experiential richness, involves the provision of enriching and satisfying experiences through active, personal and meaningful participation in, and involvement with, nature, people, places and cultures.

In many circumstances green tourism is used synonymously with ecotourism, nature-based and rural tourism, however it is important that all sectors of the industry, including the conventional and mass tourism markets, adopt biodiversity conservation and rural poverty reduction strategies and practices. In fact, it is the conventional and mass tourism markets that will provide the greatest benefits arising from the greening of the industry; not the niche markets (UNEP, 2011). Indeed Weaver (2012) suggests that there is a convergence towards sustainable mass tourism.

Adoption and promotion of green tourism will reduce the cost of energy, water and waste, enhance biodiversity, ecosystems and cultural heritage, as well as improve the tourist experience and the appeal of the destination. A reflection of the benefits arising from adopting green tourism is provided by Ringbeck *et al.* (2010) who suggest that the overall financial cost-recovery of a destination's green strategy (ratio of present value savings to present value capital expenditures) can be up to 174 per cent for investment recovery from hotel buildings' operation efficiency.

In addition to the environmental, cultural and financial benefits, green tourism can also be a valuable marketing tool providing a destination with a differential advantage over its competitors (see Sasidharan *et al.*, 2002). The green practices of destinations and providers are becoming progressively important influences on the choices of increasingly sophisticated and environmentally and culturally aware tourists. For example, an international survey by TripAdvisor identified that 38 per cent of respondents considered environmentally-friendly tourism when travelling and 38 per cent had stayed at an environmentally-friendly hotel. In addition, 9 per cent stated they had specifically sought out environmentally-friendly hotels and 34 per cent indicated that they were willing to pay more to stay in these hotels (Pollock, 2007).

Clearly, from demand and supply perspectives, the greening of the industry is very important. As the Sri Lankan government notes 'maintaining the natural beauty of the coastal environment is vital to sustaining this [tourism] industry' (NCSD, 2009, p. 43).

Methods

The primary method adopted for this study consisted of a comprehensive review of published and unpublished government and academic documents. The documentary method is used to critically analyse secondary data sources including documents and public records (Jennings, 2001). Data were also collected from twenty-one semi-structured, face-to-face interviews with business owners, tour operators, travel consultants, academics and representatives from government and non-government organizations. The interviews, conducted in July 2012, November 2012 and April 2013, were used to supplement and confirm or otherwise the desktop findings and to gain additional insights about the perceived greening of the industry. Interview participants were selected through a non-random, convenience and snowball sampling method (Coyne, 1997; Patton, 1990). The sample size for this study was determined through the use of the 'saturation' criterion, whereby interviews cease when additional interview participants fail to provide the researcher with new information (Patton, 1990). Interviews were guided by a set of predetermined questions and the data collected was analysed using NVivo software.

Sri Lanka and its tourism industry

Sri Lanka is an island country located off the southern coast of the Indian subcontinent. In 2012, there were approximately 20 million people living in Sri Lanka comprising

Sinhalese (75 per cent of the total population), Tamils (11 per cent) and Muslims (9 per cent) (Sri Lankan Department of Census and Statistics, 2012). These ethnic divisions were the source of the country's extended history of communal politics including the long-running civil war.

The country had a yearly gross domestic output of US$64 billion and a nominal per capita income of US$3,139 in 2012 (International Monetary Fund, 2012). The economy grew by 8.2 per cent in 2010 and it is expected that this trend will continue (EML Consultants, 2012). Tourism along with tea, clothing, rice production and other agricultural products are the main economic sectors of the country. Overseas employment, particularly in the Middle East, also contributes substantially to foreign exchange (Sri Lankan Ministry of Finance and Planning, 2011). In addition to the country's recent sound economic performance it has also performed relatively well in terms of the UN Human Development Index. Good literacy rates and health indices have underpinned the UN Human Development Index performance (EML Consultants, 2012).

As noted, the growth in the economy has been facilitated in part by the growth in the tourism sector. It was anticipated that travel and tourism would contribute 3.0 per cent directly and 7.9 per cent in total to the national GDP in 2011 increasing to 5.0 per cent directly per annum up to 2021. In addition, tourism and travel was expected to contribute 2.7 per cent directly to the total employment in 2011 and 7.1 per cent in total to employment in 2021 (World Travel and Tourism Council, 2011). Tourism is the fourth largest contributor to foreign exchange earnings, contributing 2.6 per cent in 2009 (Sri Lanka Tourism Development Authority, 2009), with the potential to become the largest earner (Sri Lanka Tourism, n.d.).

The recent growth in the industry is reflective of its relative resilience and its ability to recover from the impacts of the civil war and related terrorist acts as well as the tsunami. 'The ability for the industry to survive through very difficult times which included the insurrection of a separatist movement, the disruption of communications and also the recession in Europe is proof that the industry is resilient and sustainable' (Hotel Representative 3, personal communication). In the early days of the industry, international visitation grew relatively quickly with an annual increase in excess of 21 per cent experienced between 1970 and 1980 (Sri Lanka Tourism Development Authority, 2005). In the three decades since 1980 visitation was relatively stagnant as a consequence of the civil war (Sri Lanka Tourism Development Authority, 2009). During this time, 1980–2009, annual numbers remained between 400,000 and 500,000 (Sri Lanka Tourism, n.d.). During this period there were also some intermittent periods where sharp drops were experienced as a result of random terrorist acts. There was also a substantial decrease as a consequence of the tsunami in 2004 when international visitation fell from 566,202 visitors in 2004 to 349,308 in 2005.

The stagnation in international visitation ended with the conclusion of the civil war. Since 2009, there have been sharp increases in international visitation and by 2011, 855,975 international tourists had visited the country. In 2012, there was further growth, with visitation exceeding 1 million. The government is expecting the growth in international visitation to continue with approximately 2.5 million expected in 2016 (Sri Lanka Tourism, n.d.).

Other factors have also been responsible for the rapid growth in international visitation. Sri Lanka receives many of its tourists from India and, to a lesser extent, China and the Middle East. These countries, with large populations, are experiencing high levels of economic growth resulting in rapidly expanding middle classes with high levels of discretionary spending. The growth in these markets is, in part, reflected in the fact that between 2000 and 2009, the South Asia region experienced a 5.8 per cent growth in its international tourist arrivals. This growth was considerably higher than the world average of 2.9 per cent for the same period (UNWTO, 2011).

The rapid expansion of the international sector is likely to be accompanied by the expansion of the domestic market as a consequence of rising local incomes. The challenge for the government and industry is to ensure that its expansion occurs within a green economy paradigm. If this occurs it will ensure that the industry maintains or enhances the country's biodiversity, ecosystems and cultural heritage as well as contributing to poverty eradication, the equitable distribution of profits and peace-building (Upadhayaya et al., 2011).

> The tourism sector has a responsibility to minimize harmful emissions by encouraging and advocating for sustainable, carbon-neutral transport solutions and low carbon market destination combinations, to improve the use of natural resources (water and energy) and to contribute to the conservation of natural areas
>
> (Tourism Consultant 1, personal communication)

Sustainability issues in Sri Lanka

As with many countries, Sri Lanka faces considerable challenges in ensuring a green economy. Some of these include:

Loss of biodiversity

Sri Lanka has significant and diverse fauna, flora and ecosystems consisting of forests, grasslands, inland wetlands, coastal and marine ecosystems. Despite these assets there has been considerable biodiversity damage and the country is identified as one of the world's biodiversity hotspots due to the high levels of threat (NCSD, 2009). This is especially true along many parts of the densely populated coastal belt.

Coastal wetlands, particularly mangroves, have suffered considerable damage or destruction especially from the construction of beach resorts. Coral has also suffered from its use as a construction material for hotels, over-fishing and as a consequence of sewage dumping and sedimentation runoff from buildings. For example, only 7 per cent of the coral reef remains alive in Hikkaduwa, a popular tourism destination on the east coast (Gunawardana and Sanjeewani, 2009). In addition, a number of the country's national parks have been under considerable stress due to carrying capacity being exceeded (Buultjens et al., 2005). Carrying capacity will be further tested as tourism continues to expand so quickly.

The damage to the environment will have demand-side effects. The conservation and restoration of the ecosystem will also provide a highly profitable, low-cost investment for the industry (UNEP, 2011). In addition, as noted earlier, there is an increasing expectation among many tourists that the industry will respect and protect the natural environment. In addition, tourists are increasingly seeking experiences that involve contact with wildlife and pristine (or near pristine) ecosystems. An industry that does not meet the tourists' expectations will lose its competitiveness.

Finally, environmental damage and biodiversity loss will result in an increase in conflict between local communities whose livelihoods depend on the environment and the tourism industry. This will result in a loss of support for the industry (UNEP, 2011).

Water consumption

Despite having a relatively high average rainfall, the spatial and temporal distribution means that 65 per cent of the country is referred to as a dry zone, and experiences water shortages and droughts during several months in the year (NCSD, 2009). There has also been a rapid deterioration of water quality owing to pollution from industrial, agricultural and domestic wastes, increased urbanization and riverbank erosion (EML Consultants, 2012).

Water issues are a major and growing problem in many destination countries (Tapper *et al.*, 2011) and it is clearly an issue in Sri Lanka, especially in the dry and arid zone. As the industry expands there will be increasing pressure on already diminished water resources. Increased water consumption for tourism is likely to result in less availability for other uses including the subsistence needs of local populations. In addition to water consumption, tourism can also directly impact on the quality of water, for example, the discharge of untreated sewage and freshwater abstraction (UNEP, 2011).

Tapper *et al.* (2011) note that, currently in Sri Lanka, tourism water use in relation to total freshwater supplies available nationally is not a critical issue but it is of concern. In contrast, they suggest that there is a critical problem with regard to the Human Water Security Threat Index.[1] It is also not unreasonable to assume that the increasing emphasis in Sri Lanka on the development of larger, luxury, resort-style hotels with their golf courses, irrigated gardens, swimming pools, spas, wellness facilities and guest rooms, will result in significantly greater water consumption in the future. The development of smaller, pension-like establishments or campsites, in contrast, will result in far less water use (UNEP, 2011).

Waste management

Waste management is a well-recognized challenge in the industry (UNEP, 2011). In Sri Lanka solid waste management is a statutory function of all local authorities, however some are failing to take proper steps to manage solid waste disposal. It is estimated that total municipal solid waste generation is around 6,400 metric tonnes per day for all of Sri Lanka, of which only 3,770 metric tonnes per day is effectively collected (IFC, 2013). 'Sri Lanka has very limited scientifically constructed landfills . . . The present method of disposal consists largely of open dumping in low lying areas, thus impacting water bodies' (EML Consultants, 2012, p. 69). Plastic, including the proliferation of plastic water bottles, is also a substantial problem in Sri Lanka. The Government has taken steps to ban polythene products although this initiative has not been very successful (EML Consultants, 2012).

The problems associated with solid waste are also exacerbated by the lack of awareness among the domestic population of the effects of littering (Owen-Edmunds, 2009). 'Unfortunately our people, including the elites, do not appreciate the importance of not littering. People just throw their rubbish away – no matter where they are' (Academic 3, personal communication). In addition there are too few rubbish bins, and waste collection methods are ad hoc and inefficient. Clearly as the number of visitors and hotels increases so will the problems associated with waste.

The problems associated with solid waste are clearly visible in many tourism destinations and it reduces their attractiveness. For example, a study of visitors to Hikkaduwa found that 83 per cent of respondents identified pollution of the beach as severe (Gunawardana and Sanjeewani, 2009). Ratnayake and Munasinghe (2006) also note that this has occurred at most of the pilgrim sites around the country such as Sri Pada (Adam's Peak), Anuradapura, and Kataragama.

Energy and GHG emissions

Currently energy in Sri Lanka is produced from three main sources: biomass (46.08 per cent), HEP (12.36 per cent), and petroleum (41.52 per cent) (IFC, 2013), while two decades earlier nearly all power was generated from hydro sources (NCSD, 2009). There are a number of coal-fired power stations under construction (Norochchole Phase II, Sampoor in Trincomalee) (Ceylon Electricity Board, 2013). However, Norochchole coal power station was envisaged to be commissioned in the late 1980s, but due to pressure from various environmental and civil organizations it was kept on hold. Interestingly, one power station has been built in very close proximity to a designated tourism zone. 'It is hard to believe they would build such an eye-sore so close to hotels' (Hotel representative 2, personal communication).

Worldwide, tourism creates substantial GHG emissions, primarily from tourist transport (75 per cent) and accommodation (21 per cent, mainly from air-conditioning and heating systems) (UNWTO and UNEP 2008). As the industry expands and preferences increase for more energy-intense transport and more luxurious accommodation there will be increased energy use unless measures are introduced to limit usage (UNEP, 2011). The Sri Lankan tourism sector's energy requirement is expected to increase threefold by 2016 resulting in a considerable increase in carbon emissions (IFC, 2013).

In the context of energy, the hotel sector in Sri Lanka accounts for 2 per cent of the national electricity consumption (in 2011) and 49 per cent of energy consumption (in 2010) (IFC, 2013), and the energy cost in this sector stands at around 18 per cent of the total cost of operations in the hospitality industry. Major energy consuming areas of hotels include air conditioning (50 per cent of total energy consumption in a hotel), lighting, and cooking (Ceylon Chamber of Commerce, n.d.). There are currently a number of medium and large-scale hotel projects under construction and therefore there is a pressing need to ensure increased energy efficiency and the more intense use of renewables.

Climate change

As with other countries, it is expected that over the next two decades, the sea level around Sri Lanka will rise by half a metre. This will have major implications for the densely populated coastal areas, including many hotels established to cater for tourists (NCSD, 2009). Climate change will also result in dry areas becoming drier and the wet areas becoming wetter – resulting in longer droughts in dry areas and floods in wet areas. There are number of consequences likely to arise from climate change, including: increased vulnerability of coastal areas to destruction of mangroves and coral reefs, decline of ecosystems and marine habitats and damage to shelter, infrastructure and human safety. In addition, the adjacent areas of the coastal regions will experience gradual but intense salinization of inland fresh water sources (EML Consultants, 2012, p. 19). Agricultural production could fall as much as 20 to 30 per cent in the next 20 to 30 years (EML Consultants, 2012).

Sri Lanka and its approach to the green economy

The Sri Lankan government's approach to sustainable development is outlined in the *Haritha Lanka programme of action* (NCSD, 2009).[2] Within this document the government acknowledges that good governance is essential for sustainable development. To ensure good governance, the national government has established a framework at national, regional and multilateral levels. The multi-level framework, according to the government, is an attempt to have integrated decision-making at all levels of government and to devolve planning functions to the provincial and local levels of government to encourage 'participatory decision-making'. Participatory decision-making should assure that 'sustainable development with peace and justice [is] ensured for all communities' (EML Consultants, 2012, p. 24).

The major government institution charged with ensuring sustainable development is the National Council for Sustainable Development (NCSD). The NCSD is chaired by the President and is responsible for formulating and implementing the *Haritha Lanka programme of action*. The NCSD attempts to integrate environmental concerns into the economic and social development processes throughout the country. The release of the *Strategy for sustainable development* (SLSSD) in 2009 presented a vision for sustainable development through the achievement of five goals. The goals were: the eradication of poverty; ensuring competitiveness of the economy; improving social development; ensuring good governance; and ensuring a clean and healthy environment (EML Consultants, 2012). As part of its approach to sustainable development the government is addressing the challenges associated with climate change. In 2008, the Ministry of Environment established the Climate Change Secretariat, in order to adopt a comprehensive national approach to address climate change challenges. A National Climate Change Adaptation Strategy and a Public Information and Awareness Strategy have also been developed to address the challenges of climate change.

In addition to the policies outlined above there are currently about eighty laws and other regulatory measures relating to environmental protection (EML Consultants, 2012).

Sri Lankan tourism and the green economy

Clearly, the rapid expansion of the tourism sector requires careful planning and development to ensure it occurs within a green economy paradigm. Unless the sector adopts this type of approach it will not contribute effectively to sustainable development and it will also lose its appeal as a destination. Worldwide, the traditional mass tourism market based around 'sun, sea and sand' resorts has reached a steady growth stage. In contrast, ecotourism, nature, heritage, cultural and soft adventure tourism, as well as subsectors such as rural and community tourism are the rapidly expanding market segments. This expansion is expected to continue for the next two decades (UNEP, 2011). Clearly, tourists are seeking environmentally and culturally differentiated destinations and they are willing to pay up to an estimated 25 to 40 per cent more for the experience (UNEP, 2011).

Much of the past tourism development in Sri Lanka proceeded in the absence of any planning, resulting in substantial problems (see Gunawardana and Sanjeewani, 2009). However, an examination of government documents indicates that the government is cognisant of the need to green the industry. The government is also aware of the changing nature of the tourism market, its increasing emphasis on environmental and cultural preservation and an expanded range of niche products. To meet these challenges and facilitate the development of the industry, a number of policies and initiatives have been implemented. The current approach to tourism management has, to a large extent, been determined by the approach adopted in the aftermath of the tsunami and re-enforced by the post-conflict response.

A major initiative introduced with the aim of overcoming the haphazard nature of tourism planning was the Tourism Development Zones. This initiative, announced in 2005 in the aftermath of the tsunami, allowed for the establishment of twenty-four Tourism Development Zones throughout the country. The types of developments planned for a number of these zones are characterized as 'mega resorts'. In addition to supplying upmarket hotels, it is anticipated that the zones will also supply golf courses, water parks, light aircraft services and shopping malls. To ensure environmental and social safeguards were in place around these developments Strategic Environmental Assessments (SEA) were conducted for all sites prior to implementation. SEAs also addressed job creation and skills development for the local communities (EML Consultants, 2012).

In addition to improved planning, the Sri Lanka Tourism Development Authority (SLTDA) is also attempting to encourage water conservation during the planning phase of new hotels through ensuring the treatment of wastewater and reuse for gardening and toilets is included (EML Consultants, 2012, p. 69). This initiative will help enhance the 'reduce, reuse and recycle' concept which is still at a primary stage in the country. However, the government believes there has been considerable improvement in this area on the part of both communities and entrepreneurs (EML Consultants, 2012, p. 70).

Another initiative, indicating the government's approach, was the launch of the Refreshingly Sri Lanka – Visit 2011 marketing campaign by Sri Lanka Tourism. Under this campaign twelve experiences including people and culture; religious tourism; body and mind wellness; heritage, nature and wildlife; community and education, were promoted. This marketing initiative has been supported by a tourism policy aimed at developing special tourism niche markets including nature tourism, community tourism, spiritual tourism, adventure tourism, agro-tourism, culture tourism, ecotourism and wellness tourism (EML Consultants, 2012, p. 66). The government's tourism-related policy is aimed at maximizing the potential of nature-based tourism and cultural tourism since they 'have the capacity to provide conducive employment opportunities to rural youth, and thereby motivate communities to protect the natural environment that provides their livelihood, and also serve the dual purposes of environmental protection and employment generation' (Sri Lankan Ministry of Environment and Natural Resources, 2007, p. 12)

The private sector has also initiated actions aimed at greening the tourism industry. For example, the Ceylon Chamber of Commerce implemented the EU-originated SWITCH Asia programme in mid-2009, targeting 350 SMEs in the hotel sector.

> The main objective of the proposed action is to enhance the environmental performance of Sri Lankan Hotels through improvement of energy, water and waste management systems and reduce cost of operations and increase market acceptance of Sri Lankan hotels with low carbon footprint
>
> (Ceylon Chamber of Commerce, n.d.)

It is estimated that the hotel sector could potentially save approximately 20 per cent in energy and water consumption as well as waste generation (Ceylon Chamber of Commerce, n.d.; See also Ratnayake and Miththapala, 2011).

Some of the larger hotel chains in Sri Lanka, including Jetwing and Aitken Spence, and tour operators are also attempting to ensure that processes within their operations are based on the 'reuse, reduce and recycle' principles (see Hausler, 2007). For example, Jetwing state that they make a concerted effort to minimize their use of plastic water bottles in their restaurants, undertake recycling, and have asked their suppliers to reduce unnecessary packaging. They have instituted a number of practices in an attempt to reduce their energy and water usage as well as their waste (Miththapala, 2007; 2012). Jetwing Hotels suggest they have reduced their per annum carbon footprint by 22 per cent (Miththapala, 2007).

In addition, some companies have initiated and funded educational programmes concerning sustainable management. As Ringbeck *et al.* (2010) note, educational and capacity-building campaigns teaching the local tourism community about best practices are important for encouraging the implementation and promotion of green policy. The Jetwing Youth Development Project provides training for rural youth so that they are positioned to find for suitable employment within their hotels or other hospitality organizations (Miththapala, 2007). Jetwing have also trained local service suppliers including trishaw drivers so that they can become quality-accredited business partners. They also provide environmental education, in consultation with community leaders, for young people who reside near their hotels.

Walker Tours is another company pursuing environmentally friendly actions. For example, in 2011, the company constructed a wastewater treatment plant in their car-washing yard at Mattakkuliya that has resulted in a large reduction in water wastage (Walker Tours, n.d.). The company is also using carbon credits to offset the carbon emissions from its entire fleet of over 600 vehicles.

Local economic vitality

The government has recognized that pro-poor tourism (PPT) development can help alleviate poverty in Sri Lanka, as noted in a publication by the Sri Lanka Institute of

Tourism and Hotel Management with the Samurdhi Authority of Sri Lanka[3] (SLITHM and SASL, n.d.). The government believes that 'as tourism itself is a labor intensive, community driven and public resources based industry' there will be pro-poor tourism outcomes (SLITHM and SASL, n.d., p. 4). The extent to which tourism promotes local economic development depends primarily on its structure and supply chain at a destination level. The higher the leakage from the local economy, the lower the multiplier effect and the lower the economic contribution to the local economy. SLITHM and SASL (n.d.) suggest that the promotion of sustainable forms of tourism, especially in rural areas, will result in the reorientation of tourism-related income in favour of the poor, resulting in the reduction of poverty (SLITHM and SASL, n.d.). To ensure pro-poor tourism outcomes, interventions must be made to help poor people become part of the processes that drive the industry (Bolwell and Weinz, 2010). The government, investors and developers play a critical role in determining what role poorer populations will play in the tourism industry (UNEP, 2011).

In addition to being relatively labour-intensive the tourism sector is traditionally dominated by micro and small enterprises with activities particularly suited for women and disadvantaged groups (UNEP, 2011). Therefore in order to maximize the pro-poor outcomes from the development of the industry it is important to ensure support for micro and small businesses. It is also important that tourism businesses use local businesses to supply their needs and recruit and train local unskilled and semi-skilled staff as well as forming neighbourhood partnerships to ensure an improvement in the local social and natural environment (Ashley, 2006). Another major feature of an effective pro-poor tourism approach is that poor people are able to participate more effectively in the tourism product and service development. This requires that there are strong links between government planning organizations, tourism-related businesses and people from low-income backgrounds.

In Sri Lanka, SLITHM, in order to improve the employment outcomes for local people, conducts a number of training and skill improvement programmes aimed at meeting the needs of the different segments of the tourism and hospitality industry. To support their studies, students are able to access support from an educational loan scheme. In addition to the training programmes, SLITHM, with assistance from SASL, is establishing 'Samurdhi Village Restaurants' in certain villages. It is expected that these restaurants will sell community livelihood food items prepared with the resources from within the community. Finance for these ventures will be provided by the Samurdhi Bank (SLITHM and SASL, n.d.). In addition, as noted earlier, some businesses also provide training.

In the aftermath of the tsunami a number of non-government organizations (NGOs) attempted to assist the country's recovery, with some focusing on the tourism industry. A number of NGOs targeted the establishment of community-based tourism (CBT) projects in the most neglected and disadvantaged regions of Sri Lanka (Hausler, 2007). For example, the Sewalanka Foundation's Sustainable Tourism Program in partnership with the Italian NGO, Instituto Cooperazione Economica Internazionale, trained thirteen local tour guides from eastern regions of Sri Lanka in 2006. The Sinhala, Muslim and Tamil guides were local community members from Pottuville, Arugam Bay, and Panama (Hausler, 2007).

Another example of a pro-poor company established in the aftermath of the tsunami was Mirissa Water Sports PVT Ltd (MWS). MWS offers various water sports and recreational activities including whale watching, sports fishing and coastal cruises. The enterprise is owned and operated by seven underprivileged youths from Mirissa and was set up in partnership with the Build a Future Foundation. In addition, other partnerships have been set up with the tourism industry's private sector and Mirissa Water Sports to provide mentoring, training, marketing, and technical knowledge to the enterprise (Mirissa Water Sports, n.d.).

Another NGO with an involvement with tourism is the Sri Lanka Ecotourism Foundation (SLEF). SLEF, founded in 1998 with the aim of establishing Sri Lanka as an ecotourism destination, has established community-based ecotourism enterprises in rural Sri Lanka as a tool for poverty alleviation in tourism generating areas of Sri Lanka (Hausler, 2007). John Keels, a large tour operator and manager of two hotel brands has started outsourcing most of the services originally managed in-house in an attempt to create more opportunities for local entrepreneurship.

Cultural diversity

UNEP (2011) notes that the largest single component of consumer demand for more sustainable tourism comes from cultural authenticity. This demand for cultural tourism can offer opportunities for the continuation, rejuvenation and enhancement of traditions and a way of life (Chafe, 2005). In addition to the intangible benefits from cultural tourism, investment in cultural heritage offers profitable investment opportunities for the society and tourism sector. The Galle Fort, a world heritage site and an important tourism destination, provides a good example of the benefits that arise from cultural tourism. The Fort's importance as a destination has helped to ensure its conservation and preservation. In the aftermath of the tsunami, investment from foreigners and the Netherlands Government has resulted in over 120 buildings being restored, the repair of the fortification walls, restoration of some public buildings, the creation of a new maritime museum and restoration and reuse of the ancient drainage and sewerage system (Owen-Edmunds, 2009).

As noted earlier, the government is trying to move away from sun, sea and sand tourism with more emphasis being placed on cultural and nature-based tourism. This should help preserve cultural diversity.

Evaluation of the greening of tourism

It is significant that the Sri Lankan government and the private sector have acknowledged the importance of greening the economy, including the tourism industry, and a number of policies have been introduced to achieve this aim. Despite these actions, the government acknowledges that the rapid development of tourism has resulted in its encroachment into environmentally sensitive locations although these locations are often reservations, buffer zones or declared protected areas. It has been noted that the construction and continuous operation of many large-scale hotels and other venues for recreation adventure and tours are causing environmental damage to the coast, coastal vegetation and coastal stability. It is also noted that 'under these circumstances the responsible (government) agencies have to be more vigilant and enforce the law' (EML Consultants, 2012, p. 104). This demands proper coordination among state agencies that are responsible for managing designated wildlife areas, coastal zones and all forest areas of the country in particular. Unfortunately, lack of funding and poor coordination make law enforcement difficult (see Ratnayake, 2011).

Another conundrum for the government, in terms of greening the industry, has been its attempt to focus on the high-end market as well as control the development process through the declaration of the Tourism Development Zones. The Tourism Development Zones have attracted considerable criticism from many commentators and can been seen as having deleterious outcomes for the greening of the economy. Many of the proposed tourism development initiatives are seen to be in ecologically sensitive areas, and development is expected to result in significant environmental damage. According to critics this has occurred despite the existence of the Strategic Environmental Assessments. For example, the Centre for Environmental Justice (2013) notes that while Sri Lanka, in comparison with many other South Asian countries, has some of the best environmental and social protection regulations, implementation is rather weak due to unsatisfactory enforcement.

This view was supported by a Tourism Body representative 2 (personal communication) who commented:

> A number of tourism policies make mention of environmental protection and coastal conservation but little attention is paid to it in reality.

While apparently:

> In recent times, certain advancements have been made by the tourism sector . . . with positive interest in adoption of cleaner production practices in the hotel sector and recognition of the need for sustainability at policy level . . . the country's tourism sector, in general, appears to be largely focused on financial sustainability . . . Little emphasis has been placed on environmental and social aspects of sustainability.
>
> (Academic 1, personal communication)

Another criticism of the Zones is that they are reducing local economic vitality and increasing inequality through their focus on high-end developments that favour larger developers at the expense of smaller entrepreneurs (Wickramasinghe and Takano, 2007). Bowes (2006) argues that the government may have used the increased vulnerability of communities and small entrepreneurs, as a consequence of the tsunami, as an opportunity to push through tourism strategies that would drastically reduce the well-being of local coastal communities. The large tourism development may also be taking place at the expense of livelihoods in the other sectors of the economy, for example, fishing (Rice and Haynes, 2005). For example, many fishing communities were moved inland in order to provide land for tourism development. The focus on large, luxury style resorts is also likely to result in lower economic contributions to the local economy since there will be higher leakages.

Community displacement and conflict can also be exacerbated through land price inflation arising through increased foreign investment in land and houses in popular tourism destinations. Increased property prices encourage families to sell their properties and this means that young people can rarely afford to purchase homes within these areas (see Atkinson, 2004). In addition, communities may also suffer from increased interaction with tourists.

The increasing displacement of people and the threat to their livelihoods is encouraging community action, resulting in increased conflict. This has caused the government to note that

> sustainable coastal development is affected by fishermen who agitate to reoccupy their traditional fishing villages although they have been given alternate land elsewhere.[4] They act on the impulse supported by foreign and local NGOs, such action necessitating suppression by the Government in a practical manner.
>
> (EML Consultants, 2012, p. 105)

The marginalization of communities and reduced local economic vitality has also arisen, in part, due to a lack of community consultation regarding tourism development and the highly centralized nature of decision-making in the country (de Silva, 2009). It is suggested that the national government, despite the rhetoric, is reluctant to devolve powers to lower levels of government (Uyangoda, 2010). The exclusion of local authorities from planning and the lack of public consultation has led to unsuitable or impracticable tourism policies (Mulligan and Shaw, 2011) with negative implications for destinations and their communities (Robinson and Jarvie, 2008). 'The focus of sustainability seems to be largely on accommodation/hotel sector. Sustainable tourist destination/site management has been virtually ignored' (Academic 2, personal communication). Corruption and a lack of expertise at the local level exacerbate the problem.

In addition to reducing local economic vitality, the focus on large, luxury accommodation resorts with their swimming pools, golf courses, substantial gardens and air-conditioning requirements will result in increased energy and water usage and implications for the greening of the industry.

> For example, to elevate yourself in the star classification, certain features are necessitated such as air-conditioning of rooms and common areas, excessive power-consuming arrangements for lighting, etc. Even carpeting of floors wall to wall in a tropical country like Sri Lanka makes the internal air quality very low due to VOC emissions as well as harbouring micro-organisms which can cause disease.
>
> (Hotel representative 3, personal communication)

The expansion of the high-end market will also result in increases in demand for aviation and transport services (EML Consultants, 2012).

Conclusion

The importance of pursuing a green economy agenda has been acknowledged in Sri Lanka, and in response various policies and initiatives have been introduced. The government has also attempted to move the emphasis away from a mass tourism market to one based on niche markets, including cultural and eco-tourism. Finally, companies and the government are also considering the equity and educational issues related to tourism development.

The financial returns from adopting a green approach through the implementation of energy-efficient technology are also becoming increasingly apparent. Yet, despite the benefits, less than 25 per cent of tourism enterprises can be classified as 'green' although this is expected to grow to 75 per cent by 2035–37 (Sri Lankan Ministry of Environment and Natural Resources, 2007).

While the green policies and initiatives are pleasing, implementation needs to be improved. The rapid increase in tourism, and the subsequent increased pressure exerted by developers in catering for the expansion, has resulted in the industry's continued encroachment into environmentally sensitive locations (EML Consultants, 2012). It also appears that some policies introduced by the government may be counterproductive and in fact may be resulting in a less sustainable or green industry. This is of particular concern. As Ringbeck *et al.* (2010) note, pursuing short-term gain at the expense of biodiversity conservation, energy conservation and waste management will have deleterious consequences for a destination. Tourists are increasingly seeking a genuine green tourism experience and are unlikely to be deceived by public relations and a marketing-created 'green façade'. As a tourism consultant noted 'there has been a focus (green) marketing benefits rather than think of the actual environmental impacts. Green washing is one of the major issues [for the industry]'.

Notes

1   The Human Water Security Threat Index is calculated from twenty-three variables covering water catchment disturbance, pollution, water resource development, and biotic factors.
2   It is not possible to provide a full overview of all policies and initiatives; some selected major initiatives are outlined in this chapter.
3   The Samurdhi Authority which comes under the purview of the Ministry of Economic Development is one of the key institutions responsible for developing strategies to alleviate poverty in the country. One of the highly prioritized areas of this authority is the empowerment of rural youth (SLITHM and SASL, n.d.).
4   In some places these communities have been moved inland well away from the coast and their livelihoods.

References

Ashley, C. (2006) *How can governments boost the local economic impacts of tourism? Options and tools.* SNV and Overseas Development Institute: The Hague, Netherlands.
Atkinson, R. (2004) The evidence on the impact of gentrification: new lessons for the urban renaissance? *European Journal of Housing Policy*, vol. 4, no. 1, pp. 107–31.
Bolwell, D. and Weinz, W. (2010) Reducing poverty through tourism. Sectoral activities programme. *ILO Working Paper 266*, Geneva.
Bowes, G. (2006) Is tourism damaging post-tsunami recovery? *The Observer*, 31 December 2006. Accessed 1 December 2012 from www.guardian.co.uk/travel/2006/dec/31/ethicalholidays. escape.

Buultjens, J., Ratnayake, K., Gnanapala, W. and Aslam, M. (2005) Tourism and its implications for management in Ruhuna National Park (Yala), Sri Lanka. *Journal of Tourism Management*, vol. 26, no. 5, pp. 733–42.

Byrd, E.T., Cárdenas, D.A. and Greenwood, J.B. (2008) Factors of stakeholder understanding of tourism: The case of Eastern North Carolina. *Tourism & Hospitality Research*, vol. 8, no. 3, pp. 192–204.

Centre for Environmental Justice (2013)*Environmental justice and governance.* Accessed on 7 July 2013 from www.ejustice.lk/environmental-Justice_Governance.htm.

Ceylon Chamber of Commerce (n.d.) *Greening Sri Lankan hotels.* Accessed 21 May 2013 from www.greeningsrilankahotels.org.

Ceylon Electricity Board (2013) *Development programmes.* Accessed on 6 July 2013 from www.ceb.lk/sub/dp/majorprojects.aspx.

Chafe, Z. (2005) *Consumer demand and operator support for socially and environmentally responsible tourism.* Center on Ecotourism and Sustainable Development (CESD) and International Ecotourism Society (TIES). Working Paper No. 104. April 2005, Washington.

Coyne, I. (1997) Sampling in qualitative research: Purposeful and theoretical sampling: Merging or clear boundaries? *Journal of Advanced Nursing*, vol. 26, no. 3, pp. 623–30.

de Silva, M.W.A. (2009) Ethnicity, politics and inequality: post-tsunami humanitarian aid delivery in Ampara District, Sri Lanka. *Disasters*, vol. 33, no. 2, pp. 253–73.

Dodds, R. and Joppe, M. (2001) Promoting urban green tourism: The development of the other map of Toronto. *Journal of Vacation Marketing*, vol. 7, no. 3, pp. 261–7.

EML Consultants (2012) *Sri Lanka's middle path to sustainable development through 'Mahinda Chintana – Vision for the future'.* Country Report of Sri Lanka, United Nations Conference on Sustainable Development/ (Rio+20), Ministry of Environment: Battaramulla, Sri Lanka.

Furqan, A., Mat Som, A.P. and Hussin, R. (2010) Promoting green tourism for future sustainability. *Theoretical and Empirical Researches in Urban Management*, vol. 8, no. 17, pp. 64–74.

Gunawardana, M.R. and Sanjeewani, H.L.G. (2009) Planning implications and sustainability of tourism: A comparative study of Hikkaduwa and Bentota, Sri Lanka. *Journal of Tourism, Hospitality & Culinary Arts*, vol. 1, no. 2, pp. 67–85.

Hausler, N. (2007) *Pro-poor tourism development in Sri Lanka: Two years after the tsunami – missed opportunities, future potentials.* Accessed 13 December 2012 from www.mascontour.info/Media/ .../Pro-Poor%20Tourism.pdf.

IFC (2013) *Ensuring sustainability in Sri Lanka's growing hotel industry.* The World Bank: Washington, DC.

International Monetary Fund (2012) *Reports for selected countries: Sri Lanka.* Retrieved 2 February 2013, from International Monetary Fund Web site: www.imf.org/external/pubs/ft/weo/ 2012/01/weodata/weorept.aspx.

Jennings, G. (2001) *Tourism research.* John Wiley and Sons Australia: Milton, QLD.

Mirissa Water Sports (n.d.) *Mirissa Water Sports, Sri Lanka – a pro poor tourism enterprise.* Accessed 24 January 2013 from http://adlibconsulting.wordpress.com/2010/07/08/mirissa-water-sports-sri-lanka-a-pro-poor-tourism-enterprise/.

Miththapala, S. (2007) *Jetwing Vil Uyana: Green directory.* Jetwing: Colombo, Sri Lanka.

Miththapala, S. (2012) *Jetwing Sea, Negombo, Sri Lanka: Green directory.* Jetwing: Colombo, Sri Lanka.

Mulligan, M. and Shaw, J. (2011). Achievement and weaknesses in post-tsunami reconstruction in Sri Lanka. In Karan, P.P. and Subbiah, S.P. (eds) *The Indian Ocean tsunami: The global response to a natural disaster.* The University Press of Kentucky: Lexington, KY, pp. 237–60.

NCSD (2009) *National action plan for Haritha Lanka programme.* Ministry of Environment and Natural Resources: Sri Lanka.

Owen-Edmunds, L. (2009) *A critical review of the responsible tourism issues in Galle Fort, Sri Lanka using the triple bottom line approach.* AdLib Consulting. Accessed 25 May 2013 from http://adlibconsulting.wordpress.com/2010/06/15/a-critical-review-of-the-responsible-tourism-issues-in-galle-fort-sri-lanka-using-the-triple-bottom-line-approach/.

Patton, M. (1990) *Qualitative evaluation and research methods.* Sage: Beverly Hills, CA.

Pollock, A. (2007) *The climate change challenge. Implications for the tourism industry.* The Icarus Foundation: Toronto, Ontario.

Ratnayake, I. (2011) *Community environmental and tourism initiatives: A case from Sri Lankan perspective* (unpublished Doctoral dissertation). Universiti Utara Malaysia (UUM), Malaysia.

Ratnayake, I. and Munasinghe, S. (2006) *Domestic religious tourism and environmental concerns: The case of Adam's Peak (Sri Pada), Sri Lanka.* Abstract publication of the First International Symposium, Sabaragamuwa University of Sri Lanka: Sri Lanka.

Ratnayake, N. and Miththapala, S. (2011) *A study on sustainable consumption practices in Sri Lanka hotel sector.* Civil Engineering Research for Industry, Department of Civil Engineering, University of Moratuwa: Sri Lanka.

Reddy, M.V. and Wilkes, K. (2013) Tourism and sustainability. In Reddy, M.V. and Wilkes, K. (eds) *Tourism, climate change and sustainability.* (pp. 1–23). Routledge: London.

Rice, A. and Haynes, K. (2005) *Post-tsunami reconstruction and tourism: a second disaster?* Tourism Concern: London.

Ringbeck, J., El-Adawi, A. and Gautarn, A. (2010) *Green tourism. A road map for transformation.* Booz & Company: Dubai.

Robinson, L. and Jarvie, J. (2008) Post-disaster community tourism recovery: the tsunami and Arugam Bay, Sri Lanka. *Disasters,* vol. 32, no. 4, pp. 631–45.

Sasidharan, V., Sirakayab, E. and Kerstettera, D. (2002) Developing countries and tourism ecolabels. *Tourism Management,* vol. 23, pp. 161–74.

SLITHM and SASL (n.d.) *Empowerment of Samurdhi beneficiaries through pro-poor tourism development.* Accessed 11 April 2013 from www.slithm.edu.lk/.../SLITHM_Samurdhi_Training_Proposal. pdf.

Sri Lankan Department of Census and Statistics (2012) *Sri Lanka census of population and housing, 2011.* Accessed 12 January 2012 from www.statistics.gov.lk/PopHouSat/CPH2011/Pages/Activities/Reports/cph2011Pub/pop42.pdf.

Sri Lankan Ministry of Environment and Natural Resources (2007) *Sri Lanka strategy for sustainable development.* Sri Lankan Ministry of Environment and Natural Resources: Colombo, Sri Lanka.

Sri Lankan Ministry of Finance and Planning (2011) *Annual report.* Sri Lankan Ministry of Finance and Planning: Colombo, Sri Lanka.

Sri Lanka Tourism Development Authority. (2009) *Annual statistical report.* Accessed 11 March 2011 from www.sltda.lk.

Sri Lanka Tourism Development Authority. (2005) *Annual statistical report.* Accessed 11 March 2011 from www.sltda.lk.

Sri Lanka Tourism (n.d.) *Tourism for all: National strategy for Sri Lanka tourism* 2009–2012. Accessed 11 March 2011 from www.sltda.lk/sites.

Tapper, R., Hadjikakou, M., Noble, R. and Jenkinson, J. (2011) *The impact of the tourism industry on freshwater resources in countries in the Caribbean, Mediterranean, North Africa and other regions.* Tourism Concern and the Environment Business & Development Group: London.

UNEP (2011) *Towards a green economy: Pathways to sustainable development and poverty eradication.* United Nations Environment Programme: Geneva.

UNWTO (2011) *UNWTO tourism highlights 2010 edition.* Accessed 11 March 2011 from www.unwto.org/facts/eng/pdf/highlights/UNWTO_Highlights10_en_LR.pdf.

UNWTO and UNEP (2008) *Climate change and tourism, responding to global challenges.* World Tourism Organization and United Nations Environment Programme: Madrid.

Upadhayaya, P.K., Müller-Böker, U. and Sharma, S.R. (2011) Tourism amidst armed conflict: Consequences, copings, and creativity for peace-building through tourism in Nepal. *The Journal of Tourism and Peace Research*, vol. 1, no. 2, pp. 22–40.

Uyangoda, J. (2010) Sri Lanka in 2009: From civil war to political uncertainties. *Asian Survey*, vol. 50, no. 1, pp. 104–11.

Walker Tours (n.d.) *Green practices of walkers tours.* Accessed 11 April 2012 from www. walkersgreen.lk.

Weaver, D. (2012) Organic, incremental and induced paths to sustainable mass tourism convergence. *Tourism Management*, vol. 33, no. 5, pp. 1030–37.

Wickramasinghe, V. and Takano, S. (2007) Revival of tourism in Sri Lanka following the December 2004 Indian Ocean Tsunami. *Journal of Natural Disaster Science*, vol. 29, no. 2, pp. 83–95.

World Travel and Tourism Council (2011) *Tourism and travel impacts 2011, Sri Lanka.* World Travel and Tourism Council: London.

World Travel and Tourism Council (n.d.) *Economic Impact Research.* Accessed 4 June 2013 from www.wttc.org/research/economic-impact-research.

10

RESPONSES AND GREEN TOURISM INITIATIVES AT A NATIONAL PARK IN SABAH, MALAYSIA

Jennifer Kim Lian Chan

Introduction

The literature records a range of green tourism concepts but there is not yet a distinctive definition of green tourism. The principle of green tourism is sustainability and the improvement of the quality and attractiveness of the natural environment at a destination (Chun, 2006). Green tourism promotes environmental friendliness to safeguard it for future generations. It is an inevitable result of human beings' return to nature and is perceived to be a method of achieving sustainable development (Zhibo, 2012). It is an alternative form of tourism that includes sustainable tourism, responsible tourism and ecotourism – which themselves do not provide a distinct definition/concept and are overlapped, interlinked and interconnected (Mitani, 1993). Widely, the practice of green tourism includes a wise use of resources; the prevention of air, land and water pollution; and the preservation and enhancement of biodiversity quality (Scottish Enterprise Network, 2002; Scottish Enterprise, 2004). Increasingly, tour operators are moving forward in the practice of green tourism (Miller, 2001; Budeanu, 2009; UNEP and WTO, 2011; Khairat and Maher, 2012) and sustainability (Miller, 2001; Budeanu, 2009; Khairat and Maher, 2012). Simply, this enables them to sustain tourists' destinations through internal management, product development, supply chain management, customer relations and cooperation with destination areas (UNEP, 2005; Khairat and Maher, 2012). Nevertheless, the ability and authority of tour operators to act in a green manner is limited.

The green tourism initiative has become a prominent research topic and extensive attention has been given by tourism stakeholders within developed and developing countries (Khairat and Maher, 2012; Azam and Sarker, 2011; Furqan *et al.*, 2010; Lynes and Dredge, 2006). Budeanu (2009), Khairat and Maher (2012) and Curtin and Busby (1999) have indicated country differences in the motivations, barriers and challenges faced by tour operators.

In the context of Malaysia, the tourism industry provides the second largest foreign exchange earnings after manufacturing. It contributes significantly to the growth of the

Malaysian economy. Thus, it is imperative for the Malaysian government to ensure the continuous sustainable growth of the tourism industry. In view of this, green tourism development was introduced as a regional development strategy under the Malaysian government transformation program (PEMANDU, 2010). Green tourism safeguards environmentally friendly practices and contributes to sustainable growth and development. Likewise, the practices of green tourism lead to sustainable development of local culture and the natural environment. The Malaysian government introduced green tourism practices in the East Coast Economic Region – a region that is rich in natural assets – to ensure sustainable development (Bhuiyan *et al.*, 2012). Following this, policies, regulations and guidelines are being introduced to implement green tourism development initiatives in Malaysia. Nevertheless, there are challenges to be faced in relation to green tourism and the green economy in Malaysia. These include the lack of knowledgeable and competent human resources, and sufficient facilities and finance to support the green technology. More importantly, the directions and strategies to enable Malaysia to move intoa green economy is still unclear, especially in the tourism sector.

Hence, this chapter presents an exploratory qualitative research work, identifying the concepts, key motivations, directions and strategies from tour operators and park officers with regard to green tourism initiatives at Kinabalu National Park (KNP) in Sabah, Malaysia.

The research objectives are:

(a) To explore the concept of green tourism, the key motivations and types of tourism resources in developing green tourism initiatives.
(b) To analyse directions and strategies from tour operators and park officers with regard to initiatives in green tourism.

Concept of green tourism

Green tourism refers to sustainable tourism practice which takes into account the mutual needs of the ecology and environment, local people, businesses enterprises and the tourists themselves (Azam and Sarker, 2011). Highly interrelated with sustainable development, environmental protection, biological diversity, human health and other principles (Zhibo, 2012), it covers issues such as business efficiency, environmental management, waste management, green transport, social responsibility and biodiversity (Chun, 2006). Green tourism refers to the reduction of environmental costs and enhancement of environmental benefits of tourism. Strategies are developed to reduce negative environmental and social impacts of tourism operations located in rural or urban areas of any country (Azam and Sarker, 2011). In Japan, green tourism is an effective rural revitalization method (Mitsuhashi and Kim, 2007). Green tourism, similar to ecotourism, covers a holiday experience in which the natural environment and cultural heritage is protected and not destroyed by the holiday activity (Scottish Enterprise Network, 2002; Scottish Enterprise, 2004). Dodds and Joppe (2001) view the concept of urban green tourism as comprising four components: environmental responsibility, local economic dynamics, cultural diversity and experiential richness.

Green tourism initiatives

Budeanu (2009) notes two motive categories in practising tourism sustainability, namely external drivers and organizational benefits. According to Khairat and Maher (2012, p. 1389) external drivers include the avoidance of a negative public image and reputation with regard to environmental and social concerns; building a positive public image for marketing purposes and developing a competitive market advantage; regulations, licences and environmental legislation of tour operation; industry trends and customer demands; and product development based on customers' preferences for holiday products. Organizational benefits refer to new staff skills and competences; enhanced product quality; cost savings; increased operational efficiency; and business opportunities through design and innovation (Budeanu, 2009). All these criteria vary in accordance with the perception and practice of green tourism. Frey and George (2010) state that the financial benefit arising from responsible tourism management is a powerful motivator for the latter. However, it is also a barrier due to the high costs involved (WCED, 1987).

Predominantly, tour operators prefer to create alliances and adopt their own standards of environmental best practice under the guidance of industry associations without making further investment. Although the tour operating sector is the key point for translating the principles of responsible or green tourism into operational changes, strategies need to be integrated with the wider development strategy with effective multi-stakeholder participation (Siti–Nabiha et al., 2011).

Green tourism practices

Green tourism practices can be implemented by tour operators in five main areas: supply chain management, internal management, product management and development, customer relations and cooperation with the destination (UNEP, 2005; Khairat and Maher, 2012). Awards and eco-labels can help consumers to identify tourism products that are environmentally benign and encourage producers to pay more attention to the environment (Font and Tribe, 2001). Eco-labels enable tourism enterprises to develop high quality environmentally friendly tourism products/services, and tourists are able to make informed choices when selecting a holiday package (Sasidharana, Sirakayab and Kerstetter, 2002). The aim of eco-label certification is to foster responsible environmental, social and cultural behaviour to produce and consume an environmentally-friendly product (Furqan et al., 2010). Likewise, awareness-raising tools can be used by tour operators to influence tourist behaviour towards green tourism (Budeanu, 2007), by promoting appropriate behaviour in pre-departure information through a fair portrayal of the destination and the local culture, and raising awareness on sustainability issues throughout the tour, excursions and in any post-holiday information (UNEP, 2005; Khairat and Maher, 2012). Strategies by tour operators can include educating or communicating sustainability messages to tourists, developing/adopting a responsible tourism code of conduct, and training for travel agents/tour operator sales staff (UNEP, 2005).

Efforts have been taken to promote green tourism, which is relatively new in Malaysia (Furqan et al., 2010); and the implementation of environmental initiaves is still low due to unattractive benefits when compared with costs, and lack of knowledge (Siti-Nabiha *et al.*, 2011).

Research method

An exploratory qualitative method using in-depth interviewing was adopted for the data collection. This method was deemed relevant as little is known about the subject matter which required detailed, clear explanations and descriptions from the tour operators and park officer. The use of purposive sampling allows a much deeper understanding, as respondents who were expressive were able to describe clearly their personal experiences (Williams and Soutar, 2000) and how they were involved in the process of tour operations and tour packages as well as tourist experiences. The sample respondents comprised twenty-one local tour operators selling Kinbalu National Park tour packages in Kota Kinabalu, Sabah and one research director of Kinabalu National Park. A semi-structured interview protocol was employed to ensure sufficient flexibility and freedom for respondents to respond; the same questions were asked. A single phrase or several significant statements grounded in the respondents' own descriptions were used to enhance the reliability and validity of the findings. The interviews were conducted using tape recordings and lasted an average of 30–45 minutes. Given the qualitative nature of the interviews, there was no predetermined sample size; the interviews continued until the level of information and theoretical insights reached saturation (no new information emerged from the responses). Data collection stopped after twenty-one interviews when there was no new insight in the responses. Data (on-site cross-sectional) were collected over a 3-month period from March to May 2013. Each interview was preceded by an introduction to explain salient details about the interviewer and the research project, to clarify the interviewee's role and importance in the research, to explain what was required of him/her in the interview as well as their right to withdraw from the interview. All of the respondents were very partici-pative and open, as the researcher had clearly explained the aims of the research and properly addressed the respondents by name to establish close rapport. Respondents were informed that they would be contacted again to validate the transcribed semi-structured interview.

Data analysis included transcribing the audio-recorded semi-structured interviews verbatim into typed text. A phenomenological approach and thematic analysis was used to analyse the data. Data were categorized according to themes and patterns that emerged during the data analysis. The themes or categories of responses were based on research objectives and linked to the theoretical constructs of: the green tourism concept, motivations, strategies and directions.

Findings and discussion

Meaning of the concept of green tourism

The interview responses on the concept of green tourism can be categorized into nine themes (see Table 10.1). The themes that emerged were conservation, minimization of negative impacts, ecotourism, sustainability, benefits to the local community, responsible tourism, environmental friendliness, travel experience and reuse concept.

TABLE 10.1 Interpretation of green tourism from the tour operators' perspectives

Theme	Interview responses from tour operators and the Sabah Park Officer
Conservation (Chun, 2006; Azam and Sarker, 2011; Zhibo, 2012; Font and Tribe, 2001)	Conservation for next generation (C1, C16) Protecting the destination's attractiveness (C2, C4, C5, C7, C8) Preserving nature for business sustainability (C9, C10) Conserving nature and greenery (C11, C15, C18, C19, C20) Protecting certain places only, e.g. jungle, forest (C14)
Minimize negative impact (Azam and Sarker, 2011; Scottish Enterprise Network, 2002; Font and Tribe, 2001)	Reducing negative impact on nature through packaging (C7) Reducing impact to destination (C11, C14, C17, C21) Low impact on forest and natural resources (C20)
Ecotourism (Scottish Enterprise Network, 2002)	Similar to definition of ecotourism (C6, C8, C9, C10, C13) More about nature (C12) Preserving nature and greenery (Sabah Park)
Sustainability (Mitani, 1993; Zhibo, 2012)	Sustainability of destination (C1, C3) Alternative tourism, sustainable tourism (C19)
Benefits to local community (Azam and Sarker, 2011; Mitsuhashi and Kim, 2007)	Involved with the local community in tourism development (C8, C11) Improve the well-being of local people (C9) Help local community (KNP)
Responsible Tourism (Mitani, 1993)	Responsible travel to natural area without degradation of nature (C9) Same as responsible tourism (C19)
Environmentally friendly	Using eco-friendly products (C14) Environment-friendly operations (C21)
Travel experiences (Dodds and Joppe, 2001)	Bringing the tourists to unexplored areas, nature and adventure (C19) Appreciating 'greenness' (C14)
3R encouragement	Encourage use of recycle, reduce and reuse concept (C21)

A significant number of respondents interpreted green tourism as conserving and protecting nature, reducing negative impacts on natural resources and the destination, and as ecotourism. Interestingly, travel experiences were least mentioned by tour operators. The findings are consistent with Chun (2006). According to C1 and C6, 'green tourism is to reduce the stress on the environment in order to conserve it for our next generation'. Another two respondents noted: 'we make money from nature; of course we are the ones responsible to conserve the place' (C1 and C6). This implies that the concept and practices of green tourism are related to business sustainability, preservation of nature and responsibility for the next generation.

Many respondents indicated that green tourism was to minimize the negative impact on nature. 'As tour operators, we can package the product to have less negative impact on the environment, such as use green engine cars to reduce carbon dioxide emissions to avoid air pollution' (C7). 'At KNP, there is an abundance of flora, too much CO_2 will kill it' (C20). This is consistent with Azam and Sarker (2011) who noted that green tourism refers to reducing negative environmental impacts.

The findings from tour operators at the Park showed that their definition of green tourism was similar to ecotourism, which is consistent with the findings of the Scottish Enterprise Network (2002). A few respondents noted that 'green tourism is not promoted by government but ecotourism is, so we are more familiar with ecotourism rather than green tourism' (C8), 'this is my first time hearing about green tourism, but I think it is same with ecotourism and ecotourism is promoted by Sabah Park' (C10). 'Ecotourism means preserving the nature and greenness, and helping the local community, like involving local people to help us to take care of the place' (Sabah Park).

Some respondents indicated that green tourism implied sustainability or alternative tourism and is difficult to differentiate, which concurs with Mitani (1993). This is reflected in the following: 'It refers to the sustainability of the destination' (C1); 'to sustain the nature and environment'(C3); 'Green tourism, responsible tourism and sustainable tourism are in the category of alternative tourism, so the principles are almost the same as that of conservation, bringing tourists to unexplored areas, nature and adventure places' (C19).

Other respondents expressed green tourism as a means of benefiting local communities, including the following responses:'involve the local community to bring awareness and protect the area and to educate the tourists' (C8); 'bring benefits to the local people in the destination' (C9); 'help local communities in the area' (C11).

In short, based on the responses, green tourism can be summarized as a sustainable tourism practice which takes into account the mutual needs of ecology and the environment, local people, businesses enterprises and tourists, consistent with the definition of Azam and Sarker (2011).

Interestingly, responses indicated that green tourism refers to travel experiences, as highlighted: 'green tourism is about green conservation which focuses on flora only, like to appreciate the greenness' (C14) and 'Green tourism means bringing tourists to unexplored areas, nature and adventure' (C19). These correspond well with Dodds and Joppe's (2001) finding that green tourism encourages people to travel and explore a tourist destination.

This seems to suggest that the understanding of green tourism varies, as it is closely related to conservation, sustainability and responsible tourism and also presents a benefit to the local community. Nevertheless, these interpretations of green tourism are consistent with the concept of green tourism from previous research.

Motivation to practise green tourism

The interview responses from the tour operators indicated a range of motivations for practising green tourism. Conservation was the main motivation, followed by eight other motivations (see Table 10.2).

TABLE 10.2 Drivers to trigger tour operators to practise green tourism

Theme	Interview responses from tour operators and KNP
Organization benefits (Miller, 2001; Frey and George, 2010; Budeanu, 2009)	Sustainability and profit (C1, C3, C4, C5, C6, C7, C8, C9, C10, C12, C14, C15, C16, C17, C18, C20, C21) Quality of product (C5, C7, C9, C14, C16, C18, C19, C20, C21) New skills (C4, C11, C20) Competitive advantages (C1, C2, C7 C8, C9, C19) Cost saving (C11)
Response to customer demand (Budeanu, 2009; Khairat and Maher, 2012)	Tourist demand (C2, C3, C6, C7, C8, C12, C17, C18, C19)
Market trend	Industry trend (C3, C10, C14, C15, C18, C19, C21)
Environmental conservation (Budeanu, 2009; Khairat and Maher, 2012)	Conservation purpose (C1) Awareness of environmental issues (C4, C11, C15) Preserve the park and avoid degrading nature (KNP)
Responsible tour operators (Khairat and Maher, 2012)	Responsibility of tour operators (C2, C17)
Government's role (Miller, 2001; Budeanu, 2009; Khairat and Maher, 2012)	Government supporting ecotourism (C10)
Positive image (Miller, 2001; Budeanu, 2009; Khairat and Maher, 2012)	Create good image (C18)

The findings showed that tour operators agree that green tourism practices bring organizational benefits in terms of sustainability and profit, quality of product and guest experiences as in the following comments: 'sustainability and guests' experience are very important to us. If we continue to practise ecotourism, our tourism industry will continue stay strong'(C1); 'Profit is needed to support conservation' (C15); 'Ecotourism practices can prolong the life span of the travel product. Ecotourism brings more profits to our company and can enhance the quality of the products' (C20); 'Green tourism practices can maintain the quality of the product'. (C11, C19).

Other organizational benefits include competitive advantage, cost saving and new skills for staff: 'Ecotourism practice brings a competitive advantage for the company . . . tourists are more likely to buy especially those who know green tourism; the majority are Western tourists like Europeans, British and Australians and also, Hong Kong-ers and Taiwanese who have education backgrounds. Actually, we also have student packages and bring students to KNP. The concept of this package is to create awareness of ecotourism' (C8); 'Cost saving by reusing materials so that the cost of the building is lower than using new materials' (C11); and 'when the staff teach green tourism it also indirectly creates an awareness for them' (C11).

Showing one's own initiative was the second motivation for tour operators in practising green tourism, as evidenced: 'it's our own responsibility to do so' (C13) and 'Mount KK is the supply lead demand and tourists don't care what our company practises'. 'It is our own initiative because Sabah is my hometown' (C3); 'own initiative because I am a Sabahan, I want the place clean and sustainable' (C5; C10); 'own motivation to protect nature in Sabah' (C13); 'Personal initiative because I am a Sabahan so I want my land sustainable' (C19); 'an own initiative, to transfer the knowledge to the next generation so our children can still see Sabah's nature' (C20). This implies the strong existence of internal drivers towards conservation and being responsible tour operators; in line with the concept of green tourism.

Customer demand emerged as another key motivation, consistent with Khairat and Maher (2012). One respondent (C6) said that 'responding to customer demand . . . I experienced Western tourists asking about the green package, what elements were included. So from here you can see that Western countries are already practising green tourism well'.

Interestingly, a few respondents stated that: 'market demand is still not strong enough' (C17); 'maybe European tourists but not China markets because they don't appreciate the destination – sometimes they just throw rubbish and their behaviour is more like "I am the one who pays money so I can do everything in this place"' (C8). This concurs with Wijk and Persoon (2006) who noted that the demand for green tourism is still low.

Market trend is another motivator, as can be seen from the responses: 'Because of industry trend, you can now see a lot of operators using the terms "ecotourism", "green" or "sustainable" to attract guests . . . if we don't follow, we will be outdated – how to compete with others?' (C14); 'It is a trend; everyone is practising so our company just follows it' (C21). Other than that, reducing environmental impact is a motivator, such as stated by C1: 'Main motivation is to make sure that Sabah still has its nature, we try to protect it as much as possible' (C1); 'Green tourism is being aware about how important it is to protect the place' (C11). Likewise, it is considered the responsibility of a tour operator to practise green tourism, as evidenced: 'Tour operators have an obligation to take care of the environment . . . so we can offer it to others and the next generation' (C2); 'The tour guide has a responsibility and obligation' (C17). The findings show that green tourism can build up a positive image in the market.

Resources needed to practise green tourism

The findings showed that education/awareness, financial resources, participation and commitment of multi-stakeholders and government roles are vital in the practice of green tourism, as shown in Table 10.3 below:

Awareness emerged as an important component, as shown in the responses: 'I think awareness is essential to start to protect the destination' (C5); 'Awareness is needed amongst staff and local community' (C7); 'Awareness, because when you climb a

TABLE 10.3 Resources required to practise green tourism

Theme	Interview responses from tour operators and KNP
Education/awareness	Public awareness through education (C3, C4, C5, C10, C11, C12, C13, C14, C16) Educate the local people (C7, C8, C17) Educational programme for students (C20)
Financial resources	Funding (C1, C2, C8, C9, C10, C15, C16, C17, C18,) To support training programme (C19) To improve public facilities (C20) Manpower (KNP) Staff training (KNP) Information, signature to the tourists (KNP)
Participation of multi-stakeholders	Efforts by everyone (C1, C7) Volunteers (C2) Cooperation among stakeholders (C12, C21)
The role of government	Rules and regulation enforcement (C1) Support from government (C10, C11) Awareness creation (C14, C17) Improve the management of KNP (C6, C7, C20)
Facilities	Proper facilities (KNP) Basic infrastructure – waste management system, energy generator, water supply not to degrade condition of park (KNP)

mountain you can see rubbish along the way and it is damaging to its image . . . as a tour operator we create awareness and educate the tourists . . . Educate the local people to keep the area clean and not to destroy any vegetation'. (C8).

Responses showed that awareness is created through education to promote green tourism: 'Education is needed for local people to take care of the place' (C17); 'Awareness is important as a signal' (C14); 'Education is important to create awareness' (C10).

The level of awareness among tourists, as evidenced from responses, indicated that Malaysian or South Asian tourists are more concerned about price over sustainability compared with the Western market, as reflected in the following: 'there is no point for us to promote green tourism because tourists don't know what it is and don't even care about the impacts of tourism on the environment; what they care about is price' (C19).

Financial resources are required to practise green tourism, to support the training programme and improve public facilities. 'First of all we need to know what things we need to sustain so that actions can be taken . . . money is definitely one of them, funding from the government' (C1); 'Sabah Park has to pay money to local people to clear the rubbish in KNP' (C8); 'Facilities and money for tree planting' (C15); 'Funds is the main resource to practise ecotourism, e.g. NGOs and government to improve public facilities not only for the normal people but for the disabled' (C20).

Also, tour operators have limited resources and authority to practise green tourism as it is more dependent on the government. For example C10 said: 'We do not have much financial resources and power to do anything in the destination, e.g. facilities such as water coolers for water refill'. Frey and George (2010) also found that despite the general positive attitude towards responsible tourism management, businesses are not investing time and money into changing management practices because of resource constraints.

The commitment and participation of multi-stakeholders is needed to achieve the goal of green tourism. A number of respondents articulated that 'The most important thing is effort by everyone, such as SP, SSL, and stakeholders like us being the middle man and the tourists' (C1); 'Participation from tourism tour operators, e.g. operating the restaurant, resort and tours' (C21). This implies that the practice of green tourism is a complex and complicated task and requires support, commitment, participation, cooperation and collaboration among the stakeholders, as pointed out by Risteski et al. (2012).

Government roles are important in promoting green tourism. The local authority is expected to coordinate and facilitate the participation processes, such as providing training to the various stakeholders involved, as pointed out by Siti-Nabiha et al. (2011). This is supported by the responses: 'There are policies initiated by the government . . . to ensure everybody is obeying the rules and regulations' (C1); 'Support from government is needed because without government support I don't think this can be done' (C10); 'Government has to create awareness and confirm it in action – and not approve the investor to cut the tree for building more hotels. If only say but no action not point to create awareness for public' (C14).

Indeed, the involvement of multi-stakeholders is very significant in practising green tourism (Waligo et al., 2013). The government or local authority (KNP) is less cooperative with tour operators, as pointed out by C17: 'We give advice to KNP, like preparing a car park outside to avoid vehicles being driven into it, which causes air pollution, but now KNP has set a policy which prohibits vans and buses from parking inside it. KNP set this rule not due to environmental factors but traffic jam and safety issues.'

The findings from KNP show that resources are needed to practise green tourism; they include awareness, manpower, facilities and basic infrastructure, funding or budget, and staff training: 'Manpower is the main resource to protect the park, like rangers and cleaners . . .'; 'proper facilities to improve tourist satisfaction, basic infrastructure is important for the practice of green tourism. . . . staff training also needed . . . more training for staff to attend' (KNP).

Directions and strategies from the tour operator for initiatives in green tourism

Two directions and strategies, related to reuse strategy, awareness strategies, profit allocation, human resource training, pricing and research and development, emerged from the interview responses.

TABLE 10.4 Directions and strategies from tour operators

Theme	Interview responses
Directions: Conservation	Preservation (C1, C7, C9, C13)
Commitment	Keep contact with local authority (C7)
	Play active role in NGOs and associations (C17)
Improve the local community living standard	Help local people (C7, C9, C10)
Strategies: 3R practice	Reduce, reuse and recycle (C4, C7, C8, C11, C17, C18, C19, C20, C21)
Create awareness	Educate tourists/customers (C4, C7, C11, C12, C19, C20)
Supply chain management	Careful in supplier selection (C11, C14)
Profit allocation	Part of profit used for conservation (C1, C9, C15)
Staff training	Campaign (C2)
	Skilled staff (C11, C20)
Keep the price high	To maintain the quality of products (C10)
Support R & D	Invite specialists from overseas to perform research in KNP (C13)

The findings revealed two directions, that is, conservation and improvement of the local community living standards. The former can be seen from the responses: 'Our company's core value and guiding principle is to conserve and protect our natural environment. We are committed to the conservation of the environment and practise sustainable and responsible tourism by giving back to the community and environment where we operate from' (C1); 'our direction is to protect our nature while doing business' (C13). The latter is evidenced from the following: 'We will ensure that every tour will allow our guests to buy souvenirs along the way to the KNP, it helps local communities to earn business' (C10).

The strategies implemented by tour operators can be categorized into three areas. First, the reduce, reuse, and recycle (3R) practice is applied in internal management, as evidenced: 'We only do whatever we can like reusing the paper and recycling tins and mineral containers' (C21). Awareness is created by some respondents through websites, to 'share the knowledge of ecotourism with our travel agents and tourists' (C12).

Three interviewees responded, 'a part of the profit will be used to aid selected conservation projects' (C1); '5 per cent of our profit will go to conservation' (C9); and 'A part of our income will go to conservation like tree planting and sponsorship' (C15). Staff training enables tour operators or guides to be aware about green tourism and to be able to educate tourists. C2 articulated that 'familiarization trips and staff training are provided by the organization to learn more about sustainable tourism'.

Selection of the right suppliers is another strategy for tour operators as indicated by the following: 'We choose and make sure our suppliers are also offering environmental friendly products' (C11); 'our packages are designed to be nature and environment friendly, involving activities like kayaking, climbing, biking and river cruises (without engine)' (C14).

Another three strategies implemented by respondents were commitment of tour operators, avoidance of price wars to degrade the quality of nature, and support of research and development in KNP: 'Actively committed to traditional culture and the environment. Educate the tourists, keep in contact with KNP re. any comments received from clients. We also ensure our guides inform our clients the rules and regulations set by KNP' (C7); and 'we are tour operators who are under associations like MATTA, KOKTAS – I am also involved in the tour guide association. The local authority will collaborate with these associations to organize any events, and as a tour operator we will participate accordingly' (C17). Fierce competition within the tour operator industry and also price wars force operators to sacrifice profit margins to maintain market share (Buhalis, 2000). Because the profit margin is low, the quality of the product is also low. However, one response noted was: 'We have kept the price high to make sure the quality of service is great for our guests' (C10). Support of research and development was a strategy mentioned by C13, 'we invite overseas specialists to KNP because some species are unique only to KNP'. Table 10.4 summarizes the directions and strategies from tour operators in the different categories.

The directions and strategies from KNP's responses included local community involvement, zone division, licence management, cooperation with other associations and plant conservation.

Conclusions, contributions and future research

In summary, the concept of green tourism is closely associated with conservation, minimization of negative impacts, ecotourism, sustainability, benefit to the local community, responsibility and environment-friendliness, travel experience and the reuse concept. Eight motivators for practising green tourism were identified from tour operators. For KNP, conservation to avoid degrading the park environment was the main motivation. Awareness of green tourism, financial support, staff training, participation of multi-stakeholders, the role of government, manpower, facilities and basic infrastructure are vital for practising green tourism. Two directions and several strategies were identified from the tour operators' responses, while directions and strategies from KNP to implement the practice of green tourism were local community involvement, zone division, licence management, cooperation with other associations and plant conservation. The role of rangers in KNP is very important to protect the ecological system and to limit human construction and activity in KNP.

The findings contribute to an understanding of the concept and practice of green tourism, with directions and strategies for green tourism initiatives for the National Park in Sabah based on the tour operators and park officer perspectives. The limitations of the study arise from the sample selection, which focused solely on local tour operators and excluded the perspectives of tourists and the local community. Therefore, future studies should focus on the tourists' attitudes towards green tourism with special reference to KNP, local residents' attitudes towards green tourism, and the roles of the government and local community to design green tourism strategies.

This chapter has pointed out that awareness or educational programmes on green tourism, the involvement and committment of multi-stakehoders as well as having sufficient funding and facilities are vital to support the practice of green tourism at Kinabalu National Park in Malaysia. However, in the transition to a green economy, Malaysia is facing a series of challenges which include the development of human resources in term of skills, knowledge and competencies and know-how for resource-efficient technologies for a green economy. Likewise, the implementation of green tourism development in Malaysia requires strong cooperation between federal and state authorities and stakeholders – the government, NGOs, private and higher learning institutions in terms of implementing appropriate policies, regulations and guidelines to strengthen green tourism development. Accordingly, the capacity-building programme in terms of human resources and local involvement is vital to support the implementation of green tourism in Malaysia (Bhuiyan *et al.*, 2012).

Acknowledgement

The funding for this project was made possible through a research grant obtained from the Ministry of Higher Education, Malaysia under the Long Term Research Grant Scheme 2011 [LRGS grant no: JPT.S (BPKI)2000/09/01/015Jld.4(67)]. Special thanks to Ms Tay Kai Xin who assisted in data collection.

References

Azam, M. and Sarker, T. (2011) Green tourism in the context of climate change towards sustainable economic development in the South Asian region? *Journal of Environmental Management and Tourism*, vol. 1, no. 3, pp. 6–15.

Bhuiyan, M.A.H., Siwar, C., Ismail, S.M. and Adham, K.N. (2012) *Green tourism for sustainable regional development in East Coast Economics Region (Ecer)*. Ontario International Development Agency.

Budeanu, A. (2007) Sustainable tourist behaviour: A discussion of opportunities for change. *International Journal of Consumer Studies*, vol. 31, no. 5, pp. 499–508.

Budeanu, A. (2009) Environmental supply chain management in tourism: The case of large tour operator. *Journal of Cleaner Production*, vol. 17, no. 16, pp. 1385–92

Buhalis, D. (2000) Relationships in the distribution channel of tourism: Conflicts between hoteliers and tour operators in the Mediterranean region. *International Journal of Hospitality and Tourism Administration*, vol. 1, no. 1, pp. 113–39.

Chun, S.S. (2006) A study on the demand for green tourism and training program for rural residents. *International Journal of Tourism Sciences*, vol. 6, no. 1, pp. 13–31.

Curtin, S. and Busby, G. (1999) Sustainable destination development: The tour operator perspective. *International Journal of Tourism Research*, vol. 1, no. 2, pp. 135–47.

Dodds, R. and Joppe, M. (2001) Promoting urban green tourism: The development of the other map of Toronto. *Journal of Vacation Marketing*, vol. 7, no. 3, pp. 261–7.

Font, X. and Tribe, J. (2001) Promoting green tourism: The future of environmental awards. *International Journal of Tourism Research*, vol. 3, no. 1, pp. 9–21.

Frey, N. and George, R. (2010) Responsible tourism management: The missing link between business owners' attitudes and behaviour in the Cape Town tourism industry. *Tourism Management*, vol. 31, no. 5, pp. 621–8.

Furqan, A., Som, A.P. and Hussin, R. (2010) Promoting green tourism for future sustainability. *Theoretical and Empirical Research in Urban Managment*, vol. 8, no. 17, pp. 64–74.

Khairat, G. and Maher, A. (2012) Integrating sustainbility into tour operator business: An innovative approach in sustainable tourism. *Tourismos: An international multidisciplinary journal of tourism*, vol. 7, no. 1, pp. 213–33.

Lynes, J.K. and Dredge, D. (2006) Going green: Motivations for environmental commitment in the airline industry: A case study of Scandinavian Airlines. *Journal of Sustainable Tourism*, vol. 14, no. 2, pp. 116–38.

Miller, G. (2001) Corporate responsibility in the UK tourism industry. *Tourism Management*, vol. 22, pp. 589–98.

Mitani, S. (1993) Green tourism, environmentally sound rural tourism in Japan: Recommendations for improvement of Japanese green tourism practices. www.arno.unimaas.nl/show.cgi?fid= 15252, accessed 30 May 2013.

Mitsuhashi, N. and Kim, J. (2007) A study on developing green-tourism in mountainous rural area of Japan: A case study of Ajimu District, Usa City, Oita Prefecture. www.ncl.ac.uk/cre/ research/ageing_countryside_UK_Japan_seminar.htm, accessed 30 May 2013.

PEMANDU (2010) *Economic transformation program*. Performance Management Unit, Prime Minister Department. Percetakan Nasional Malaysia Berhad: Kuala Lumpur.

Risteski, M., Kocevski, J. and Arnaudov, K. (2012) Spatial planning and sustainable tourism as basis for developing competitive tourist destinations. *Procedia – Social and Behavioral Sciences*, vol. 44, pp. 375–86.

Sasidharana, V., Sirakayab, E. and Kerstetter, D. (2002) Developing countries and tourism ecolabels. *Tourism Management*, vol. 23, pp. 161–74.

Scottish Enterprise Network (2002) *The green tourism agenda*. Natural Capital: Edinburgh.

Scottish Enterprise Network (2004) *Perspectives on international best practice green tourism*. Natural Capital: Edinburgh.

Siti-Nabiha, A., George, R., Wahid, N.A., Amran, A., Abustan, I. and Mahadi, R. (2011) A field survey of environmental initiatives at selected resorts in Malaysia. *World Applied Sciences Journal*, vol. 12, pp. 56–63.

UNEP (2005) *Integrating sustainability into business – A management guide for responsible tour operations*. United Nations: Paris.

UNEP and WTO (2011) Towards a green economy. In Pratt, L., Rivera, L. and Bien, A. (eds) *Tourism investing in energy and resource efficiency*. UNEP: Nairobi.

Waligo, V.M., Clarke, J. and Hawkins, R. (2013) Implementing sustainable tourism: A multistakeholders involvement management framework. *Tourism Management*, vol. 36, pp. 342–53.

WCED (1987) *Our common future*. Oxford University Press: Oxford.

Wijk, J.V. and Persoon, W. (2006) A long-haul destination: Sustainability reporting among tour operators. *European Managment Journal*, vol. 24, no. 6, pp. 381–95.

Williams, P. and Soutar, G.N. (2000) Dimensions of customer value and the tourism experience: An exploratory study. *Visionary Marketing for the 21st Century: Facing the Challenge*, vol. 28, pp. 1415–21.

Zhibo, D. (2012) The current situation of green tourism in China: 2012 International conference on affective computing and intelligent interaction. *Lecture Notes in Information Technology*, vol. 10, pp. 72–5. L.L. Jia: Taipei.

11

THE POTENTIAL OF ENERGY TOURISM

A multiple case study on renewable energy-based tourist attractions

Lena-Marie Lun, Michael Volgger and Harald Pechlaner

Introduction

> Fifteen years ago the subject of renewable energies was a mere niche topic, nowadays everybody is talking about it and for South Tyrol it represents an important flagship.
>
> (Member of a city administration; EURAC, 2012 [translation])

This quotation taken from the present study alludes to a current trend within the globally changing patterns of environment, economy and society. Increasingly confronted with the fundamental challenge to retain and enhance their competitiveness in the market, traditional and aspiring tourism destinations are picking up on this trend. Thus, at the interface of destination competitiveness (Ritchie and Crouch, 1993) and destination development (Butler, 1980), tourism research now strives to incorporate the aspect of sustainability (Butler, 1999).

Many discussions evolving around tourism and sustainability emphasize the mediatory and indirect role played by renewable energies in creating sustainable tourism (Michalena, 2008; Dalton *et al.*, 2009; Michalena and Tripanagnostopoulos, 2010). This oblique role refers to applying renewable energy technologies to implement low-carbon tourism – for example by constructing energy-efficient accommodation or providing sustainable means of transport. However, beyond these more general aspects, new niches in tourism have also arisen, such as energy tourism (Jiricka *et al.*, 2010). This niche focuses on the direct use of renewable energies as major elements of tourist attractions.

In the context of an increased transition towards a 'green economy' within Europe (EEA, 2010), renewable energy-based attractions may contribute to a green orientation also within the tourism system. Being a concept that is based on minimized carbon emissions, resource-efficiency as well as social inclusion (UNEP, 2011), a green economy requires innovative approaches throughout all segments of the economy. Thus, tourist attractions incorporating renewable energies can add to the process of reviewing economic paradigms.

The multiple case studies discussed here advances our knowledge about these recently emerging forms of energy tourism by critically looking at four examples of renewable energy-related tourist attractions. These include the currently planned *Klimaerlebniswelt* in Bolzano (South Tyrol, Italy), two established science centres – the *Klimahaus Bremerhaven 8°Ost* in Bremen (Germany), and the *Welios: Energie.Erlebnis.Haus* in Wels (Austria) – and the infotainment centre *Fertighauszentrum Blaue Lagune* in Wiener Neudorf (Austria). The four discussed tourist attractions share the ambition to help visitors directly experience ecological sustainability in the form of renewable energy production, soft mobility, and energy-efficient building.

By applying a mixed methods approach (Howe, 2004), we have tried to take adequate account of the complexity of the subject. The qualitative method contributes to better understanding of the contexts, preconditions and success factors in all four cases. However, we also conducted a quantitative analysis to estimate the potential demand for the case of the planned *Klimaerlebniswelt* in Bolzano.

Overall, we strive to critically assess the thematic focus of renewable energy-based attraction points, and provide an insight into the environmental, social, and economic preconditions and implications for successfully developing and managing such tourist attractions. Furthermore, we examine the existing demand for one of these attraction points, as well as the tourists' willingness to pay for it. In summary, this study tries to contribute to the concept of the 'green economy' approach in the field of tourism (Reddy, 2013).

Literature review

Tourist attractions

For decades, tourist attractions – a main motivation for travelling – have represented a core element of tourism research (Lew, 1987; Leiper, 1990; Wall, 1997; Peters and Weiermair, 2000; Swarbrooke, 2001; Richards, 2002). An early definition by Lew (1987, p. 554) identified tourist attractions as: '[. . .] all those elements of a "non_home" place that draw discretionary travelers away from their homes. They usually include landscapes to observe, activities to participate in, and experiences to remember.' However, Leiper (1990) has criticized this definition, and questioned the literal ability of attractions to influence the behaviour of visitors.

Research on their typology or classification accompanied the discussion on the definition of tourist attractions. Using the three elements 'nucleus', 'inviolate belt' and 'zone of closure', Gunn (1988, p. 49) applies a spatial approach to classifying attraction points and recommends paying attention to all three elements in order to attract the interest of visitors. MacCannell (1976, p. 41) suggests an even broader understanding of tourist attractions: 'I have defined a tourist attraction as an empirical relationship between a *tourist*, a *sight*, and a *marker* – a piece of information about a sight.' Leiper (1990) integrated the concepts of Gunn (1988) and MacCannell (1976) to set up an understanding of attraction systems that is still valuable. He suggested that tourist attractions are sub-systems, whose existence implies the interconnection of a human being, an informative element, and a nucleus as a central element (Leiper, 1990). Applying a demand perspective, he distinguished three types of nuclei:

(1) A primary nucleus, which directly influences a traveller's decision to visit a specific destination;
(2) A secondary nucleus, which is known beforehand by a traveller, but does not influence her/his itinerary;
(3) A tertiary nucleus, which is not known before a visit, but is discovered upon arrival at a destination (Leiper, 1990).

More recent publications focus on tourist attractions in the context of services and experiences, which research acknowledges as an opportunity to valorize attractions (Peters and Weiermair, 2000; Bieger et al., 2003; Bieger and Gräf, 2004). These authors argue that attraction points gain additional value by putting them into a scene, combining them with services, and developing them into a memorable experience for visitors.

'Worlds of experience' as tourist attractions

A focal point of tourism research has developed at the junction between tourism and experience (Pine II and Gilmore, 1999). Interactive involvement of visitors is gaining new importance within destination strategies since it can substantially contribute to enhancing products and offers. Furthermore, creating experiences at the convergence of tourism production and tourism consumption is a topic that has found its way into literature under the concept of 'experiencescapes' (O'Dell and Billing, 2005).

Destinations are increasingly trying to stand out by combining tourist attractions with experiences, meaning multifunctional establishments – which in German literature are summarized under the umbrella term *Erlebniswelten* (worlds of experience) (Franck and Roth, 2001; Hinterhuber and Pechlaner, 2001; Steinecke, 2001) – are gaining in importance. They appear as materializations of experience-based offers and are able to meet the visitor's desire for authenticity, individuality, and entertainment all at the same time. Thus, 'worlds of experience' coincide with the shifting demands of today's society. Steinecke (2001, p. 69 [translation]) understands 'the consumer's hunger for experiences as the central motor for the boom and acceptance of these establishments'.

The term 'world of experience' is associated with a multitude of different facilities, with science parks and infotainment centres, which we discuss below, being only two examples. The focus on spectacular offers, a clear profile, consistent management and administration, a well-known lead person, multifunctional packages, and hierarchical access can be identified as common success factors of 'worlds of experience' (Steinecke, 2001). 'Worlds of experience', moreover, have a wider strategic role within the territorial context of a destination. They tend to integrate into regional clusters and show a reciprocal relationship with these clusters. On the one hand, their development is often fundamentally influenced by these clusters, and on the other hand, their existence influences the development of clusters and destinations (Bieger, 2001).

In particular, when presenting technical or scientific topics – such as renewable energies – 'worlds of experience' can constitute a promising opportunity to attract visitors. According to Scherrieb (2003), they can provide a broad range of possibilities for transmitting a message to the audience, if their instigators accept that ultimately visitors are addicted to entertainment and not to learning. He argues that visitors should have the option to engage their own fantasy and imagination in order to make knowledge attractive in the long-term.

Sustainability- and renewable energy-based tourist attractions

Tourism in the context of sustainability has been widely discussed in the literature over the past 20 years (Pigram, 1990; Bramwell and Lane, 1993; Hall and Butler, 1995; Stabler, 1997; Butler, 1999; Liu, 2003; Reddy and Wilkes, 2012; Buckley, 2012). The definitions of sustainable tourism are manifold. For instance, Bramwell and Lane (1993, p. 2) define it as being 'a positive approach intended to reduce the tensions and friction created by the complex interactions between the tourism industry, visitors, the environment and the communities which are host to holidaymakers'. According to Prosser (1994), four societal forces drive the search for sustainability in tourism: dissatisfaction with existing products, growing environmental awareness and cultural sensitivity, the realization by destinations that they possess precious but vulnerable resources, and lastly the changing attitudes of developers and tour operators.

Tourism, being a phenomenon that basically deals with travelling from one place to another, as well as activities performed at these places, contributes to changing environments, society, and economy. Renewable energies, as a major topic in sustainability, are playing a growing role in the construction and running of tourism facilities. It is right to acknowledge that tourism managers are more and more trying to reduce the potential impacts of their activities on climate change.

Beyond that, tourist destinations also increasingly use the production and consumption of renewable energies as thematic pillars for tourist attractions. Especially in Germany, Austria and northern Italy, numerous initiatives, often called 'energy-regions', have emerged within the last few years. Such regions usually contain one or more renewable energy production site(s) and – based on this production site – try to promote renewable energies as an element of an attraction point (e.g. Energie in Südtirol, 2008; Könighofer, 2009; Regionales Energiekonzept ökoEnergieland, 2011; Bioenergie Regionen, 2012–15). Besides these 'energy-regions', single establishments such as science centres exist. These are not necessarily focused on a specific production site, but nevertheless use the ample theme of renewable energies as a core topic (e.g. Konzeptstudie Bremerhaven, 2009).

Renewable energies as a novel theme for business tourism and increasingly also for a wider public have also been discussed (Jiricka *et al.*, 2010). However, research on energy tourism and related attraction points is rather limited; hence this study tries to contribute further to this discussion.

Data and methodology

To best address the complexity of the subject 'renewable energy-based tourist attractions', we applied a research design based on mixed methods. In other words we followed the rationale of others in the field who define the task as requiring 'answers beyond simple numbers in a quantitative sense or words in a qualitative sense. A combination of both forms of data can provide the most complete analysis of problems.' (Creswell and Plano Clark, 2007, p. 13).

According to Creswell and Plano Clark (2007), mixing qualitative and quantitative data requires a systematic approach. One way of combining data comprises embedding qualitative into quantitative data, or vice versa, whereby one of the data types plays a subordinate role within the overall design (Creswell and Plano Clark, 2007). In this context, we applied a research design that embeds a quantitative part into a mainly qualitative study.

Qualitative approach

We discuss four cases of attraction points that use renewable energies and their manifold aspects as a central thematic element to develop a 'world of experience'. These cases are:

- *Klimahaus Bremerhaven 8°Ost*, a science centre located in Bremerhaven (Germany), which has attracted around 1,204,000 visitors per year since its opening in 2009, and whose core topics are climate, climate change, and renewable energies;
- *Welios: Energie.Erlebnis.Haus*, a science centre located in Wels (Austria), which has attracted around 100,000 visitors altogether since its opening in 2011, and whose core topic is renewable energy;
- *Fertighauszentrum Blaue Lagune*, which can be described as an infotainment centre, located in Wiener Neudorf (Austria), which has attracted around 200,000 visitors per year since its foundation in 1991/1992, and whose core topic is energy-efficient modular building;
- *Klimaerlebniswelt Südtirol*, a 'world of experience' based on the topic of renewable energies, which is currently planned for Bolzano (Autonomous Province of South Tyrol, Italy) and which is intended to become a core attraction point for a destination trying to position itself as a pioneer in the field of renewable energies.

To better understand the preconditions and implications of the four attraction points above, nineteen semi-structured interviews were conducted with selected stakeholders. These included representatives of the 'worlds of experience' as well as local representatives from different economic sectors, environmental organizations, public administration, and cultural or educational organizations. The interviews were conducted from May to June 2012 either face-to-face or by telephone.

Following a series of orientation questions, which were slightly adapted to the various interview partners, we asked the interviewees to give their opinions and estimations about several aspects. These included the current economic situation of the destination (with particular regard to tourism), the topic of sustainability and renewable energy-based tourist attractions, their potential positive or negative impacts, as well as success factors for developing such attraction points.

The interviews were recorded and transcribed. The analysis process was inspired by the qualitative content analysis of Mayring (2002). To reduce the complexity of the interviews' content, we defined three primary categories – general framework, positive effects, and challenges – and allocated all relevant references found within the interviews to these categories.

Quantitative approach

Embedded into the above-mentioned qualitative approach, we furthermore included a quantitative analysis; however this analysis was only applied to the case of the currently planned *Klimaerlebniswelt*. A survey, based on a standardized questionnaire, was aimed at obtaining data on the expected demand and potential resulting revenues of such an attraction point.

To account for the different target groups of such an attraction point – guests and residents – we implemented two different surveys. The first survey targeted guests, and thus focused on the two most promising source markets (Germany and Italy). Germany and Italy account for about 82 per cent of the guests visiting the region in question (ASTAT, 2013). The survey was representative of the population over 14 years old for Germany ($n = 500$) and over 15 for Italy ($n = 1,000$). It was intended to obtain information on the degree of interest in a renewable energy-based tourist attraction, on the importance of such an attraction point as a travel motive, and on the maximal willingness to pay for visiting it.

The second survey targeted the inhabitants of the region around the planned attraction point, South Tyrol, as well as the school directors of the South Tyrol and neighbouring region of Trentino. The two regions' pupils and students are considered to be interesting target groups for such an education-related attraction point. Additionally, currently sojourning tourists in the region of South Tyrol were also surveyed. In total, this second survey had a sample size of 384 (inhabitants: 150; school directors: 65; sojourning tourists: 165). Within this second survey – in addition to the interest, the importance of the travel motive, and the willingness to pay – we also asked about the respondent's interest in specific thematic areas, such as different types of renewable energies or sustainable mobility.

Renewable energy-based attraction points: success factors, impact and demand

Success factors and challenges of renewable energy-based tourist attractions

Results from the qualitative interviews suggest that renewable energy-based tourist attractions necessitate fundamental considerations regarding the target visitors. According to Jiricka *et al.* (2010), we can distinguish between expert-oriented and experience-oriented energy tourism, whereby the former aims at technology-seeking visitors and the latter at entertainment-seeking visitors.

Expert-oriented visitors, such as architects, designers, consultants, building contractors, and companies in general, represent a potential target group that in terms of numbers is significantly smaller than experience-oriented visitor groups. The latter target group has no particularly deep affinity with renewable energies and is mainly interested in interactively experiencing the topic. Thus, put bluntly, renewable energy-based tourist attractions that do not go into depth about technical details may be attractive for a higher number of visitors. However, results also show that attraction points that exclusively focus on expert-oriented visitors, such as the *Fertighauszentrum Blaue Lagune*, can be successfully established.

Additionally, the analysis of the interviews concerning the four scrutinized cases suggests that certain requirements and framework conditions ought to be fulfilled in order to render renewable energy-based attractions as thriving points for tourism:

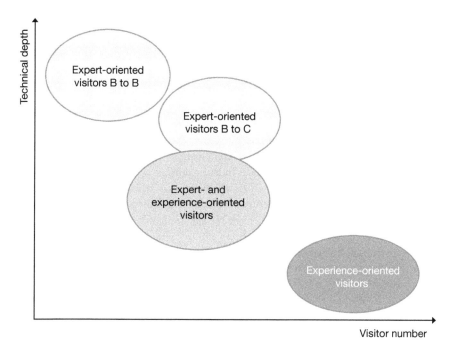

FIGURE 11.1 Expert-oriented versus experience-oriented energy tourism
Source: EURAC (2012)

- availability and integration of a strong partner network comprising companies, public administration, politics and media, and willingness of all partners to cooperate;
- taking into consideration the three aspects of location, strategic orientation, and management;
- logical and consistent embedding into the entire destination and urban/regional development strategies;
- establishing and preserving local authenticity and consistently implementing this authenticity within all products and offers;
- strong support from the private economic sector regarding long-term financing;
- outstanding and unique optical design;
- creating emotional experiences;
- collaborating with a professional marketing organization for all external communication.

The following quote from a representative of one of the case studies underlines these points: 'We cross-linked and synchronized with a lot of institutions and . . . thus have important collaboration partners on a scientific level, but we also cooperate closely with the local tourism organizations and with environmental educational institutions . . . and the whole sustainability branch' (CEO of one of the four analysed attraction points; EURAC, 2012 [translation]).

Findings indicate that the above-mentioned aspects, together with the decision to focus on either technology-seeking or entertainment-seeking visitors, represent essential success factors for implementing renewable energy-based attraction points.

Socio-economic impacts of renewable energy-based tourist attractions

The multiple case study indicates that renewable energy-based tourist attractions can represent a regional centre of competence that merges several key functions of regional and destination development: pooling of competences, awareness-raising among the population, local and international image-building, linkage of information, promotion of cultural identity, networking, and ultimately the creation of regional economic value. Successful renewable energy-based tourist attractions can act as trendsetters and customer magnets within a destination since they tend to positively influence the influx of visits to other attraction points of the destination.

Moreover, the destination and region not only profit from generating economic value through visitor arrivals and spending, but overall through the development of new workplaces, orders to local companies, and potentially also through increased export activities of these companies. Furthermore, the government also profits from increased tax revenues originating from these workplaces in the region. For instance, according to the managers, the *Klimahaus Bremerhaven 8°Ost* generated approximately 1.3 million euros in tax revenues within the first year of operation.

Additionally, renewable energy-based tourist attractions can also act as a centre of education for sustainable development. They are considered to be adequate, informal, and innovative learning environments and offer opportunities to raise awareness among young people about technical professions.

A representative of a 'world of experience' even indicated that: 'besides – and this can hardly be measured in a monetary way – there occurred a real shift of sentiments and a change in awareness among the inhabitants of the city since we opened' (CEO of one of the four analysed attraction points; EURAC, 2012 [translation]).

Growing into a competence centre, a renewable energy-based tourist attraction can launch a spearhead regarding the thematic positioning of a destination, not just from a tourism point of view, but concerning the entire orientation of a location's economy (cluster building). Through intensive cross-linking of green economy businesses, cooperation can be intensified and thus innovation, research, and development supported in the long term.

Interest in and willingness to pay for the Klimaerlebniswelt

The surveys on the German and Italian markets indicated that there is a high interest (willingness to visit) in the renewable energy-based tourist attraction *Klimaerlebniswelt* in South Tyrol, Italy. A total of 63 per cent of the surveyed Germans (representative of the population over 14 years old) and 50 per cent of the surveyed Italians (representative of the population over 15) declared an interest in visiting this attraction point. In this context, younger and higher-income groups showed a higher degree of interest than other groups.

A renewable energy-based attraction point such as the *Klimaerlebeniswelt* can fulfil all three functions of an attraction point (primary, secondary, and tertiary nucleus) as depicted by Leiper (1990; Figure 11.2). Indeed, the results suggest that a renewable energy-based tourist attraction, such as the planned *Klimaerlebniswelt*, represents – to a considerable extent – a direct travel motive. The results showed that 8.6 per cent of the German sample and 33 per cent of the Italian sample indicated that they would travel to South Tyrol especially to visit this attraction point. Another 19 per cent (German sample) and 30 per cent (Italian sample) acknowledge a lesser but still apparent influence on their willingness to visit the destination. Among the tourists surveyed while sojourning in South Tyrol, more than 90 per cent declared that they would (potentially) be willing to visit the *Klimaerlebniswelt*. Regarding local residents, the degree of willingness amounted to 90 per cent and for school directors up to 97 per cent.

The results from the quantitative study furthermore indicate that among all target groups a high interest in different thematic sub-areas prevails; overall the highest importance is attached to the subjects' 'generation of renewable energies', followed by 'sustainable mobility' and 'energy-efficient building'. For example, 73 per cent of the tourists surveyed while residing in South Tyrol stated that they had a high or medium interest in the thematic area 'generation of renewable energies'; for school directors this percentage was 87 per cent, and for residents, 75 per cent.

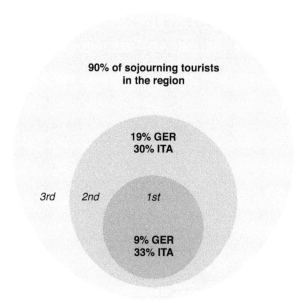

1st . . . directly influencing a traveler's decision to visit a specific destination (primary nucleus)
2nd . . . known beforehand to a traveler, but influencing his-her itinerary to a lesser degree (secondary nucleus)
3rd . . . not known before a visit, but discovered upon arrival in a destination (tertiary nucleus)

FIGURE 11.2 Attracting functions of renewable energy-based attraction points (using the *Klimaerlebniswelt* as an example)

Source: EURAC (2012)

Interestingly, among the types of renewable energies, 'solar energy', followed by 'hydroelectric power' and 'wind energy' generated the most interest. 'Geothermal energy' and 'biomass energy' aroused less interest. For example, 75 per cent of sojourning tourists, 79 per cent of residents, and 93 per cent of school directors pronounced a high or medium interest in 'solar energy'. Concerning different forms of sustainable mobility, overall, the interest in 'electric cars' ranked highest.

Taking into account the survey on German and Italian markets, respondents declared an average maximal willingness to pay an entrance fee of 10 euros per person (median value) for a 1-day experience at the planned renewable energy-based attraction *Klimaerlebniswelt*. We constructed a demand function for the attraction point (see Figure 11.3) and – considering the trade-off between visitor numbers and price – derived the highest revenues for entrance fees between 10 and 20 euros. Within this range, revenues were quite similar, reaching a peak with a relatively high entrance fee of 20 euros. Applying these prices, according to the survey, yearly visitor numbers reaching 800,000 to 1,000,000 people seem possible.

However, we call for cautionary interpretation of these numbers, since discrepancies generally arise between the declared willingness to use or pay (all the more if based on very limited information) and the actual decision to purchase a product or service (Völckner, 2005). Thus, these numbers tend to overestimate actual willingness to use and pay, and should be considered the ceiling of what is achievable. As a comparison, other successful attraction points in the region of South Tyrol (e.g. the Gardens of Trauttmansdorff with the integrated South Tyrol Museum of Tourism *Touriseum*; South Tyrol Museum of Archaeology with the *Iceman Ötzi* exhibits) attract 200,000 to 400,000 visitors per year. This would mean that the *Klimaerlebniswelt* would have the potential to become the most important attraction point of the region.

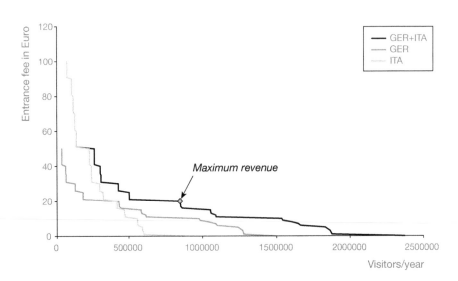

FIGURE 11.3 Estimated demand function for the *Klimaerlebniswelt* (extrapolated to potentially interested customers)

Source: EURAC (2012)

The other cases of renewable energy-related attraction points analysed here show in part even higher visitor numbers (e.g. more than 1.2 million for the *Klimahaus Bremerhaven* in Germany), or partly also lower numbers (e.g. 200,000 in the case of the *Fertighauszentrum Blaue Lagune* in Austria).

This wide range of (potential) visitor numbers is a key message from the multiple case study. As has been suggested by several interviewees, the differences depend on the scope of the target group (experience-oriented vs expert-oriented), the quality of the offer (contents, cutting-edge technology, optical presentation), logistics, management, and the quality of communication.

Conclusion

Taking into consideration the transition towards a green economy, this study contributes to evaluating the idea of using renewable energy-based attraction points for developing or enhancing green tourism within a destination. Combining a qualitative with a quantitative study within a multiple case study design, the study investigated some framework conditions for successfully developing and managing renewable energy-based tourist attractions. It further considered success factors, consequences, and demand structures – the latter in particular detail for the case of the planned *Klimaerlebniswelt* in Bozen/Bolzano (South Tyrol, Italy).

Beginning with the demand structure, all surveyed groups (local residents, sojourning and potential guests, and scholars/school directors) were interested or even highly interested in visiting a renewable energy-based attraction. In particular, younger and higher-income groups showed a high willingness to visit.

Renewable energy-based 'worlds of experience' exhibited high relevance as attraction points. They show similar (if not higher) potential for attracting people compared with offers such as museums. In detail, the collected survey data shows that renewable energy-based attraction points may play a role as primary, secondary, and tertiary nuclei (Leiper, 1990).

However, considerable variance exists in the actual and potential success of these attraction points. This clearly highlights the fact that renewable energy-based attractions are not self-propelling, but require a number of preconditions. First, reflections about target groups are critical. It seems wise to seriously consider both the expert-oriented (architects, planners, constructors, businesses, etc.) and experience-oriented target groups. Those cases that have managed this balancing act attest to higher success. The creation of 'worlds of experience' that can also target the emotional level and implement interactive elements might be a feasible approach in this context. These findings are consistent with the results of Jiricka *et al.* (2010).

Second, authenticity is critical. This means that a renewable energy-based attraction point needs to be integrated into the positioning of the destination and the strategies of regional development in a logical and consistent manner. A 'green region' might be a good context for integrating a renewable energy-based attraction. Moreover, being a cross-sectoral topic, it is crucial to establish or embed this into a strong interdisciplinary network that integrates specialized renewable energy industries with tourism (destination management organizations and single businesses) and public administration. Activating and maintaining such networks requires high governance efforts (Pechlaner and Volgger, 2012).

Third, both product quality and communication are critical. Product quality refers to the two elements of presenting up-to-date technology, and to the requirement of presenting it in an optically fashionable manner. Here, some topics such as producing renewable energies, sustainable mobility, and energy-efficient buildings seem to create more interest than others. Communication might mean collaborating with professional marketing organizations as well as integrating into the destination marketing.

When considering the results of this study, some limitations need to be taken into account. Various recognized methods – direct ones, such as the open-ended question format applied here, or indirect ones – exist for measuring a consumer's hypothetical willingness to pay. All these approaches are subject to considerable uncertainty in their results (Miller *et al.*, 2011). Moreover, discrepancies between indicated and actual willingness to pay and willingness to use or visit tourist attractions are quite common (Völckner, 2005). Since indications tend to exceed actual numbers, reported estimations regarding entrance fees and visitor numbers are likely to overestimate actual demand. In particular, interest in and the willingness to pay for the *Klimaerlebniswelt* in Bozen/Bolzano (South Tyrol, Italy) requires cautious interpretation because this particular attraction point is still in the phase of planning and has not yet been realized. Finally, despite the multiple case study design the number of analysed examples is rather small and restricted to central European countries. Thus, we can generalize the findings only to a limited extent.

> However, overall, the results of our multiple case study suggest that renewable energy-based tourist attractions seem to be an instrument to realize the potentials of energy tourism. Their effects may be positively judged from an economic point of view, but go well beyond that, and include education, and promotion of research and development . . .
> [T]his establishment is certainly our spearhead in the thematic positioning of the city and it has a certain image factor. . . . It is decisive for the future orientation and manifestation of our region's economy. . . . And it is also essential to encourage young people to embark on technically-oriented careers.
> (CEO of one of the four analysed attraction points;
> EURAC, 2012 [translation])

References

ASTAT (2013) *Tourismus in Südtirol. Tourismusjahr 2011/12*. Bozen/Bolzano.

Bieger, T. (2001) Von der Unternehmensperspektive zur Destinationsperspektive – integrierte strategische Planung für Erlebniswelten. In Hinterhuber, H.H., Pechlaner, H. and Matzler, K.(eds) *IndustrieErlebnisWelten. Vom Standort zur Destination* (pp. 21–33). Erich Schmidt: Berlin.

Bieger, T. and Gräf, H. (2004) Das Konzept Attraktionspunkte: Ein Innovationskonzept für standortgebundene Dienstleistungen. In Bruhn, M. and Strauss, B. (eds) *Dienstleistungs-innovationen* (pp. 497–525). Gabler Verlag: Wiesbaden.

Bieger, T., Laesser, C. and Bischof, L. (2003) Das Konzept, Attraktionspunkte –Theoretische Grundlagen und praktische Folgerungen. In Bieger, T. and Laesser, C. (eds) *Attraktionspunkte. Multioptionale Erlebniswelten für wettbewerbsfähige Standorte* (pp. 123–33). Haupt Verlag: Bern/ Stuttgart/Wien.

Bioenergie Regionen (2012–15) Vorhaben zum Aufbau regionaler Strukturen im Bereich Bioenergie. www.bioenergie-regionen.de/bioenergie-regionen-2012–2015/liste-der-21-bio energie-regionen/, accessed 5 July 2013.

Bramwell, B. and Lane, B. (1993) Sustainable tourism: An evolving global approach. *Journal of Sustainable Tourism*, vol. 1, no. 1, pp. 1–5.

Buckley, R. (2012) Sustainable tourism: Research and reality. *Annals of Tourism Research*, vol. 39, no. 2, pp. 528–46.

Butler, R.W. (1980) The concept of the tourist area lifecycle of evolution: implications for the management of resources. *Canadian Geographer*, vol. 24, pp. 5–12.

Butler, R.W. (1999) Sustainable tourism: A state_of_the_art review. *Tourism Geographies: An International Journal of Tourism Space, Place and Environment*, vol. 1, no. 1, pp. 7–25.

Creswell, J.W. and Plano Clark, V.L. (2007) *Designing and conducting mixed methods research*. Sage: Thousand Oaks, CA.

Dalton, G.J., Lockington, D.A. and Baldock, T.E. (2009) Case study feasibility analysis of renewable energy supply options for small to medium-sized tourist accommodations. *Renewable Energy*, vol. 34, no. 4, pp. 1134–44.

EEA (2010) *The European environment – state and outlook 2010: synthesis*. European Environment Agency: Copenhagen.www.eea.europa.eu/soer/synthesis/synthesis/at_download/file, accessed 8 January 2014.

Energie in Südtirol (2008) Südtirol: Zukunftsweisende Energiepolitik. Erneuerbare Energie im Aufwind. *Wirtschaft im Alpenraum*. September/October 2008, pp. 72–104, www.wianet.at/ uploads/tx_wiasonderthemenneu/Energie-Suedtirol-Homepage.pdf, accessed 5 July 2013.

EURAC (2012) *Klimaerlebniswelt Südtirol. Energie, Nachhaltigkeit und Innovation.Machbarkeitsstudie. Endbericht*. Study on behalf of the Autonomous Province of South Tyrol, Italy. European Academy of Bolzano, Institute for Regional Development and Location Management: Bolzano [unpublished document].

Franck, J. and Roth, E. (2001) Freizeit-Erlebnis-Konsumwelten: Trends und Perspektiven für den Tourismus in Deutschland. In Kreilkamp, E., Pechlaner, H. and Steinecke, A. (eds) *Gemachter oder gelebter Tourismus? Destinationsmanagement und Tourismuspolitik*. Linde Verlag: Wien. Vol. 3, pp. 89–99.

Gunn, C.A. (1988) *Vacationscape designing tourist regions*. Van Nostrand Reinhold: New York.

Hall, C.M. and Butler, R.W. (1995) In search of common ground: reflections on sustainability, complexity and process in the tourism system – a discussion between C. Michael Hall and Richard W. Butler. *Journal of Sustainable Tourism*, vol. 3, no. 2, pp. 99–105.

Hinterhuber, H.H. and Pechlaner, H. (2001) Mit Erlebniswelten in gesättigten Märkten neue Pionierphasen einleiten. In Hinterhuber, H.H., Pechlaner, H., and Matzler, K. (eds) *IndustrieErlebnisWelten. Vom Standort zur Destination.* (pp. 11–200. Erich Schmidt: Berlin.

Howe, K. (2004) A critique of experimentalism. *Qualitative Inquiry*, vol. 10, no. 4, pp. 42–61.

Jiricka, A., Salak, B., Eder, R., Arnberger, A. and Pröbstl, U. (2010) Energetic tourism: exploring the experience quality of renewable energies as a new sustainable tourism market. *Sustainable Tourism IV*, vol. 139, pp. 55–68.

Könighofer, K. (2009) Multifunktionales Energiezentrum Kötschach-Mauthen.Modellsystem zur Erreichung der Energieautarkie, *Berichte aus Energie- und Umweltforschung*, Nr. 60, Bundes-ministerium für Verkehr, Innovation und Technologie (ed), www.energiesystemederzu kunft.at/edz_pdf/0960_energiezenrum_koetschach_mauthen_edz-814146.pdf, accessed 5 July 2013.

Konzeptstudie Bremerhaven (2009) Konzeptstudie 'Klimastadt Bremerhaven' – Analysen, Perspektiven, Empfehlungen -Alfred-Wegener-Institut für Polar- und Meeresforschung,

Bremerhaven. www.bremerhaven.de/downloads/397/27498/Klimastadt_Bremerhaven.21488. pdf, accessed 5 July 2013.

Leiper, N. (1990) Tourist attraction systems. *Annals of Tourism Research*, vol. 17, pp. 367–84.

Lew, A.A. (1987) A framework of tourist attraction research. *Annals of Tourism Research*, vol. 14, pp. 553–75.

Liu, Z. (2003) Sustainable tourism development: a critique. *Journal of Sustainable Tourism*, vol. 11, no. 6, pp. 459–75.

MacCannell, D. (1976) *The tourist: A new theory of the leisure class.* Schoken Books: New York.

Mayring, P. (2002) *Einführung in die qualitative Sozialforschung: eine Anleitung zu qualitativem Denken*, 5. Aufl. Beltz: Weinheim/Basel.

Michalena, E. (2008) Using renewable energy as a tool to achieve tourism sustainability in Mediterranean islands. *Études caribéennes*, vol. 11.

Michalena, E. and Tripanagnostopoulos, Y. (2010) Contribution of the solar energy in the sustainable tourism development of the Mediterranean islands. *Renewable Energy*, vol. 35, pp. 667–73.

Miller, K.M., Hofstetter, R., Krohmer, H. and Zhang, J.Z. (2011) How should consumers' willingness to pay be measured? An empirical comparison of state-of-the-art approaches. *Journal of Marketing Research*, vol. 48, no. 1, pp. 172–84.

O'Dell, T. and Billing, P. (2005) *Experiencescapes: Tourism, culture and economy.* Copenhagen Business School Press: Copenhagen.

Pechlaner, H. and Volgger, M. (2012) How to promote cooperation in the hospitality industry: Generating practitioner-relevant knowledge using the GABEK qualitative research strategy. *International Journal of Contemporary Hospitality Management*, vol. 24, no. 6, pp. 925–45.

Peters, M. and Weiermair, K. (2000) Tourist attractions and attracted tourists: How to satisfy today's 'fickle' tourist clientele? *The Journal of Tourism Studies*, vol. 11, no. 1, pp. 22–9.

Pigram, J.J. (1990) Sustainable tourism: Policy considerations. *Journal of Tourism Studies*, vol. 1, no 2, pp. 2–9.

Pine II, B.J. and Gilmore, J.H. (1999) *The experience economy, work is theatre and every business a stage.* Harvard Business School Press: Boston, MA.

Prosser, R. (1994) Societal change and the growth in alternative tourism. In Cater, E. and Lowman, G. (eds), *Ecotourism: A sustainable option?* (pp. 19–37). John Wiley: Chichester.

Reddy, M.V. (2013) Global tourism and travel industry: Performance during the double-dip recession and recommendations for transition to a green economy, *The World Financial Review*, www.worldfinancialreview.com/?p=2740, accessed 5 July 2013.

Reddy, M.V. and Wilkes, K. (2012) (eds) *Tourism, climate change and sustainability.* Routledge: Abingdon.

Regionales Energiekonzept ökoEnergieland (2011) Klima- und Energie Modellregion, Europäisches Zentrum für erneuerbare Energie Güssing GmbH, www.oekoenergieland.at/images/Down loads/Modellregion/20101109_Umsetzungskonzept_oekoEnergieland_KLIEN.pdf, accessed 5 July 2013.

Richards, G. (2002) Tourism attraction systems. Exploring Cultural Behavior. *Annals of Tourism Research*, vol. 29, no. 4, pp. 1048–64.

Ritchie, J.R.B. and Crouch, G.I. (1993) Competitiveness in international tourism: A framework for understanding and analysis, *Proceedings of the 43rd Congress of the Association Internationale d'Experts Scientifique due Tourisme on Competitiveness of Long- Haul Tourist Destinations*, San Carlos de Bariloche, Argentina, October 17–23, pp. 23–71.

Scherrieb, H.R. (2003) Fallbeispiel 2: Inszenierung einer Landschaft – Schaffung von kleinen und grossen Erlebniswelten. In Bieger, T. and Laesser, C. (eds) *Attraktionspunkte. Multioptionale Erlebniswelten für wettbewerbsfähige Standorte* (pp. 123–33) Haupt Verlag: Bern/Stuttgart/Wien.

Stabler, M. (1997) *Tourism and sustainability: Principles to practice*. CAB International: Wallingford.

Steinecke, A. (2001) Erlebniswelten und Inszenierungen im Tourismus: Die Thematisierung des touristischen Raumes. In Kreilkamp, E., Pechlaner, H. and Steinecke, A. (eds) *Gemachter oder gelebter Tourismus? Destinationsmanagement und Tourismuspolitik* (pp. 67–87). Linde Verlag: Wien.

Swarbrooke, J. (2001) Key challenges for visitor attraction managers in the UK. *Journal of Leisure Property*, vol. 1, no. 4, pp. 318–36.

UNEP (2011) *Towards a green economy: Pathways to sustainable development and poverty eradication*. Green Economy Report, United Nations Environment Programme. www.unep.org/green economy, accessed 8 January 2014.

Völckner, F. (2005) Methoden zur Messung individueller Zahlungsbereitschaften: Ein Überblick zum State of the Art, *Research Papers on Marketing and Retailing*, vol. 30, Universität Hamburg: Hamburg.

Wall, G. (1997) Tourism attractions: points, lines, and areas. *Annals of Tourism Research*, vol. 24, no. 1, pp. 240–3.

12

ECO-CERTIFICATION AND LABELLING PROGRAMMES OF HOTELS IN CHINA

Policy perspectives for sustainable tourism and a 'greener' economy

Fu Jia and Ralph Wahnschafft

Introduction

In its Twelfth 5-Year Plan (2011–15), the Chinese government made a full-scale commitment to carry forward the concept of a 'green' economy. The tourism and hotel industry is widely recognized as one of the core economic sectors. Along with the increasing domestic demand for entertainment, leisure, tourism and related services, Chinese consumers now demand not only more but also better tourism and hotel services. At the same time, China also faces growing environmental challenges. Growing energy consumption, water scarcity, water and air pollution and waste pose many problems, including in tourist destinations. Various 'top down' regulatory measures, standards and programmes have been implemented by the national and local governments aiming at making China's hotels 'greener'. Meanwhile, hotels and their managers have also initiated their own resource-saving and cost-reduction programmes, thus contributing to the economic and environmental sustainability of the industry from the 'bottom up'. This chapter reflects on the importance of complementarity: A 'greener' economy will only be achievable if both public and private sectors work together, pursuing similar objectives and implementing compatible approaches.

At the outset, this chapter provides an overview of the contribution of the tourism sector and hotels to China's rapid economic growth. Then, the concerns over sustainability of the hotel industry are recounted through major stakeholders' perspectives, namely, the national policy-makers, the local policy-makers, the hotel owners and managers and tourist visitors and consumers. The hotel star-rating system and related policies are explained, together with the application of eco-certification and labelling programmes. Major international eco-certification programmes, including the International Standards Organization (ISO) standard system, EarthCheck, Green Globe, Green Key, The Sustainable Tourism Eco-Certification Program (STEP), Luxury Eco Certification Standard (LECS), and their adaptation in China are reviewed. Analysing the so-called 'top down' regulatory systems, the chapter also explains and compares the two main national Green Hotel rating systems, which are used far more widely throughout the country. Selected independent voluntary environmental conservation programmes, part of the 'bottom up' initiatives, are also discussed. Based on empirical studies, the chapter brings forward some prevailing perceptions and remaining issues of these programmes. It concludes with some recommendations for policy-makers and the industry in general which could facilitate further progress towards a 'greener' hotel industry in China.

Tourism services and hotels: contributing to China's rapid economic growth

Ever since China embarked on its economic reforms in the late 1970s, international inbound tourism has grown rapidly, often by double digits, year after year. Construction of international hotels boomed throughout the 1990s and beyond. Today, China's hotel industry comprises 12,038 star-rated hotels, with revenue in the first quarter of 2013 reaching 53.628 million RMB (approx. US$8.768 million) (National Tourism Administration of China – CNTA, 2013). The 2008 Olympic Games, 2010 Shanghai Expo and other large international conference events, trade fairs, business and educational programmes have regularly brought many visitors to China and to its unique and worldwide renowned tourist attractions. During more recent years, the country has seen some levelling off in the arrivals of foreign tourists. The global economic and financial crisis, as well as public health issues such as the Severe Acute Respiratory Syndrome (SARS) and the Influenza A (H1N1) epidemic, temporarily posed serious challenges for China's tourism industries. Today, however, new tourist markets are emerging, resulting again in an increase in international visitors to China. It is estimated that approximately 137 million visitors entered China in 2013, with the expenditure reaching around US$49.3 billion (China Economic Information Network, 2013). Recent tourism trends include growing diversification in tourist activities and experiences, development of new destinations and new services, such as ecotourism, in order to cater for more affluent international visitors.

Rapid urbanization, modernization and economic expansion in China have lifted millions of people out of poverty and have created a rapidly growing middle class, as well as a wealthy business elite. Together with the growth in disposable incomes, demand for entertainment and leisure, tourism and related services have all grown tremendously. In 2012, China's 1.35 billion inhabitants (not including residents of Hong Kong SAR, Macao and Taiwan) undertook 2.96 billion trips (approx. 2.2 trips per person per year) (National Bureau of Statistics of China, 2013). Much of the domestic travel occurs during public holiday periods and mostly comprises family visits. However, China's domestic market for commercial tourism services may soon become the largest in the world. Today, Chinese consumers demand not only more but also better tourism services. This trend is expected by many to continue well into the future. Today, the Chinese middle class is already larger than the entire population of the United States. In 15 years, the Chinese middle class is expected to reach 800 million (Thraenhart *et al.*, 2012). China's outbound tourism is also seen by many as a vibrant and expanding market for the years to come.

Concerns over sustainability of international and domestic tourism in China

As economic progress unfolds, China also faces growing natural resource constraints and environmental challenges. Scarcity of drinking water, water and air pollution, waste disposal and wastewater management already pose serious problems in several cities around the country, including tourist destinations. Statistics show that per capita water and energy/electricity consumption of hotel guests is typically much higher than the average per capita consumption in the residential sector. According to the China Hotel Association, the average electricity consumption per unit of floor area of hotels is ten times higher than that of urban residential areas, while water consumption is five times higher. More luxurious forms of consumption and continuously increasing demand of hotels for energy and food are also widely seen as contributing to long-term price increases.

Large hotels can generate considerable amounts of additional traffic and local waste streams, for which adequate local infrastructure may not always exist. Enhancing sustainability in tourism is a globally agreed goal, most recently reaffirmed at the Rio+20 United Nations Conference on Sustainable Development (United Nations General Assembly Resolution, 2012). However, analysing and addressing the challenges and identifying feasible and acceptable ways to enhance sustainability in the hotel sector requires comprehensive local and national studies, as well as stakeholder consultations and prudent policy decision-making, which this chapter hopes to facilitate.

For *national policy-makers* seeking to promote a 'greener' economy, one of the main tasks is to develop a regulatory framework that supports the expansion of the national hotel and tourist industry, but also ensures its efficient use of resources while minimizing environmental impacts. Local employment opportunities are also important concerns. In China, sustainable tourism development has been identified as an important area for policy-making ever since 1992, the year which the National Tourist Administration declared 'Friendly Sightseeing Year'.

For *local policy-makers*, one of the main challenges is to enhance the attractiveness of the locality for tourists, particularly in areas where destinations compete for visitor attention and tourist expenditure. In addition to ensuring adequate local infrastructure as well as public security and safety, close cooperation with local businesses and coordinated public relations will always be essential, in particular for successful destination marketing.

For *hotel owners and managers*, tourist customer satisfaction and the successful marketing of tourist services is imperative. Whereas high-end hotels emphasize comfort, services, wellness and exclusivity, managers of budget tourist accommodation attract their customers with competitive prices. In China, as in many other countries, hoteliers observe and anticipate tourism development trends, including an expected greater demand for 'greener' hotels. However, hoteliers also observe that a large number of the tourists who perceive themselves as 'green' are rarely willing to compromise on location, comfort or price. Hence, hoteliers have to decide which environmental protection measures to implement and how best to publicize their 'green' hotel measures, if they decide to do so.

Tourist visitors/consumers have the choice to reflect on their preferences as they plan their tourist activities and programmes. At the time that tourists are making their reservation decisions, most of them do not as yet know what product or what level of service to expect. Independent quality ratings, including ratings of hotel facilities and services, have an important role to play in providing market transparency. Star rating systems are a common measure used to rate hotel facilities. Star rating systems are typically designed and administered by government authorities in collaboration with the concerned industry associations. In addition, a considerable number of national and international 'green hotel' rating and eco-labelling programmes have emerged which aim to provide (prospective) hotel guests with assurance of adherence to sustainability and environmental principles, concepts and measures.

This chapter provides a brief analytical overview of the evolving hotel rating systems in China, in particular with regard to the aforementioned sustainability concerns. It is based on information collected and reviewed during desk research, internet searches and telephonic and in-depth on-site interviews with regulatory entities, hotel management and guests in several Chinese cities, including Beijing, Shanghai, Tianjin, Kunming, Hangzhou and Ningbo. The chapter places particular emphasis on the more recent Chinese domestic 'Green Hotel' eco-certification and eco-labelling programmes which have thus far received only limited recognition beyond China.

Hotel classification and star rating systems in China

A hotel classification and star rating system, namely, the antetype of the current Classification & Accreditation for Star-rated Tourist Hotels was first introduced in China in 1988 with a focus on those hotels licensed to accommodate foreign visitors. The rating system was subsequently revised and improved several times, respectively in 1993, 1997, 2003 and 2010. Star rated hotels are those which have been certified by the National Tourism Administration of China (CNTA). Star rated hotels typically provide better facilities and services than non-rated hotels. Hotels are rated as one, two, three, four or five star hotels.

Since 2003, the star rating system has applied to all hotels, not just to hotels that were approved for hosting foreign guests. Furthermore, a new 'platinum 5-Star' level was added over and above all other levels. During recent years CNTA and other authorities have more vigorously implemented follow-up checks to confirm compliance with the rating system. Various media reports have indicated that a number of hotels were stripped of their star ratings due to violations or non-compliance.

The analysis of the CNTA databank suggests a number of recent industry trends which can be summarized as follows: (a) China's hotel industry has grown continuously, in particular in the up-market categories. (b) China's hotel industry is also increasingly diversifying. Today, accommodation services are provided not only by a growing number of large and small chain hotels, but also by serviced apartments/apart-hotels, boutique hotels, economy hotels, budget hotels, youth hotels, hostels, inns, motels, guesthouses and some other forms of privately rented accommodation. (c) Together with the rapid expansion of accommodation capacities, average hotel occupancy rates have tended to decline.

Between 2003 and 2010, the hotel rating system and the criteria used have evolved considerably. In addition to assessing the facilities, other aspects such as environmental protection and emergency preparedness are also considered. However, the star rating

---

BOX 12.1 KEY FACTS OF CHINA'S HOTEL INDUSTRY IN THE ELEVENTH 5-YEAR PLAN PERIOD (2005–2010)[1]

- China registered 13,991 star rated hotels at the end of 2010, including 595 5-star hotels, 2,219 4-star hotels and 6,268 3-star hotels (CNTA, 2010).
- Between 2005 and 2010 the room inventory of star rated hotels grew by an average of 6.3 per cent per year. Growing at an annual average rate of 16 per cent, the increase in the 5-star category outpaced other categories.
- Star rated hotels comprised 28 per cent of China's registered tourism enterprises, accounting for 53 per cent of fixed assets, 40 per cent of operating revenues and 61 per cent of employment, generating 72 per cent of business tax revenues.
- About 1,000 of the hotel properties are associated with one or another hotel chain. There are currently some seventy hotel brands in China, including forty international hotel chains. Several of the domestic Chinese hotel brands have started to gain international recognition.
- The revenue per available room (RevPAR) and gross operating profit (GOP) of 5-star hotels operated by domestic hotel groups has improved and is now comparable to those of the international hotel groups.

---

system does not provide customers with information on hotel sustainability projects or initiatives. Hence, both hotel operators competing in an increasingly competitive market place and hotel guests concerned with environmental conservation may find separate eco-labelling informative and useful.

International eco-certification programmes of hotels in China

Certification of the International Standards Organization for the hospitality industry

The ISO has established a number of general global quality and environmental management standards for manufacturing and service industries which are also applied in the hospitality industry. The relevant ISO standards are ISO 9001 (quality management), ISO 14001 (environmental management), OHSAS 18001 (occupational health and safety), as well as ISO 22000 (food safety standard).

The ISO 14001 certification was published in 1996 and amended in 2004. It provides a road map for companies seeking to improve their operational efficiency and environmental credentials. Under the ISO guidelines, licensed auditors are invited to assess the environmental performance of participating companies. Audits may include measurement of energy consumption, recycling efforts and other aspects. Participating hotels are obliged to periodically retake on-site audits if they wish to remain certified.

One of the main institutions overseeing ISO quality assessment in China is the China Environmental United Certification Center (CEC). ISO Certification is popular among companies engaged in international trade. A considerable number of hotels in China participate in the ISO assessment and certification process and many of them announce their certification on their respective hotel websites. Ibis Hotels China Headquarters and its first three hotels in Beijing, Shanghai and Wuxi reportedly obtained ISO 9001 certification in June 2009, making Ibis the first ISO certified economy hotel chain in China. Fourteen more Ibis hotels are scheduled to obtain ISO certification in the near future (Accor Greater China Communications Team, 2013).

International eco-certification and eco-labelling programmes used by hotels in China

Eco-certification and eco-labelling means any programme that offers a 'logo' or a 'marketing brand' that leads the consumer to believe that their choice of accommodation implements good environmental practices (Honey, 2002). Eco-certification schemes are mostly created by private companies, as well as by non-governmental or non-profit organizations. Like the ISO certification programmes, private eco-certification and labelling depend entirely on the voluntary participation of hotels.

Certification schemes can be distinguished by their method. While process-based certification schemes set up a system for monitoring and improving performance, performance-based methods state the goals or targets that must be achieved before any certification is issued. Most of the more widely used private eco-certification schemes are process-based schemes which allow participating companies to use their eco-labels as soon as they meet the minimum requirements and commit to performance improvements over time. Various hybrid schemes combining elements of both methods can also be found.

Most eco-certification programmes charge an enrolment or a membership fee. Fees are used to cover administrative costs and to support advertising and promotion of the logo or the label. On-site assessments by independent auditing experts are typically charged separately. Some programmes stagger their fees according to the assessed volume of business of their clients. Larger hotels are expected to pay higher fees for the use of the eco-label.

Today, there exist a considerable number of local, national and international 'green' hotel rating and certification programmes, mostly in Europe, North America and other countries of the Organisation for Economic Co-operation and Development (OECD). Many of these programmes were launched in the wake of the 1992 Rio Earth Summit. A study undertaken by ECOTRANS for the World Tourism Organization in 2001 found no less than 104 voluntary eco-labelling, eco-awards and eco self-commitment programmes, all aimed at enhancing sustainability in tourism-related services (UNWTO, 2002). This chapter discusses only those programmes that have issued certifications to hotels in China.

Founded in 1987, EarthCheck is one of the oldest and most widely applied private environmental standards and eco-labelling systems for the hospitality industry.[2] EarthCheck is a voluntary performance-based programme. It monitors the hotel performance in terms of water and energy consumption, waste management, paper use, pesticide use, cleaning and hygiene product use, as well as local community involvement. Hotels that implement a plan of action and practical measures to improve their performance and achieve the goals set by EarthCheck will receive certification. Hotels are inspected by independent auditors. The EarthCheck certification is not permanent and can be withdrawn if the hotel does not continue its efforts on a regular basis.

Today, more than a thousand hotel and other tourism business operators in more than sixty countries hold EarthCheck compliance certifications, including some fifty up-market hotel properties in China, most of which are associated with international hotel chains, such as Crown Plaza, Holiday Inn, Intercontinental, Radisson Plaza, Shangri-La Hotels, Novotel and Traders Hotels.

Green Globe is also a globally operating sustainable tourism certification company.[3] Green Globe is an affiliate member of the United Nations World Tourism Organization (UNWTO) and is partly owned by the World Travel and Tourism Council (WTTC). Green Globe offers environmental certification not only to hotels, but also to other travel-related enterprises, including airports. The EarthCheck and the Green Globe eco-certification programmes cooperated closely in the past, however, more recent announcements issued in 2010 and thereafter suggest that the two programmes intend to pursue their marketing more independently in the future.

Green Globe International, Inc. announced in August 2011 that it had received the registration certificate from China's trademark registry, which is valid until December 2020. Thus, the Green Globe eco-certification and labelling programme can be expected to expand in China in the months and years ahead.

There are also two international eco-certification and labelling programmes under the name Green Key. One of these programmes is hosted by the Danish non-profit organization Foundation for Environment Education (FEE). Its participants and clients are mostly located in Europe and include hotels associated with hotel brands such as Radisson Blu, Park Inn, Rezidor, Starwood and others. The Danish Green Key programme does not operate in North America.

The second Green Key programme operates mostly in North America. It was launched in 1997. Membership of the programme includes some 3,000 hotel properties, mostly in Canada and the United States, as well as in a growing number of other countries.[4] At the time of the research for this study, neither of the two Green Key eco-certification and labelling programmes were operating in China.

STEP was launched in 2007 by Sustainable Travel International (STI). Since the beginning of 2012 the STEP process has officially been recognized by the Global Sustainable Tourism Council (GSTC). STEP is currently certifying hotels in the United States, Canada, the United Kingdom, Australia and Brazil. Applicants can decide at what level they want to be certified. To date, only a few dozen companies and chain hotels have gone through the STEP process. Only a few properties in China are STEP certified. Most of these are located in Taiwan Province of China.[5] Beyond eco-certification, STI also provides travel assistance, booking and other services primarily to 'green-minded' travellers.

STI has also launched a separate certification programme for luxury properties, focusing on 5-star hotels. Taking into account the special challenges facing high-end properties that seek to go 'green', STI has developed a stringent but achievable LECS. LECS certification requires an on-site audit. According to the company's website, a total of sixty-one 5-star hotels located in different cities of China are participating in the auditing programme administered by Leading Quality Assurance (LQA), an STI subsidiary.[6]

There are still several more eco-certification and labelling programmes, including Green Leaf, Green Seal, Travelife, EU Eco-Label, among others. These programmes play a role in other important national or regional markets, mostly in North America and Europe, but can rarely be found in China. Hence, they are not further discussed in this chapter.

Private, commercial eco-certification and eco-labelling programmes have not as yet been able to gain a very significant market share in the Chinese hotel industry. Only less than 4 per cent of the star-rated hotels in China hold one or other form of international private commercial eco-certification. Most hotels that do so are in the up-market category, notably 4-star and 5-star hotel properties, which are often associated with international hotel brands.

Managers of hotels that primarily cater for domestic business travellers and tourists may implement their own environmental conservation and cost-reduction programmes but appear to be less interested in international certification, in part because of communication difficulties and the costs involved, and in part because most international eco-labelling programmes do not as yet seem to offer a Chinese language equivalent of their labels. EarthCheck is reportedly considering providing its label in Chinese. However, as long as most domestic travellers are not yet familiar with foreign hotel eco-labels and their meaning, there is little commercial incentive for hotels to acquire them.

Chinese 'green hotel' rating and certification programmes

The China green hotel rating system

The first initiative to introduce a 'green hotel' rating system in China dates back to 2003 and to the publication of China Hotel Association's standards for 'green' hotels. In 2005, the State Council called for the setting up of a more stringent nationwide 'green hotel' rating and certification system. The programme was subsequently developed by the Ministry of Commerce, the National Development and Reform Commission (NDRC), the Ministry of Environmental Protection, the Standardization Administration, the State-owned Assets Supervision and Administration Commission, the National Tourist Administration and China Hotel Association.

The Green Hotel regulation GB/T21084 was drafted in 2007 by the aforementioned entities and became effective on 1 March 2008. A National Green Hotel Committee was established in 2008 to guide and oversee implementation of the regulations. In addition, several subsidiary working groups were established at the provincial level.

Application procedures are similar to those governing the ISO 14000 Environmental Management System: hotels submit applications on a voluntary basis. The assessment

---

BOX 12.2 MEASURES REQUIRED BY THE CHINA GREEN HOTEL RATING SYSTEM[7]

- Installation of meters to monitor energy and water consumption and conduct energy audits. Indoor temperatures in common areas are recommended to be kept at no lower than 26°C during summer time, and no higher than 20°C in winter time.
- Reduction in use of packaging and disposable products, including reduced frequency of changing towels and bed sheets (unless requested otherwise by guests) and using paper-smart technologies.
- Compliance with national and regional standards on the discharge of pollutants and emissions, including reducing and separating solid waste, handing over hazardous waste and recyclable materials to qualified agents for disposal or recycling and applying only organic fertilizer and natural insecticidal methods.
- Promotion of public health by offering non-smoking rooms and floors and ensuring good ventilation and insulation of walls, doors and windows, offering relative humidity for the indoor climate, providing clean drinking water and daily disinfection of toilet equipment and facilities.

---

institution determines a rating, which is communicated to the applicant within a short period of time. Hotels are encouraged to undertake self-assessments. Hotels may then apply for on-site inspections which are carried out by independent professional assessors. All hotels that pass the on-site assessment will be granted official approval in the form of a plaque and a certification. Hotels will need to pay an initial application fee (4000 Yuan RMB or approx. US$ 700, at the time of the preparation of this study) which includes an on-site inspection and the later issuing of a plaque and a certificate. Hotels are also responsible for the travel costs of auditors. The eco-certification typically remains valid for a period of 4 years and reviews are carried out every 2 years. The plaque and the certificate are meant to be displayed for the information of (prospective) hotel guests. The Green Hotel certification scheme differentiates five levels of achievement symbolized by the number of ginkgo leaves in the certification, with five leaves representing the highest level. In addition, the programme also seeks to assess and promote the 'greening' of hotel and restaurant supply chains.

A first *China Green Hotel Development Report* assessing the impact of the programme was released in 2010. According to the report, about 700 hotels had been certified as Green Hotels under the China Green Hotels Certification Programme. A nationwide survey was also carried out in 2011 in an attempt to quantify actual achievements. The survey estimated that the water consumption saved in 2010 equalled about 1.5 times the volume of West Lake (approx. 15.45 million m³), and the electricity consumption saved was equal to 5 months' electricity consumption of a medium-sized Chinese city (National Green Hotel Committee, 2011).

FIGURE 12.1 Sample plaque of China Green Hotel[8]

The China Green Tourist Hotel rating system

During recent years, a similar yet different hotel eco-certification and eco-labelling programme has emerged in China, largely based on a regional initiative of the Zhejiang Province of China. This standard is primarily based on Zhejiang Province Standard LB/T007–2006 and was activated on 23 March 2006. The standard differentiates between 'Golden Leaf Level' and 'Silver Leaf Level'. The application is open to tourist hotels having been in operation for 1 year. Once granted, the certificate is valid for a 5-year period. Upon expiry, a reassessment and re-certification may take place upon the request of the hotels. The China Tourist Hotel Star-rating Committee is the executing agency of the programme. As of August 2012, a total of 2,439 hotels – equivalent to nearly 20 per cent of all hotels in China – had been issued with China Green Tourist Hotel certifications (806 'Golden Leaf' and 1,633 'Silver Leaf'), with Jiangsu Province, Beijing and Shanghai having the most certified hotels. Notably, almost all 'Golden Leaf' hotels are star-rated hotels, while some 'Silver Leaf' holders are not.

Comparative assessment of the two China Green Hotels certification programmes

While the two hotel eco-certification programmes are comparable in terms of their requirements concerning water quality, waste water disposal, air quality and air pollution from boilers, there are also several differences. The China Green Hotel system attaches relatively more importance to energy conservation, food safety and occupational health and safety, while the China Green Tourist Hotel programme is more

FIGURE 12.2 Sample plaque of China Green Tourist Hotel[9]

specific and more demanding with regard to efficiency of electricity use and solid waste management.

While the China Green Hotel eco-certification programme secured only some 700 hotels as subscribers over its start-up period of the first few years, the parallel China Green Tourist Hotel eco-certification scheme secured more than three times as many participants. The China Green Tourist Hotel programme appears to be more flexible in terms of implementation, enjoying significantly greater acceptance by the hotel industry, especially star rated hotels.

Under both programmes, most of the certified hotels are located in the main cities, in the more affluent provinces and along the eastern and southern coasts. In smaller cities and towns, in the northern and western provinces, eco-certification of hotels is still more of an exception.

In some resort areas, such as on Hainan Island and in some cities where tourism plays a more prominent role in the local economy, such as in Guangxi Province, some local hotel industry associations can be observed actively advocating the 'greening' of existing and new hotels.

Additional efforts are currently under way to further promote the uptake of both programmes. The China Hotel Association has identified the 'greening' of hotels as a priority for the ongoing Twelfth 5-Year Plan period. In 2010, a first China Green Hotel Expo was organized in Beijing to promote new concepts for 'green' hotel designs. The China Green Hotel Committee recently also launched a nationwide campaign to promote low-carbon tourism and environmental protection. Some one hundred certified green hotels participated in the campaign, attracting the attention of the public and social media, and raising the environmental awareness of Chinese consumers.

Hotel environmental conservation programmes without certification

A considerable number of hotels in China are also implementing their own independent voluntary resource conservation programmes from the 'bottom up' without taking part in any external eco-certification, or without advertising any logos, even if they would be entitled to do it.

As in other countries, China has a growing number of resorts and boutique hotels which offer unique travel or accommodation experiences. Such hotels are often located within or near important historic, scenic, natural or cultural sites of touristic interest. The management of up-market hotels in such locations is typically more aware of the potential environmental concerns of their guests. Some of these resorts articulate their environmental protection programmes in detail in their promotional materials, on their websites and in the guestrooms. In this case, eco-certification can be considered dispensable. There are also some specialist hotels that function as technology demonstration centres, providing commercial accommodation at the same time. The Himin Solar Valley Micro-Emission Hotel in Dezhou, Shandong Province, is one such example.[10] Other examples of unusual hotel design are the 5-star Xiang Xiang Xiang Pray House Hotel near Changzhi, which was built from shipping containers, and the Crosswaters Ecolodge near Nankun Mountain National Park, Guangzhou, which was designed by ecolodge architecture specialist Hitesh Metha in accordance with Feng Shui principles, using mostly bamboo and other locally available building materials.[11]

Some international hotel chains have also established their own trademark to characterize and publicize their environmental policies and programmes. The Accor hotel chain, for example, launched its own 'Planet 21' Sustainability Programme, which has its own logo. The designated cost-saving and resource-conservation measures are implemented by most of the hotels associated with the chain, including its associated properties in China (Accor Greater China Communications Team, 2013). Most hotels of the Accor Hotel Group are still independently eco-certified, but the creation of their own brand names can save operators payment of recurrent inspection and eco-labelling subscription fees.

Empirical studies: prevailing perceptions and remaining issues

One of the co-authors conducted more than twenty in-depth interviews with senior hotel management staff with a view to assessing prevailing perceptions on eco-certification and eco-labelling programmes. The feedback received from hotel industry representatives is summarized below.

- Insufficient commitment and financial support from governments was often cited as one reason for a comparatively slow dissemination and uptake of the 'green hotel' programmes in China. At present, all programme costs of assessments and eco-certification are covered by the hotel industry itself. Several hotel managers expressed an expectation of greater recognition of their own voluntary and independent 'bottom up' initiatives and good practices.

- Flexibility and adaptation of eco-certification standards to local conditions: Given that China is a very large country with varying regional and local climatic conditions and resources, it will be essential to further explore possibilities for a more flexible adaptation of national standards to local conditions. Some hotels reported difficulties in achieving established standards, goals and targets. Beyond national standardization, eco-certification programmes could allow, and perhaps encourage, appropriate adjustments by participating companies.
- Balancing guest satisfaction and environmental performance: Hotel management and staff interviewed for this project regularly pointed out the challenge of meeting expectations of hotel guests in a sustainable manner. In particular, the managers and staff of the more up-market hotels noted that providing quality services for tourists intrinsically requires more resources. 'Green hotel' programmes are therefore clearly not acceptable for the hotel industry concerned if they include any measures that might compromise the comfort of hotel guests.

Conclusions and recommendations

Recent reforms of the general star rating system for hotels in China and the more rigorous control of its correct implementation have greatly helped to provide market transparency and enabled consumers to make more informed choices.

Throughout China, hotels and their management can be observed striving to upgrade facilities and services with a view to improving sales and revenues in an increasingly competitive market.

Even though eco-certification and eco-labelling of hotels is still a rather new concept for China, the related programmes, and in particular the recently launched national China Green Hotel and China Green Tourist Hotel programmes, have rapidly gained popularity. In total, nearly 30 per cent of all star rated hotels in China hold one or other type of eco-certification.

In China, the national eco-certification and eco-labelling programmes are significantly more important than the international ones. The national campaigns to make the hotel and tourism industries in China more environmentally conscious and 'greener' have been met with considerable enthusiasm and success, however, a variety of additional policies and practical measures could still be considered to further enhance the sustainability of the hotel and tourism sector. These could include some of the following:

- Incentivizing greater participation: Notwithstanding the active participation in general, there still remains a considerable number of hotels that do not participate in the 'green hotels' programme as yet. Hence, the government of China and its national, regional and local authorities might consider providing some direct or indirect incentives to encourage additional participants to join the programmes. Such measures could include tax credits or other forms of subsidies which can make environmental audits less costly and, therefore, more acceptable.

- Dialogue with management of hotel chains and hotel business associations: Advocacy aimed at motivating newcomers to join the 'green hotel' campaigns may give priority attention to the dialogue with management of hotel chains and hotel business associations. The largest Chinese hotel chains are Home Inns and Hotel Management (848 properties), Green Tree Hotel (600 properties), China Lodging Group (including Hanting Hotels and Inns) (580 properties), 7 Days Inn (568 properties), Jinjiang Inns (400 properties) and Jinjiang Hotels (346 properties) (Tophotelprojects, n.d.). Several of the Chinese hotel chains have already signalled their intention to improve their environmental performance.

- Raising public awareness of more sustainable consumption patterns: In March 2013, a China Green Hotels Conference was held in Sanya, Hainan Island, to launch an informative report on energy-saving and emission-reduction measures implemented by 100 green hotels, also intended as a contribution to the Global Reporting Initiative (Meadin, 2012). These and similar environmental education and awareness campaigns can significantly stimulate domestic demand for 'greener' hotels.

- Continuous development of industry standards and capacity building: Hotel industry standards may periodically be reviewed and amended in line with technology and policy development. At the above-mentioned conference, a first proposal for a national standard to regulate carbon emissions of the hotel industry was reportedly presented and discussed (National Green Hotel Committee, 2013a). The China Green Hotel Development Report 2013 also includes a detailed listing of energy-saving options, including equipment and suppliers and technical guidance (National Green Hotel Committee, 2013b). The National Green Hotel Committee periodically also offers related training programmes.

- Dialogue with hotel companies engaged in hotel modernization and new hotel construction: At almost any given time, there are approximately 500 or more ongoing or planned hotel modernization, expansion or new construction projects in China. In 2011, many major new projects were inaugurated, including one of the largest hotel projects in China, the Sanya Beauty Crown Hotel on Hainan Island, which is expected to feature 6,000 rooms, once fully completed. Installations for indoor temperature, climate and illumination control, as well as energy and water conservation are comparatively inexpensive if already considered during building design and construction. Wherever possible, advocacy aimed at 'greener' hotel buildings should seek opportunities for dialogue with hotel property developers, architects and building designers at an early stage of project planning.

- Dialogue with online hotel booking platforms: Online booking platforms, such as Ctrip, Elong and others, are significant and influential stakeholders in the Chinese tourist hotel market. At present, only a few specialized online hotel booking platforms provide consumers with information on environmental performance. Eco-certification of hotels could reach a much higher level of importance if online booking platforms were to include eco-labels in their product information.

- Consideration of mandatory eco-certification for specific environmentally sensitive tourist regions: As part of the continuing expansion and diversification of tourism in China a growing number of up-market seaside, mountain, desert and other nature resorts are being developed, including in environmentally sensitive areas.

**BOX 12.3 RECOMMENDATIONS FOR ENHANCING A
'GREENER' HOTEL AND TOURISM ECONOMY
IN CHINA**

- Incentivizing greater participation of the private sector
- Continued dialogue with management of hotel chains and hotel business associations
- Continuous development of industry standards and capacity building
- Dialogue with hotel companies engaged in hotel modernization and new hotel construction
- Dialogue with online hotel booking platforms.
- Consideration of mandatory eco-certification for specific environmentally sensitive tourist regions.

The government might consider making compliance and Green Hotel certification mandatory in selected locations or regions in order to protect the natural heritage of some of these environmentally sensitive tourist destinations, such as in Hainan Island, Inner Mongolia, Tibet, or other regions.

Notes

1   Source: Setting milestones for China's hotel industry in Liu and Lu (2012, p. 112).
2   See EarthCheck webpages, www.earthcheck.org, http://cn.earthcheck.org/, www.earth check.org/media/59479/FAQ_CN.pdf, accessed 8 December 2012.
3   See Green Globe webpage, www.greenglobeint.com, Green Globe Certification Standard, http://greenglobe.com/green-globe-certification-standard/, accessed 8 December 2012.
4   For further information, please see www.greenkeyglobal.com, accessed 7 August 2013.
5   For detailed information, please see: www.sustainabletravelinternational.org, accessed 7 August 2013.
6   For information, please see: www.leadingquality.com/Default.aspx, accessed 7 August 2013.
7   Source: www.chinahotel.org.cn/lsfd/gjbz.asp, accessed 6 August 2013.
8   Source: www.chinahotel.org.cn/lsfd/#, accessed 8 August 2013.
9   Source: www.ahmd.com.cn/show.asp?id=5259, accessed 8 August 2013.
10 See also www.chinasolarvalley.net, accessed 6 August 2013.
11 For details, see http://h-m-design.com/, accessed 6 August 2013.

References

Accor Greater China Communications Team (2013) Accor Greater China Fact Book, www.accor. com/fileadmin/user_upload/Contenus_Accor/Presse/Country/China/Press_Kits_2011/20130 712_accor_greater_china_fact_book_en_01.pdf, accessed 8 August 2013.
China Economic Information Network (2013) Touristic industry report in China for the 4th quarter of 2012, http://202.106.125.32:90/doc/hyk34/2013030200041.pdf, accessed 24 July 2013.
CNTA (2010) Statistical Bulletin for Star-rated Hotels in 2010, accessed 17 October 2012.

CNTA (2013) Quarterly report of star-rated hotels, first quarter, www.cnta.gov.cn/files/chizijing/2013, accessed 24 July 2013.

Honey, M. (ed.) (2002) *Ecotourism and certification: Setting standards in practice*. Island Press: Washington, DC.

Liu, S.J. and Lu, K.L. (2012) *Essential China Travel Tends 2012* (electronic publication). www.chinatraveltrendsbook.com/dragon-edition/download, accessed December 2012.

Meadin (2012) Mr LI Jian announces the launch of China Green Hotel Development Report for the Year of 2012, http://info.meadin.com/fh_jckd/82211_1.shtml, accessed 25 July 2013.

National Bureau of Statistics of China (2013) Statistics bulletin for the economic and social development in the year of 2012. www.stats.gov.cn/tjgb/ndtjgb/qgndtjgb/t20130221_402874525.htm, accessed 6 August 2013.

National Green Hotel Committee (2011) *China Green Hotel Development Report*. National Green Hotel Committee: Beijing.

National Green Hotel Committee (2013a) China Green Hotel Exchange will be held in March in Sanya, www.chinahotel.org.cn/show.asp?id=14691, accessed 25 July 2013.

National Green Hotel Committee (2013b) Launch of China Green Hotel Development Report for the Year of 2013, www.chinahotel.org.cn/show.asp?id=15907, accessed 25 July 2013.

Thraenhart, J., Chang, K. and Arlt, W. (2012) The changing Chinese traveler. *Essential China Travel Trends 2012* (electronic publication), pp. 14–7, www.chinatraveltrendsbook.com/dragon-edition/download/, accessed 7 December 2012.

Tophotelprojects (n.d.) Global hotel projects and hotel chain on-line databases, www.tophotelchains.com/en, accessed 8 December 2012.

United Nations General Assembly Resolution A/66/L.56 (2012) *The future we want* (incl. paragraphs: 130–31 on sustainable tourism), https://rio20.un.org/sites/rio20.un.org/files/a-conf.216l-1_english.pdf.pdf, accessed 7 December 2012.

UNWTO (2002) *Voluntary initiatives in tourism, worldwide inventory and comparative analysis of 104 eco-labels, awards and self-commitments*. UNWTO: Madrid.

13

WORKING TOWARDS A TRANSITION TO A GREEN ECONOMY IN SMALL ISLAND DEVELOPING STATES

The Seychelles

Rachel Welton

Introduction

This chapter is set against the backcloth of continued growth in the travel and tourism industry, even during the economic turndown of recent years (WTTC, 2013). However, the economic benefits of such growth are not evenly distributed between all countries and while some developing nations such as China and India are seeing unprecedented growth in tourism's contribution to GDP, this is not the case for many small island developing States that often have a high economic dependence upon tourism (Reddy, 2013).

In 2012, the Rio+20 United Nations Conference on Sustainable Development report, *Our common vision*, acknowledged the particular vulnerabilities of small island developing states, such as their small size, remoteness, narrow resources and export base and the exposure to a large range of impacts from climate change. Disturbingly, it highlighted that limited economic progress had been made by these states in terms of poverty reduction and debt sustainability (UN, 2012, p. 33). The report also emphasized that well-designed and managed tourism can make a significant contribution to sustainable development within a country and affirmed that a green economy is an important tool for achieving sustainable development (UN, 2012, p. 9). The transition to a green economy offers an opportunity for the Seychelles to respond to the dual challenges of sustainability (poverty alleviation, social development and the exploration of natural resources) and the impacts of climate change. The Seychelles provides a good example of the challenges and opportunities faced by small island developing states in moving towards sustainable tourism as part of their economic development.

The Republic of the Seychelles is heavily reliant upon tourism to generate wealth and contribute to the economic stability of the country. It is being adversely affected by the global economic recession and the impacts of climate change. These simultaneous crises are creating changes to biodiversity, affecting fuel supply and usage, food and water resources; and the essential income streams upon which the country relies, which in turn could compromise the future sustainability of the Seychelles as a tourism destination. This chapter will provide an in-depth exploration of tourism within the Seychelles by way of reviewing the tourism product, the tourist markets, tourism development and tourism strategy. This is followed by an account of key tourism initiatives being undertaken in the Seychelles to respond to the uncertainties brought about by the changing external factors of climate change and economic crisis. These initiatives are examined for their efficacy in developing a green economy.

Tourism, greenhouse gases and impacts of climate change

Tourism has an integral reliance upon climate; the climate is frequently the reason why tourists travel between generating and destination regions. Significant changes are occurring within the climate system, 'Warming of the climate system is unequivocal, as is now evident from observations of increases in global average air and ocean temperatures, widespread melting of snow and ice and rising global average sea level' (IPCC, 2007, p. 30). The UNWTO (2008) identifies four broad categories of climate change impacts that will affect the competitiveness and sustainability of island tourism destinations such as the Seychelles. The first category is direct impacts which include sea level rises, increases in the sea temperature, and changes in storm frequency and intensity. These impacts could result in problems of groundwater salination, coral bleaching, loss of natural defences, such as mangroves and beach erosion. These changes will increase costs to tourism destinations as they will require additional emergency preparedness, and higher operating costs with increased insurance and expensive energy backup systems, etc. (UNWTO, 2008).

The second category is the indirect environmental change impacts on the tourism industry which are often highly sensitive to environmental conditions. Changes to water supplies, biodiversity loss, altered agricultural production, increased natural hazards, coastal erosion, damage to infrastructure and increased vector-borne diseases will all impact on tourism destinations to varying degrees (UNWTO, 2008). UNESCO (2013) is concerned that some World Heritage Sites will be detrimentally affected by climate change; often these resources are critical for tourism destinations like the Seychelles.

The next category of impacts is that of mitigation policies that seek to reduce GHG emissions that could have an impact on tourism flows. These policies could make transportation between generating and destination regions more expensive for tourists and are likely to adjust the attitudes of tourists to different transport modes resulting in changing travel patterns. Long-haul destinations such as South East Asia, Australia and the Caribbean have registered their concerns about this (Bartlett, 2007; Boyd, 2007, Caribbean Hotels Association and Caribbean Tourism Organisation, 2007); this concern is mirrored by the Seychelles government.

The final category of climate change impacts is indirect societal change. Climate change is thought to pose a threat to future economic growth. The Stern Report concluded that while a 1°C change to global temperatures might improve GDP, further changes would reduce GDP and this might lead to a reduction in consumption per capita of 20 per cent (Stern, 2006). The knock-on effect for the tourism industry would be to reduce tourism demand as fewer people became able to afford to travel.

Tourism, the global economy and climate change

While the global economic crisis continues in many developed countries, the tourism sector has so far remained fairly resilient and is one of the fastest growing sectors in the world. In 2012 international tourist arrivals exceeded 1 billion. Growth of 3 to 4 per cent p.a. is predicted to continue with new markets emerging, such as those in China and India (UNWTO, 2012). The predicted growth of the tourism sector is something of a double-edged sword, as on the one hand it provides economic opportunities, while on the other it could increase the sector's contribution to global GHG emissions and increase other negative environmental impacts. Tourism's current share of global CO_2 emissions is estimated to be 5 per cent but is predicted, in a 'business as usual' scenario, to increase by 161 per cent by 2035 (UNWTO, 2008). As nations tighten their GHG reduction targets and consumers from many developed countries tighten their belts, tourism destinations are facing new challenges and opportunities in influencing destination choices (Gössling, 2011; Gössling et al., 2008; UNWTO, 2008).

The economic importance of tourism to the Seychelles

Tourism is the most important pillar of the Seychelles economy, accounting for approximately a quarter of its gross domestic product (IMF, 2012). The Seychelles has had quite a dramatic turnaround in its economic status over the last 5 years, now being seen as an illustration of how to develop effective growth in an African economy and maintain a good environmental record. This was not the case in 2008 when the IMF was forced to intervene and set in place stringent financial reforms to prevent the financial collapse of the islands.

The Seychelles government has had to implement radical structural economic reforms and this has included a number of green tourism initiatives. Developing the green economy could possibly help the Seychelles improve its competiveness while at the same time limiting some of the risks associated with climate change impacts.

Tourism in the Seychelles

The following section provides a detailed understanding of the tourism context of the Seychelles by establishing the 'pull factors' in the destination, the generating region of tourists, the development, organization and strategy of tourism.

The Seychelles is a series of 116 granite or coral islands in the Indian Ocean, situated to the north-east of Madagascar. The central islands (including Mahé, Praslin, and La Digue) are granite and the outlying islands are coral atolls. The granite islands are frequently used as the promotional image for Seychelles tourism, with their pristine golden sandy beaches, typified by Figure 13.2. As a result of the relative isolation and the comparatively late arrival of humans, many of the islands' plants and animals are endemic to the Seychelles. The key 'pull' factors for tourism are based around the

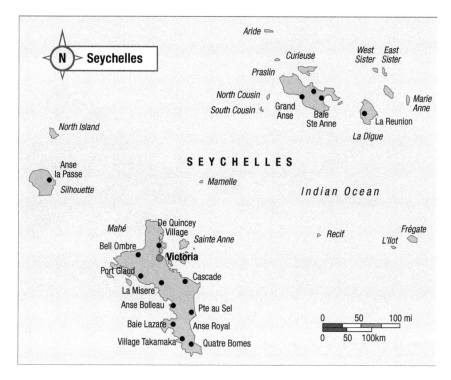

FIGURE 13.1 Map of Seychelles

Seychelles' natural environment and its climate. There are diverse and unique eco-systems, including many endangered species, such as the giant tortoise, which features on the national flag, see Figure 13.3 (Nature Seychelles, 2010).

World Heritage Sites

There are two UNESCO World Heritage Sites managed and protected by the Seychelles Islands Foundation (SIF). Aldabra was designated in 1982 as a prime example of a raised coral atoll and is significantly less disturbed than most other atolls in the Indian Ocean and elsewhere in the world. It has been extremely well protected and visitors are only allowed by written permission.

The second World Heritage Site, Vallée de Mai, was inscribed in 1983 as an outstanding example of a low- and intermediate-altitude palm forest characteristic of the Seychelles. Vallee de Mai houses the Cocoa de Mer palm (Figure 13.4), and is only one of two places in the world where the plant grows naturally. There are a number of tourist routes through the forest and written interpretation is used to inform visitors. There is also a small entrance fee that the SIF uses to pursue its conservation objectives. Between 41 per cent and 48 per cent of visitors to the Seychelles visit Vallee de Mai (UNEP, 2010).

FIGURE 13.2 A granite island scene typical of the Inner Islands
Source: Welton (2012)

FIGURE 13.3 Giant tortoise
Source: Welton (2012)

FIGURE 13.4 Cocoa de Mer at Vallee de Mai
Source: Welton (2012)

In addition to these two sites there are currently seven National Parks designated by the government to help protect and enhance the natural environment of the Seychelles. There is a good record of designating protected areas, which now cover 45 per cent of the total land mass (UNEP, 2010).

Tourism growth and development

The first official recording of tourist arrivals was in 1982, with 47,280 arrivals. During the last three decades tourism has grown steadily and in 2011 arrivals reached 194,476. The strategic document *Vision 21: Tourism development in Seychelles 2001–2010* lays out the guiding vision for tourism development stating: 'Tourism in the Seychelles shall continue to be developed to the highest standards for the optimum social and economic benefit of the Seychellois people while maintaining a commitment to the protection and conservation of the natural environment and biodiversity'(STB, 2000). A maximum carrying capacity of 200,000 tourists per annum was set out in Vision 21 (STB, 2000). However, in 2007, the government acknowledged the severity of their economic situation and launched an addendum to Vision 21: *Strategy 2017: creating our nation's wealth together* (STB, 2000). This is a 10-year plan to double the GDP of the country through focused fisheries and tourism expansion programmes, the development of the financial services industry, and the growth of other economic sectors. It contains a new goal of 360,000 tourist arrivals by 2017 and increases to the average daily spend from US$150 to US$215. In 2012, 208,034 tourist arrivals were recorded, surpassing the 200,000 threshold for the first time (SNBS, 2013).

The generating regions and market characteristics

The tourism sector in the Seychelles is heavily dependent upon the European market, which accounts for almost 72 per cent of arrivals (SNBS, 2013). The major generating countries within Europe are France, Italy, Germany, UK, Eire and Russia. The consequences of this are that most tourists take a long-haul flight. The associated carbon emissions concern the Seychelles Tourist Board as emissions from the global tourism industry are anticipated to increase by 150 per cent by 2035 (compared with 2005) (UNWTO, 2008). Predictions suggest that such emissions will become more important in the decision-making of tourists from Europe (Gössling, 2011; UNWTO, 2008).

Holidays to the Seychelles are expensive, with the cheapest accommodation being approximately £150 per person per night and the most expensive running into thousands of pounds. Consequently this restricts the types of tourists that are able to go to this exclusive destination. Many competing destinations offer unadorned luxury at a lower price. The distinguishing features of tourists that visit the Seychelles are that they require a high quality tourist product and an exceptional natural environment. They are not looking for luxurious trimmings, but for a well-protected natural environment that has an abundance of different flora and fauna. These tourists tend to be well educated, with high incomes that enable them to travel to exotic places to pursue their interests.

Transportation to and within the Seychelles

The overwhelming majority of tourists reach the Seychelles by air and the fostering of relationships with international airlines is essential for the growth of the tourism market. There is one international airport at Mahé. The national airline, Air Seychelles, has been crucial to the Seychelles. Air Seychelles started operations in 1977 and connected Mahé with eleven destinations in Africa, Asia and Europe. There are thirteen domestic air services within the Seychelles, enabling tourists to island-hop quickly. There is also a well-developed pedestrian ferry service providing good links between the main islands. Tourists can also charter private ferries. As the islands are relatively small, tourists tend to hire cars for a day rather than a prolonged period. Buses are regularly used by both tourists and locals to transport them around the islands. Tourists typically stay on the three main islands, Mahé (58 per cent); Praslin (24 per cent); and La Digue (6 per cent). An increasing number of tourists (4 per cent) stay on yachts or private boats (SNBS, 2013).

The structure and organization of tourism in the Seychelles

The planning and coordination of the tourism industry in the Seychelles was, until recently, dominated by the public sector. The Seychelles Tourism Board (STB) sits within the Ministry of Tourism and Transport, and these organizations act as both facilitator and regulator. The Ministry's Tourism Development Division consists of four sections: Tourism Planning, Human Resources Development, Quality and Standards, and the Seychelles Tourism Board. In 2008, as a response to the IMF intervention to reform the country's economy, the Seychelles government decided to privatize the Seychelles Tourism Board and all tourism marketing activities. The reorganization included an increase in private sector Board members as well as the creation of two private sector sub-boards, namely, Destination Marketing and the Tourism Academy with 50 per cent of the marketing budget now funded by the private sector (Mintel, 2009). Linked to this is the Seychelles Tourism Advisory Board (STAB), whose membership is drawn largely from the private sector, and which advises on all aspects of the tourism industry.

This section has established that the natural environment is extremely well protected through effective regulation. The management of the tourism sector has been dominated by the public sector but is increasingly being influenced by the private sector. The opening up of the market place and ambitious targets for tourism growth provides both opportunities and challenges for tourism stakeholders and the government.

Green tourism initiatives in the Seychelles

This section identifies a number of tourism stakeholder green initiatives regarding concerns about the carbon footprints of tourists and the economic conditions imposed by the IMF to aid the transformation of the economy. These are taken from a wider study of the impacts of climate change within Indian Ocean Island tourism destinations (Welton, 2012).

Carbon-neutral

As established previously, the Seychelles is reliant upon long-haul flights. Recently Air Seychelles stopped providing flights to and from Europe and has become a regional carrier within Africa. This is reflected in the latest data which show slightly less reliance upon the European market and an increase of 14 per cent in interregional visitors from South Africa and the United Arab Emirates (SNBS, 2013). During 2008 a renowned German professor gave media interviews in Germany encouraging Germans to travel locally to Sylt Island (a German island in the North Sea) and not to the Seychelles, in order to reduce their carbon footprint. STB felt that its destination was being singled out and tourists, who might not have previously considered their tourism carbon footprint, would now demand 'off-setting' actions to ameliorate associated GHGs. Seychellois stakeholders consider that tourists from Europe tend to be more 'environmentally aware', particularly those from Germany and Scandinavia; and this news story exacerbated STB's apprehension that tourists might stop taking long-haul flights. This also raises a bigger question regarding responsibility for emissions from long-haul flights, is it for the generating or the receiving region to resolve?

There have been a number of positive outcomes from the bad publicity in Germany. It united the stakeholders within the Seychelles, and a number of initiatives evolved, such as education workshops on tourism and climate change, and the development of a carbon audit for many aspects of tourism within the Seychelles from large resorts to small entrepreneurs (Welton, 2012). Vignette 1 is an illustration of an initiative by Nature Seychelles to develop the first carbon-neutral nature reserve.

BOX 13.1 COUSIN ISLAND CARBON-NEUTRAL NATURE RESERVE

Vignette 1: Cousin Island Carbon-Neutral Nature Reserve

Nature Seychelles is a non-profit environmental organization involved in a wide range of activities to improve the natural environment. Conservation activities on the Reserve include monitoring the island's biodiversity, research, re-introduction of endangered species such as the Seychelles Magpie robin, ecotourism and education. Cousin has received international awards for its conservation and ecotourism efforts.

The Cousin Island carbon-neutral nature reserve project involves a rigorous carbon footprint assessment, assurance process and investment in high quality carbon credits to offset the footprint. Nature Seychelles launched the initiative in 2010 during World Tourism Day. It is a multi-agency project involving Nature Seychelles, Seychelles Tourism Board and the British High Commission in Seychelles.

The Reserve welcomes thousands of tourists each year, mainly from Europe. In recognition of the environmental impact of these visitors to Cousin and after media reports in Europe urging citizens not to travel to long-haul destinations such as the Seychelles, Nature Seychelles took the decision to make the Reserve carbon-neutral.

The Reserve's carbon footprint was measured by looking at various activities associated with visitor arrivals to Cousin and its operations. Since 1968 the island's habitat has been restored, with the result that 85 per cent is now covered by natural tropical vegetation. Based on available scientific information, the amount of annual carbon that the island can absorb was netted off against the footprint. The remainder of the footprint was offset using carbon credits purchased from a carefully selected and independently verified clean cook stove project in Darfur, Sudan.

Adapted from Birdlife International (2013)

Carbon off-setting

There is no formal tourism off-setting scheme implemented or endorsed by the Seychelles government. Tourism stakeholders have a lack of confidence in the transparency of some 'off-setting' schemes and were anxious they might be perceived as 'greenwashing' (Welton, 2012). The Seychellois public are however encouraged to participate in the United Nations plant-a-tree scheme (Figure 13.4). Tourism stakeholders who supported this initiative recognized the limited impact the Seychelles contribution to the reduction of GHG emissions would make globally, but wanted to convey to the Seychellois and tourists that every little helps and the project was seen as a conduit for raising awareness of climate issues.

La Digue project

The smallest of the three main islands that most tourists visit is La Digue. It is only 3km long and 2km wide and is also the least developed of the tourist islands. One project that is currently being undertaken here is to remove cars from the island and make its resorts carbon-neutral by 2020. Vignette 2 provides an insight into the tensions between tourism development and protection of the biodiversity on La Digue.

BOX 13.2 LA DIGUE ISLAND AND THE CRITICALLY ENDANGERED SEYCHELLES PARADISE-FLYCATCHER

Vignette 2: La Digue Island and the critically endangered Seychelles Paradise-flycatcher

The Seychelles government is now investigating the possibility of making La Digue carbon-neutral after Cousin Island Special Reserve. The government is in the process of phasing out all fossil fuel vehicles on La Digue so that only bicycles (Figure 13.5), ox carts (Figure 13.6) and electric vehicles will be allowed on the island, as part of the goal to reduce the Seychelles carbon emissions. The implementation of sustainable tourism initiatives can be fraught with the competing objectives of tourism stakeholders, as this case illustrates. Tourists visit La Digue for the isolated beaches (Anse Source d'Argent), the wildlife (Seychelles Paradise-flycatcher and giant tortoise) and limited tourism development (ox carts and small-scale tourist accommodation) which all combine to provide a subtle relaxed atmosphere. While ox carts and bicycles enhance the laid-back culture of the island, local residents are reluctant to give up use of their fossil fuel vehicles and negotiations between government and community groups are protracted.

More recently there has been a problem with illegal felling of mature trees on La Digue. The felling included several native tree species used by the endangered Seychelles Paradise-flycatcher, *Terpsiphone corvina*, a bird sought by wildlife tourists but dwindling in numbers. The owner of the section of land made an application to develop a tourism resort but the Department of Environment had put this on hold to conduct an environmental impact assessment in line with regulations. In the interim, the owner apparently went ahead with land clearing, which required authorization from the Department of Environment. Consequently, the land owner and the contractor who undertook the works were fined 50,000 Seychelles Rupees each (about US$ 4,000) by the environment authorities. According to sources on La Digue those fined are refusing to pay and have their own case against the government.

This instance shows that while there may be a national goal to make La Digue carbon-neutral, if local residents do not have this shared goal it can make implementation of sustainable tourism initiatives extremely difficult to achieve.

Adapted from Birdlife International (2011)

FIGURE 13.5 Tourists on La Digue are encouraged to cycle
Source: Welton (2012)

FIGURE 13.6 Ox-pulled coach used to transport tourists from the ferry to accommodation
Source: Welton (2012)

Planning development and governance in the protection of the environment

The Seychelles government has a long history of using planning regulations to protect the environment. For example, no more than 50 per cent of any island can be used for any development and a minimum of 50 per cent is kept in pristine condition (Vision 21). Tourism is developed on only eleven of the 116 islands. The Seychellois are very proud of this and stakeholders state that there is nowhere else in the world where half the territorial extent of a nation is actually under conservation (Welton, 2012). Unlike some competing destinations, tourism has not grown particularly rapidly in the Seychelles and there has always been a policy that has limited growth, through strict building regulations and the requirement for local Seychellois to be involved in the investment.

Tourism stakeholders have a common understanding that these self-limiting factors have actually been beneficial, and without these policies the pristine environment could have been lost. Hence, there is a clear message that the Seychellois did not want mass tourism with the ripple effects of environmental and social problems that could arise (Welton, 2012). They want to conserve, not over-develop, and they see a limit as to how much development is sustainable. These views are mirrored by the President of the Seychelles in Vignette 3. The values of the President and the Seychellois have a resonance with the core themes within the concept of a green economy.

Regulations

The Seychelles has stringent requirements for gaining planning permission to develop a tourism resort. These include the investor conducting a full environmental impact assessment, more recently climate change impacts are also reviewed. STB ensures that

---

BOX 13.3 AN ABRIDGED INTERVIEW WITH THE PRESIDENT OF THE SEYCHELLES

Vignette 3: An abridged interview with the President of the Seychelles where he reaffirmed his commitment to balancing economic development with environmental protection.

'As tourism is our main economic activity, we felt it was important to marry the two activities by developing our tourism business model as the "ecotourism" model, where economic development and the protection of our cultural and environmental diversity are fused into our planning systems. I also believe that we must preserve the environment we have in order to ensure that our people have a healthy life, because by respecting nature and nurturing it, people experience vast health benefits and lead a better quality of life.'

Source: Spencer (2012)

the development process rigorously monitors the resorts to ensure compliance with planning conditions. If all aspects of the conditions are met, an operating licence will be issued. Research by Welton (2012) found a number of resorts had had operating licences revoked and there seemed a tacit understanding that this was in the pursuit of raising both environmental and quality standards in the industry. Although regulations are in place the government has found itself at the centre of a controversial proposal to develop a new tourism resort, and has been accused of 'green-washing', an accusation strongly denied by the Minister for Tourism and Culture. Vignette 4 illustrates the government's position.

BOX 13.4 AN ABRIDGED INTERVIEW WITH THE TOURISM AND CULTURE MINISTER, ALAIN ST. ANGE

Vignette 4: An abridged interview with the Tourism and Culture Minister, Alain St. Ange

'This is a game of politics, nothing else. The people of the Seychelles know how important tourism is for our economy. Our young people need employment opportunities. Those who alleged that all jobs in new resorts will be taken by foreigners are not telling the truth. STA has been intensifying training of Seychellois to start a career in the hospitality industry.

Yes, there will eventually be a limit for more developments, but not just yet. New resorts means more jobs for our people, more opportunities to even start new businesses related to tourism. Those opposed have not said a word where they would find jobs for young Seychellois if not in the tourism sector.

Seychelles has weathered the global economic crisis of 2008 and the Eurozone crisis much better than many other countries. This is a result of a concerted effort to improve the business climate and by finding new markets for our resorts. Success is evident here and while there are challenges, those are met head on. I think we are all aware that environmental protection is the key for our success as a tourism destination. Let me give you an example. When the Constance Ephelia [a tourism resort] was built, the same people cried that the mangrove forest would be destroyed by the project. You have been there several times and seen that instead, the mangrove forests have increased in size because now they get active protection from staff of the resort. More mangroves have been planted and this is continuing. It shows that it is possible to find a balance between environment and resorts. It is costly but this is factored into our hotel tariffs. There are always new challenges arising but I think we have the mechanism in the Seychelles to solve such issues.

Any new resort, this one at Cap Ternay and the other one at Police Bay, or those on Praslin or other islands, will always be subject to a very stringent process of EIA. We have learned from past shortcomings and will continue to learn as we go along. Trying to stop developments without answering where the bread and butter for our people should then come from is futile.'

Source: Wolfganghthome (2013)

The Seychelles Sustainability Tourism Label

In 2011, STB launched a certified sustainability label. The Seychelles Sustainability Tourism Label (SSTL) is applicable to all tourism businesses and aims to encourage more sustainable ways of conducting business to safeguard the biodiversity and the culture of Seychelles. The components of the SSTL are set out in Vignette 5.

Investment in tourism resources

The Seychellois government restricts the number of visitors by limiting the number of bed spaces available in the accommodation sector. The number of accommodation establishments has been growing steadily over the last 5 years. In 2007, there were 167 compared with 244 in 2012. Improvements to the quality of the resorts are being pursued and large hotel groups such as Shangri-la, Raffles and Emirates are investing in new resorts (STB, 2013a). This is in response to the increasingly competitive nature of the international tourist market to ensure the Seychelles is able to increase tourist satisfaction and can continue to secure premium prices, resulting in increased spend by the tourists.

Car hire is regulated by the Seychellois government in the Investment Promotion Act (1994), which encourages domestic investment in the tourism sector and prohibits non-Seychellois from entering the market. The Act also restricts the number of hire vehicles that an investor can own, to thirty. This policy seems to be successful with many small operators entering the market, and as a result very little money leaves the country through economic leakage.

There is limited evidence of renewable energy being used within the Seychelles, as the cost of renewable energy was perceived by tourism stakeholders as being more costly than burning fossil fuels. Stakeholders acknowledge the benefits of photovoltaic energy, wind energy, and hydro-energy, but the perceived cost of the initial outlay

---

BOX 13.5 THE SEYCHELLES SUSTAINABILITY TOURISM LABEL

Vignette 5: The Seychelles Sustainability Tourism Label

The project was initiated by the Seychelles Tourism Board in collaboration with the GOS-UNDP-GEF Programme Coordination Unit and with funding from the Global Environment Facility (GEF)

The tourism business needs to apply to participate in the scheme and pay an application fee of between 400 and 1,000 euros depending on size. In order to be certified by the SSTL a hotel needs to demonstrate that it has adopted a minimum number of sustainable business practices.

To achieve the SSTL, participating hotels need to meet basic criteria. The standards include: Management, Waste, Water, Energy, Staff, Conservation, Community and Guests. To date three hotels have been awarded the SSTL.

Source: STB (2013a)

was a major deterrent. The lack of adoption of renewable energy technologies by private investors has frustrated government officials, and to overcome this resistance they are in the process of changing the building regulations, to ensure new developments are required by law to invest in some renewable energy; the prevailing belief is that the tourism industry can probably absorb the set-up costs (Welton, 2012).

Education

Outside of the tourism sector there is a climate change technical officer employed in the President's Office and the government has set up the Sea Level Rise Foundation to encourage education in schools, and to support young people taking relevant degrees, to establish increased human capacity to tackle climate change within the country.

A high proportion of the Seychellois population work within the tourism sector. Figure 13.7 shows a local Seychellois entrepreneur cooking and selling produce at the weekly tourist market on Mahé. However, few senior managers within the resorts are Seychellois. To address this, the Seychelles Tourism Academy has been established to improve productivity and service quality through apprenticeship, pre-service and in-service training and to increase representation of Seychellois in management roles.

FIGURE 13.7 Seychellois tourism entrepreneur
Source: Welton (2012)

Conclusion

The Seychelles, like many other small island developing states, (as recognized by the UN at the Rio+20 Conference on Sustainable Development), continues to face the concurrent challenges of developing sustainable tourism against the backcloth of the economic downturn and the impacts of climate change.

The Seychelles tourism destination is in a very vulnerable position. Already the Seychelles tourism stakeholders claim to be observing the impacts of climate change and the global economic recession; they could also be disadvantaged by the tourists' choice of destination. The sustainability challenge for the Seychellois is finding effective mechanisms to maintain and enhance the islands' environmental capital which is their unique selling point, while at the same time growing the tourism economy. Reddy (2013) observes that international organizations have been strongly advocating the green economy approach as it has the potential to achieve low-carbon, socially inclusive, sustainable tourism growth and to meet the combined carbon mitigation scenarios of the tourism sector.

In the Seychelles the economic benefits of tourism can be garnered through increasing the length of stay and daily spend of tourists and reducing economic leakage. The current target of 360,000 tourists by 2017 appears rather ambitious given the time it would take to increase the accommodation stock and the environmental challenges inherent in developing such capacity. Concentrating on 'high end' tourists and ensuring that local people invest in tourism has helped to keep the economic benefits of tourism within the country.

The implementation of sustainable tourism initiatives, such as the carbon-neutral nature reserve and La Digue island, the Seychelles Sustainability Tourism Label, and GHGs audits illustrates the proactive response that permeates from the top of government through to small guest house entrepreneurs. These projects demonstrate a collaborative approach by tourism stakeholders, a likely factor in their success. In addition, a critical success factor is the value given to the natural environment by the Seychellois, borne out by regulation.

The rate of growth of tourism has been relatively slow comparative to other destinations in the Indian Ocean such as the Maldives and Mauritius. This is partially due to having a cap on the number of tourists and also enforcing this via limiting the bed spaces available. The organization of tourism is well advanced and there is general recognition that tourism planning, supported by a strong government presence in regulation and enforcement has paved the way for more sensitive development in the future. The new resort investments are providing the foundation for achieving the new tourist targets, but this could compromise the environmental values that are espoused within the tourism strategy and by the President, Jean Michael. This approach for the future is broadly in line with the UN (2012) Rio+20 recommendations for sustainable development. Particularly, with the use of cultural tourism and ecotourism to encourage the promotion of investment in sustainable tourism and the recommendation that policy-makers should take a leadership role in developing appropriate policies through an inclusive and transparent process, and not by applying rigid rules.

The main ingredients of the path to a green economy in the Seychelles are an appreciation of the natural environment which is propagated within the Seychellois culture, effective regulation,and proactive tourism stakeholders, all combining to produce innovative green responses. The Seychelles is a good illustration of potentially mutual reinforcing benefits that flow from tourism growth, environmental protection and social well-being and this provides them with some reasons to be optimistic about the future resilience of the Seychelles as a tourism destination.

References

Bartlett, L. (2007) Australia fears that jet flight guilt could hit tourism, *Agence France-Presse*, www.onecaribbean.org/content/files/unwtoclimatechangereport.pdf, accessed 3 March 2011.

Birdlife Partnership (2011) Cousin habitat danger for Seychelles Paradise-flycatcher, *Birdlife International*, www.birdlife.org/community/2011/12/habitat-danger-for-seychelles-paradise-flycatcher/, accessed 10 April 2013.

Birdlife Partnership (2013) Cousin Island special reserve carbon neutral, *Birdlife International*, www.birdlife.org/community/2010/09/cousin-island-special-reserve-carbon-neutral/, accessed 10 April 2013.

Boyd, A. (2007) Carbon tax threatens to ground Asia tourism, *Asian Times*, www.atimes.com/atimes/Asian_Economy/ID19Dk01.html, accessed 11 March 2011.

Caribbean Hotels Association and Caribbean Tourism Organisation (2007) Position paper of global climate change and the Caribbean tourism industry, www.caribbeanhotelassociation.com/mbrsonly/AnnualReport/CHAAnnualReport07.pdf, accessed 20 October 2010.

Gössling, S. (2011) *Carbon management in tourism: Mitigating the impacts of climate change.* Routledge: Abingdon.

Gössling, S., Peeters, P. and Scott, D. (2008) Consequences of climate change policy for international tourist arrivals in developing countries. *Third World Quarterly*, vol. 29, no. 5, pp. 873–901

IMF (2012) Seychelles: Fifth review under the extended arrangement, request for modification performance criteria, and financing assurances review, IMF Country Report No. 12/260, September 2012, www.imf.org/external/pubs/ft/scr/2012/cr12260.pdf, accessed 6 January 2013.

IPCC (2007) *Climate change 2007: Synthesis report.* A contribution of Working Groups I, II and III to the Fourth Assessment report of the Intergovernmental Panel on Climate Change [Core Writing Team, Pachauri, R.K. and Reisinger, A. (eds)]. IPCC: Geneva, Switzerland.

Mintel (2009) *Travel and Tourism – Seychelles.* Mintel Group: London.

Nature Seychelles (2013) Natural Environment of the Seychelles *www.natureseychelles.org/*, accessed 26 May 2013.

Reddy, M.V. (2013) Global tourism and travel industry: Performance during the double-dip recession and recommendations for transition to a green economy. *The World Financial Review.* Accessed 18 January 2014 at: *www.worldfinancialreview.com/?p=2740*

Seychelles National Strategy (2007) www.tralac.org/files/2012/12/Seychelles-strategy2017.pdf, accessed 26 March 2013.

SNBS (2013) *Visitor statistics April 2013*, May 2013 edition.

Spencer, R. (2012) Black gold has been detected in Seychelles, *The Guardian*, 2 February 2012, www.the-report.net/seychelles/feb2012/28-q-a-james-michel-president-of-the-republic-of-seychelles, accessed 30 May 2013.

STB (2000) *Vision 21 tourism development in Seychelles 2001–2010.* www.sey-tess.com/other_items/, accessed 26 March 2013.

STB (2013a) *The Seychelles Islands another world. Accommodation in the Seychelles*, www.seychelles. travel/en/plan_your_visit/accommodation.php, accessed 22 March 2013.

STB (2013b) Seychelles launches sustainable tourism label logo, *The Seychelles E-Newsletter*, www. seychelles.travel/newsletter/home/index.php?ii=76&si=194&ai=1024, accessed 26 March 2013.

Stern, N. (2006) *Stern review: The economics of climate change*. HM treasury report, www.hm-treasury. gov.uk/independent_reviews/stern_review_economics_climate_change/stern_review_report.cf, accessed 2 February 2013.

UN (2012) *The future we want. Our common vision Rio+20*. United Nations: New York.

UNEP (2010) Vallee de mai nature reserve Seychelles, www.unep-wcmc.org/sites/wh/pdf/Vallee, accessed 23 April 2013.

UNESCO (2013) World Heritage Site Listing, http://whc.unesco.org/en/statesparties/lk, accessed 22 March 2013.

UNWTO (2008) *Climate change and tourism: responding to global challenges*. World Tourism Organization: Madrid, Spain

UNWTO (2012) *Tourism highlights*, *2012 edition*, Madrid, Spain. http://mkt.unwto.org/en/publica tion/unwto-tourism-highlights-2012-edition, accessed 23 June 2013.

Welton, R. (2012) Coastal tourism: the response of Indian Ocean island tourism destinations to climate change, PhD Thesis, Nottingham Trent University at Nottingham, UK.

Wolfganghthome (2013) Emirates top leadership in Seychelles in talks for even closer cooperation. http://wolfganghthome.wordpress.com/2013/05/24/emirates-top-leadership-in-seychelles-in-talks-for-even-closer-cooperation/, accessed 3 June 2013.

WTTC (2013) *WTTC Travel & Tourism Economic Impact 2013*, accessed 18 January 2014 at: www. wttc.org/site_media/uploads/downloads/world2013_1.pdf.

14

DESTINATION UKRAINE

Tourism litmus of the transition to a green economy

Viktoriya Kiptenko and Pavlo Doan

Introduction

The green economy concept is attractive to transition economies such as Ukraine. This country has a number of reasons for greening besides Chernobyl. Apart from the essence of eco- and eco-agro-activities, tourism drives a variety of opportunities and options for sustainable consumption. The aim of this scoping study is to assess different pathways and the effects of greening tourism in the country. The international impetus frames responses from tourism industry entities, NGOs and state institutions. Scenarios (bottom-up or otherwise) differ depending on the above actors' interactions and spatial focuses (i.e. the Carpathian, the Crimea, local tourism systems). Innovative activities have proved to be the litmus of the transition to a green economy in business, social and educational aspects as they have sought the appropriate legal environment and mechanisms for implementation.

Different sources have outlined the potential of a greening economy to solve Ukraine's transition development problems (from the viewpoint of both natural and social sustainability), which have included energy overuse, soil erosion and lack of fresh water, on top of poor waste management, strong heavy industry and fifteen nuclear plants, including Chernobyl (some of the most recent being UNEP, 2011; Martyniuk and Ogarenko, 2012; UNEP, 2012; and Kononeko, 2013).

A number of international and domestic institutions estimate that the pace of the green economy concept in Ukraine will be slow and gradual because although it is an attractive idea, there are a number of limiting factors (for the most comprehensive overview of the available environmental information see European Environment Agency, 2011).

Despite promising progress towards the Millennium Development Goals (UNDP, 2013) the Environmental Performance Index suggests that between 2000 and 2010 although this country had improved slightly, it was still showing poor performance, with the most significant inhibitory effects being attributed to the situation with water resources (ecosystems effect), agriculture and fisheries. Deeper analysis reveals negative trends in terms of forests (forest loss, in particular), CO_2 emissions in electricity generation, ecosystem vitality, and air quality (effects on human health) (Yale University, 2012).

The international vision of the green economy model has inspired extensive discourse in academic, business and public circles. The concept of dynamic elaboration by world and regional institutions has broadened the mechanisms already practised around the world in different spheres. Starting from the sustainable development motion set out by the *Our common future* report (1987) the focus of its approach has been transformed through the decade landmarks of the Rio Earth Summit (1992), the Johannesburg World Summit on Sustainable Development (2002) and finally Rio+20 (2012), which induced the tourism industry to advance the motto 'put green on the same page as growth' (eTN Global Travel Industry News, 2013). At the same time the latest UNEP (UN Environment Programme) and UNWTO (UN World Tourism Organization) background report provides clear and comprehensive guidelines on the international perspective of the definition, challenges and opportunities, as well as the enabling conditions, for tourism greening (UNEP and UNWTO, 2012).

Our scoping study therefore aims to show the range of opportunities and options for sustainable consumption in tourism. There have been a great number of conferences, workshops and seminars which have prompted greening in Ukraine in different areas of its economy. However, we have limited our analysis to organic agriculture and some notions of eco-building and eco-dwelling, speculating on the impact of their integration with tourism in terms of benefiting the country's sustainable development. A better understanding of the current initiatives (which are mostly bottom-up and outward facing) reveal the urgency of the need for shifts in legislative, public and business domains for green tourism and greening the economy of Ukraine.

'Legislating' the green economy concept in Ukraine

Nowadays a key role in efficient greening is played by the explicit regulation(both from a conceptual and practical viewpoint) for the green economy model in Ukraine. Since its independence in 1991, Ukraine has gradually been processing background environmental legislation but still lacks a comprehensive strategy for a green economy.

Table 14.1 shows how the outside influence of international norms of sustainable development and green economy implementation have been strengthened by the national legal framework in the field of ecology (environmental management), sustainable growth and rural development. A significant step was taken in 2001 with the adoption of the Law of Ukraine on Environmental Protection. In the same year the state established rules of product standardization which were reinforced in 2005 with certification requirements. These documents formed the basis for the later adoption of other legislation related to rural development and national environmental policy. However, the withdrawal in July 2011 of the Implementation Programme of the Decisions Made at the World Sustainable Development Summit (adopted in 2003) signalled financing concerns. Ukraine adopted the Decree on Technical Regulations of Environmental Labelling elaborated in compliance with the Eco-labelling regulations of the European Parliament (EP) and Council (EC) in 2011. This enactment played a considerable role in the actual implementation of the green economy tools, as we represent later, particularly in relation to tourism.

TABLE 14.1 Key Ukraine legislation for the regulation of green economy development

Type of document	Document title	Date of adoption	Date of last change	Adoption authority
Law	Law of Ukraine on Environmental Protection	25 June 1991	18 November 2012	Verhovna Rada of Ukraine
	Law of Ukraine on the Ratification of the Convention on Access to Information, Public Participation in Decision-Making and Access to Justice in Environmental Matters★	6 July 1999	6 July 1999	
	Law of Ukraine on Standardization	17 May 2001	2 December 2012	
	Law of Ukraine on Adoption of the State Programme on Adaptation of Ukrainian Legislation to the Laws of the European Union★	18 March 2004	1 October 2011	
	Law of Ukraine on the Basic Principles (strategy) of the State Environmental Policy of Ukraine until 2020	21 December 2010	21 December 2010	
Bylaws	Combined Implementation Programme of Decisions Made at the World Summit on Sustainable Development for 2003–2015★	26 April 2003	withdrawn 7 July 2011	Cabinet of Ministers of Ukraine
	Decree on Making Arrangements for Implementation of International Environmental Standards ISO 14000★	13 October 2004	13 October 2004	Ministry of ecology and natural resources of Ukraine
	Order on Approval of the List of Products Subject to Mandatory Certification in Ukraine	1 February 2005	1 February 2013	State committee of Ukraine for technical regulation and consumer policy
	Decree on Approval of the State Programme of Ukrainian Village Development until 2015	19 September 2007	19 September 2007	Cabinet of Ministers of Ukraine
	Order on Approval of the Concept of National Environmental Policy of Ukraine until 2020	17 October 2007	17 October 2007	
	Order on Approval of the National Plan for Environmental Protection for 2011–2015	25 May 2011	1 April 2013	

★ legislative and executive acts related to international norms

Source: Authors – based on Verhovna Rada of Ukraine (2004)

Ukrainian public, academic and business sectors have interpreted the role of the travel industry in the sustainable development of the economy through 'rural green tourism'. The term comes from the Union for Promotion of Rural Green Tourism in Ukraine which was actually the first entity that aimed to unite efforts to promote principles of sustainability in tourism. The NGO registration by the Ministry for Justice of Ukraine in 1996 provided the legal framework for further penetration of the 'rural green tourism' concept in the Law of Ukraine on Tourism (1995, 2001, 2004) and the Law of Ukraine on Private Farming (2003).

With its roots at the beginning of the twentieth century, during the last few decades rural tourism in Ukraine has broadened its outlook and now presents three types of green tourism: agro-tourism, rural recreation and ecotourism (Ministry of Culture of Ukraine, 2009).

The practice has shown the successful diversification of green rural tourism from both the services (innovative tourism products) and the spatial patterns view. Besides the traditional (home and farmstead) agro-touristic activities widely represented in the Carpathian region together with neighbouring Polissia and Podillia Uplands, on the Black and Azov coasts and the River Dnieper banks, the thematic and ethnographic routes effectively combine environmentally friendly activities. Ecotourism in various forms (ethnic, pilgrimage, cave, castle and architectural, archaeological, nature and historical tourism; winter and summer activities, suburban and seaside recreation) prevails in national parks and other protected areas and their (mostly rural) neighbourhoods (Ministry of Culture of Ukraine, 2009; Jerzy and Krzysztof, 2012).

Such a discourse, however, can create confusion. It appears that in Ukraine the enthusiastic development of 'rural green tourism' directly supplants the essence of sustainability of tourism in practice. Even researchers and policy-makers often take the label of 'green tourism' (meaning rural-/agro- and eco-tourism) for granted to mean sustainable development and/or a tourism green economy (e.g. Ministry of Culture of Ukraine, 2009; Potapenko, 2012; Kononeko, 2013).

International insights on related definitions and perspectives (Medlik, 2003; UNEP and UNWTO, 2005; UNEP and UNWTO, 2012) suggest that apart from the alternative tourism concept, sustainable development can apply to any kinds of the activities, in tourism in particular, that are in harmony with their physical, social and cultural environments, which explains the interrelation (but not overlap) of rural-/agro-/eco-tourism and sustainable tourism activities. In addition, the latter sustained indefinitely in a social, economic, cultural, and environmental context is understood as tourism in the green economy. understanding. The Global Sustainable Tourism Criteria provide a framework to try to evaluate the greening of tourism practice and business. The sustainability-related challenges enhance the focus and correct understanding of the contexts, which seeks its correct application in legal, public and business practice in Ukraine.

There is a contextual concern, however. Despite the state prioritizing tourism to provide sustainable development in the country through the Law of Tourism of Ukraine (1995, 2001, 2004), the Strategy of Tourism and Resorts Development (2008) makes no mention of 'green' (or eco/rural) tourism. However, it does aim to comply with the environmental standards, to elaborate and implement modern methods of environmental-risk evaluation, and to mandate the ecological expertise for protected areas of tourism. The final stage of the above Strategy envisages balancing all the elements of tourism and resort development as socially responsible, environmentally friendly and economically efficient activities (Order on Adoption of Strategy of Tourism and Resorts Development, 2008).

'Green rural tourism' likewise lacks a legal framework. Several bills regarding green and rural tourism failed to be adopted in the Ukrainian Parliament during the period 2003–7. The Law of Ukraine on Tourism, nevertheless, makes a distinction between rural and ecological (green) tourism and asserts that both are key priorities of the state tourism policy together with inbound and domestic tourism. This Law establishes regulations with regard to the rules and requirements for certain types of tourism, which, however, fail to legislate for green and/or rural and/or eco tourism. Very general basic principles for economic activity in green recreation are currently covered by the Civil Code, the Commercial Code and the Law of Ukraine on Private Farming. To legislate for a green economy in tourism, in Ukraine, thus means the introduction of international approaches but without any solid concept comprehension, appropriate (domestic) legal framework or mechanism for implementation. This country lacks a comprehensive strategy to approach the challenges of energy and greenhouse emissions, efficient water consumption and waste management, and loss of biodiversity together with maintaining built and cultural heritage, planning and governance.

Bottom-up integration

Alternative tourism, indeed, constitutes the firm foundation for the penetration of a green economy in Ukraine. The (mostly) NGO initiatives (with wide promotion and easy access on the Web (Magazine Organic UA, 2013; Union for Promotion of Rural Green Tourism in Ukraine, 2013) provide examples of how rural recreation activities can integrate with organic agriculture.

One of the most representative and valuable institutions of eco-farming is the Federation of Organic Movement of Ukraine (FOMU). This organization provides information about green farming in general, consults about the criteria for organic land management, organizes forums, conferences and meetings, and participates in international farming fairs and exhibitions etc. FOMU is one of the members of the International Federation of Organic Agriculture Movements (IFOAM). Ukrainian businesses (BIOlan Ukraine Association, Organic Standard Ltd and Ukragrofin) also participate in IFOAM, while the Ukrainian non-governmental organization Zhyva Planeta is an associate member. A number of NGOs advance eco-gardening, the main ones being the Swiss-Ukrainian project 'Development of Organic Market in Ukraine' funded by the Research Institute of Organic Agriculture (FIBL, Switzerland), the national public organization, Club of Organic Farming, the Association of Organic Goods Producers 'Pure Flora', the non-governmental organization the 'Association of Organic Farming and Gardening' (AOZIS), and the German non-profit public organization 'Ecoconnect'.

Ukrainian organic farming nowadays cultivates and supplies the international market with crops, legumes, bran, flour, pasta, honey, sugar, dried fruits, nuts, oil and wine, while satisfying the country's demand for chicken, beef, pork, lamb, sausages, milk, butter, yogurt, sour cream, cottage cheese, chicken eggs and quail eggs, etc. Organic products are starting to enjoy increased advertising campaigns including public service announcements (PSAs), street advertisements on billboards and illuminations, and TV commercials. In addition, a network of eco-food shops and counters have sprung up around the country (for example Nature Boutique, Eco-lavka, GoodWine, Organic era, Eco idea, Zdorova lavka).

Launched in Ukraine (Kyiv, 2008) the International Conferences on Development of the Organic Sector in the Central/Eastern Europe and Central Asia countries have widened their scope to Tbilisi (Georgia), Astana (Kazakhstan), and Izmir (Turkey) forming an international platform for best practice exchange in order to better direct the entities, NGOs and institutions. The outcome has demonstrated the beneficial interrelation of organic food production and environment protection, biodiversity and ecotourism. The mutual impacts have helped to raise the attractiveness of rural tourism and promote local and organic production.

Since 2010, at the domestic level the positive results of such integration have been represented at the annual Eco-Vacation fair, which unites the efforts of the Union for Promotion of Rural Green Tourism in Ukraine and the Federation of Organic Movement of Ukraine. The fair along with workshops, presentations and folklore promotes the producers of organic food and has programmes such as 'Ukrainian village welcomes' and 'European village in Ukraine'. The best practice exchange serves to benefit both homes and farmsteads to diversify and create truly innovative green products and services. Alongside the nationwide events a number of regional initiatives (mostly in the Carpathian and the Crimea) include fairs of organic food, visits to ethnographic homesteads and exhibitions of arts and crafts together with energy-saving technology presentations, folklore festivals, conferences and training courses.

The more complex effects include the promotion of eco-building practices, which are mostly developed in Ukraine on a volunteer basis. The basic adobe and straw house construction has its roots way back in Ukrainian history. Hundreds of such dwellings (mostly brick-lined during the last century), and dozens of newly built houses, sometimes powered by solar battery, represent facilities that will enable greater cooperation to see the growth of tourism in the central part of Ukraine (e.g. Poltava, Kyiv, Zhytomyr, Dnipropetrovsk regions). The eco-built homesteads often focus on environmentally oriented living space with organic farming, folklore and customs, and summer camps for children, workshops, culture and education events.

The authors participated in and monitored the pioneer demonstration centre of ecological technologies, Teteryvskyi Kish, (94 km from the capital of Kyiv towards the regional centre Zhytomyr) from its establishment in March 2012. The centre is located in a rural area on the banks of the Teteriv river. The private owners of a 2-hectare plot of land have provided this area for sustainable activities of volunteers and interested 'green' ginger groups. The invited volunteer instructors have already involved participants in the piecemeal erection of straw-block houses during the traditional Ukraine 'Toloka' (when the host invites relatives, friends and neighbours to construct the house together) (see Figures 14.1 and 14.2).

The same 'toloka' principle has contributed to alpine-park and organic agriculture (including apiculture) initiatives. A solar battery is due to be installed this year. Based on a family-values idea, indigenous to the Slavic and Cossack culture of Ukrainians, they have been able to organize regular events, at least monthly, including master-classes, traditional holidays and folklore expeditions on short and long-term bases (Figures 14.3 and 14.4).

FIGURE 14.1 Author's picture of 'Teterivskyi Kish' initiation Toloka

FIGURE 14.2 Author's picture of 'Teterivskyi Kish' house in September 2012

FIGURE 14.3 Author's picture of alpine class during summer camp in June 2012

FIGURE 14.4 Author's picture of Ukrainian garland practice during summer camp in June 2012

The 'Teteryvskyi Kish' dwellers interact with the villagers on the other bank of the river and involve them in order to learn about their lifestyle and customs.

The centre widely exchanges experiences and practice with a growing number of so-called eco-settlements across Ukraine. These colonies reflect the movement of volunteers to almost-dead villages, abandoned areas or just newly privatized land spots (mostly around urban areas of the country) to revive them on an environmentally friendly basis. The movement itself is very similar to other practices around the world. In Ukraine, however, the family values enrich or, in some cases, absorb the environmental concerns, as in Russia, where the idea originated. The general Slavic focus in Ukraine, moreover, has widened with the introduction of medieval customs of Cossack communities in the eco-settlement lifestyle. They often call themselves 'family eco-steads', using a wider understanding of traditional beliefs and farming methods to safeguard the natural, social and cultural environment. From the touristic perspective, nevertheless, the family-stead dwellers are cautious in many cases. It is estimated that there are around eighty such family eco-stead settlements around the country. The capital regions of the country (Kyiv, Zhytomyr, Chernigiv), the Carpathian and the Crimea prosper the most in this respect. The centripetal diffusion, nowadays mostly eastwards, enthusiastically calls for cooperation, largely through the Internet and social media (Real Expo, 2013).

The wide spectrum of outcomes achieved by NGOs and ginger groups feed the environmental, social and cultural (including educational) aspects of tourism integration with truly green activities. Such bottom-up initiatives have gained the support of numerous international funds and institutions. Groups including 'Vidrodzennya' and 'Eurasia', TASIS programmes and the EU-UA Cooperation Committee, the International Chamber of Commerce and European Council, the Foundation for Environmental Education and the International Federation of Organic Agriculture Movements, in addition to financial aid are promoting an academic and public movement towards deep discussion and the search for effective steps to strengthen the green economy in Ukraine.

Eco-labelled destinations in Ukraine

Ukraine as a tourist destination has in recent years steadily enriched its green image with eco-labelled sites (Figure 14.5).

The Agency for Ecological Certification and Labelling, as a subdivision of the Ukrainian non-governmental organization, Zhyva Planeta (Ukrainian representative office of the ICEA – Environmental and Ethical Certification Institute) pioneered the green economy path in Ukraine in 2003. The agency verifies a wide range of products and services (food and beverages, goods, commodities, different types of services and 'green office' requirements) for conformity with international, European, and national organic standards and the environmental certification ISO 14024. This authority also licenses (by resolutions) the usage of international, European and national environmental labelling symbols. The accreditation ISO/Guide 65 (EH 45011) 'General requirements for institutions that manage products certification systems' confirms the quality of certification. Moreover Zhyva Planeta is a participant of the Global Eco-labelling Network (GEN), a member of the International Federation of Organic

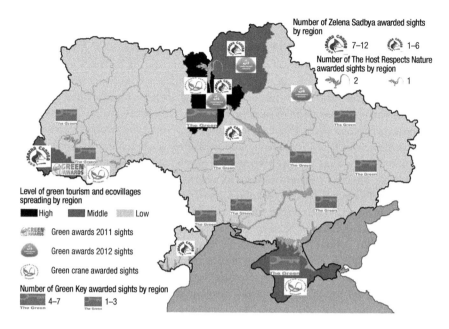

FIGURE 14.5 Eco-labelled destinations in Ukraine

Agriculture Movements (IFOAM) and a counterpart of the Association of Ukrainian Accredited Authorities for Conformity Evaluation.

One of the most developed domains of eco-labelling in Ukraine applies to food and beverages. In 2009 the Ukrainian Parliament added the Law of Ukraine on Safety and Quality of Food and introduced provisions on genetically modified organisms (GMOs). Since that time the producers of food and beverages have been obligated to mark the presence or absence of GMOs in products with appropriate signage ('with GMO' or 'without GMO'). Due to this requirement many actors in the industry have changed their manufacturing technology to exclude GMOs from their goods. Ukrainians have chiefly benefited from this move, and since 2009 they have had a reasonable choice and can shop more carefully. Ecological demands thus require domestic food quality improvements and encourage technological innovations in agriculture and the food industry. Above all, the new 'ecological way of thinking' and respective transformation of the economy gives it a boost.

Ukraine was a pioneer of the eco-labelling system based on ISO 14000 among the former USSR countries. Currently just one eco-sign has international recognition. The Agency for Ecological Certification and Labelling, Zhyva Planeta, introduced the so-called 'green crane' mark (its appearance is similar to the shape of a crane) and registered it with the Ministry for Justice of Ukraine in 2002. The international programme of ecological labelling, ISO 14024, embraced the green crane mark in 2003. Along with the Ukrainian mark some other signs came into the country (e.g. the EU 'Organic farming', German 'BIO-Siegel', French 'AB' (agriculture biologique), UK 'Soil association', USA 'USDA Organic', Canadian 'Ecologo', and the Russian 'Leaf of life').

The Agency for Ecological Certification and Labelling also provides control over office organizations with 'green office'initiatives. It verifies the conformity of entities management to the Standard of Ukraine on Ecological Norms of Administrative Services (offices). The certification comprises evaluation of materials and natural resources usage efficiency, energy conservation, environmental quality of working areas, waste management, and the purchase of goods and services. Organizations that pass the audit obtain the certificate of conformity and the right to use the green crane label. Unfortunately, none of the Ukrainian companies have yet gone through certification.

This Agency for Ecological Certification and Labelling administers two official types of certificates in tourism, approved in accordance with the international standard system, ISO 14024. The first concerns tourism in general and responds to the Standard of Ukraine on Ecological Norms of Tourist Services. This type of certification covers management, working out tourist routes in compliance with ecological norms, waste policy, energy conservation, greening of transport in tourist agencies and ecotourism households. The second type of certificate targets hotels, motels and other accommodation facilities. In conformity with the Standard of Ukraine on Ecological Norms of Temporary Accommodation Services the Agency audits energy, water and waste management, the use of detergents and cleaning products, the quality of amenities (materials they are made of) and food. The key priority relates to the enterprises' influence on the environment. Approved institutions are allowed to use the green crane label and can obtain a corresponding certificate of quality.

Just three entities in Ukraine had gone through official certification as of mid 2013. The first of the Ukrainian green accommodation enterprises was the hotel complex 'Artemida' located near Yalta city, in Crimea (2011). During construction of that hotel trees were cut down to clear the land for building. Besides, most of the flora of the surrounding landscape belongs to rare or endangered species (Agency for Ecological Certification and Labelling, 2011). The next certificate was given to the mountain hotel 'Kovcheg'in 2012, located at the top of Megura mountain (the Carpathians, 1313m). This estate has a fully independent energy supply based on renewable sources: wind generators, solar panels and collectors, wood boiler and diesel-generator (Mountain Hotel Kovcheg, 2012). The latest 'green crane' (at the end of 2012) was for the hospitality complex 'Kozatskyi Stan' located near the capital city of Kyiv (Agency for Ecological Certification and Labelling, 2012).

Besides this agency, which is the official certification institution, there are several non-official private companies who have introduced eco-labelling activities in Ukraine. One of the main ones is the international non-profit organization 'Green Dossier Information Centre'. Located in Kyiv, the organization has worked out its own criteria for eco-certification of tourist businesses in Ukraine and created the label 'The host respects nature'. Its labelling criteria include evaluation of personnel, systems of guest relations, water and power consumption, use of detergents, waste, nutrition, internal climate of the enterprise, greenery, ecological enlightenment, management and cooperation with partners, suppliers and transport, etc. Green Dossier certification successfully adapted its international experience to the national peculiarities of small and medium-sized tourist enterprises and got the approval of the Ukrainian Council for Tourism and Resorts, the Ministry of Culture and and the Ministry of Ecology and Natural Resources. Since 2010, five enterprises including four hotels and one café have passed the certification. Besides already being marked with the 'green crane' certification, the mountain hotel Kovcheg in the Carpathians has attained the 'host respects nature' mark, as have the hotel 'Kosiv' (Kosiv, Ivano-Frankivsk region), the homestead 'Zhyvytsia' (Kosiv, Ivano-Frankivsk region) and the boutique and spa hotel 'Sesony SPA' (near Obuhiv, Kyiv region) together with the kneipp-café 'Kupidon' (Kyiv city) (Green Dossier, 2013).

The rural (green) tourism, which is considered to be the starting point for the green economy path in Ukrainian tourism, has its own system of eco-certification for homesteads, introduced by the Union for Promotion of Rural Green Tourism in 2004. The 'Zelena Sadyba' (Green Homestead) has certification criteria similar to those previously mentioned and the international standards. The elaborated categorization system increases certification levels from the first to the third and validates conformity with the requirements for 2 years. The network of labelled homesteads consists of seventeen in total, including twelve in the Zakarpattya region, two in the Kyiv region and one in the Odesa, Cherkasy and Chernigiv region (Union for Promotion of Rural Green Tourism in Ukraine, 2013).

Participation in programmes of The Foundation for Environmental Education (FEE) (Green Key and Blue Flag) has also elevated the greening efforts of Ukraine. Green Key is currently one of the largest systems of eco-labelling in the world, for accommodation, campsites, restaurants and attractions. Currently a number of Ukrainian hospitality enterprises have the Green Key label, including the Aquapark Goluboy Zaliv (Blue Bay) and the Aquatoria marine animals' theatre (both located in Yalta, Crimea) together with Maison Blanche Bed and Breakfast hostel (Kyiv)and eighteen Green Key hotels. A third of the Green Key hotels are based in the capital city of Kyiv (mainly those of the famous chains, Maison Blanche, Radisson and Intercontinental). Another chain, Reikartz, together with the Radisson hotels predominates among the labelled accommodation facilities in the Crimea (three establishments), Lviv (three) and Mykolaiv (two) along with the regions of Kharkiv, Zaporizhzhya, Dnipropetrovsk, Donetsk and Odesa (each having one hotel). In addition, the Radisson Blue Resort (Bukovel, Ivano-Frankivsk region) successfully meets international standards (Green Key, 2013).

The Blue Flag is a voluntary labelling system for marinas and beaches in accordance with sustainable development principles. The Ukrainian network of Blue Flag sites includes twelve beaches and one marina in the coastal southern regions of the country (the Crimea and Odesa) (Blue Flag, 2013).

Domestically the spread of the green economy since 2011 has been promoted by Green Awards Ukraine which, among other things, nominates tourism and best education green projects. Included among these projects are the eco-resort Izki (Mizhgir'ya, Zakarpattya region), the eco-homestead Maison Blanche (Kyiv region) and eco-hotel ShishkiNN (Chernigiv region) along with the eco-path 'Zhuravlyna' in the Mizhrichenskyi regional landscape park (between the Dnieper and Desna rivers) and eco-art therapy for children with impaired psychological development (Sumy region) (Green Awards Ukraine, 2012).

Conclusion

Numerous inhibitory factors have impacted the low environmental performance in Ukraine. The underdeveloped legal framework and lack of finance have hampered the growth of the green economy model. The international norms of sustainable development and green economy implementation need more sophisticated national legislation and public instruments in the field of ecology (environmental management), sustainable growth and rural development.

In addition, the confusion of terminology has impeded a clear understanding of the green tourism concept apart from the eco- and eco-agro-activities in rural recreation. The basis and principles of sustainable development in tourism have missed having a comprehensive state strategy, which can multiply the benefits of tourism integration with the green economy model.

However, the wide spectrum of bottom-up initiatives has assisted Ukraine's transition to sustainable development with innumerable conferences, workshops and seminars to prompt greening in Ukraine. NGOs, assisted by many international institutions have been urging for the integration of sustainable practices into tourism (rural, in particular) and organic farming. The eco-building movement has been inspired by a combination of organic farming and tourism advantages in different forms providing for diversification and the elaboration of innovative tourism products. The developing network of home and farmstead entities and eco-settlements has encouraged volunteers and ginger groups to undertake green economy practices. The initiatives have complex social and educational implications, hence the businesses seeking the appropriate legal environment and mechanisms for implementation.

The clear steps forward in eco-labelling since the start of the last decade have improved the image of Ukraine as a destination. The pioneer efforts of several NGOs have gained international recognition and, eventually, public approval in terms of state regulation. A few official and unofficial eco-labelling systems have nevertheless elevated the tourism litmus test of the green economy transition in Ukraine along with international certification systems (e.g. Green Key and Blue Flag).

Insights on organic agriculture and eco-building and eco-dwelling initiatives have demonstrated the benefits of their integration with tourism. The scoping picture of mostly bottom-up and outside international initiatives reveals the urgent need for acute shifts in legislative, public and business spheres in order to promote green tourism and economic growth in Ukraine.

References

Agency for Ecological Certification and Labelling (2011) *The first ecologically certified hotel comes into sight in Ukraine.* Agency for Ecological Certification and Labelling: Kyiv. Available from: www.ecolabel.org.ua/novini/156-new.html (Accessed 2 July 2013).

Agency for Ecological Certification and Labelling (2012) *Hotel and restaurant complex 'Kozatskyi Stan' successfully eco-certified.* Agency for Ecological Certification and Labelling: Kyiv. Available from: www.ecolabel.org.ua/novini/419-new.html (Accessed 2 July 2013).

Blue Flag (2013) *Awarded sites in Ukraine.* Blue Flag: Copenhagen. Available from: www.blueflag.org/menu/awarded-sites/2013/northern-hemisphere/ukraine (Accessed 6 July 2013).

eTN Global Travel Industry News (2013) *ICTP President: Time to focus on visitor impact as well as the economy*. eTN Global Travel Industry News: Haleiwa, HI. Available from: www.eturbo news.com/34012/are-we-moving-toward-sustainable-travelism (Accessed 24 June 2013).

European Environment Agency (2011) *Ukraine country fiche-green economy*. European Environment Agency: Copenhagen. Available from: www.eea.europa.eu/themes/regions/pan-european/ virtual-library/Ukraine-Green-economy (Accessed 5 July 2013).

Green Awards Ukraine (2012) *Green Awards Ukraine portal*. Green Awards: Kyiv. Available from: www.greenawards.info/en/home.html (Accessed 12 July 2013).

Green Dossier (2013) *Ecological certification for tourist business*. Green Dossier: Kyiv. Available from: http://ecolabeling.wordpress.com (Accessed 6 July 2013).

Green Key (2013) *Awarded sites in Ukraine*. Green Key: Copenhagen. Available from: www.green-key.org/menu/awarded-sites/ukraine (Accessed 2 July 2013).

Jerzy, W. and Krzysztof, W. (2012) Geography of tourism of Central and Eastern Europe countries. In Lyubitsewa, O., Kiptenko, V., Malska, M., Rutynskiy, M. and Zin'ko, Y. (eds) *Geography of tourism of Ukraine*. (pp. 452–3; 479–81) Department of Regional Geography and Tourism of Wroclaw University, Poland.

Kononeko, O.(2013) Development of green economy in Ukraine as a display of transformation processes. *Kyivsky Geographichny Shorichnyk*, vol. 8, pp. 77–80.

Magazine Organic UA (2013) *Ukrainian organic news*. Magazine Organic UA: Kyiv. Available from: *http://organic.ua* (Accessed 24 June 2013).

Martyniuk, A. and Ogarenko, Y. (2012) *Resource efficiency gains and green growth perspectives in Ukraine*. Friedrich-Ebert-Stiftung: Berlin. Available from: http://library.fes.de/pdf-files/id-moe/09398. pdf (Accessed 3 July 2013).

Medlik, S. (2003) *Dictionary of travel, tourism & hospitality*. (3rd edn). Butterworth Heinemann: Kent.

Ministry of Culture of Ukraine (2009) *The peculiarities of green tourism development in Ukraine (overview based on media materials)*. DZK: Kyiv. Available from: http://mincult.kmu.gov.ua/mincult/uk/ publish/article/183838 (Accessed 6 July 2013).

Mountain Hotel Kovcheg (2012) *Mountain Hotel 'Kovcheg' successfully passed eco-certification*. Mountain Hotel Kovcheg: Dolyshniy Shepit village. Available from: www.megura.net/eco-sertificat (Accessed 10 July 2013).

Order on Adoption of Strategy of Tourism and Resorts Development (2008) (SI 1008-p). Available from: http://zakon2.rada.gov.ua/laws/show/ (Accessed 6 July 2013).

Potapenko, V. (2012) *Strategic priorities for Ukraine's safe development on the basis of 'Green Economy'*. National Institute for Strategic Studies: Kyiv.

Real Expo (2013) *Family eco-settlements in Ukraine*. Real Expo: Kyiv. Available from: www. zagorodna.com/uk/ekologiya/ekologichni-poselennya-ukrajni/rodovi-ekoposelennya-v-ukrajni.html (Accessed 5 July 2013).

UNDP (2013) *Millennium development goals in Ukraine*. United Nations Development Programme: Kyiv. Available from: www.undp.org.ua/en/millennium-development-goals/mdgs-in-ukraine (Accessed 9 July 2013).

UNEP (2011) *Organic agriculture: A step towards the green economy in the Eastern Europe, Caucasus and Central Asia region. Case studies from Armenia, Moldova and Ukraine*. Instaprint: Geneva.

UNEP (2012) *Ukraine. Country study summaries*. Green economy Advisory Services. UNEP: Paris. Available from: www.unep.org/greeneconomy/Portals/88/documents/advisory_services/ countries/Ukraine (Accessed 5 July 2013).

UNEP and UNWTO (2005) *Making tourism more sustainable: A guide for policy-makers*. United Nations Environment Programme: Paris. Available from: www.unep.fr/shared/publications/ pdf/DTIx0592xPA-TourismPolicyEN.pdf (Accessed 26 June 2013).

UNEP and UNWTO (2012) *Tourism in the green economy. Background Report.* WTO: Madrid. Available from: www.unep.org/greeneconomy/Portals/88/documents/ger/ger_final_dec_2011/Tourism (Accessed 26 June 2013).

Union for Promotion of Rural Green Tourism in Ukraine (2013) *Ukrainian network of farmsteads.* Union for Promotion of Rural Green Tourism in Ukraine: Kyiv. Available from: www.greentour.com.ua/ukrainian/catalog (Accessed 2 July 2013).

Verhovna Rada of Ukraine (2004) *The law of Ukraine on tourism* (Cm 324/95-). Available from: http://zakon4.rada.gov.ua/laws/show/1282–15 (Accessed 6 July 2013).

Yale University (2012) *2012 EPI and pilot trend results: EPI score.* Yale Center for Environmental Law and Policy: New Haven, CT. Available from: http://epi.yale.edu/dataexplorer/indicator profiles?ind=EPI (Accessed 14 July 2013).

15

ECOTOURISM AS A MECHANISM FOR ACHIEVING A GREEN ECONOMY IN DEVELOPING COUNTRIES

Experiences from Ghana

Patrick Brandful Cobbinah, Rik Thwaites and Rosemary Black

Introduction

The green economy has been increasingly recognized in the international discourse as a global approach and an alternative development paradigm in mitigating atmospheric carbon content, reducing poverty and ensuring sustainable development (UNEP *et al.*, 2011). Although there is no internationally agreed definition of the green economy, one of the most widely cited definitions is provided by the United Nations Environment Programme (UNEP, 2011, p. 2) which describes the green economy as 'one that results in improved human well-being and social equity, while significantly reducing environmental risks and ecological scarcities. It is low carbon, resource efficient and socially inclusive'. With its focus on poverty reduction, social inclusiveness, environmental conservation and carbon emission reduction, the green economy is now regarded as providing a pathway towards achieving sustainable development (UNEP, 2011).

While developed countries are more concerned with reducing carbon emissions in their transitioning into the green economy, Khor (2010) argues that developing countries are committed to reducing poverty and achieving sustainable growth. With a low-carbon profile and rich natural capital assets in developing countries, UNEP *et al.* (2011) have identified key sectors that may contribute to the greening of developing country economies including: energy access, waste, ecotourism, agriculture, sustainable urbanization and forestry. The focus of this chapter is on the potential of ecotourism to contribute to the green economy in a developing country, using a case study from Ghana.

Ecotourism, as a niche form of tourism and a development philosophy, has grown and gained global influence as a sustainable development and environmental conservation strategy (Courvisanos and Jain, 2006; Western, 2012) and has attracted attention from both development proponents such as academics and development agents such as national governments and donor countries. Early definitions of ecotourism focused on describing nature-based tourism activities (Wallace and Pierce, 1996). Ceballos-Lascurain was one of the first to define ecotourism as 'travelling to relatively undisturbed or uncontaminated natural areas with the specific objective of studying, admiring and enjoying the scenery and its wild plants and animals as well as any existing cultural manifestations found in these areas' (Ceballos-Lascurain, 1987, p. 14).

Over the past three decades, different definitions have gone beyond the descriptive elements of locations and activities to include various normative elements or outcomes. Based on a content analysis of forty-two selected definitions (thirty from academic literature and twelve from government and non-governmental organization [NGO] sources), Donohoe and Needham (2006) identify six tenets central to the concept of ecotourism: nature-based by providing opportunity to experience natural areas; preservation and conservation by creating awareness of ecosystem requirements and ensuring cooperation between providers and community; environmental education by increasing awareness and understanding of natural and cultural heritage; sustainability by achieving equity and social justice and integrating conservation and development; distribution of benefits by improving the quality of life of local people; and ethics/ responsibility by adopting an ethics-based environmentally, socially and culturally responsible approach.

Thus, ecotourism and the green economy are both sustainable development concepts that seek to protect the natural environment and deliver sustainable outcomes to people. Although the concept of sustainable development is highly contested, Kates *et al.* (2005) assert that it hinges on three key pillars: economic development, social development and environmental protection, which are mutually reinforcing at the local, national and global levels. Whereas the green economy is a global strategy for achieving sustainable development, ecotourism is generally a local or community level strategy that has the potential to contribute to sustainable development.

As suggested earlier, the green economy focuses on poverty reduction, environmental conservation, social inclusiveness and carbon emission reduction as the pathway to achieving sustainable development. However, the literature (e.g. Courvisanos and Jain, 2006; Honey, 2008) suggests that ecotourism can contribute to the green economy through environmental conservation, social inclusiveness and poverty reduction by generating revenue/income, creating employment opportunities and empowering local communities as well as reducing local communities' dependence on the natural environment for their livelihood in terms of resource extraction. UNEP *et al.* (2011) recognize that the rich natural resources in many developing countries offer the potential for ecotourism to be a key contributor to growing the green economy and thus conserving the environment by reducing local communities' dependence on natural resources and generating employment opportunities, especially important in local communities without the resources for engaging in industrial activities.

On the other hand, there are well-known negative impacts of ecotourism, especially in Africa, such as limited benefits to the local community (Charnley, 2005; Chiusti *et al.*, 2011), depletion of natural and ecological resources (Kamauro, 1996; Ormsby and Mannie, 2006) and indoctrination and invasion of foreign culture into local communities (Clifton and Benson, 2006) which can be detrimental to the pursuit of the green economy. For example, Chiusti et al.'s study (2011) reveals that there are very limited socio-economic benefits of ecotourism in both the Mahenye Ecotourism Venture in Chipinge District, Zimbabwe and the Makuleke Ecotourism Initiative in South Africa because of poor governance and discriminative policies.

Similarly, in the Ngorongoro Conservation Area in Tanzania the local community has been excluded in participating and benefiting from ecotourism because of the lack of policy direction and weak institutions (Charnley, 2005). Kamauro (1996) also asserts that the Maasai National Park in Kenya and the Ngorongoro Conservation Area in Tanzania have been severely depleted as a result of increased demand for firewood used for cooking and heating in tourist camps and lodges. One of the key issues of ecotourism operationalization is therefore to understand and manage these impacts, as ecotourism should aim to minimize the negative impacts and maximize the positive impacts on the environment and local communities. Thus, ecotourism operationalization should be appropriately planned and managed to deliver the outcomes proposed by the green economy. This will require formulation and implementation of policies at the national and local levels as well as the international legal framework which UNEP (2011) argues are central to the idea of the green economy.

Green economy initiatives and challenges in Sub-Saharan Africa tourism

Across Sub-Saharan Africa, the green economy has been recognized by many countries (e.g., South Africa, Ethiopia, Ghana and Namibia) as one of the drivers of sustainable national development. Although the concept of the green economy remains unclear in the African context because of different institutional interpretations and similarities with the sustainable development concept, the German Society for International Cooperation (GIZ) indicates that the green economy is necessary for Africa's development, as it provides economic opportunities for economies dependent on natural resources (GIZ, 2013). In addition, African economies' vulnerability to climate change makes the green economy a relevant approach to sustainable development (UNEP, 2011). Many countries in Sub-Saharan Africa are promoting initiatives directed towards achieving a green economy, although they are at different stages. These initiatives focus on transport, housing, energy, agriculture, forestry and tourism (UNEP et al., 2011).

In relation to tourism, UNEP and the United Nations World Tourism Organization (UNWTO) explain that a green economy can result when tourism activities are maintained or sustained indefinitely by engaging adequately with social, economic, cultural and environmental goals (UNEP and UNWTO, 2012). Africa, being the fastest-growing tourism destination in the world, recorded an average annual growth of 6.4 per cent between 2000 and 2010 (WTTC, 2010). Tourism is therefore recognized as one of the few strategies for achieving sustainable poverty reduction in many countries in Sub-Saharan Africa (UNEP and UNWTO, 2012). Many governments, donor organizations, private sector organizations and NGOs have developed tourism initiatives directed towards achieving the green economy.

The governments' role mainly revolves around policies and programmes which create an enabling environment for tourism to succeed, including political and economic stability, safety of visitors and favourable conditions for investors (Spenceley, 2010; UNEP and UNWTO, 2012). Among the government-led tourism-oriented green economy initiatives are the Ecotourism Strategy in Seychelles (Seraphine, 2010); Namibia's Conservancy Programme,which allows local residents the rights to use wildlife on their lands; and sustainable tourism policies developed by the governments of South Africa and the Gambia (UNEP and UNWTO, 2012) as well as Botswana's policy to support high-value tourism while minimizing impacts (Spenceley, 2010).

The activities of donor organizations (multilateral and bilateral agencies) are vital to tourism development and green economy initiatives in Sub-Saharan Africa, especially in the areas of financial support, technical assistance and professional development (Spenceley, 2010; UNEP and UNWTO, 2012). Examples of donor initiatives include the International Finance Corporation's Anchor Investment Programme in Mozambique which creates stable land tenure in protected areas such as the Maputo Special Reserve and leverages investment from operators with good environmental practices; the World Bank's Transfrontier Conservation Area Programme in Mozambique; and the UNWTO's Sustainable Tourism Eliminating Poverty initiative (UNEP and UNWTO, 2012). Other donor initiatives are the United Nations Industrial Development Organization's Collaborative Actions for Sustainable Tourism Project which promotes coastal biodiversity conservation, management and monitoring in nine East and West African countries; the United States Agency for International Development's Global Sustainable Tourism Alliance in Mali; and other tourism interventions in protected areas of Rwanda, Mozambique, Kenya and Tanzania (UNEP and UNWTO, 2012) as well as the Norwegian Agency for Development Cooperation programme on tourism infrastructure and community-based natural resource management in Zambia, South Africa, Tanzania, Mozambique, Uganda and Malawi (Spenceley, 2010; UNEP and UNWTO, 2012).

There are many private sector initiatives that also promote sustainable tourism towards achieving the green economy in Sub-Saharan Africa, including the Great Plains Conservation which applies carbon offset programmes to finance conservation; and the Banyan Tree (a hotel group) which supports initiatives to connect communities and conservation NGOs. A number of private organizations are also certified as promoting sustainable tourism and green economy initiatives in Africa, including Masakutu in The Gambia; Singita in South Africa, Tanzania and Zimbabwe; the Mantis collection in South Africa, Rwanda, Zambia and Mozambique; and Nkwichi Lodge (UNEP and UNWTO, 2012).

NGOs, both local and international, are playing key roles in green economy initiatives in the tourism sector. These initiatives include the International Gorilla Conservation Programme which supports Mountain Gorilla conservation in the Virunga Massif between Rwanda the Democratic Republic of Congo and Uganda; the Netherlands Development Organization's (SNV) Poverty Reduction through Tourism Programme in Tanzania, Rwanda, Mozambique, Zambia, Mali, Ghana, and Kenya; and the Conservation International NGO initiative in tourism infrastructure development in Ghana (Spenceley, 2010; UNEP and UNWTO, 2012).

However, there a number of challenges in using tourism as a medium to achieve green economy objectives in Sub-Saharan Africa. According to GIZ (2013), while the legal and regulatory framework necessary to promote the green economy remains in its infancy stage across Sub-Saharan Africa, the lack of clarity of the meaning of the concept of a green economy has resulted in inadequate knowledge and awareness of the green economy's potential for job creation and economic growth. Other challenges include poor human and institutional capacity and inadequate collaboration between the various stakeholders (GIZ, 2013). These challenges appear to undermine green economy initiatives in many countries in Africa.

Within this context of ongoing uncertainties surrounding tourism's potential to contribute to the green economy, this chapter presents an example from Ghana on ecotourism's potential to green the economy. Using the Kakum Conservation Area (KCA), the most visited ecotourism destination in Ghana, as the case study, the chapter considers the contribution of ecotourism development to achieving the green economy, particularly in relation to poverty reduction, social inclusiveness and environmental conservation in the communities around the KCA.

Background to ecotourism in Ghana

Ghana is located in West Africa within the tropical region and is bounded to the west by Cote d'Ivoire, to the east by Togo, to the north by Burkina Faso and to the south by the Gulf of Guinea (see Figure 15.1). Ghana has ten administrative regions and is rich in ecotourism resources including national parks, historical sites, beaches and game reserves (Tamakloe, 2000). As illustrated in Figure 15.1, some of the major ecotourism destinations in Ghana include Bia, Bui, Mole National Parks, Kakum Conservation Area, Shai Hills, Ankasa, Kogyae and Bomfobiri Resource Reserves, Owabi Wildlife

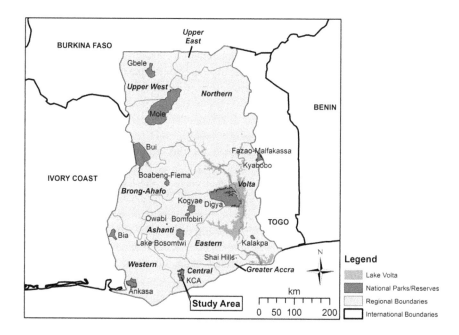

FIGURE 15.1 Major ecotourism destinations in Ghana
Source: Charles Sturt University Spatial Analysis Unit (2013)

Sanctuary, Buabeng Fiema Monkey Sanctuary, Lake Bosomtwi and several coastal wetlands (Asiedu, 2002). Most of the ecotourism resources in Ghana are found in rural areas where poverty levels are high and many remain undeveloped.

Although these ecotourism resources and destinations exist in Ghana, the sector faces many challenges such as limited community involvement (Bediako, 2000; Asiedu, 2002). According to Bediako (2000) the ecotourism sector is accorded low priority in the national development framework particularly by the Ghana Wildlife Division (GWD), the organization responsible for managing protected and natural areas in Ghana. This situation has resulted in poor quality and inadequate provision of tourist services and infrastructural facilities and lack of interpretation, which has in turn limited the level of tourist visitation and employment and income generation at the local level (Bediako, 2000; Asiedu, 2002). In addition, the low commitment to destination development in rural communities, in Asiedu's (2002) view, means ecotourism has not achieved its potential to reduce poverty in those local communities. Asiedu (2002) asserts that the development of these ecotourism destinations and associated tourism activity has the potential to spread direct and indirect benefits across the country that could result in significant improvements in the living conditions of the poor which could contribute to advancing the objectives of the green economy.

A further challenge identified by Bediako (2000) arises from the limited level of community involvement in ecotourism development in Ghana. Bediako (2000) finds that local communities around ecotourism destinations are dissatisfied by their limited involvement in ecotourism development and disappointed by the outcomes. Haligah (1998) and Asiedu (1998) argue that local disillusionment resulting from limited outcomes from, and community engagement in, ecotourism could threaten environmental conservation efforts in Ghana. According to Asiedu (2002, p. 8), if such local disillusionment is not resolved, this 'could endanger the very principles upon which ecotourism is founded leading to local disinterest in it'. From this we can infer that there would be a likely consequence for the objectives of the green economy to create a socially inclusive society, reduce poverty and conserve the environment.

Methodology

A qualitative research approach was adopted for this study using semi-structured interviews, in-depth interviews and secondary data analysis. Based on the identification of twenty-seven communities within a 1–10km range of the KCA (Appiah-Opoku, 2011), the four communities of Abrafo, Mesomagor, Adadientem and Nuamakrom were selected as research study areas to provide diversity in geographic location, proximity to the KCA and proximity to existing ecotourism attractions (see Figure 15.2). Following consultation with community leaders, ten residents from each of the four communities were purposively selected based on their understanding and experiences with ecotourism in the KCA and were interviewed on their experiences in terms of benefits from and challenges of ecotourism.

To gather background information on ecotourism and its management in the KCA, semi-structured interviews were also undertaken with representatives of four institutions: GWD responsible for the management of the KCA; Ghana Heritage and Conservation Trust (GHCT) responsible for ecotourism development and management in the KCA;

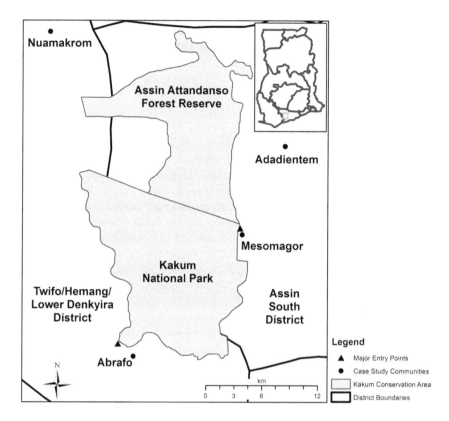

FIGURE 15.2 Location of the KCA in the district context
Source: Charles Sturt University Spatial Analysis Unit (2013)

Conservation International (CI) NGO who were key contributors to the design and development of ecotourism facilities in the KCA; and Ghana Tourism Authority (GTA) responsible for implementation of tourism policies and plans in Ghana.

Ecotourism and the green economy: the case of the KCA, Ghana

Physical characteristics of the KCA

Covering a land area of 360km^2, the KCA is located about 30km north of Cape Coast, the Central Regional capital. The KCA lies in the Upper Guinea forest zone in southern Ghana (Eggert *et al.*, 2003) between longitude 1°30' W – 1°51' W and latitude 5°20' N – 5°40' N. The major rainy season is from March to July while the period from September to November marks the minor rainy season (Monney *et al.*, 2010). The KCA is endowed with faunal diversity with mammals such as elephants, potto and Demidoffs galago; species of primates such as black and white colobus; reptiles such as dwarf crocodile and serrated tortoise; and a total of 266 bird species and about 405 species of butterflies IUCN (2010). Moreover, the KCA is a reserve that represents the diminishing tropical evergreen forest located within the semi-deciduous forest zone (Appiah-Opoku, 2011). According to Eggert *et al.* (2003) logging activities in the KCA began in the 1930s and intensified between the 1950s and 1980s due to poor supervision by the Ghana Forestry Department. In 1989, the Central Region Administration suspended logging activities.

Background and purpose of the KCA

In 1992, the KCA was officially and legally gazetted as a national park and resource reserve by the Wildlife Reserves Regulations (Ll 1525) under the administrative jurisdiction of the GWD (IUCN, 2010). As illustrated in Figure 15.2, the KCA comprises the Assin Attandanso Resource Reserve and the Kakum National Park. These two reserves were established to protect the watersheds of the Kakum River and other rivers which supply the water needs of Cape Coast and the surrounding communities (IUCN, 2010).

The KCA has also been described as seeking to restore and maintain the integrity of the rapidly diminishing rain forest reserve while diversifying the tourism product offerings of Ghana, providing environmental education to both tourists and local communities and promoting economic development in the surrounding local communities (CI, 1998; Appiah-Opoku, 2011). With the assistance of the CI NGO, ecotourism was introduced in 1995 as a catalyst to facilitate effective management of the KCA and to stimulate development in the local communities (CI, 1998). Ecotourism development started with the construction of a canopy walkway (major ecotourism facility) by the Government of Ghana and the CI NGO and the establishment of a tree platform in the KCA by the GWD. In addition, other community and privately owned attractions such as the craft village, the traditional bamboo orchestra, the bee-keeping centre and the monkey sanctuary have developed outside the reserve to leverage off the KCA developments.

Characteristics of communities around the KCA

Politically the KCA straddles the Twifo-Hemang Lower Denkyira District (THLDD) and Assin South District (see Figure 15.2). Based on an early socio-economic survey (GWD, 1996) and the 2010 national population and housing census, about a quarter of the total population of the two districts live in the communities bordering the KCA (Akyeampong, 2011; GSS, 2012). These two districts are predominantly rural, with THLDD having 75 per cent and Assin South District 100 per cent rural populations (GSS, 2012). Agriculture is the dominant economic activity in these districts employing over 70 per cent of the total population in both districts (GSS, 2012), though in the communities bordering the KCA over 90 per cent are engaged in small-scale agriculture (Monney *et al.*, 2010).

Management of the KCA and ecotourism

The management of the KCA has been the legislative responsibility of the GWD under the Ghana Forestry Commission. With the introduction of ecotourism into the KCA in

1995, the GHCT, a non-profit NGO was established by the CI NGO to manage ecotourism in the KCA on behalf of the Ghana government and to generate funds for the management of the KCA. Given the location of ecotourism attractions (e.g. canopy walkway) within the KCA, the GHCT has been collaborating with the GWD to manage the KCA.

Contribution of ecotourism to the green economy in the KCA

As earlier identified, ecotourism has the potential to contribute to sustainable development by engaging local communities, reducing poverty and conserving the environment, though this has not always been the experience. The following section explores the experiences of communities around the KCA in Ghana on the implementation of ecotourism and interprets these in the context of successes and challenges in its contribution to the green economy.

Successes of ecotourism's contribution to the green economy in the KCA

Given its proximity to the Central Regional capital, Cape Coast and Ghana's national capital, Accra, the KCA is the primary ecotourism destination in Ghana. As a result, the study findings indicate that the total tourist visitation to the canopy walkway in the KCA has been increasing over the years. Given that the canopy walkway is the major source of attraction, the study findings show that it is the first point of visit by tourists to the KCA. As a result, the GHCT only keeps records on tourist visitation to the canopy walkway. Between 2000 and 2011, the number of tourist visits to the canopy walkway in the KCA more than tripled. As illustrated in Figure 15.3, domestic tourist numbers have increased over the past years while international tourist numbers have remained stable.

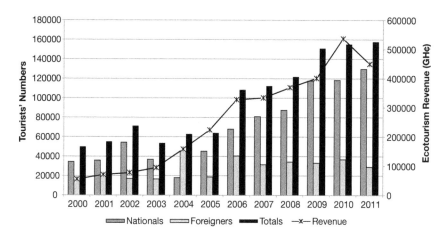

FIGURE 15.3 Tourist visitation to and ecotourism revenue from the canopy walkway in the KCA

Note: As of 17 June 2013, US$1= Ghana Cedis [GH¢] 1.9.

Source: Derived from GHCT Ecotourism Records (2012)

The increasing visitation to the canopy walkway in the KCA has been accompanied by an increase in revenue from entry fees as presented in Figure 15.3. According to the GHCT, ecotourism revenue from the canopy walkway in the KCA is shared between the Government of Ghana (51 per cent) and the GHCT (49 per cent). Officials from GWD and GHCT explained that the government revenue from ecotourism goes into consolidated funds for the development and benefit of the entire country while the rest contributes to the management and maintenance of the KCA.

In addition to revenue generation, community residents at major entry points to the KCA (Abrafo and Mesomagor) believe that the introduction of ecotourism into the KCA has fostered a relationship of cooperation between the communities and the GWD and GHCT. This has led to the creation of employment opportunities for a limited number of community members in the KCA such as tour guiding and cleaning. Further, local people believe that their cooperation with the GWD and GHCT in the development of ecotourism and management of the KCA is a key factor in attracting tourists to the area. Ecotourism within the KCA gives the community the opportunity to provide tourists with experiences outside the reserve and thus generate additional income by sharing their cultures and interacting with tourists, and through the sale of farm produce. This, they assert, means they are committed to supporting the protection of the KCA because it attracts tourists to their communities: 'For us in this community, the tree platform [ecotourism attraction] always makes us renew our commitment to protect the park [KCA] because it supports the development of our traditional bamboo orchestra and provides jobs for some of our people' (Mesomagor 5, June 2012).

A number of community ecotourism attractions have been developed around the major entry points to the KCA. The Abrafo craft village has provided training for local residents to use their creative skills in basket weaving, traditional dress-making (*kente*) and bead-making. The bee-keeping centre in Abrafo displays traditional honey production practices. And in Mesomagor, the traditional bamboo orchestra offers a special cultural experience to tourists. Interviews with community members indicate that while these ecotourism activities provide employment and income for some community residents, others are happy with the international recognition of their communities and the regular interaction with tourists: '. . . Because of the park [KCA] and the tourists who come here, we have a website and the name of this community is on the internet.' (Mesomagor 8, June 2012).

Interviews with the local community also identified the empowerment of women as a benefit resulting from ecotourism development. For example, in Mesomagor, interviewees explained that because of tourist visitation to the KCA and their community to see the traditional bamboo orchestra, some local women have been trained as cooks and now provide local food for tourists. Some expressed the view that the traditional bamboo orchestra not only provides income to households, but has also contributed to women's involvement in community-level decision-making, and that, together, these contribute to a low incidence of gender discrimination, enhanced respect and improved well-being for women in the community:

> We [women's group] cook indigenous foods such as plantains, fufu . . . We feel
> happy doing that because it is refreshing cooking for a whiteman . . . it's not

> because we get money from that to support our families but the community leaders also involve us in taking decisions about the community's development.
>
> (Mesomagor 1, June 2012)

The above discussion reveals that ecotourism in the KCA contributes to the development of the green economy in terms of poverty reduction, environmental conservation and social inclusion. Tourist entry fees make a direct contribution to the management and thus environmental conservation in the KCA. Opportunities for direct employment in the KCA and the development of community ecotourism ventures outside the reserve generate income in local communities and thus contribute to the alleviation of poverty. The involvement of women in ecotourism activities providing them with a role in income-generation and decision-making raises their position within the community and thus contributes to the social inclusion objective of the green economy. The recognition of local benefits arising from ecotourism also raises support for the management of the KCA and thus reinforces the environmental conservation objective.

However, the above discussion draws heavily on perspectives expressed in the communities located at the main entry points to the KCA (e.g. Abrafo and Mesomagor) which attract the majority of tourist visits to the region. Communities further away from the major entry points to the KCA (e.g. Nuamakrom and Adadientem) have different perspectives to offer, that may enhance our understanding of the experience of developing ecotourism and the challenges that may limit ecotourism's contribution to achieving the green economy.

Challenges of ecotourism's contribution to the green economy

Prior to the gazettal of the KCA in 1992, communities in the vicinity of the reserve engaged in off-farm seasonal activities such as hunting and gathering of snails, mushrooms, firewood, raffia palm for roofing, pestle and mortar for making local food (*fufu*), chewing sticks for cleaning teeth and canes used for basket-weaving. These forest-based activities supported their subsistence needs, but also provided some income outside their small-scale farming (Baidu-Ntiamoa, 2002; KCA, 1997). With the gazettal of the KCA, these forest-based activities ceased, removing the opportunity for seasonal income generation and their supply of forest goods to supplement food supplies, as well as other needs such as medicines and construction materials.

In the memory of many local community members, ecotourism was introduced around the same time as the KCA was gazetted (1990s) and they attribute the ban on hunting wildlife in the forest to the introduction of ecotourism, rather than to the establishment of the Conservation Area. They consider that the hunting ban has not only removed an important supplementary food source and source of income, but has resulted in an increase in the wildlife population and an increased occurrence of farm raids in the surrounding communities. Many community participants expressed the view that ecotourism and conservation have compounded the poverty situation of households in communities surrounding the KCA. Barnes *et al.* (2003) confirm the impact of farm raids, finding that about 300 households living around the KCA lose 60 per cent of their crops annually to farm raids by wildlife. Interviews also indicated that there have been no compensation payments made to local farmers experiencing such losses. Thus with the constant threat from wildlife, the loss of crops and the loss of access to forest products, many local people have expressed an antagonistic attitude towards ecotourism.

Negative views of ecotourism were also expressed in terms of the lack of benefits arising from ecotourism, unmet promises and a lack of commitment from the government and a lack of inclusion of local people in the decision-making process. According to community and agency interviewees, the introduction of ecotourism into the KCA by the government and the CI NGO has created a perception among both residents and government institutions that ecotourism in the KCA is a national project. Local people expressed the frustration of people who have been excluded from the process of development of ecotourism and from its benefits. Despite promises from the government about the benefits that would come to them from the establishment of the KCA and development of ecotourism, many local people, particularly those living away from the major tourist entry points (e.g. those in Nuamakrom and Adadientem) have experienced no benefits from ecotourism development.

While seeing increasing numbers of tourists, residents of communities around the KCA assert that they are excluded from the benefits of increasing revenues, as these are shared between the government and the GHCT. They believe that they should receive a share of the ecotourism revenue, but there is no existing policy or framework for the development of ecotourism and managing and distributing its impacts (both positive and negative). While the GHCT official explained that 51 per cent of ecotourism fee revenues go into government consolidated funds for development of the whole country, local residents expressed disappointment with the limited development interventions that have been introduced into their communities. They complained about the poor state of infrastructure (e.g. roads) and lack of social services (e.g. piped water) in their communities, demonstrating to them the lack of commitment from government to support development in their communities. These negative attitudes towards ecotourism were expressed more strongly by residents of Nuamakrom and Adadientem:

> the government takes all the revenue from ecotourism in the KCA and keeps on promising us development . . . If the government cares about us, it will spend some of the revenue to construct our road and provide us with piped water.
>
> (Nuamakrom 4, May 2012)

Interestingly, they remain supportive of conservation of the KCA for reasons such as this: 'It [KCA] is very important to us because the stream from which we fetch water takes its source from the park . . .' (Adadientem 9, July 2012).

Residents from communities at the major entry points to the KCA identified another challenge for ecotourism related to the operation of ecotourism activities within their communities such as the traditional bamboo orchestra in Mesomagor and the craft village in Abrafo. Visitor numbers have been lower to these attractions than to products within the KCA such as the canopy walkway. Residents believe that these community-based attractions have been less effective at attracting visitors, attributing this to poor marketing, the poor state of the infrastructure, particularly roads, and the poor quality of services provided to tourists. In Mesomagor, the low and variable numbers of tourists was linked by interviewees to poor road conditions and lack of electricity in the community.

The Abrafo residents attributed the low numbers of tourists to poor marketing by the GHCT and GWD because of the weak relationship between the craft village and these two institutions. Residents suggested that these ecotourism attractions have not met their potential in terms of delivering employment and income generation to their community. While residents in Abrafo and Mesomagor are concerned about the limited benefits, those in Adadientem and Nuamakrom consider the distance of their communities from the major entry points as the reason that they have no community ecotourism attractions, and no tourist visitation and thus no benefits from employment, income generation and engaging with tourists.

These results suggest that ecotourism has actually contributed little to poverty reduction in these communities surrounding the KCA and has certainly not met people's expectations for employment and income-generation. In fact, the loss of access to forest resources and increased crop and property damage from wildlife incursions onto farms has actually compounded poverty issues. Further, the limited opportunity to engage with tourists, the lack of a share in direct revenue from entry fees, the unmet promises and perceived lack of commitment from the government to deliver improved infrastructure and services, and the perception that ecotourism is a government project that excludes local involvement and opportunity, all point towards a failure of eco-tourism to meet the green economy expectation of social inclusion. Moreover, though support for conservation in the KCA was often expressed by the community, the frustration and antagonism expressed by some towards ecotourism may spill over into negative attitudes towards conservation and potentially drive activities that are contrary to the objectives of environmental conservation.

Discussion and future directions

The introduction of the green economy as an alternative development paradigm has encouraged the international community, national and local governments and NGOs to adopt new development strategies that focus on poverty reduction, social inclusiveness, carbon emission reduction and environmental sustainability. Although the green economy literature has identified ecotourism as one opportunity for greening the economy, studies on ecotourism show that there are well-known negative impacts of ecotourism such as depletion of natural and ecological resources (Ormsby and Mannie, 2006) and indoctrination and invasion of foreign culture into local communities (Clifton and Benson, 2006). In addition, the lack of ecotourism policies in many developing countries has resulted in a situation where many attractions remain either undeveloped or underdeveloped (e.g. Bediako, 2000; Charnley, 2005). In this case study of the KCA, the local communities' key concerns in relation to ecotourism are their of lack of ecotourism revenue benefits and the incidence of farm raids by wildlife from the KCA as a result of hunting bans.

In addition, while residents of communities located at the entry points to the KCA maintained that ecotourism activities in their communities have been less effective because of limited employment and income-generating opportunities, others from communities located further away expressed their disappointment with the lack of ecotourism attractions in their communities. Data from community interviews show that some community residents have developed an antagonistic and apathetic attitude towards ecotourism because of the farm raids, the limited perceived benefits from ecotourism and the lack of ecotourism attractions in some local communities. This situation has the potential to threaten the sustainability of ecotourism attractions and the key tenets upon which ecotourism is founded (Donohoe and Needham, 2006), given that the livelihoods of the communities surrounding the KCA are based on small-scale agriculture and previously on forest resources in the KCA.

The persistent nature of poverty and the volatile economic conditions in Ghana and many developing countries further complicate the ideals of the green economy because these issues directly affect the natural environment and policy decisions relating to the local communities. However, the successes of ecotourism in helping to alleviate poverty, contribute to social inclusion and support environmental conservation as presented in this case study are cause for some optimism regarding ecotourism's capacity to contribute to the green economy in Ghana. However, this case study has also discussed the various ways in which ecotourism does not contribute to the green economy in Ghana.

In an era of global commitment towards achieving sustainable development, the contributions and challenges of ecotourism presented in this case study present an opportunity to minimize the negative impacts and maximize the positive impacts of ecotourism in Ghana through planning and management to deliver sustainable outcomes proposed by the green economy. Thus, ecotourism's potential to contribute to the green economy in Ghana could be enhanced through the formulation and implementation of national and local ecotourism policies which set out the development and management practices that could ensure improved engagement with the local community and equitable distribution of ecotourism benefits. Given the local communities' strong support for the conservation of the KCA, an appropriate ecotourism policy with an equitable impact distribution mechanism has the potential to deliver wider benefits to the local communities in relation to employment and income-generation, community empowerment and environmental conservation, thus contributing to the green economy.

However, in the context of the KCA where the government has a major interest in ecotourism because of its revenue-generating capacity and limited involvement of local communities, it is uncertain if future ecotourism policies will focus on integrating and involving local communities in ecotourism and ensuring equitable distribution of ecotourism benefits.

Conclusion

This case study suggests that ecotourism's contribution to the green economy in Ghana is a paradox. On the one hand community perception indicates that ecotourism has contributed to a limited extent to environmental conservation, social inclusiveness, reduction of local communities' reliance on forest resources and poverty reduction through employment creation, but it is also perceived to have compounded poverty in some of the communities around the KCA. The study findings show that while ecotourism attractions are concentrated in some of the communities, the negative impacts such as farm raids are experienced across all the communities bordering the KCA. The lack of clear policies to implement the concept of ecotourism has also resulted in local dissatisfaction through limited opportunities for engagement in tourism and limited benefits. If these challenges are not addressed, it is likely that ecotourism in the local communities will continue to remain underdeveloped and cannot be potential drivers for advancing conservation, social inclusion and poverty reduction initiatives and promoting the green economy.

Future research regarding ecotourism's potential to contribute to the green economy especially in developing countries could focus on understanding the green economy concept from the perspective of local institutions on the role of community engagement as well as the practicability of the ecotourism concept as an alternative development paradigm in local communities. In addition, the barriers that impede ecotourism implementation towards transitioning into the green economy could be explored.

In the Sub-Saharan African context, the study findings indicate that there is no universal approach to achieving the green economy through tourism. Despite the various green economy oriented initiatives, tourism development in Africa is faced with many challenges. Transition into the green economy through tourism in Sub-Saharan Africa therefore requires the cooperation and commitment of the various stakeholders (e.g., governments, NGOs, private sector, donor organizations) towards sustainable implementation of tourism. This approach will ensure that tourism engages with the political process of delivering wider poverty reduction outcomes and environmental conservation benefits, which are imperative to achieving the objectives of the green economy.

Acknowledgement

This study forms part of a PhD thesis which is funded by Charles Sturt University, Albury, Australia. The authors are particularly grateful to the Faculty of Science, Charles Sturt University for sponsoring this study.

References

Akyeampong, O. A. (2011) Pro-poor tourism: residents' expectations, experiences and perceptions in the Kakum National Park area of Ghana, *Sustainable Tourism*, vol. 19, no. 2, pp. 197–213.

Appiah-Opoku, S. (2011) Using protected areas as a tool for biodiversity conservation and ecotourism: A case study of Kakum National Park in Ghana, *Society and Natural Resources*, vol. 24, no. 5, pp. 500–10.

Asiedu, A.B. (1998) An overview of issues in domestic tourism promotion in Ghana, *Legon Journal of Humanities*, vol. 11, pp. 67–84.

Asiedu, A.B. (2002) Making ecotourism more supportive of rural development in Ghana, *West African Journal of Applied Ecology*, vol. 3, pp. 1–16.

Baidu-Ntiamoa, Y. (2002) Indigenous versus introduced biodiversity conservation strategies: the case of protected area systems in Ghana. In Weber, W. (ed.) *African rainforest ecology and conservation*. Yale University Press: New Haven, CT, pp. 385–394.

Barnes, R.F.W., Boafo, Y., Nandjui, A., Umaru-Farouk, D., Hema, E.M., Danquah, E. and Manford, M. (2003) *An overview of crop-raiding by elephants around the Kakum Conservation Area*, Elephant Biology and Management Project, Africa Programme, Conservation International: Washington, DC.

Bediako, V.J. (2000) Sustainable ecotourism development in Ghana: A case study of the Kakum National Park, MPhil Thesis, Department of Geography, Norwegian University of Science and Technology at Trondheim, Norway.

Ceballos-Lascurain, H. (1987) The future of ecotourism, *Mexico Journal*, January, pp. 13–14.

Charnley, S. (2005) From nature tourism to ecotourism? The case of the Ngorongoro Conservation Area, Tanzania, *Human Organization*, vol. 64, no. 1, pp. 75–88.

Chiusti, S., Mukoroverwa, M., Karigambe, P. and Mudzengi, B.K. (2011) The theory and practice of ecotourism in Southern Africa, *Journal of Hospitality Management and Tourism*, vol. 2, no. 2, pp. 14–21.

CI (1998) Creating solutions for the 21st century, Annual report, Conservation International NGO at Washington, DC.

Clifton, J. and Benson, A. (2006) Planning for sustainable ecotourism: The case for research ecotourism in developing country destinations, *Journal of Sustainable Tourism*, vol. 14, no. 3, pp. 238–54.

Courvisanos, J. and Jain, A. (2006) A framework for sustainable ecotourism: application to Costa Rica, *Tourism and Hospitality Planning and Development*, vol. 3, no. 2, pp. 131–42.

Donohoe, H.M. and Needham, R.D. (2006) Ecotourism: the evolving contemporary definition, *Journal of Ecotourism*, vol. 5, no. 3, pp. 192–210.

Eggert, L.S., Eggert, J.A. and Woodruff, D.S. (2003) Estimating population sizes for elusive animals: the forest elephants of Kakum National Park, Ghana, *Molecular Ecology*, vol. 12, no. 6, pp. 1389–1402.

GIZ (2013) *Green economy in Sub-Saharan Africa: Lessons from Benin, Ethiopia, Ghana, Namibia and Nigeria.* GIZ: Eschborn, Germany.

GSS (2012) *2010 population and housing census: Summary report of final results.* Sakoa Press: Accra, Ghana.

GWD (1996) *Kakum National Park and Assin Attandanso Resource Reserve, Management Plan.* Forestry Commission: Accra, Ghana.

Haligah, I. (1998) *The underutilized tourist resources at the Kalakpa Resource Reserve*, Bachelor of Arts Honours Thesis, Department of Geography and Resource Development, University of Ghana, Legon-Accra.

Honey, M. (2008) *Ecotourism and sustainable development: Who owns paradise?* Island Press: Washington, DC.

IUCN (2010) *Parks and reserves in Ghana; Management effectiveness assessment of protected areas.* IUCN: Gland, Switzerland.

Kamauro, O. (1996) Ecotourism: suicide or development? Voices from Africa, *Sustainable Development*, no. 6, UN Non-governmental Liaison Service: Geneva.

Kates, R.W., Parris, T.M. and Leiserowitz, A.A. (2005) What is sustainable development? Goals, indicators, values, and practice, *Environment: Science and Policy for Sustainable Development*, vol. 47, no. 3, pp. 8–21.

KCA (1997) Facing the storm: Five years of research in and around Kakum National Park, Ghana, *Proceedings of Kakum Conservation Area Research Colloquium*. Conservation International: Washington, DC, pp. 15–18.

Khor, M. (2010) Preliminary notes on the green economy, in the context of sustainable development, Presentation of the Executive Director of the South Centre in the Panel of the Green Economy at the Inter-sessional debates of Rio Plus 20, January 10–11.

Monney, K.A., Dakwa, K.B. and Wiafe, E.D. (2010) Assessment of crop raiding situation by elephants (*Loxodonta africana cyclotis*) in farms around Kakum Conservation Area, Ghana, *International Journal of Biodiversity and Conservation*, vol. 2, no. 9, pp. 243–9.

Ormsby, A. and Mannie, K. (2006) Ecotourism benefits and the role of local guides at Masoala National Park, Madagascar, *Journal of Sustainable Tourism*, vol. 14, no. 3, pp. 271–87

Seraphine, B. (2010) Seychelles ecotourism strategy for 21st Century (SETS 21): A review of ecotourism products, sites and activities in the Seychelles, Compilation of baseline information and review, Seychelles Tourism Board, Seychelles.

Spenceley, A. (2010) *Review of tourism product development interventions and best practices in Sub-Saharan Africa*, Synthesis Report, Report to the World Bank, 3 December 2010, World Bank: Washington, DC.

Tamakloe, W. (2000) State of Ghana's environment – Challenges of compliance and enforcement, Report, pp. 1–3, Ghana Environmental Protection Agency: Accra, Ghana.

UNEP (2011) Towards a green economy: Pathways to sustainable development and poverty eradication, a synthesis for policy makers, www.unep.org/greeneconomy/portals/88/documents/ger/GER_synthesis_en.pdf, accessed 16 May 2013.

UNEP and UNWTO (2012) *Tourism in the green economy, background report*. UNEP and UNWTO: Madrid, Spain. www.unep.org/greeneconomy/Portals/88/documents/ger/ger_final_dec_2011/Tourism, accessed 2 January 2014.

UNEP, UNCTAD and UN-OHRLLS (2011) Green economy: Why a green economy matters for least developed countries, www.unep.org/greeneconomy/Portals/88/documents/research_products/, accessed 16 May 2013.

Wallace, G.N. and Pierce, S.M. (1996) An evaluation of ecotourism in Amazonas, Brazil, *Annals of Tourism Research*, vol. 23, no. 4, pp. 843–73.

Western, D. (2012) Ecotourism: From small beginnings to global influence. In Briker, K.S., Black, R. and Cottrell, S. (eds) *Sustainable tourism and the millennium development goals: Effecting positive change*. Jones and Bartlett Learning: Burlington, MA, pp. xvii–xx.

WTTC (2010) *The 2010 Travel and Tourism Economic Research*. Economic Data Research Tool, World Travel and Tourism Council: London.

16

LOCAL FOOD

Greening the tourism value chain

Susan L. Slocum

Introduction

The world is attempting to circumvent previously exploitive economic policy agendas by trying to mitigate a number of global crises, including resource, fuel, and water scarcity, as well as increasing poverty. Food production draws heavily on natural resources, uses 70 per cent of the available clean water and has been criticized as a leading cause of carbon emissions and pesticide pollution (FAO, 2011). However, agriculture also employs 40 per cent of the world's population. Therefore, the agriculture sector is a critical component in efforts to green the economy.

Global food transport is increasing at a faster rate than food production itself, raising the role food plays in the economic and political landscape and resulting in a growing number of countries and industries relying on the international food trade (Ercsey-Ravasz *et al.*, 2012). Many value-chain analyses have investigated the vertical relationship between buyers and suppliers and the movement of food from producers to consumers (Mather and Greenberg, 2003; Fold and Larsen, 2008) and the resulting unequal power distribution, entry barriers, and dispersal of rewards towards developed nations (Bolwig *et al.*, 2010). The result has been a policy push by governments to increase exports as a diversification strategy for small-scale agriculture. However, the lack of international food standards has increased consumers' awareness of food safety and quality, as well as amplifying the compliance costs for agricultural producers increasingly dependent on the international food industry (Henson and Humphreys, 2010).

Long-distance hauling of agricultural goods has fuelled growing concern by consumers. Weatherell *et al.* (2003) argue that food consumers in developed countries are motivated by intrinsic (food quality and appearance), extrinsic (retail and shopping experience), and credence (healthiness, environment and rural welfare) factors which have caused an upswing in a 'buy local' movement. Food safety and quality issues have made headlines following food-borne illness in the UK (BSE in beef), Asia (bird flu in poultry), and the USA (salmonella in cantaloupe). Not only do these diseases affect humans, but the international transportation of food helps spread these diseases to local agricultural livestock. Rising awareness of the environmental consequence of food miles and the resulting carbon footprint of food has also raised questions on the impact global food chains have on the health of the environment (Jaffee and Henson, 2004). Small-scale agriculture and the 'family farm' are quickly diminishing worldwide, a result of waning incomes to farmers, which has changed pastoral landscapes and impoverished rural regions (Ilbery *et al.*, 2005). Mass agricultural transport has increased the need for pesticide usage, chemical ripening agents, antibiotics, and other potentially toxic substances, adding fuel to the food debate by a growing health-conscious society (Delind, 2006). Furthermore, global food chains have alienated consumers from food production methods. Mounting debates over the sustainability of globalized food chains have brought attention to the benefits of local food networks, resulting in a new interest in 'farm-to-fork' movements prevalent in many developed countries. The localization of food supply chains means simply that food should be consumed as close to the point of origin as possible, reducing the number of intermediaries and pushing for a distribution channel that moves directly from on-farm production to the consumer's fork (Seyfang, 2008).

Consumer interest in local food networks has also been transferable to tourism sectors. Food tourism, defined as 'the desire to experience a particular type of food or the produce of a specific region' (Hall and Sharples, 2003, p. 10) covers a vast number of epicurean opportunities for tourists (Okumus *et al.*, 2007). The inclusion of local food in tourism industries is well documented in academic, policy, and development circles. This paper explores the rising 'farm-to-fork' movement as a form of sustainable development, then provides literature-based research to investigate the inclusion of local food in tourism value chains as a method to green the tourism industry. Using a review of academic publications, this chapter will address consumer/tourist preferences for local food and the advantages of utilizing local food networks in relation to sustainable consumption, environmental impacts, rural development, and tourism industry benefits. This chapter will also address current 'green' tourism initiatives regarding locally sourced food and regional labelling. The goal is to combine supply and demand attributes from a variety of disciplines to show the underlying benefits and green options that food and tourism partnerships can provide. It is argued here that while the consumer movement towards local food and the growth of food tourism is a viable sustainability strategy that can contribute towards the greening of the tourism value chain, it is critical to assess how local food is incorporated to judge its effect on the greening of the tourism value chain.

Food tourism

The growing 'eat local' movement has been approached as a strategy for sustainability due to the increased benefits to local economies, communities, and the environment. It has been argued that the globalization of food distribution and the pressure to standardize food production has eroded the culinary heritage of regions (Slocum and Everett, 2010) and is closely associated with the destruction of local culture and the invasion of Western food values (Tregear, 2003). This process has also distanced consumers from climate and seasonality of food, disassociating consumers from food production methods. Ilbery and Kneafsey (1998) suggest that food and drink tourism can reassert cultural distinctiveness. The rise in programmes and policy supporting the local food movement has resulted in a number of innovative 'farm-to-fork' initiatives and alternative food networks (Cox *et al.*, 2008). Food tourism, or the incorporation of local food in the tourism sector, is increasingly being recognized as a form of sustainable tourism that supports regional development by strengthening local production through backward linkages in food and tourism supply-chain partnerships (Telfer and Wall, 1996; Renko *et al.*, 2010) and supports the enhancement of the tourism experience through the consumption of cultural distinctiveness (Rusher, 2003). Specifically, rural areas where food production constitutes a large percentage of the economic output, food tourism has been found to strengthen a region's identity, sustain cultural heritage, ease fears of global food homogenization, support a region's economic and socio-cultural foundation (Everett and Aitchison, 2008), and facilitate support for family farms (Chesky, 2009). Through the promotion of wineries/breweries, agritourism, farmers' markets, farm shops, local recipes, or locally sourced restaurant meals, local food promoted to the travelling public has become a foundation of regional development (Schnell, 2011). Schnell writes, 'Nearly absent in 1993 promotions, 'eating locally' is now a cornerstone of tourism advertising' (p. 281).

Sustainable consumption

Sustainable consumption and production patterns have received much attention internationally. The United Nations Conference on Sustainable Development (United Nations, 2012) recognized the need for regional and national initiatives to promote sustainable consumption since 'fundamental changes in the way societies produce and consume are indispensable for achieving global sustainable development' (p. 2). While it is acknowledged that sustainable consumption and production should be flexible enough to handle varying levels of development and capacities in different countries, the United Nations' 10-year framework encourages the promotion of sustainable consumption in a manner that supports new market development and opportunities for products and technologies (United Nations, 2012, p. 4). It could be argued that local food distribution and consumption falls within this realm.

Re-localizing food chains is a new approach to increasing sustainable consumption and has led to a rise in demand for local produce through direct marketing channels (e.g. farmers' markets, farm shops, and Consumer Supported Agriculture) (Pretty *et al.*, 2005). Numerous studies have shown that a key driver in local consumption is increased freshness of produce, better taste, and a perceived healthier alternative that lacks chemical additives (Stagl, 2002; Delind, 2006; Schnell, 2011). As consumers become more aware of the benefits of sourcing local food, these behaviours are being transferred to consumption patterns while traveling (Torres, 2002).

Sustainable consumption is defined as

> the use of goods and related products which respond to basic needs and bring a better quality of life, while minimising the use of natural resources and toxic materials as well as the emissions of waste and pollutants over the life cycle, so as not to jeopardise the needs of future generations.
>
> (Seyfang, 2006, p. 384)

It involves: socially-embedded economies of place and the development of networks between consumers and growers; boosting ethical and social capital around food supply chains; educating consumers about the origin of food and the impacts of different production methods; creating support mechanisms which are absent when food comes from distant origins; and strengthening local economies and markets against disruptive external forces of globalization (Norberg-Hodge *et al.*, 2000). Sustainable consumption also incorporates seasonality of produce as a means to reduce the carbon footprint associated with food distribution (discussed in the next section).

In relation to sustainability, the connection between nature and society plays a vital role in food-based consumption (Littig and Grießler, 2005). Eating habits can be viewed as an expression of culture (Reynolds, 1993) and the preservation of traditional foodways is a substantial part of cultural identity, and thus cultural sustainability (Marzuki *et al.*, 2013). Gössling and Hall (2013) divide sustainable consumption into four categories which highlight the role of tourism in the agri-food system (pp. 29–36). The 'business as usual' approach defines sustainability in purely economic terms and food consumption is based on a wide variety of mass commodities, especially meat products, and is characterized by scientific input into food processes. This approach is encouraged by mass tourism, resulting in significant standardization and a high level of media attention placed on food service products. A 'green growth' approach seeks to balance the economic, environmental and social aspects of sustainability and encourages greater efficiency through the promotion of green economic growth via technological and market solutions (i.e. waste reduction and increased food output per capita). In tourism, out-of-home consumption is encouraged with mass customization of food and hospitality services. The development of niche food-based experiences for high-end markets uses regional food branding and advertising and promotes food and tourism lifestyles. The 'traditional sustainable' approach is based on traditional methods of food production that promote food security for the rural poor. The emphasis is placed on small-scale agriculture that is culturally and ecologically sensitive to local needs. In tourism, this approach limits the development of food services and places more emphasis on concepts of hospitality. The 'steady-state' approach is characterized as the balancing of natural capital/natural systems within consumption practices. It incorporates sustainable yields together with environmental conservation where sufficiency is more important than efficiency. Tourism encourages the growth of organic or other specialized services, the joining of food and lifestyle, and a focus on domestic promotion or incorporating the costs of emissions for international markets.

The academic literature suggests that there are demographic and psychographic differences in tourism consumption patterns (Telfer and Wall, 2000). While some studies show that tourists prefer food to which they are accustomed (Bélisle, 1984; Momsen, 1998), other studies show that there is an increasing interest in trying local foods (Sharkey and Momsen, 1995; Telfer and Wall, 2000). Telfer and Wall (2000) find that nationality plays a large role in distinguishing tourists' preferences although Sharkey and Momsen (1995) find more correlation between traveller typologies than nationality in food preferences. However, in the emerging concept of 'slow travel' and 'slow food', where 'slow' is a state of mind, the journey itself becomes intrinsic to the tourism experience and locality, culture and engagement becomes increasingly important (Gardner, 2009). Visentin (2011) echoes these findings by stating that contemporary tourism is evolving to include independent trips, easily accessible destinations, slow rhythms, a propensity to explore traditions and a strong inclination towards authenticity. These traits have resulted in the growth of agritourism activities, nature-based holidays and cultural exploration, where food plays a vital role in the travel experience and supports sustainable consumption for tourists.

Environmental impacts

The environmental impact of globalized distribution versus local food networks is contested within academic literature. While the industrial food system has been highly criticized for its carbon footprint (Patel, 2007), Purcell and Brown (2005) demonstrate that the efficiency of local production is highly dependent on local transportation systems, farming methods, and chemical applications. While Webber and Matthews (2008) claim that up to 11 per cent of food-related greenhouse gas emissions come from food trans-port alone, local food grown out-of-season in greenhouses may actually use more energy than long-distance transport systems (Wallgren, 2006). Gössling and Hall (2013) compare greenhouse gas emissions by production and transport type and conclude that while air transport is the most CO_2-demanding, transport by road is still carbon-intensive. Economies of scale suggest that long-distance hauling of food actually has less environmental impacts than short-distance transport of smaller quantities (Stagl, 2002). Bridle and Bonney (2010) propose that long-distance food transport only outsources the environmental consequences of food production, whereas local food tends to internalize these impacts and makes consumers more conscientious about environ-mental costs.

Above and beyond the obvious transportation issues in the environmental impacts of food, chemical agents necessary to transport food long distances have become increas-ingly controversial. These chemicals are primarily used to extend shelf life, transport, packaging and synthetic refortification (Delind, 2006). As regulations have increased to inform consumers about the use of these chemical agents, private and public labelling organizations have also increased. Local food, on the other hand, allows the consumer to know where their food originates, therefore making the supply chain transparent for the consumer (Stagl, 2002). Organic produce, a mass agricultural sector in itself, reduces the production and use of synthetic agents and offers a healthier choice for consumers (Choo and Jamal, 2009). Lastly, precious water is quickly becoming a high-priced commodity. With over 70 per cent of the world's clean water earmarked for agriculture (Sage, 2012) the efficiency of agricultural production in arid regions adds to the debate on the environmental impacts of food production.

Very few empirical studies have approached tourism demand for locally sourced food products and the perceived environment stewardship values behind such demand. Farmers' market studies have documented the rising environmental perceptions of local food, although how this translates to the travelling public remains obscure. Torres and Momsen (2004) investigated Cancun's hospitality linkages and found that only seafood was sourced locally due to the local chef's perceptions that tourists preferred imported food. However, Sims (2009) found that local food products in the Lake District, England appealed to visitors who worry about the environmental consequences of contemporary agriculture because it restores meaningful connections between consumers and the regions that produce their food. Enteleca Research (2001) found that 65 per cent of tourists in England believed that local food helps the environment. Curtis and Cowee (2009) established that gourmet chefs in Las Vegas, Nevada were more concerned about production, favouring organic produce, than they were about the marketability of their products, implying values of environmental stewardship. Research has shown that, in general, tourists remain unaware of the environmental impact of their travel behaviour (Hillery *et al.*, 2001), although it is hard to tell if this translates into their eating habits and food purchase behaviour as well. As Choo and Jamal (2009) remind us, local food is only as environmentally sustainable as the on-farm practices employed in local farms.

Sustainable development

Traditional industries, such as farming, face new challenges with increasingly globalized supply chains, price-competitive marketing strategies employed by food service providers, and a growing discrepancy between input costs and commodity prices (Bianchi, 2013). These global processes have reduced the earning potential of rural farmers, creating a new wave of rural poverty prevalent in most countries worldwide (Douwe van der Ploeg, 2012). Many authors have documented the 'crises' facing rural communities including the reduction of traditional industries (Sims, 2009), outward migration (Tregear, 2003), and decreasing farm incomes (Ilbery *et al.*, 2005). Everett and Slocum (2013) argue that agricultural producers are facing pressures to diversify their offerings and distribution networks in an attempt to secure a viable future, which has been encouraged through national agricultural policy initiatives. Building local partnerships in food provision has been shown to increase backward linkages, creating indirect and induced effects that keep a larger portion of agricultural revenue in the local economy (Telfer and Wall, 1996). Furthermore, green agricultural production has been shown to benefit local farmers. For example, The Food and Agriculture Organization of the United Nations reports that organic farms are more economically profitable through reducing pesticide usage by 71 per cent and energy consumption by 35 per cent in Europe and 30 per cent in the United States. Furthermore, investment aimed at increasing the productivity of the agricultural sectors has proved twice as effective in reducing poverty as in any other economic sector. The result is that food is increasingly becoming part of the sustainability agenda for many communities, and emphasis has been placed on food and tourism partnerships to supplement the agricultural sector and broaden the scope of regional development schemes in rural areas (Hall and Sharples, 2003).

Tourism is known as an industry with high economic leakages, resulting from the corporate ownership of tourism businesses (Telfer and Wall, 2000). Slee *et al.* (1997) argue that local food can greatly enhance the economic impact of tourism, leaving a larger percentage of tourism revenue in the local economy. Renko *et al.* (2010) contend that the benefits gained by uniting local food and tourism include enhanced environmental quality through the preservation of small sustainable agricultural production, provision of viable economic alternatives specifically designed for small and medium-sized farms, and the improvement of the quality of life for farmers, farm workers and rural communities by supporting new distribution channels within the tourism sector that increase the profitability of rural farms and create jobs. Ollenburg and Buckley

(2007) also discovered that communities that embrace agritourism-specific activities, such as farm stays and private hunting reserves, have an enhanced quality of life due to increased recreational opportunities, diversified economic bases and retention of farmland. Everett and Aitchison (2008) agree with previous research, recognizing that local food and tourism can boost the socio-cultural basis within communities, instilling cultural pride and bringing together members of society.

Tourism industry benefits

The sustainability of the tourism industry, itself, is an important consideration when assessing socially-conscious or environmentally-friendly value-chain changes, such as the addition of local food in the tourism offer. There is evidence that sourcing locally is less cost-effective, resulting in higher prices due to the reduced economies of scale (Everett and Slocum, 2013; Gössling and Hall, 2013). However, previous research suggests that consumer preferences and willingness to pay for locally grown produce is also higher (McCluskey and Loureiro, 2003; Carpio and Isengildina-Massa, 2009), allowing farmers and restaurants the opportunity to charge price premiums to recover increased supply costs. While this theory has not been tested in tourism markets, local food has been shown to capture up to a 25 per cent premium by local consumers (Curtis and Cowee, 2009).

Food represents approximately one-third of travel expenditure (Bélisle, 1983; Meler and Cerovi, 2003), and Quan and Wang (2004) consider food consumption a primary activity that motivates tourists to travel because food is one of the major activities and sources of expenditure of a trip. Laesser and Crouch (2006) claim that travellers interested in local food are likely to spend more, and Kim et al. (2011) found that food tourists, those who travel specifically to a food-related event, tend to be insensitive to increases in price. Therefore, it is possible to incorporate the higher cost of local food sourcing and pass these expenses on to the consumer, preserving profit margins for tourism businesses.

The key to successful promotion of local food, however, lies in the marketing, labelling, and visibility of local produce to the tourists (Jansen-Verbeke, 2009). One of the key elements that motivates consumers in the farm-to-fork movement is linking their food with local growers (Sims, 2009), and 'preserving the identity of farmers on product labels is important for connecting with consumers, distinguishing the product from those of competitors, and providing traceability to the consumers' (USDA, 2012, p. 1). Therefore, acknowledging the specific location of food origins and telling stories about the farm from which the food is sourced boosts this connection, creating a feeling of authenticity in the dining experience which can justify the price premiums charged by restaurants (Mak et al., 2012). Encouraging seasonal consumption informs consumers of local agricultural practices as well as decreasing expectations that favourite recipes will always be available, but it may also create additional work in menu development (Curtis and Cowee, 2009). In order for businesses to be sustainable in food tourism, a new educational component to tourism marketing may be required to educate consumers about the benefits of local produce, regional farms, traditional recipes and seasonality, as a means to serve-up a quality food experience.

Local and green tourism initiatives

Labelling and certification for local food is still sporadic in tourism destinations and tends to be promoted at the county, state or other regionalized level (Ilbery *et al.*, 2005). While many empirical studies discuss the success of local-labelling in traditional consumer markets, very few measure specific successes in tourism markets. There are too many 'local' food labels to discuss in one article, but some research has emphasized best practice in local food promotional efforts. Lin *et al.* (2011) highlight the success of Taiwan's attempt to unite their destination image with local food production, recipes, and dining experiences for tourists. They found that providing a united message in food promotion reduced confusion in relation to the destination image and emphasized that 'clear and strong brand identity' (p. 44) is a prerequisite for successful food-based campaigns. Lange-Vik and Idsø (2013) discuss the successful partnership between Destination Røros, a destination marketing organization, and Rørosmat in Norway. Rørosmat is a cooperative of local food producers whose aim is to make Røros a culinary region based on fresh, local produce. Destination Røros has focused on five areas including: a host programme training for tourism employees in the region; environmental certification for tourism businesses; sustainable waste management systems; local food training; and sustainable value creation. The success of the destination marketing campaign is attributed to 'the tight networks and synergies between different strategies and stakeholders' (p. 94).

What has become more common in food labelling is Geographical Indication (GI) certifications which cover agricultural products and foodstuffs that are produced, processed and prepared in a given geographical area using recognized know-how (such as Florida juice or Cuban cigars) or foodstuffs closely linked to a geographical area (such as bourbon whiskey or Roquefort cheese). Bowen and Zapata (2008) found that the GI certification for tequila has increased tourism for the impoverished region in Mexico while simultaneously increasing the mass corporate production that is threatening the environment necessary for agave production. Bruwer (2003) shows how the development of wine routes in South Africa, based on the Stellenbosch GI, have supported small and medium-sized wineries, increased visitation numbers, and allowed substantial price premiums to be charged, resulting in 78 per cent of business revenues being generated through wine tourism activities. López and Martín (2006) show how the *Tradition along the Road*, a GI certification associated with the legendary Road to Santiago combining products from France, Spain and Portugal, has led to numerous community development projects around agro-food partnerships that 'are re-injecting new life into these regions, not only economically but also by strengthening them socially' (p. 176).

There is also a growing interest in 'green' hospitality initiatives that incorporate local food along with other environmentally and socially conscious business practices in the hospitality industry. The World Bank, in an assessment of national certification schemes for tourism, recognizes the 'provision of purchasing of local food and equipment from local community' as an important component of green certification (Dodds and Joppe, 2005, p. 38). Large-scale distributors, such as Sysco and US Foodservices, have begun to incorporate local food as a means of reducing their carbon emissions and lowering their operating costs (Wright, 2013). Organizations such as Safe and Local Supplier Approval (SALSA) in the UK offer food safety, local partnerships and regional networks for restaurants and hotels that want to be certified for incorporating locally sourced food as part of their green-business planning. South Carolina's Green Hospitality Alliance includes environmentally preferred purchasing, with a strong emphasis on local food production and agricultural support, as a prerequisite for green-certification across the State (DHEC, 2013).

Conclusion

Agriculture is a key component of the world's economy, and its inclusion in greening the value chain of any sector is vital to the success of sustainable development initiatives. Local food offers a variety of sustainable options to support tourism economies and businesses, but the addition of local food is not necessarily a 'green' solution per se. The importance of how local food is incorporated remains at the heart of the discussion. Gössling and Hall's (2013) 'steady-state' approach, which balances natural capital and supports sufficiency over efficiency, provides the most viable approach for encouraging sustainable consumption in tourism industries. This policy encourages lifestyle characteristics that unite environmental stewardship with support for local economies and emphasizes a 'slow' approach and sense of place within the tourism experience. It also supports Bridle and Bonney's (2010) observation about internalizing the environmental costs by increasing the consumers' awareness of the impacts that food production has on a region. Through transparency, sourcing locally brings a personal touch to farm production, and tourists are better able to support efforts that reduce carbon emissions and the amount of chemical additives in the food they consume (Stagl, 2002). The environmental impact of local food is strongly dependent on local growing practices which, if communicated to tourists, can support sustainable consumption patterns through seasonality and reduced food additives (Choo and Jamal, 2009). As suggested by Renko et al. (2010), new avenues of distribution that encourage price premiums for producers can help slow rural to urban migration, preserve family farms and support the traditional heritage of a region. In turn, the sustainability of tourism is supported through increased cultural expression, the preservation of lifestyles, and increased authenticity of experiences for the tourist (Everett and Aitchison, 2008). Successful farm-to-fork programmes must rely heavily on limpidity through communication channels that inform tourists of the benefits of local food, local growing practices, and traditional food heritage. These messages are increasingly being transferred through green certification or labelling which incorporate local food in the sustainability agenda.

References

Belisle, F.J. (1983) Tourism and food production in the Caribbean, *Annals of Tourism Research*, vol. 10, no. 3, pp. 497–513.

Bélisle, F.J. (1984) Tourism and food imports: The case of Jamaica, *Economic Development and Cultural Change*, vol. 32, pp. 819–42.

Bianchi, R. (2013) From agriculture to rural: agritourism as a productive option. In Sidali, K., Spiller, A. and Schulze, B. (eds) *Food agriculture and tourism: Linking local gastronomy and rural tourism* (pp. XIII-XV), Springer: Heidelberg, Germany.

Bolwig, S., Ponte, S., du Toit, A., Riisgaard, L. and Halberg, N. (2010) Integrating poverty and environmental concerns into value-chain analysis: A conceptual framework, *Development Policy Review*, vol. 28, no. 2, pp. 173–94.

Bowen, S. and Zapata, A.V (2008) Geographical indications, terroir, and socio-economic and ecological sustainability: The case of tequila, *Journal of Rural Studies*, vol. 25, pp. 108–19.

Bridle, K. and Bonney, L. (2010) Food for thought: Biodiversity management on farms – links to demand driven value chains, *Social Alternatives*, vol. 29, no. 3, pp. 31–8.

Bruwer, J. (2003) South African wine routes: some perspectives on the wine tourism industry's structural dimensions and wine tourism product, *Tourism Management*, vol. 24, no. 4, pp. 423–35.

Carpio, C.E. and Isengildina-Massa, O. (2009) Consumer willingness to pay for locally grown products: The case of South Carolina, *Journal of Agribusiness*, vol. 25, no. 3, pp. 412–26.

Chesky, A. (2009) Can agritourism save the family farm in Appalachia? A study of two historic family farms in Valle Crucis, North Carolina, *Journal of Appalachian Studies*, vol. 15, no. 1 & 2, pp. 87–98.

Choo, H. and Jamal, T. (2009) Tourism on organic farms in South Korea: A new form of ecotourism? *Journal of Sustainable Tourism*, vol. 17, no. 4, pp. 431–54

Cox, R., Hollowa, L., Venn, L., Dowler, L., Hein, R., Kneafsey, M. and Tuomainen, H. (2008) Common ground? Motivations for participation in a community-supported agriculture scheme, *Local Environment: The International Journal of Justice and Sustainability*, vol. 13, no. 3, pp. 203–18.

Curtis, K. and Cowee, M. (2009) Direct marketing local food to chefs: Chef preferences and perceived obstacles, *Journal of Food Distribution*, vol. 40, no. 20, pp. 26–36.

Delind, L. (2006) Of bodies, places, and culture: Re-situating local food, *Journal of Agricultural and Environmental Ethics*, vol. 19, pp. 121–46.

DHEC (2013) Green Hospitality Program, www.scdhec.gov/environment/lwm/recycle/green_hospitality/index.htm, accessed 13 June 2013.

Dodds, R. and Joppe, M. (2005) CSR in the Tourism Industry? The status of and potential for certification, codes of conduct and guidelines, Study prepared for the CSR Practice Foreign Investment Advisory Service, www.turismdurabil.ro/literatura/csr/additional_documents/I-CSR+in+the+Tourism+Industry, accessed 13 June 2013.

Douwe van der Ploeg, J. (2012) Poverty alleviation and smallholder agriculture: The rural poverty report 2011, *Development and Change*, vol. 43, no. 1, pp. 439–48.

Enteleca Research (2001) Tourists' attitudes towards regional and local food, MAFF and the Countryside Agency, www.tourisminsights.info, accessed 22 May 2013.

Ercsey-Ravasz, M., Toroczkai, Z., Lakner, Z. and Baranyi, J. (2012) Complexity of the international agro-food trade network and its impact on food safety, *PLoS ONE* vol. 7, no. 5, p. e37810, doi:10.1371/journal.pone.0037810.

Everett, S. and Aitchison, C. (2008) The role of food tourism in sustaining regional identity: a case study of Cornwall, South West England, *Journal of Sustainable Tourism*, vol. 16, no. 2, pp. 150–67.

Everett, S. and Slocum, S. (2013) Food and tourism, an Effective Partnership? A UK based review, *Journal of Sustainable Tourism*, vol. 21, no. 7, GEA/Report/2011.

FAO (2011) FAO/OECD Expert Meeting on Greening the Economy with Agriculture, Paris, France, September 2011, www.fao.org/fileadmin/user_upload/suistainability/Presentations/Naqvi.pdf, accessed 9 April 2015.

Fold, N. and Larsen, M.N. (eds) (2008) *Globalization and restructuring of African commodity flows*. Nordic Africa Institute: Uppsala.

Gardner, N. (2009) A manifesto for slow travel, *Hidden Europe Magazine*, vol. 25, pp. 10–14.

Gössling, S. and Hall, C.M. (2013) Sustainable culinary systems: an introduction. In Hall, C.M. and Gössling, S. (eds) *Sustainable culinary systems: Local food, innovation, tourism, and hospitality* (pp. 3–44). Routledge: New Zealand.

Hall, C.M. and Sharples, L. (2003) The consumption of experiences or the experiences of consumption? An introduction to the tourism of taste. In Hall, C.M., Sharples, E., Mitchell, R., Macionis, N. and Cambourne B. (eds) *Food tourism around the world: development, management and markets* (pp. 1–24). Butterworth-Heinemann: Oxford.

Henson, S. and Humphreys, J. (2010) Understanding the complexities of private standards in global agri-food chains as they impact developing countries, *Journal of Development Studies*, vol. 46, no. 9, pp. 1628–46.

Hillery, M., Nancarrow, B., Griffith, G. and Syme, G. (2001) Tourist Perceptions of Environmental Impacts, *Annals of Tourism Research*, vol. 28, no. 4, pp. 853–67.

Ilbery, B. and Kneafsey, M. (1998) Product and place: promoting quality products and services in the lagging rural regions of the European Union, *European Urban and Regional Studies*, vol. 5, no. 4, pp. 329–41.

Ilbery, B., Morris, C., Buller, H., Maye, D. and Kneafsey, M. (2005) Product, process and place: An examination of food marketing and labelling schemes in Europe and North America, *European Urban and Regional Studies*, vol. 12, pp. 116–32.

Jaffee, S. and Henson, S.J. (2004) *Standards and agri-food exports from developing countries: rebalancing the debate*, World Bank. Policy Research Working Paper 3348, The World Bank: Washington, DC.

Jansen-Verbeke, M. (2009) The territoriality paradigm in cultural tourism, *Turyzm/Tourism*, vol. 191, no. 2, pp. 27–33.

Kim, Y.H., Kim, M., Goh, B.K. and Antun, J.M. (2011) The role of money: The impact on food tourists' satisfaction and intention to revisit food events, *Journal of Culinary Science & Technology*, vol. 9, no. 2, pp. 85–98.

Laesser, C. and Crouch, G.I. (2006) Segmenting markets by travel expenditure patterns: The case of international visitors to Australia, *Journal of Travel Research*, vol. 44, pp. 397–406.

Lange-Vik, M. and Idsø, J. (2013) Rørosmat: the development and success of a local food brand in Norway. In Hall, C.M. and Gössling, S. (eds) *Sustainable culinary systems: Local food, innovation, tourism, and hospitality* (pp. 85–98). Routledge: New Zealand.

Lin, Y., Pearson, T.E. and Cai, L.A. (2011) Food as a form of destination identity: A tourism destination brand perspective, *Tourism and Hospitality Research*, vol. 11, no. 1, pp. 30–48.

Littig, B. and Grießler, E. (2005) Social Sustainability: a catchword between political pragmatism and social theory, *International Journal of Sustainable Development*, vol. 8, no. 1&2, pp. 65–79.

López X.A. and Martín, B.G. (2006) Tourism and quality agro-food products: An opportunity for the Spanish countryside, *Tijdschrift voor Economische en Sociale Geografie*, vol. 97, no. 2, pp. 166–77.

McCluskey, J.J. and Loureiro, M.L. (2003) Consumer preferences and willingness to pay for food labeling: A discussion of empirical studies, *Journal of Food Distribution Research*, vol. 34, no. 3, pp. 95–102.

Mak, A., Lumbers, M. and Eves, A. (2012) Globalisation and food consumption in tourism, *Annals of Tourism Research*, vol. 39, no. 1, pp. 171–96.

Marzuki, S., Hall, C.M. and Ballantine, P. (2013) Sustaining halal certification at restaurants in Malaysia, In Hall, C.M. and Gössling, S. (eds) *Sustainable culinary systems: Local food, innovation, tourism, and hospitality* (pp. 256–74). Routledge: New Zealand.

Mather, C. and Greenberg, S. (2003) Market liberalisation in post-apartheid South Africa: The restructuring of citrus exports after 'deregulation', *Journal of Southern African Studies*, vol. 29, no. 2, pp. 393–412.

Meler, M. and Cerovi_, Z. (2003) Food marketing in the function of tourist product development, *British Food Journal*, vol. 105, no. 3, pp. 175–92.

Momsen, J. (1998) Caribbean tourism and agriculture: New linkages in the global era? In Klak, T. (ed.) *Globalization and Neoliberalism: The Caribbean Context*, (pp. 115–33). Lanham, MD and Oxford, UK.

Norberg-Hodge, H., Merrifield, T. and Gorelick, S. (2000) *Bringing the food economy home: The social, ecological and economic benefits of local food*. ISEC, Rowman & Littleman: Dartington, UK.

Okumus, B., Okumus, F. and McKercher, B. (2007) Incorporating local and international cuisines in the marketing of tourism destinations: The cases of Hong Kong and Turkey, *Tourism Management*, vol. 28, no. 1, pp. 253–61.

Ollenburg, C. and Buckley, R. (2007) Stated economic and social motivations of farm tourism operators, *Journal of Travel Research*, vol. 45, no. 4, pp. 444–52.

Patel, R. (2007) *Stuffed and starved: markets, power, and the hidden battle for the world's food system*. HarperCollins: Toronto, ON.

Pretty, J., Ball, A., Lang, T. and Morrison, J. (2005) Farm costs and food miles: An assessment of the full cost of the UK weekly food basket, *Food Policy*, vol. 30, no. 1, pp. 1–19.

Purcell, M. and Brown, J.C. (2005) Against the local trap: scale and the study of environment and development, *Progress in Development Studies*, vol. 5, no. 4, pp. 279–97.

Quan, S. and Wang, N. (2004) Towards a structural model of the tourist experience: An illustration from food experience in tourism. *Tourism Management*, vol. 25, no. 3, pp. 297–305.

Renko, S., Renko, N. and Polonijo, T. (2010) Understanding the role of food in rural tourism development in a recovering economy, *Journal of Food Products Marketing*, vol. 16, pp. 309–24.

Reynolds, P. (1993) Food and tourism: towards an understanding of sustainable culture, *Journal of Sustainable Tourism*, vol. 1, no. 1, pp. 48–54.

Rusher, K. (2003) The Bluff Oyster festival and regional economic development: Festivals as culture commodified. In Hall, C.M., Sharples, E., Mitchell, R., Macionis, N. and Cambourne, B. (eds) *Food tourism around the world: development, management and markets* (pp. 193–205). Butterworth Heinemann: Oxford.

Sage, C. (2012) *Environment and food*. Routledge: London.

Schnell, S. (2011) The local traveler: farming, food, and place in state and provincial tourism guides, 1993 – 2008, *Journal of Cultural Geography*, vol. 28, no. 2, pp. 281–309.

Seyfang, G. (2006) Ecological citizenship and sustainable consumption: Examining local organic food networks, *Journal of Rural Studies*, vol. 22, pp. 383–95.

Seyfang, G. (2008) Avoiding Asda? Exploring consumer motivations in local organic food networks, *Local Environment*, vol. 13, no. 3, pp. 187–201.

Sharkey, D. and Momsen, J. (1995) Tourism in Dominica, West Indies: Problems and prospects, *Caribbean Geography*, vol. 6, no. 1, pp. 40–51.

Sims, R. (2009) Food, place and authenticity: local food and the sustainable tourism experience, *Journal of Sustainable Tourism*, vol. 17, no. 3, pp. 321–36.

Slee, B., Farr, H. and Snowdon, P. (1997) The economic impact of alternative types of rural tourism, *Journal of Agricultural Economics*, vol. 48, no. 1–3, pp. 179–92.

Slocum, S.L. and Everett, S. (2010) Proceedings from the Fourth International Conference on Sustainable Tourism: Food tourism initiatives: Resistance on the ground. In Brebbia, C.A. (ed.) *The sustainable world*. WIT Press: England.

Stagl, S. (2002) Local organic food markets: potentials and limitations for contributing to sustainable development, *Empirica*, vol. 29, pp. 145–62.

Telfer, D. and Wall, G. (1996) Linkages between tourism and food production, *Annals of Tourism Research*, vol. 23, no. 3, pp. 635–53.

Telfer, D. and Wall, G. (2000) Strengthening backward economic linkages: local food purchasing by three Indonesian hotels, *Tourism Geographies*, vol. 2, no. 4, pp. 421–47.

Torres, R. (2002) Towards a better understanding of tourism and agriculture linkages in the Yucatan: Tourist food consumption and preference, *Tourism Geographies*, vol. 4, no. 3, pp. 282–306.

Torres, R. and Momsen, J. (2004) Challenges and potential for linking tourism and agriculture to achieve pro-poor tourism objectives, *Progress in Development Studies*, vol. 4, no. 4, pp. 294–318.

Tregear, A. (2003) From Stilton to Vimto: using food history to re-think typical products in rural development, *Sociologia Ruralis*, vol. 43, no. 2, pp. 91–107.

United Nations (2012) Rio+20 United Nations Conference on Sustainable Development: provisional agenda - outcome of the conference. www.unep.org/rio20/portals/24180/Docs/a-conf.216-5_english.pdf, accessed 3 January 2015.

USDA (2012) New study explores innovation and opportunities for diverse local food distributors, USDA Agricultural Marketing Service, Release No. 0096.12, www.ams.usda.gov/AMSv1.0/ams, accessed 10 May 2013.

Visentin, C. (2011) Food, agri-culture and tourism. In Sidali, K., Spiller, A. and Schulze, B. (eds) *Food agriculture and tourism: Linking local gastronomy and rural tourism* (pp. XIII–XV). Springer: Heidelberg, Germany.

Wallgren, C. (2009) Local or global food markets: A comparison of energy use for transport, *Local Environment: The International Journal of Justice and Sustainability*, vol. 11, no. 2, pp. 233–51.

Weatherell, C., Tregear, A. and Allinson, J. (2003) In search of the concerned consumer: UK public perceptions of food, farming and buying local, *Journal of Rural Studies*, vol. 19, no. 2, pp. 233–44.

Webber, C. and Matthews, S. (2008) Impacts of food choices in the United States, *Environmental Science and Technology*, vol. 42, no. 10, pp. 3508–13.

Wright, W. (2013) *Supply chain information: Accommodations and food.* Supply Chain Information, http://gogreenplus.org/environmental-business-help/supply-chain-information/supply-chain-information-accommodations-food, accessed 25 June 2013.

17

THE ROLE OF GREEN EVENTS IN A GREEN ECONOMY

Bill Merrilees, Dale Miller and Amelia Green

Introduction

Events are a very distinctive and visible component of the tourism sector and a good 'bellwether' of progress to sustainability. A green economy requires rebooting an economy to one based on sustainability principles. Tourism and its related components such as events, can make a major contribution to the green economy. An effective way to make such a green economy contribution is to draw lessons from best practices in the tourism and events domain, which is what this chapter does. The chapter first documents the literature on green events and argues that very limited progress has been made. Most events have made minimal progress to sustainability and are best described as token efforts.

Second, the chapter investigates 'exemplar cases' of green events. Special emphasis is on the Burlington Ribfest, Burlington, Ontario, Canada, which is portrayed as Canada's largest Ribfest, but more importantly it is the greenest Ribfest. A local Rotary Club, in conjunction with 300 volunteers, makes an extraordinary effort to achieve a very high rate of waste diversion for what is one of the City of Burlington's major tourist attractions.

Finally, the chapter examines how the lessons from exemplar events can be mainstreamed and thus ramp up the diffusion of green principles in the mainstream event industry.

Green events

The literature on green events is not extensive. The seminal literature review is Laing and Frost (2010), with few major additions since then, other than Lawton and Weaver (2010), and Merrilees and Marles (2011) in particular. The scope of the current chapter emphasizes community events, rather than business events or major sporting events. The green business event literature is summarized in Mair and Jago (2010) and Merrilees and Marles (2011). The green sporting event literature is summarized in Laing and Frost (2010). Although outside the scope of the current study, in the context of green sporting events, the International Olympic Committee (2013) notes that the decision to locate the 2012 London Olympic Games in East London enabled environmental revitalization of industrial wasteland. The decision also laid the foundation for economic growth in a previously struggling section of the city through the creation of business and job opportunities. The Committee claims that their approach of integrating sustainability in all aspects of operations, and establishing an independent commission to monitor and publicly evaluate those operations, has set new standards for sustainable construction and development practice. An Independent Commission credits London as 'the most sustainable Games ever' (p. 2), but adds there is always more to be done (Commission for a Sustainable London, 2012, 2013).

Laing and Frost (2010) use a particular framework to organize their literature review. This is also a useful way to classify the precise green activities of a specific event. They organize the literature explicitly around the following sections:

- participation of key stakeholders;
- operational issues;
- promoting a message through green events.

The first matter, participation of key stakeholders, is clearly very important for community events, compared with, say, business events, where employees and conference organizers tend to be involved. Operational issues can be divided into various sub-components, essentially reflecting the different ways that events conduct environmental activities. The operational sub-components used by Laing and Frost include, in order:

- public transport access;
- waste management;
- alternative fuels and other power options;
- logistical issues, including more local sources;
- audits to monitor progress.

This excellent framework, suggested by Laing and Frost (2010), can be extended slightly by more carefully targeting and perhaps optimizing the operational mix of environmental operational activities. Very few green community event studies have even attempted to measure the mix of green activities. In a birding festival study, Lawton and Weaver (2010) rank the green activities as follows:

1   Waste minimization (dominated by re-use of signage or banners)
2   Recycling (cans and bottles collected, and bins and/or recycling)
3   Energy-conserving transport (including buses and carpooling)
4   Other energy savings (reduced electricity usage).

The percentage of use drops markedly as you move down the list, with 90 per cent of birding festivals active with waste minimization, then down to 40 per cent active with recycling. Perhaps these first two items should be combined, with an emphasis on waste minimization and recycling. Third on the list was efficient transport (with

30 per cent of birding festivals active with this green mix component), and finally down to less than 10 per cent with other energy savings. The relevance of this mix can be highlighted by comparing it to that for business events. Merrilees and Marles (2011) identify almost the reverse mix for a business event, with more opportunity and capability of business events cto create other energy savings and often not making much effort with waste minimization and recycling.

The case study of the Burlington Ribfest uses the Laing and Frost (2010) classification of green event issues, and the two studies (Lawton and Weaver, 2010; Merrilees and Marles, 2011) which analyse the mix of green activities. Next, the exemplar case, the Burlington Ribfest, is presented and discussed.

Burlington Ribfest as an exemplary green event

Burlington City as a relatively green context for a potential green event

A major consideration for staging green events is the city context in which they are located. The contention is that a relatively green city, often referred to as 'an environmentally friendly' city, provides a more supportive context for developing and staging a green event. Further, the argument will be that the green city context was not necessarily critical for the birth of the green event. Rather, ongoing year-by-year support from the City of Burlington was important for greening the event. The authors maintain that the green connection between the Burlington Ribfest and the City of Burlington is synergistic; each positively supports the other, such that the collective green impact is greater than the sum of the two parts.

In Canada, Burlington is one of the neater, cleaner cities in the Greater Toronto Golden Horse-shoe, and borders Lake Ontario, 60km South-West of Toronto. The Ribfest website (www.canadaslargestribfest.com) provides extensive photos and maps illustrating the nature and location of the event. It is a relatively affluent, upmarket city of about 175,000. Urban planning has been gradually influenced by (Ontario) provincial planning, including directions to increase housing densities and reduce landfill waste. In March 2004, the Government of Canada launched a programme to encourage Canadians to reduce their greenhouse gas emissions by one tonne (per person) each year. Recycling and composting were two areas highlighted by the 'one-tonne challenge' (Government of Canada, 2004). In June 2004, the Ontario Ministry of Environment established a 60 per cent waste diversion goal for the province to be achieved by 2008 (Ministry of the Environment, 2004). So there is a subtle set of connecting influences, in that the Ontario province influences the City of Burlington, which in turn influences events in Burlington such as Ribfest.

Since Burlington has historically been neat and clean, with generally pleasant parks and mainly light industrial usage, it has a head start to being a green city, at least moderately. A consultative process in 2002 led to a new city brand with the environment as one of the four pillars. The new logo (still in use) included three coloured swishes representing the aspirational objective of environmental quality of air, water and land (yellow, blue and green). The 2002 rebranding was quickly adopted by local partners including Tourism Burlington, and later embodied in the 2004–6 Strategic

Plan. Recent changes have elevated the environment even further. The new 2012 vision is 'Burlington: where people, nature and business thrive'. Thus nature has moved from just being important to taking centre stage.

The more explicit green branding of Burlington City was embryonic in the 2002–2004 years leading up to the greening birth of Ribfest in 2004. Gradually, since then, the green city branding has strengthened. Similarly since 2004, the greening of the Ribfest has strengthened. The synergy between the two is evident in numerous city-based communications, including from the Mayor. In the months surrounding the event each year, local newspapers interview local councillors, who describe the Ribfest in terms such as 'a showcase of Burlington as a destination for families, music lovers and tourists' (*Inside Halton* [hereafter IH] 03.09.2010), 'one of Burlington's signature events' (IH 22.08.2008) and an 'end of summer ritual' (IH 30.08.2006). Another representative comments that: 'the Ribfest is a wonderful, special event for all Burlingtonians because everyone has fun, and everyone can participate' (IH 25.08.2006). Among the 'ribbers' (rib cooking teams), the Burlington Ribfest is considered the 'crown jewel in the ribbing schedule' (IH 27.08.2008). One ribber claims the success of the event and its 'almost flawless system of recycling', shows that the organizers could 'write a book on how to throw a ribfest' (IH 06.09.2011).

Origins of Ribfest: Serendipity

When Bob Peeling joined the Burlington Lakeshore Rotary Club in 1995, he was given the task of finding a new fundraising source for the club. After a chance meeting with Larry Murphy, a renowned ribber from Alabama, Peeling, and John Thorpe, a past Rotary president, began planning the launch of a Ribfest in Burlington. Together, they visited a similar event in Columbus, Ohio in search of ideas (*The Hamilton Spectator* [hereafter THS] 01.09.2011). The initial idea for the Burlington Ribfest could be seen as serendipity, which is not simply chance, but also a willingness and capability to respond to what seem like random opportunities (see Merrilees *et al.*, 1998).

The first Burlington Ribfest, held over the Labour Day long weekend later in that same year (1995), comprised just four ribbers. Despite pouring rain, the event sold out and made the club $850 (IH 01.09.2010; *The Burlington Post* [hereafter TBP] 01.09.2011). Clearly this was a humble start to what would become a very major event. [All $ amounts are in Canadian dollars to preserve the relativities and authenticity, and to avoid discrepancies with fluctuating exchange rates. Typically the Canadian dollar is discounted about 10 per cent below the US$]

Birth of a green event: 2004: More serendipity

Increasingly conscious of the amount of waste produced over the 4-day event each year (THS 06.09.2011), previously estimated at 30 tonnes (ACISS, 2004), Rotary members were keen to help implement a waste management plan proposed by volunteer Barbara Frensch. After meeting with Paul Kaldick, the Rotarian in charge of event logistics at the time, Frensch organized a group of thirty-seven volunteers to pilot a recycling and composting programme for the 2004 Burlington Ribfest (ACISS, 2004).

Again, one might attribute the green birth in part to serendipity, not unlike employees in big companies being responsible for many innovations. That year, the volunteers comprised members of a local non-profit organization dedicated to environmental maintenance and rehabilitation, employees from a province-wide home safety inspection business, local residents and high school students (TBP 17.09.2004).

Blue barrels designated for recycling were placed beside standard garbage bins within the site, a lakeside park in the Burlington Downtown. Volunteers operated waste-sorting stations and collected rubbish from tables during the event (THS 06.09.2011). The bags, barrels and gloves used were donated by regional and city councils (ACISS, 2004). Despite primitive resources, 5.30 tonnes of waste was diverted from a landfill site nearby on Bronte Road (TBP 20.09.2006; THS 28.04.2006; IH 30.04.2006). Signalling hope for the future of the event's environmental programme, the volunteers identified very few waste items that could not be recycled or composted given sufficient human resources (ACISS, 2004).

Glitter, awards and buzz: Recognition of environmental achievements

Frensch attributes the early success of the programme to the openness of Rotary to her proposal and the enthusiasm of volunteers (ACISS, 2004). From 2005 onward, the programme, and its success, continued to expand (see Table 17.1). Not all the figures are available for the entire period; however, a broad improvement in tonnes diverted and composted is discernible. Allowing for greater attendance, as shown, an improvement in tonnes diverted or composted per capita can also be discerned. In the first 2 years of the scheme, the per capita diversion was less than 0.0001 tonnes, whereas the last 3 years average around 0.0002, more than a doubling in the per capita waste diversion tonnage.

TABLE 17.1 Environmental Outcomes 2004–2012

Year	Attendance	Waste diversion rate %	Diverted & composted (tonnes)	Recyclables (tonnes)
2004	120,000 (TBP 07.09.2004)	N/A	5.30	(not recycled)
2005	131,000 (IH 06.09.2006)	N/A	9.80	4
2006	95,000 (IH 06.09.2006)	N/A	13.70	3
2007	145,000 (TBP 04.09.2008)	N/A	16	4
2008	148,000 (IH 09.09.2009)	89	27.98	9.58
2009	175,000 (IH 09.09.2009)	79	21.16	12.93
2010	139,000 (IH 16.08.2011)	82	28.6	9.50
2011	152,000 (IH 07.09.2011)	88	27.24	8.27
2012	156,000 (TBP 04.09.2012)	86	39.37	10.02

Sources: attendance data from *The Burlington Post* (TBP) and *Inside Halton* (IH); other data from Canada's Largest Ribfest (2013a)

In 2006, the Mayor of Burlington presented Frensch with a Civic Recognition Award for her efforts to improve and protect Burlington's environment. Thus she became an example to the community (THS 28.04.2006; IH 30.04.2006). Since then, the event has continued to receive accolades for environmental management. Frensch's efforts gained further recognition in 2008 with a Conservation Award of Excellence (IH 23.05.2008).

Burlington's reputation for hosting the most successful festivals in Ontario prompted selection of the city to host the 2009 Festivals and Events Ontario (FEO) Annual Conference (IH 29.02.2008). In 2010, the Recycling Council of Ontario presented event organizers with a Waste Minimization Gold Award. Referring to the Ribfest as 'one of the most environmentally-sound public events in the country' (IH 15.04.2011), FEO named the event the Best Greening Festival for 3 consecutive years from 2010 to 2013 (TBP 08.03.2013).

Other Rotary Clubs across Canada hoping to emulate the event's success, seek out Peeling and Thorpe (event co-founders) for advice (IH 25.08.2006). There are now more than twenty-five similar fundraising events in Ontario alone (TBP 01.09.2011). In terms of environmental performance, the event is recognized as a model for other festivals in the province, in the media (IH 18.08.2010) and by the Recycling Council of Ontario (Canada's Largest Ribfest, 2013b). Since 2007, other Burlington-based events such as the Sound of Music Festival, Halton EcoFest, the Jazz 'n' Blues Festival and Cancer Relay for Life have attempted to adapt the Ribfest's waste management programme for their own purposes (IH 26.08.2007).

Economic significance of the Ribfest including tourist economic impact

An independent study commissioned in 2003 estimated the total economic benefit of the Ribfest to be $1,162,000 (IH 26.10.2005). In 2010, the figure was approximately $3 million (IH 03.06.2010). In 2009 alone, the festival attracted 175,000 attendees and raised more than $320,000 (IH 09.09.2009; IH 08.09.2010). With free admission and no subsidies from the City of Burlington, the organizers absorb the $500,000 it costs to run the event each year (IH 03.06.2010). In 2010, the festival was awarded a $98,610 grant from a Federal government funding programme supporting events, which stimulate the local economy by drawing a significant number of tourists (IH 03.06.2010). The grant was allocated to marketing campaigns targeted at new markets including northern United States, other parts of Ontario and Québec, as well as special celebrations for the Ribfest's fifteenth anniversary (IH 03.06.2010). These enhancements were expected to increase the event's economic impact by $800,000 (IH 03.06.2010).

More than $2.3 million was raised for local, national and international charities in the 16 years to 2011 (TBP 01.09.2011). In addition to tourism, the economic spin-off and charity funding, the event's co-founders recognize enjoyment as a further means through which the event benefits the community (IH 26.10.2005). Members of local government refer to the number of people who volunteer for community events such as the Ribfest, as an indication of the care and concern Burlington citizens have for each other (IH 29.12.2010).

Green functional developments since 2004

Having demonstrated the successful outcomes above, it is now appropriate to backfill and articulate the detailed operational changes that have contributed to the growing success of greening the Burlington Ribfest event. To structure this section, the authors adopt the schema by Laing and Frost (2010) who use the following components:

- participation by stakeholders;
- operational issues;
- promoting a message through green events.

While generally using the same three sub-headings, the authors prefer to use the more direct term 'environmental education' instead of promoting a message. Further, the approach by Laing and Frost (2010) concludes operational issues with the need to conduct audits to monitor progress in achieving green objectives. In fact, the environmental impact outcomes have been dealt with above, noting that a hallmark of the Ribfest is the excellent audit trail that the organizers have recorded.

Participation by stakeholders: volunteers

Volunteers are a key stakeholder group. Since 2008, an average of 300 volunteers have been involved in the event annually (IH 19.08.2009). Typically, high school students obtaining volunteer hours, adult citizens, members of local community groups and Rotarians (TBP 20.09.2006) are among those who sign up for one or more 4-hour shifts (IH 18.08.2010). Supervisors, also engaged on a volunteer basis, are responsible for tasks such as recruiting and rostering volunteers, vendor education and evaluation, set-up and removal of physical infrastructure, sorting waste and communicating with the media (IH 08.08.2007). In 2011, a local single mothers' support group was one of the four charities and community organizations selected each year to receive a portion of the tips collected at beer tents during the event. In return, these groups assist the drive to sign up more volunteers (IH 25.08.2011).

By 2008, the thirty-seven volunteers involved in the 2004 pilot recycling programme had grown to eighty-one (TBP 11.09.2008). In recent years, husband and wife Ron and Ann Oatman have worked with Frensch to manage the festival's environmental programme (IH 18.08.2010). In an open letter published in a local newsletter, they describe the continuing support of volunteers as an 'invaluable asset' and the 'backbone' which make the 'monumental mission' possible (IH 08.10.2010).

Other groups such as a breast cancer awareness organization set up booths at the event to raise awareness and collect donations for their cause (IH 10.09.2010). Further non-environmental initiatives such as the 'Ride to the Ribs' motorcycle ride, first held in 2009, have been added to the event over the years, resulting in an even broader range of stakeholders. The proceeds of tickets purchased to enjoy a hot breakfast and participate in a scenic ride to the event go directly to Crime Stoppers of Halton, the community group responsible for organizing the side event (IH 29.08.2011).

Participation by stakeholders: other groups including vendors

As well as gaining the cooperation of the attendees and vendors, the organizers work with support service providers such as noise monitoring experts, public safety authorities and regional health inspectors before, during and after the event (IH 26.10.2005; IH 06.09.2006).

In 2006, the organizers made recycling and organics collection mandatory for vendors, and various education-oriented practices ensured higher levels of cooperation from both vendors and attendees (TBP 20.09.2006). The fast pace at which the ribbers work to prepare the ribs and manage their stalls can make manually sorting waste into organics, recyclables and garbage difficult (ACISS, 2004). Those who do not follow the specified waste sorting guidelines are unable to return the following year (IH 26.08.2007). To encourage cooperation, a competition is held to identify the vendor who sorts the waste produced by their own stall most accurately (TBP 07.08.2005). Each vendor must sign a contract that stipulates the exclusive use of biodegradable products such as fibre-based food containers for serving the ribs (IH 20.08.2008), corn starch-based beer cups and wooden cutlery (Canada's Largest Ribfest, 2013b). Before introducing these requirements in 2008, vendors were given 1 year to research biodegradable alternatives (IH 20.08.2008). Transparent bags are used for ease of sorting and monitoring (IH 26.08.2007).

Operational issues

Equipped with designated funding for environmental responsibility, organizers introduced a larger and more formalized '100 per cent Green Program' in 2008 (IH 11.07.2008). Additional waste management initiatives included green containers for biodegradable waste to accompany the existing blue containers for recycling and more stations where attendees can take their waste to be sorted by 'Recycling Staff' (Canada's Largest Ribfest, 2013b). The number of containers and stations continues to grow with increases in crowd size. In 2010, there were three main recycling stations and eight sub-stations throughout the venue (IH 18.08.2010). Volunteers collect waste left on tables and bring it to the nearest recycling station (IH 18.08.2010). Throughout the event, volunteers check that items have been sorted correctly. Recyclable waste or organics misplaced with garbage, such as diapers and plastic wrappers, which attendees bring onto the site, are recovered by hand (TBP 11.09.2008). Correcting contamination before pick-ups is vital. Hamilton Recycling Ltd. donates their services, visiting the park three times on each day of the 4-day event to collect the recovered waste (TBP 17.09.2004; TBP 11.09.2008).

Plastic water bottles remain the largest component of waste. Attendees are encouraged to make use of the water re-filling stations by bringing their own re-usable water bottles or purchasing a refillable souvenir water container on site. Used cooking grease is collected and recycled into bio-diesel or fertilizer (TBP 20.09.2006). All grey water created during the event is pumped into the same filtration system as the city's sewage (ACISS, 2004).

Reducing gas emissions and congestion in the Burlington Downtown core is a continuing goal of the festival. To encourage alternative modes of transport while also decreasing traffic and parking issues, a shuttle bus service and secure bike storage programme were introduced in 2006 and 2008 respectively. The minimal fee charged for these services contributes to the fundraising efforts. In 2008, more than 600 attendees used the valet bike service, which volunteers from Community Living Burlington managed. The $740 raised from the service was forwarded directly to that charity (IH 03.09.2008).

Rain is a continuing theme in the story of the Ribfest (TBP 01.09.2011). For instance, attendance in 2010 (140,000) was 35,000 less than the previous year due to heavy rain on the first 2 days. The effect of that drop in attendance on profit was estimated at $50,000 (IH 08.10.2010). However, the lakeside waterfront position and thick green grass of Burlington's Spencer Smith Park are noted as value-adding components of the event's ambiance, and thus points of differentiation from the numerous other ribfests across Canada and America (IH 30.08.2006; IH 29.08.2007).

Educating stakeholders about environmental issues

The third pillar in the Laing and Frost (2010) schema for evaluating green events was what they called 'promoting a message through green events', which the current authors term 'educating stakeholders about environmental matters'. As Laing and Frost (2010) note, some events have their overarching theme as green, such as the Slow Food festivals in Melbourne and San Francisco. However, more generally, events like Ribfest, have their own particular theme, such as music, crafts or birding, and the green message is a by-product of the main activity.

Frensch, who helped motivate the move to green, began proactive efforts to educate festival attendees, vendors and community members about the importance of waste management from 2004 (IH 30.04.2006). While most stakeholders were initially supportive of the event's recycling efforts, an explicit attempt was made in 2006 to create awareness that depositing organics in landfills emits methane gas, but composting does not (ACISS, 2004).

Each sorting centre has visible instructions detailing where items go (IH 18.08.2010). At the 2011 event, the authors observed large, colourful and detailed posters indicating how to disperse particular scrap items. The posters alone were a major educational tool. Educating attendees and answering questions about the waste management programme are considered key functions of volunteers across all areas (IH 19.08.2009).

Vendor education takes place on the day before the festival when the physical infrastructure is set up (IH 22.08.2007). Through an ongoing collaboration with media partners, information about the event's environmental programme is communicated in local newspapers (ACISS, 2004), on the Ribfest's website, digital newsletters, signage at the event (Canada's Largest Ribfest, 2013b) and recycling-themed t-shirts worn by the volunteers (TBP 07.08.2005).

Highlights of the Burlington Ribfest

It is clear that Burlington Ribfest is an exemplar green event, especially for an event where the main purpose is not inherently green. The event is hugely successful for providing family-oriented leisure to the local community and visitors, generating millions of dollars for charities and adding millions of dollars to the local economy. The chapter documents the operational approaches taken to green the event, and quantifies the outcomes in terms of the environmental footprint. The overall environmental success is symbolized by many awards and recognitions. As per Lawton and Weaver (2010), waste minimization and recycling are the two most important components of the green event mix. Green transport options, such as the shuttle service, are a long way back in third place (see also Merrilees and Marles, 2011).

Each of many detailed features contributes to the success, and that is noteworthy in its own right. However, there seem to be two standout features which are, first, the tight green integration of the event and the green city and, second, the tight green integration of the attendee stakeholder group with the event itself.

In terms of the integration between the event and the City of Burlington, the Mayor of the City of Burlington highlighted the ongoing success of the Ribfest in a 2005 end-of-year address, where he also commented: 'Our economy is strong, we have made great strides in protecting our natural environment and we have significantly enhanced the quality of life for people living in our city' (IH 28.12.2005). The following statement from a journalist reporting on the Ribfest in 2011 refers directly to the synergy between the event and its host city: 'since 2004, organizers have worked toward creating a ribfest that reflects society's concern about preserving and protecting our environment' (TBP 02.09.2011). As the Ribfest website adds: 'The environment is important to all of us, and what better way to show our appreciation for beautiful Burlington than to ensure that this event produces only biodegradable waste and 100 per cent recyclable material' (Canada's Largest Ribfest, 2013b).

A second highlight builds on the integration of all stakeholders to the green cause and the success of the event; stakeholders who include the City, Rotary, volunteers, ribbers, vendors and attendees. It is worth emphasizing the inclusivity towards the biggest stakeholder group of all, namely the attendees. In one sense, attendees can be perceived as passive, receiving the one-way green education messages noted above. Yet, in many ways, attendees are proactive in generating green outcomes. As recognized, some attendees bring their own refillable water containers. Further, the event relies on attendee cooperation, in returning waste products to the recycling station and supporting the volunteers in doing their job and generally buying-in to the green event concept. The positive involvement of the attendees essentially means that they are co-creating the green experience, rather than being passive.

Lessons from exemplar events

In many countries, there are hundreds of community events with a potential to upgrade their degree of greenness. Many of these community events are trying to increase their greenness but from a low base and with limited success. For example, in Goderich, Ontario, in 2010, the Goderich Celtic Roots Festival in 2010 tried to get biodegradable cup containers, but found that they were very expensive. This problem would seem to reflect a limited sourcing capability, related to the scale of the festival. Other events appear to be able to achieve such a task. At the same festival in 2011, containers were placed for waste and recycling. However, they were not easily distinguished from each other and, on observation, people placed items in the wrong bin.

Given the likely different clusters of approaches to green events, it would be rash to think that most could reach the Burlington Ribfest standards quickly. Less-green events could aim to reach an average standard, while the middle and high performing green events could aim for the top, namely the Burlington Ribfest standard.

From low to middle green event standard

Goderich Celtic Roots Festival is typical of the low green community events. A predominant characteristic of such a status is the lack of emphasis on green matters and the lack of coordination of green activities. Organizers of such events need to get together and set some basic goals and means of achieving them. All staff and volunteers should be informed about these approaches and their importance. Ideally, these processes should be developed to enable the staff and volunteers to buy-in to the new approach. This essentially means that the green aspect of the event is being rebranded (Miller *et al.*, 2013).

Waste management is the biggest potential component of greening a community event. So presenting sufficient well-labelled bins, with very clear instructions and encouragement are a major tool. As a minimum, waste/landfill and recycling are the two main types of bins, but there is also scope to have more than one type of recycling and also a green waste bin. Having different colours and perhaps different images on bins are a useful way to go. The objective over time should be to reduce the percentage of waste going to landfill.

From middle to high performing (best practice) green community events

As the Burlington Ribfest case study shows, it takes a sustained effort over many years to move to green event best practice. Once an event has achieved and maintained the middle level standard for say 4–5 years, it should be ready to progress to or at least attempt the next level, namely best practice green events. Again, another 4–5 years' effort is required.

To an extent, progression up the ladder of green performance requires a deliberate strategy by the event organizers to be a sustainable event. Ad hoc measures of more and better bins by themselves will not elevate the event sufficiently. Bold objectives seem to preface bold actions. A deliberate strategy to make a particular event more green essentially requires the organizers to rebrand the event. A recent wider study suggests a need to be very sure of the purpose of the event and to engage all stakeholders (Miller *et al.*, 2013).

In terms of appropriate green actions, the Ribfest provides a benchmark as to the relevant green mix: namely about three parts waste minimization, two parts recycling and one part more efficient transportation options. However, to achieve a sufficient size of impact, event organizers need to be somewhat innovative in their approaches. In the case of Burlington Ribfest, the rigorous and energetic way that the waste-sorting stations were organized from the outset in 2004 is an excellent example.

Additional factors increase the green performance of an event. Laing and Frost (2010) end their operational issues with the suggested need to audit the ongoing green impact over time. This factor was missing from Lawton and Weaver (2010), as were more quantitative measures of environmental impact. In contrast, as Table 17.1 shows, Burlington Ribfest has been carefully monitoring their environmental impact scorecard, which provides sound evidence of impact and motivation to continue to improve. Winning various environmental awards and praise adds further motivation to the organizers, and other stakeholders.

Another important contributing strategic success factor is the desirability of integrating key stakeholders into the green cause. The Rotary Club, in the current case study, is a pivotal stakeholder. The City is also a more subtle stakeholder. Most of the case study discussion on operational issues focused on the two big stakeholder groups, volunteers and vendors, but mention was also made of attendees. Vendors were almost micro-managed in terms of guidelines, down to small wooden cutlery, a good sign of striving for best practice. Volunteers are at the heart of the green event, in itself a clever, innovative and strategic decision. So in total, it is not just a matter of being inclusive and involving all key stakeholders; it also embraces the way that inclusivity is encouraged. It is all about stakeholder engagement (Miller *et al.*, 2013).

Finally, another important contributing success factor is the nexus between the Ribfest event and the City. The authors identified this as a second highlight of the Burlington Ribfest. The intertwined network between a green event and a green city is synergistic and greatly facilitates the likely sustainability success of both parties. Such a synergy may not always happen, but the option is there. Again, it takes time to build such an event-city relationship. Usefully, it opens up another trigger for moving to a green event – perhaps the City (with green aspirations), rather than the event organizers, could take the initiative in approaching a particular event to go green? In any case, the Burlington Ribfest case could be helpful in developing such a relationship. Indeed, there may be cases where the province or nation takes the lead, which partly explains the London Olympics' greening activities.

Conclusions

Green events can have many positive outcomes. All stakeholders stand to gain. In the case of Burlington Ribfest, the benefits include funds for charities, a stronger city economy, a richer lifestyle for the community, tourist development and most importantly, a more environmentally friendly footprint. The quantitative measures of environmental outcomes are particularly significant in the exemplar case study.

The Burlington Ribfest has an economic impact of $3 million, which essentially means a green economy impact of $3 million. Symbolically, the impact on the city is even greater because it means that the Burlington City economy also is defined in green terms, by its largest event, the Ribfest. Other Burlington City events and business conferences take a lead from this example. Further Ribfests throughout Ontario also take a lead from the Burlington Ribfest demonstration. The impact of the Ribfest has multiplied from a single green event to the wider green economy. Thus, while the event is short-term, its impacts can be far-reaching and enduring.

In particular, the benefits to charities, the economy and the environment are cumulative. All stakeholders influence and are influenced by the green nature of the event and activate what is a type of multiplier effect. The many stakeholder groups, including Rotary, the City, volunteers, waste management service providers, vendors, ribbers and attendees all motivate and interact with each other, creating synergies that are greater than the individual contributions. In turn, the demonstration and educational benefits transcend the event and multiply to other settings, including household recycling, other ribfests, other events, city governance and management and provincial governance and management. In short, green events such as the Burlington Ribfest are significant for the wider green economy.

The Burlington Ribfest narrative is compelling. Careful reading reveals humble beginnings that have been enthusiastically built up at a rapid rate. While the event has not quite achieved 100 per cent green, it has come very close to that mark and is destined to reach it in the near future. Both the broad strategy and the detailed operational management developments of Burlington Ribfest can inspire and stimulate other events to emulate its actions and achievements.

References

ACISS (2004) Volunteer organizer pleased with Ribfest recycling efforts, www.aciss.ca/k-com munity.htm, accessed 15 June 2013.

Canada's Largest Ribfest (2013a) Recycling at Ribfest, www.canadaslargestribfest.com/about.php? page=recycling, accessed 14 July 2013.

Canada's Largest Ribfest (2013b) Canada's Largest Ribfest 100 per cent Green *Program,* www.canadaslargestribfest.com/about.php?page=green, accessed 15 June 2013.

Commission for a Sustainable London 2012 (2013) Making a difference: post-games report, www.cslondon.org/wp-content/uploads/downloads/2013/03/CSL-Making-a-Difference-2013.pdf, accessed 3 July 2013.

Government of Canada (2004) Your guide to the one-tonne challenge, www.quest.uwinnipeg.ca/ quest-north/otctipsguide.pdf, accessed 18 June 2013.

International Olympic Committee (2013) London 2012 facts & figures, www.olympic.org/ Documents/Reference_documents_Factsheets/London_2012_Facts_and_Figures-eng.pdf, accessed 2 July 2013.

Laing, J. and Frost, W. (2010) How green was my festival: Exploring challenges and opportun-ities associated with staging green events, *International Journal of Hospitality Management,* vol. 29, no. 2, pp. 261–67.

Lawton, L.J. and Weaver, D.B. (2010) Normative and innovative sustainable resource management at birding festivals, *Tourism Management,* vol. 31, no. 4, pp. 527–36.

Mair, J. and Jago, L. (2010) The development of a conceptual model of greening in the business events tourism sector, *Journal of Sustainable Tourism,* vol. 18, no. 1, pp. 77–94.

Merrilees, B. and Marles, K. (2011) Green business events: Profiling through a case study, *Event Management,* vol. 15, no. 4, pp. 361–72.

Merrilees, B., Miller, D. and Tiessen, J. (1998) Serendipity, leverage and the process of entrepreneurial internationalization, *Small Enterprise Research: The Journal of SEAANZ,* vol. 6, no. 2, pp. 3–11.

Miller, D., Merrilees, B. and Yakimova, R. (2013) Corporate rebranding: An integrative review of major enablers and barriers to the rebranding process, *International Journal of Management Reviews,* vol. 6, no. 3, pp. 265–89. doi: 10.1111/ijmr.12020.

Ministry of the Environment (2004) Ontario's 60% Waste Diversion Goal – A Discussion Paper, www.ene.gov.on.ca/stdprodconsume/groups/lr/@ene/@resources/documents/resource/std01 _079752.pdf, accessed 18 June 2013.

PART 3

Research implications and emerging issues

18

A MICRO–MACRO ASSESSMENT OF CLIMATE CHANGE AND VISITORS TO THE GREAT BARRIER REEF, AUSTRALIA

Tazim Jamal, Bruce Prideaux, Hana Sakata and Michelle Thompson

Introduction

Climate change was recognized by the Davos Declaration on Climate Change as the greatest challenge to the sustainability of tourism in the twenty-first century (UNWTO, 2007). While adaptation and mitigation initiatives are gradually emerging, tourism policy-making and leadership by public and private sector stakeholders are slow to follow, despite increasing concern about extreme weather events and tourism's contribution to climate change (see Scott, 2011). The CO_2 emissions from all forms of tourism accounted for just under 5 per cent of the world total or 1,307 million tons in 2005, and are estimated to increase by 130 per cent from 2005 to 2035 (UNWTO, UNEP and WMO, 2008, cited in de Grosbois and Fennell, 2011). This chapter discusses micro-level issues and macro-level implications related to environmental awareness, perceptions and actions of tourists at the Great Barrier Reef, Australia. Proactive sustainability action by the tourism industry and policy-makers will be needed as societal perceptions shift and structural changes are initiated in response to climate change. The chapter argues for targeted educational, communication and social change strategies at the micro- and macro-levels in order to facilitate the transition by various tourism stakeholders towards a green economy locally and globally.

Visitors are key stakeholders in the tourism system, but research is equivocal on their travel attitudes and behaviour (see next section), and on their importance to tourism in the green economy. Sustainable tourism scholars today are still grappling with how much responsibility visitors have to undertake for ethical behaviour, learning or civic action in this complex new world of extreme weather, global warming, and unpredictable climate futures. Ecotourism, with clearer principles of nature education and aspiration for behaviour change, offers some hope here, but research in this area is nascent. In the context of marine tourism, limited visitor research has been undertaken on the cumulative impacts of humans and climate change on the Great Barrier Reef and other coral reefs worldwide (De'ath et al., 2012). The purpose of this chapter is therefore twofold: (i) to conduct a micro-level exploratory study of visitors to the tropic North Queensland region that encompasses Cairns and the World Heritage listed Great Barrier Reef; and (ii) to identify and discuss some macro-level key policy, planning and destination management issues and themes related to climate change, in order to enable a green economy and conserve the vital biodiversity of this iconic destination. Specific issues investigated are:

- Do the reef visitors recognize they are in a World Heritage Area?
- What are their knowledge and beliefs about climate change?
- Does climate change awareness (or lack thereof) mediate their preferences and actions?
- What role can reef visitors play personally in climate change impact management?
- What are the implications for proactive ethical action by tourism stakeholders towards a green economy at the local and global level?

Climate change and tourism: Awareness and action at the reef

Among the future research priorities identified in Buckley's (2012) review of social and environmental impacts, responses and indicators for the tourism sector globally was 'the effects of individual perceptions of responsibility in addressing climate change' (p. 528). Existing visitor studies have found significant gaps between awareness and action, described as an 'attitude-behaviour' gap even among international tourists who seemed aware of global warming and climate change, but were reluctant to alter their own travel behaviour or contribute to carbon offset schemes (Becken, 2004; Huebner, 2012; Mair, 2011). Perceptions of the freedom to travel and the right to leisure in long-haul destinations appear to be firmly engrained in many Western developed economies, giving rise to the belief that individuals have a sacrosanct right to enjoy their holiday spaces (see Becken, 2007; Hares et al., 2010). 'Public interest' in these tourist-generating countries is often determined in terms of economic and market interests that support growth based on increased consumption; these interests and values influence views on individual rights and the freedom to consume travel and tourism (Bartle, 2009).

There are relatively few studies on tourist perceptions and actions in relation to climate change in World Heritage Sites. Scott et al. (2009) explored climate change scenarios with a wide range of visitors in the mountainous landscapes of Waterton National Park, Canada (a World Heritage Site). On the Great Barrier Reef, Turton et al. (2009) used an extensive multi-stakeholder process to examine the climate–resource relationship and tourism. Stakeholders present at the workshops did not include tourists, however. Ramis and Prideaux (2013) found that tourists were sensitive to changes in the condition of the reef and that climate change may have a major impact on visitation patterns in the future. The exploratory research presented below investigates climate change-related knowledge, perceptions and ethical actions of visitors to the Great Barrier

Reef (micro-level). Implications for social responsibility and societal change in the context of climate change and tourism in the green economy are discussed in the latter half of the chapter, along with some related themes and issues (macro-level).

The Great Barrier Reef, Australia

Background and setting

Located within this complex region, the boundaries of this study extend from Cairns south to Mission Beach and north to Cape Tribulation. The economic significance of tourism in this region is well documented (Prideaux and Falco-Mammone, 2010), but less is known about the potential impacts of climate change. Impacts on vertebrate populations, birdlife, temperature, rainfall and weather, plus landscape changes caused by extreme weather events are expected to have a significant impact on tourism (Ramis and Prideaux, 2013; Turton *et al.*, 2009). Increases in water temperature above 2°C (IPCC, 2007) are expected to have severe implications for the health of coral reefs, fisheries and coastal ecosystems. The Great Barrier Reef has undergone eight mass bleaching events since 1979 (1980, 1982, 1987, 1992, 1994, 1998, 2002 and 2006), with the most severe in 1998 and 2002 affecting about 42 per cent and 54 per cent of reefs respectively (Berkelmans *et al.*, 2004; cited in Hall, 2008). In addition, the cumulative effects of a range of environmental and human impacts need to be factored in. Local anthropogenic issues, such as pollution, over-fishing, agricultural run-off and other sources of sediment discharge, increase the vulnerability of reef ecosystems to climate change-related effects such as ocean acidification. Increasing impacts from incidents such as cyclones and Crown of Thorns invasion (COTS – predatory star fish that eats coral polyps) attacks continue to raise concerns about the threats facing this iconic destination (De'ath *et al.*, 2012; see also Bryant, 2013; Larwood, 2012). The Queensland State Government's approval of extensive dredging programmes to open coal ports within the Great Barrier Reef Marine Park boundaries, and continued ocean acidification and sea level rises, contribute further uncertainty to the efforts of the Australian Federal government's reef management authority, the Great Barrier Reef Marine Park Authority (GBRMPA), to manage individual and cumulative impacts on the reef (see GBRMPA, 2009a, 2009b). However, proactive management strategies implemented by the Great Barrier Reef Marine Park Authority and supported by tour operators to address issues such as over-fishing (e.g., through implementing green zones and strict regulatory oversight), have contributed to the reef being recognized as the best-managed coral reef system in the world.Collectively, future climate change-induced impacts are anticipated to adversely affect visitor experiences and enjoyment, such as diving at the reef (Zeppel, 2012). Yet, too little is known of visitor knowledge, perceptions and actions related to climate change and impacts on the reef. The exploratory study reported below is a preliminary investigation of these visitor-related issues. Within the study region, most reef tour operators departing from Cairns and Port Douglas, the two key towns in the study area, have Australian ecotourism certification, and a few have advanced eco-certification. Reef tours range from day visits to reef islands and pontoons moored on the reef to overnight dive and whale watching trips.

Data gathering and analysis

Data collected was based on a self-administered questionnaire distributed to tourists departing the region from the domestic terminal of Cairns International Airport. Collection occurred during a high visitation period (July to September 2012). Data collection days were randomized within weekdays. The questionnaire was four pages long and took approximately 10–12 minutes to complete. The questionnaire included questions on socio-demographic information, motivations for visiting the region, activities undertaken, plus issues related to climate change and sustainability at the GBR. Overall relationships to climate change in terms of knowledge, perception and ethical actions were also examined (e.g. choosing ecotourism-certified reef operators). As English was the only language used on the questionnaire, the sample was restricted to visitors who could read and write in English. Respondents included both domestic and international visitors. The sample consists of 368 valid responses from participants, with a response rate of 92 per cent. Closed-ended responses were analysed using SPSS 20 statistical software. Non-parametric tests were used to test the closed responses as the data was distribution free and ordinal and nominal in nature. As with any survey of this nature, care should be taken in generalizing these results over a larger population.

Results

Profile of reef visitors

The sample consisted of 51.5 per cent males and 48.5 per cent females. Respondents originated from both Australia (53 per cent) and overseas (47 per cent). International visitors originated mainly from Europe (28.6 per cent), which included the UK and Ireland (10.9 per cent) and Germany (3.8 per cent), as well as North America (11.2 per cent). Ages ranged from 19 to 85 years. The main age groups of respondents for this period were: 20–29 years (24.1 per cent), followed by 50–59 years (20.5 per cent), 30–39 years (12.9 per cent), 40–49 years (12.9 per cent), 60–65 years (9.9 per cent), and under 20 years (8.6 per cent). Less than half (43.2 per cent) reported that they held a degree or higher university qualification, had finished secondary education (21.3 per cent), had a diploma (16.7 per cent), had a trade or TAFE qualification (10.7 per cent) or other kinds of education (8.1 per cent). The main employment categories were professionals (25.1 per cent), students (18 per cent) and retired/semi-retired (16.1 per cent). Other occupations included public service (8.7 per cent), self-employed (8.2 per cent), management (6.6 per cent), tradesperson (5.5 per cent), clerical (3.6 per cent), domestic duties (2.7 per cent), service industry (2.5 per cent), retail (2.2 per cent) and manual/factory worker (0.8 per cent).More than half of the respondents (64 per cent) reported visiting the GBR on that trip and 36 per cent had not been to the GBR. Of those who reported visiting the GBR on that trip, it was a first visit for 71.4 per cent and the remainder were repeat visitors. Leisure was the main orientation of these visitors. The most common activities related to the reef were snorkelling (50.8 per cent) followed by swimming (35.2 per cent), glass-bottom boat and semi-submarine coral viewing (29 per cent) and visiting other islands in the region (20.8 per cent). The results showed no significant difference ($p = 0.673$) between international and domestic respondents' participation in a marine biologist-led snorkel tour, which is an activity offered by a number of reef tour operators. Very low participation in marine biologist tours was observed for both international (8.3 per cent) and domestic respondents (7.1 per cent). (Note: some reef operators include a marine biologist-led snorkel tour in their offering, while others charge for this activity, with prices averaging around AU$20). Participants were also asked to rate their experience at the GBR. A high proportion (83.9 per cent) of the participants reported that they had a 'good' experience at the GBR, 14.3 per cent reported that their experience was 'fair' and only 1.8 per cent rated their experience as 'poor'.

Recognition and importance of World Heritage designations in the Cairns region

Approximately half of the respondents (51.2 per cent) reported that they noticed World Heritage designated sites in the Cairns region. About a third of respondents who noticed a World Heritage Area (WHA) in the region were able to name either or both sites. The results indicate that the Great Barrier Reef WHA (31.9 per cent) is slightly better recognized than the Wet Tropics WHA (28.5 per cent), which is also in the region. Overall, the results indicated a generally poor recognition of the World Heritage brand despite the fact that the region's main selling proposition is based on these two World Heritage Areas. Results also indicated that World Heritage status may not greatly affect tourism visitation to Cairns. When asked if they would still have made this trip to Cairns if the Great Barrier Reef *lost* its World Heritage status, a high percentage of visitors responded affirmatively (Yes 84.2 per cent, No 15.8 per cent).

Climate change impacts on the Great Barrier Reef: Concerns and deterrents

Concern about damage to the Great Barrier Reef

Participants were highly concerned about the impact of climate change on the GBR (see Table 18.1). There was a significant difference in responses between genders, χ^2 (3, n = 343) = 13.738, p = 0.003. Females reported significantly higher concerns ('Not at all concerned' 3.0 per cent, 'A little concerned' 10.8 per cent, 'Concerned' 34.7 per cent and 'Very concerned' 51.5 per cent) than males ('Not at all concerned' 4.5 per cent, 'A little concerned' 15.9 per cent, 'Concerned' 47.7 per cent and 'Very concerned' 31.8 per cent). The chi-squared test for independence did not detect significant differences by origin (p = 0.682). The sample was too small to test significance within age groups or educational background.

TABLE 18.1 Level of concern that climate change will damage the Great Barrier Reef

Level of concern	Respondents (%)
Not at all concerned	3.7
A little concerned	13.1
Concerned	41.9
Very concerned	41.3

It is interesting to note that participants were not nearly as concerned about climate change reducing their quality of life as they were about its impact on the Great Barrier Reef. A little over one quarter (26.4 per cent) were 'very concerned' that climate change would reduce their quality of life and a further 39.7 per cent were 'concerned'. Just over a third of the sample showed little to no concern: 24.1 per cent were a little concerned, and 9.8 per cent were not at all concerned. There were no significant differences found on the main demographic variables of gender, origin, age or educational background.

Climate change-related deterrents to visiting: Coral bleaching

The questionnaire asked about deterrents to visiting the GBR. Close to 30 per cent (29.4 per cent) reported that they would still have visited Cairns even if the GBR was affected by a major coral bleaching event described in the questionnaire as 'when the coral dies because of high water temperatures'. While 19.3 per cent answered 'no', the majority (51.3 per cent) of respondents were ambivalent. We did not observe significant differences in the reaction between genders ($p = 0.808$). Significant difference was found only in regard to the origin of the respondents, χ^2 (2, $n = 228$) = 8.753, $p = 0.013$. The results indicated that international respondents would be less likely to visit Cairns if a major coral bleaching event occurred. Only 13.2 per cent of domestic and 23.4 per cent of international respondents responded that they would not have visited, and 39.6 per cent of domestic and 22.6 per cent international respondents reported that it would not have affected their decision to visit Cairns. About half of both domestic (47.3 per cent) and international respondents (54 per cent) responded 'maybe'. The sample size was too small to test age group and educational background.

Visibility/clarity of viewing

Participants were asked if they would still have visited Cairns if water at the GBR was known to be murky. Only 25.3 per cent reported yes, 34.4 per cent reported no and 40.3 per cent reported that they may have still made their trip to Cairns, depending on the level of murkiness. There was no significant difference in reactions across gender ($p = 0.428$). However, respondents' origins did matter, as shown by the statistically significant result obtained (χ^2 (2, $n = 221$) = 12.561, $p = 0.002$). International respondents reported more negative responses (Yes 17.3 per cent, No 40.6 per cent and Maybe 42.1 per cent) than domestic respondents (Yes 37.5 per cent, No 25 per cent and Maybe 37.5 per cent). The sample size was too small to test age group and educational background.

Knowledge, perceptions and ethical action

Knowledge level and belief on the cause of climate change

Respondents were asked to rate their own level of knowledge about climate change. More than half of the respondents (59.7 per cent) reported that they had some knowledge, 23.6 per cent reported having a little knowledge and 13.4 per cent said that they had a high level of knowledge. Only 3.4 per cent reported that they had no knowledge about climate change. There was no significant difference in their responses across gender ($p = 0.179$), origin ($p = 0.566$), generations ($p = 0.472$) or educational background ($p = 0.105$).In addition, participants were prompted to respond to an open-ended question on what they believed was the 'single greatest cause' of climate change. A total of 278 responses were received and categorized. A high proportion (63.8 per cent) believed that climate change was mainly caused by human-induced (anthropogenic) activities. Causes reported included energy use, fossil fuel, over-population, human greed, urbanization and capitalism. A low proportion perceived that it did not exist (2.0 per cent) or that it occurred as part of a natural cycle (4.8 per cent).

Perceived seriousness of climate change

Participants were asked to rate how serious a problem climate change was. Most people considered climate change as a serious problem, as shown in Table 18.2. International visitors were found to be significantly more likely to rate climate change as a 'very serious' or worse problem than were Australian visitors. The figure for international visitors was 70.1 per cent compared with 54.0 per cent for domestic visitors (χ^2 (1, $n = 354$), $p = 0.02$).

There is a statistically significant difference between those who considered climate change to be a very serious or even worse problem and those who considered it to be less than a very serious problem, based on education level ($p = 0.013$). As Table 18.3 shows, the more educated a person is, the more likely they are to consider climate change to be a very serious or worse problem. Two thirds (65.9 per cent) of those with a diploma or higher formal education considered climate change to be a very serious or worse problem compared with just 46.8 per cent of those with a less formal education.

TABLE 18.2 Perceived seriousness of climate change

Level of seriousness	Respondents (%)
Not serious at all	5.6
A little serious	9.6
Somewhat serious	23.7
Very serious	40.4
The biggest environmental issue we face	18.6
The single biggest issue we face	2.0

TABLE 18.3 Perceived seriousness of climate change vs. level of education

Seriousness of climate change	Secondary	Trade/ TAFE	Diploma	Degree	Other education
Less than 'very serious'	53.4%	52.8%	36.2%	35.2%	23.1%
'Very serious' or worse	46.6%	47.2%	63.8%	64.8%	76.9%

Commitment to meaningful action

Respondents were asked if they believed they could make a meaningful contribution to reducing the impact of climate change. The results indicate that a significant percentage of respondents (61 per cent) believed they were making an effort to address their own impact on climate change. The remaining respondents considered that climate change was too big an issue for one person (16 per cent); they had tried to change, but it was too difficult (3 per cent); it would require a major lifestyle change that they were not willing to make now (12.8 per cent); or yes, they would make an effort to address their own impact, but sometime in the future (9.9 per cent).

There is a statistically significant difference (χ^2 (6, n = 343) = 16.514), p = 0.011) between those who claimed to be trying to reduce their impact on climate change now and those who were not, based on age group. Respondents aged 40 years and older were significantly more likely to be trying to reduce their impact now, compared with their younger counterparts (71.0 per cent vs. 50.0 per cent). Further, there is a statistically significant difference (χ^2 (4, n = 327) = 10.498), p = 0.033) between people who were trying to reduce their impact on climate change now and those who were not, based on education level (see Table 18.4). People who had obtained a diploma or better were much more likely than those with less formal education to indicate that they were presently trying to reduce their own personal impact on climate change (65.5 per cent vs 52.3 per cent).

There also appears to be a relationship between perceived climate change knowledge and the belief that the respondent can make a meaningful contribution to reducing the impact of climate change. While the sample size was not large enough to claim statistically significant differences, there was a clear pattern that indicated the more climate change knowledge a person had, the more likely s/he was to act to try and reduce climate change impacts in a meaningful way. Figure 18.1 highlights the relationship between climate change knowledge and commitment to reducing impacts. Of respondents who stated they had a high level of climate change knowledge, 76.6 per cent were trying to reduce their impact. In comparison, those with little or no knowledge were the least likely to have a commitment to action to reduce climate change.

Booking environmental tours

Participants were asked if they had a preference for booking tours that had environmental accreditation. Close to half (46.4 per cent) answered 'Depends', 22.8 per cent answered Yes, and 30.8 per cent answered No. The probability that a person will prefer to book an environmentally accredited tour appears to depend on their level

Table 18.4 Climate change reduction contribution by level of education

Climate change reduction contribution	Secondary	Trade/ TAFE	Diploma	Degree	Other education
Trying now	50.0%	57.1%	77.8%	60.7%	65.4%
Not trying now	50.0%	42.9%	22.2%	39.3%	34.6%

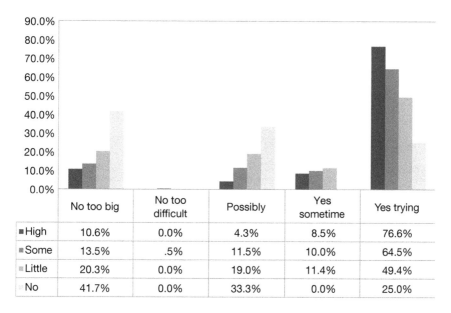

	No too big	No too difficult	Possibly	Yes sometime	Yes trying
■ High	10.6%	0.0%	4.3%	8.5%	76.6%
■ Some	13.5%	.5%	11.5%	10.0%	64.5%
■ Little	20.3%	0.0%	19.0%	11.4%	49.4%
No	41.7%	0.0%	33.3%	0.0%	25.0%

FIGURE 18.1 Climate change knowledge vs level of commitment to making a meaningful contribution to reducing the impact of climate change

of education; people who have a diploma or higher in terms of formal education are significantly more likely to prefer to book such tours than those with less formal education (52.2 per cent vs 26.3 per cent; $p = 0.02$). This finding supports results from previous findings in ecotourism research (Musau and Prideaux, 2003).

Even though there was not a statistically significant difference between climate change knowledge and preference for booking tours that had environmental accreditation, those who felt they had a high degree of climate change knowledge were more likely to book a tour that was environmentally accredited. Only 11.1 per cent of those who claimed to have no climate change knowledge preferred to book such tours, compared with 52.2 per cent of those with a self-professed high level of climate change knowledge.

Vacation destination choice

Respondents were asked if they looked for a place that was actively protecting its environment, when selecting a vacation destination. Less than a quarter (22.5 per cent) indicated 'Never', 48.4 per cent indicated 'Sometimes', 25.9 per cent indicated 'Most of the time' and only 3.1 per cent selected 'Always'. The majority of respondents, regardless of their level of climate change knowledge, who reported being either concerned or very concerned about climate change impacting the GBR, did not seem to factor in the environment when choosing a vacation destination. However, even those most knowledgeable about climate change seldom 'always' selected a vacation destination that was actively protecting its environment. Figure 18.2 shows the relationship between knowledge of climate change and the likelihood of respondents

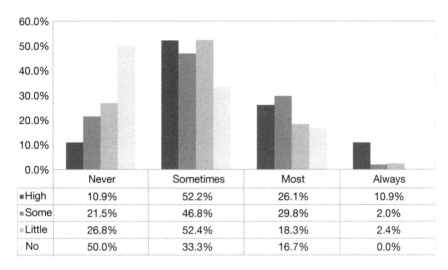

	Never	Sometimes	Most	Always
■High	10.9%	52.2%	26.1%	10.9%
■Some	21.5%	46.8%	29.8%	2.0%
■Little	26.8%	52.4%	18.3%	2.4%
No	50.0%	33.3%	16.7%	0.0%

FIGURE 18.2 Climate change knowledge vs vacation destination choice

always selecting destinations that protect the environment. Just 10.9 per cent of respondents who said they had a high level of climate change knowledge stated 'always' and 26.1 per cent said 'most of the time'. Statistically significant differences between this variable and climate change knowledge however could not be verified due to the small sample size.

Profile of 'believers and doers'

The emerging results suggest that developing a profile of climate change-savvy (self-typed), highly serious, and action-oriented respondents with a high level of climate change knowledge might be useful. This sub-group, that we call 'believers and doers', is characterized as follows: respondents identify themselves as having a high level of knowledge about climate change; they consider climate change to be very serious or worse, and they are acting to try and reduce their personal impact on climate change in a meaningful way. The size of this group from our sample was surprisingly small, at just thirty-one people out of 368.

We then looked at this group in terms of four demographic variables: age, origin (Australian or international), education level and gender. Compared with the sample as a whole, this sub-group has more males than females (63.3 per cent vs 51.5 per cent). There is little difference in terms of origin, with 54.8 per cent of this sub-group coming from Australia compared with 53.7 per cent for the overall sample. Respondents in this small sub-group had a higher level of formal education than the overall sample, with 90.0 per cent having a diploma or higher, compared with 68.0 per cent of the entire sample. In terms of age, the group skews towards being older than the overall sample, with 77.4 per cent aged 40 years and older compared with 53.4 per cent for the sample as a whole. This group is not unlike some ecotourist profiles in terms of education and age (Tao *et al.*, 2004).

Discussion

The above-reported exploratory study of visitors at Cairns airport offers some preliminary insights into environmental awareness, perceptions and ethical actions of visitors to the GBRWHA, in relation to climate change and sustainability. The following discussion focuses on issues related to the awareness–action gap, the level of concern about climate change and a possible role for education.

Bridging the awareness–action gap

The exploration of knowledge, environmental behaviours and actions offers some interesting insights in this study, with socio-demographic factors playing a distinctive role. Education level was found to be important in relation to climate change knowledge and contributing to reducing climate change impacts, as well as in choosing environmentally accredited tours at the destination. The more formal education the participants had, the more likely they were to perceive climate change as a very serious or even worse problem. For example, 90 per cent of the 'believers and doers' sub-group had a high school diploma or better, compared with 68 per cent of the sample.

Not surprisingly, anthropogenic causes were identified as the single greatest contributor to climate change by a high proportion (63.8 per cent) of the 278 responses to this question. Knowledge played a significant role with respect to social action. Individuals with higher levels of knowledge were more likely to believe that they could make a meaningful contribution to reducing the impacts of climate change, and were also more likely to book environmentally accredited tours. But, despite the relatively high level of education, and a strong perception of climate change being a serious issue, neither this nor knowledge about climate change seemed to influence them strongly towards choosing a holiday destination that was actively protecting its natural environment.

This awareness–action gap among respondents, previously identified in the literature as an 'attitude–behaviour' gap, has been observed by other researchers cited earlier in the chapter. Becken (2007), for example, found that tourists were able to distinguish between their travel and their everyday life, and responsibility for mitigation was perceived to be greater in the home world than in their travels. The results above suggest a similar disconnect in the sense that a quality reef experience is clearly important, but ethical decisions did not follow strongly on aspects such as booking accredited tours (22.8 per cent of respondents) and seeking destinations that actively protected their environment (25.9 per cent). The visitors in our sample were a paradoxical mix. Despite what appeared to be a prioritizing of leisure over ethics described previously, they demonstrated concern about climate change impacts on the GBR, and more than half (61 per cent) said they were trying to reduce their own impact on climate change in a meaningful way. Age was a significant factor here, with respondents aged 40 years and over making a greater effort to manage their own impact than younger visitors.

Only a small number of visitors (31 out of 368) demonstrated all three characteristics of being knowledgeable, perceiving climate change to be at least very serious if not worse, and were actively trying to reduce their impact on climate change in a meaningful way. Given the relatively high education level of the whole sample, it is not surprising to see that 90.0 per cent of this small sub-group had a diploma or better compared with 68.0 per cent of the entire sample. While this sub-group is small, our overall visitor sample demonstrated that a sizeable percentage (~40 per cent) were concerned about climate change and were making an effort to reduce their personal impact.

Previous research indicates increasing awareness and ethical concern among travellers. For instance, in Higham and Cohen's (2011) study of Norwegian travellers, those concerned about their contribution to climate change continued to engage in 'air travel with a carbon conscience'. Their study comports with Gössling et al.'s (2009) research but contrasts with that of Hares et al. (2010), whose UK study showed climate denial coupled with reluctance to change travel behaviour. All studies, however, acknowledge an 'information deficit' (as mentioned by Hares et al., 2010) and seem to support the need for greater awareness-raising and information dissemination among the travelling public. The research points to the importance of raising knowledge and awareness of climate change and the potential for engaging tourists in sustainable co-creation actions. At the Great Barrier Reef, raising awareness and knowledge about climate change impacts on the reef, and the carbon impacts of travellers, are important actions for the tourism industry and other key stakeholders including destination managers and the Great Barrier Reef Marine Park Authority to engage in. Awareness-raising and information communication, sustainability education and collaborative involvement of tourists perhaps in co-creating environmentally friendly tools and strategies, are critical priorities. But making the product available may not be enough. These have to be linked to provide the resident at home and tourist elsewhere (resident-tourist) with concrete, doable acts to enable behavioural change and sustainability-oriented actions at home and in the destination. This is especially important in order to manage various drivers of inaction, noting that almost 29 per cent of our sample felt that the issue was too big to handle individually, or required a major lifestyle change that they were unwilling to make at present (see also Kroesen, 2013).

Actions indicating a proactive structural shift towards a low-carbon future

Respondents, particularly female visitors, expressed serious concern about climate change impacts on the Great Barrier Reef, and were more concerned about this than climate change impacting their own quality of life. Impacts on the quality of their reef experience were also an important concern, especially for international visitors. A coral bleaching event was perceived to be a potential deterrent. The level of concern about climate change impacts on the reef suggests that there is room for destination managers, tourism service providers and policy-makers to develop programmes that may be able to encourage GBR visitors to engage in sustainable practices. In both spaces (home and holiday), communication and various marketing strategies could be used to convey climate change information and targeted, realistic actions and practices such as adopting sustainable transportation, carbon offset programmes, energy conservation at home, localism geared towards low-carbon impacts, and communicating the belief that developing good habits can be achieved without adversely impacting on enjoyment of the holiday space. Interpretive tools, social media, the community social market plus a range of other communication strategies are available at home and abroad to strive towards low-carbon futures at home and away (Jamal and Watt, 2011).

For this to occur, destination managers and operators will need to remain informed about social and cultural shifts in visitor markets over time, and to factor evolving public knowledge, awareness and actions into their climate adaptation policies and plans, on-site interpretive materials and communication strategies. As social sentiments and political discourses shift at home and globally (see Donnelly, 2008; Pidgeon, 2011), proactive ethical actions by destination managers and service providers may become increasingly important to ensure an effective product–market match. For example, it can be anticipated that tourists will become increasingly sensitive to climate change impacts, both with respect to the reef and their own reef experience, as national governments begin to implement mandatory mitigation policies such as carbon trading.

Civic engagement and situated knowledge

Some respondents were more concerned about the impacts of climate change on the reef than about how it may affect their own quality of life. It is a well-understood phenomenon that people tend to be more concerned about climate change in spatially distanced locations than in their own backyard (see Pidgeon, 2011; Schott, 2010). This phenomenon opens up possibilities for directly engaging tourists, which includes: communicating their concerns to policy-makers and requesting greater attention and resources for reef conservation and sustainability; and engaging in social action and personal behaviour change at the destination and at home. Our results indicate that education and knowledge are significantly related to engaging in meaningful action on climate change. Hence, disseminating pertinent information on climate change and the Great Barrier Reef to create wider understanding and support for necessary policies and legislative initiatives could be a valuable strategy for policy-makers and destination managers to explore.

As the evidence for the adverse impacts of climate change begins to increase, destinations that are able to demonstrate a commitment to genuine climate change mitigation strategies are likely to gain a competitive advantage over those that are slower to act. At the destination level, an important consideration will be the development and implementation of climate-concerned communication and educational strategies targeted at destination stakeholders, including visitors, the domestic public and suppliers in tourist-originating markets. The Great Barrier Reef Marine Park Authority, which has an active climate change policy unit, supports extensive climate change research and monitoring and requires boat operators to be ecotourism certified. The difficulty for operators is that they have yet to see the cost of such programmes reflected in their annual profit statements.

The data outlined in Figure 18.2 shows that the relationship between understanding and action is still relatively low. In future, as the effect of climate change intensifies, social action that builds proactive civic participation in sustainable futures within the tourism system and outside it will become more attractive (see Hares *et al.*, 2010). As Slocum (2004, p. 433) states: 'Localizing climate change means to transform it into problems that are materially and culturally relevant to citizens and also to change what is relevant'. She is seeking a paradigm shift when she argues for *situated knowledges*

(Haraway, 1988) and thinking in different ways about oneself in relation to home and global, humans and non-humans. This will require an informed, engaged citizenry in the public sphere, speaking from a located place, to 'offer a partial perspective on why it matters that the climate is changing, and discuss how they sit in relation to this phenomenon' (Slocum, 2004, p. 432). Such a paradigm shift will need to be reflected in tourism research and practice – sustainable tourism must incorporate a tourism pedagogy that facilitates knowledge and awareness-raising among the stakeholders of tourism and climate change, the tourist included.

Future policy and practices for (marine) tourism in a green economy

In his article 'Can sustainable tourism survive climate change?' Weaver (2011, p. 5) points to an 'apathetic and fickle travelling public and a reciprocally uncommitted tourism industry'. As with other studies reported earlier in the chapter, the visitor survey findings reported here offer some hope, as they indicate that the climate change-related knowledge, concern and interest required to undertake meaningful action to manage climate change impacts are present. Such a shift may not occur without the help of legislative and policy changes that can shift part or all of the environmental cost of travel onto the consumer, a tax on carbon production for example, and implementing changes in what society views as ethical and unethical behaviour.

Our explorations above indicate that facilitating continuity in ethical action and behaviour between home and the holiday space is essential to facilitate informed civic action, and to avoid cognitive and psychological dissonance (see Donnelly, 2008). Targeted education and communication strategies about climate change, along with concrete actions towards behaviour change (e.g., through social marketing), may be needed to encourage personal action and social change in the home world (see Jamal and Watt, 2011), and to generate public support for legislative and policy initiatives to address climate change impacts in protected areas of global significance. In the micro-level visitation space, destination managers may benefit from better understanding and facilitating local-global citizenship among visitors to world heritage destinations such as the Great Barrier Reef through climate change-related education and encouraging actions such as managing personal carbon contributions at the destination. Opportunities for tourists to engage in political pressure on policy-makers to address climate change mitigation and impacts on protected areas that are a global heritage, such as the Great Barrier Reef, would constitute new and emerging roles for tourists that bear further research and investigation.

Bridging this complex micro-macro policy domain and the awareness-action gap will be no simple matter and will require a coalition of stakeholders including academics, practitioners, government and the resident-tourist (see Tiller and Shott, 2013). In the past, closing the awareness-action gap on issues such as smoking and wearing seat belts took many years, if not decades. As Pidgeon (2011) reminds us, we may not have the luxury of decades to change attitudes to climate change. Given that an increasing number of countries are beginning to introduce policies to combat climate change, destinations that implement proactive strategies to deal with this issue in a meaningful way can expect to gain a competitive advantage over destinations that fail to act.

The interrelated micro and macro perspective above places joint responsibility for social action and societal change on the supply side (the destination), and the demand side (visitor origin), as well as on the travelling public. From a research perspective, then, micro-macro approaches are needed to investigate structural constraints (e.g. sustainable transportation) and social issues (e.g., media representations, cultural–ethical dispositions of travellers, etc.). For example, what role does social media, as well as other media play (consider, for instance, supporting documentaries such as David Attenborough's BBC series that included learning-oriented segments on the Great Barrier Reef) with regard to public awareness, knowledge and social action related to World Heritage places such as the Great Barrier Reef? It could be argued that destination places such as the Great Barrier Reef offer opportunities to be *pedagogic* playgrounds for engaging (and enjoyable) experiential learning and promoting the virtues of global environmental citizenship. Sustainable tourism and ecotourism scholarship currently lack a theory of ethical action to guide the exploration of such questions. Further research is needed on the cultural and ethical dispositions of visitors in relation to climate change, such as towards (civic) participation in policy action for areas of global significance such as the Great Barrier Reef World Heritage Area.

The visitor study reported upon in this research had a number of limitations imposed by time, and practical constraints on survey design and methodology, its coverage being limited to English speakers and the complexity of the questions. The issues and themes canvassed here offer a preliminary discussion. Greater understanding of these critical agendas is needed in order to facilitate tourism in a green economy where extreme weather and other climate change impacts will be persistent, pressing issues in the twenty-first century.

Acknowledgements

Thanks to Brian Smith for assistance with survey data analysis. We would like to also acknowledge the support of The Cairns Institute, James Cook University, Smithfield, Queensland, Australia. Funding of the research was made possible with financial support of the National Environmental Research Program (NERP), a programme of the Commonwealth of Australia.

References

Bartle, I. (2009) A strategy for better climate change regulation: towards a public interest orientated regulatory regime. *Environmental Politics*, vol. 18, no. 5, pp. 689–706.

Becken, S. (2004) How tourists and tourism experts perceive climate change and carbon offset schemes. *Journal of Sustainable Tourism*, vol. 10, no. 2, pp. 114–30.

Becken, S. (2007). Tourists' perception of international air travel's impact on the global climate and potential climate change policies, *Journal of Sustainable Tourism*, vol. 15, no. 4, pp. 351–68.

Berkelmans, R., De'ath, G., Kininmonth, S. and Skirving, W.J. (2004) A comparison of the 1998 and 2002 coral bleaching events of the Great Barrier Reef: spatial correlation, patterns and predictions. *Coral Reefs*, vol. 23, pp. 74–83.

Bryant, N. (2013) Great Barrier Reef fights to retain UNESCO status. Online BBC news report, 1 February 2013. Retrieved from: www.bbc.co.uk/news/science-environment-21293736 (accessed 9 April 2015).

Buckley, R. (2012) Sustainable tourism: research and reality. *Annals of Tourism Research*, vol. 39, no. 2, pp. 528–46.

De Grosbois, D. and Fennell, D. (2011) Carbon footprint of the global hotel companies: comparison of methodologies and results. *Tourism Recreation Research*, vol. 36, no. 3, pp. 231–45.

De'ath, D., Fabricius, A.E., Sweatman, H. and Puotinen, M. (2012) The 27-year decline of coral cover on the Great Barrier Reef and its causes. Retrieved from *PNAS Early Edition:* www.pnas.org/content/early/2012/09/25/1208909109.full.pdf (accessed 9 April 2015).

Donnelly, D. (2008) Propensity for UK and German travelers to adapt travel intentions due to rising awareness of climate change issues. Retrieved from: www.ret.gov.au/tourism/Docu ments/Tourism and Climate Change/consumer_market_research_report-uk_and_germany.pdf (accessed 9 April 2015).

GBRMPA (2009a) Science information needs for the management of the Great Barrier Reef Marine Park 2009–2014. Retrieved from: www.gbrmpa.gov.au/__data/assets/pdf_file/0019/3376/ GBRMPA_Scientific_Information_Needs.pdf (accessed 9 April 2015).

GBRMPA (2009b) Great Barrier Reef outlook report 2009. Retrieved from: www.gbrmpa. gov.au/corp_site/about_us/great_barrier_reef_outlook_report (accessed 9 April 2015).

Gössling, S., Haglund, L., Kallgren, H., Revahl, M. and Hultman, J. (2009) Swedish air travellers and voluntary carbon offsets: towards the co-creation of environmental value? *Current Issues in Tourism*, vol. 12, no. 1, pp. 1–19.

Hall, M. (2008) Tourism and climate change: knowledge gaps and issues. *Tourism Recreation Research*, vol. 33, no. 3, pp. 339–50.

Haraway, D. (1988) Situated knowledges: The science question in feminism and the privilege of partial perspective. *Feminist Studies*, vol. 13, no. 3, pp. 575–99.

Hares, A., Dickinson, J. and Wilkes, K. (2010) Climate change and the air travel decisions of UK tourists. *Journal of Transport Geography*, vol. 18, pp. 466–73.

Higham, J. and Cohen, S. (2011) Canary in the coalmine: Norwegian attitudes towards climate change and extreme long-haul air travel to *Aotearoa*/New Zealand. *Tourism Management*, vol. 32, pp. 98–105.

Huebner, A. (2012) Public perceptions of destination vulnerability to climate change and implications for long-haul travel decisions to small island states. *Journal of Sustainable Tourism*, vol. 20, no. 7, pp. 939–51.

IPCC (2007) Summary for policy makers. In Solomon, S., Qin, M., Manning, Z. Chen, M., Marquia, K., Averyt, M., Tignor, M. and Miller, H. (eds) *Climate change 2007: The physical science basis. Contribution of working group 1 to the Fourth Assessment Report of the Intergovernmental Panel on Climate Change* (pp. 1–18). Cambridge University Press: Cambridge, UK and New York.

Jamal, T. and Watt, M. (2011) Climate change pedagogy and performative action: toward community-based destination governance. *Journal of Sustainable Tourism*, vol. 19, no. 4–5, pp. 571–88.

Kroesen, M. (2013) Exploring people's viewpoints on air travel and climate change: understanding inconsistencies. *Journal of Sustainable Tourism*, vol. 21, no. 2, pp. 271–90.

Larwood, C. (2012) Climate change threatens Great Barrier Reef. Online BBC news report, 22 October 2012. Retrieved from: http://news.bbc.co.uk/2/hi/programmes/fast_track/976 2256.stm (accessed 9 April 2015).

Mair, J. (2011) Exploring air travellers' voluntary carbon-offsetting behaviour. *Journal of Sustainable Tourism*, vol. 19, no. 2, pp. 215–30.

Musau, P.and Prideaux, B. (2003) Sustainable tourism – a role for Kenya's hotel industry. *Current Issues in Tourism*, vol. 6, no. 3, pp. 197–208.

Pidgeon, N. (2011) Public understanding of and attitudes towards climate change (Report 5: *International dimensions of climate change*). UK Government Foresight Office: London.

Prideaux, B. and Falco-Mammone, F. (2010) *The impacts of Cyclone Larry on tourism in the Mission Beach, Tully and the Atherton Tablelands Region one year later*. Centre for Tropical Tourism Research, James Cook University: Cairns.

Ramis, M. and Prideaux, B. (2013). The importance of visitor perceptions in estimating how climate change will affect future tourists flows on the Great Barrier Reef. In Reddy, M. and Wilkes, K. (eds) *Tourism, climate change and sustainability* (pp. 173–88). Routledge: London.

Schott, C. (ed.) (2010) *Tourism and the implication of climate change: Issues and actions*. Emerald: Bingley, UK.

Scott, D. (2011) Why sustainable tourism must address climate change. *Journal of Sustainable Tourism*, vol. 19, no. 1, pp. 17–34.

Scott, D., de Freitas, C.R. and Matzarakis, A. (2009) Adaptation in the tourism and recreation sector. In Ebi, K.L., Burton, I. and Hoeppe, P. (eds) *Biometeorology for adaptation to climate variability and change* (pp. 171–94). Springer: Dordrecht, Netherlands.

Slocum, R. (2004) Polar bears and energy-efficient light bulbs: strategies to bring climate change home. *Environment and Planning D: Society and Space*, vol. 22, no. 3, pp. 413–38.

Tao, C.H., Eagles, P. and Smith, S. (2004) Profiling Taiwanese ecotourists using a self definition approach. *Journal of Sustainable Tourism*, vol. 12, pp. 149–68.

Tiller, T.R. and Schott, C. (2013) The critical relationship between climate change awareness and action: an origin-based perspective. *Asia Pacific Journal of Tourism Research*, vol. 18, no. 1–2, pp. 21–34.

Turton, S., Hadwen, S.W. and Wilson, R. (eds) (2009) The impacts of climate change on Australian tourism destinations: Developing adaptation and response strategies – a scoping study. Retrieved from: www.crctourism.com.au/BookShop/BookDetail.aspx?d=670 (accessed 9 April 2015).

UNWTO (2007) Davos declaration climate change and tourism. Responding to global challenges. Davos, Switzerland, 3 October 2007. Retrieved from: www.unwto.org/climate/index.php; 12.11.2007.

UNWTO, UNEP and WMO (2008) *Climate change and tourism: Responding to global challenges*. UNWTO: Madrid.

Weaver, D. (2011) Can sustainable tourism survive climate change? *Journal of Sustainable Tourism*, vol. 19, no. 1, pp. 5–15.

Zeppel, H. (2012) Climate change and tourism in the Great Barrier Reef Marine Park. *Current Issues in Tourism*, vol. 15, no. 3, pp. 287–92.

19

INVESTIGATING THE TRANSITION OF THE TOURISM INDUSTRY TOWARDS A GREEN ECONOMY IN SAMUI ISLAND, THAILAND

Gunjan Saxena, Nisarat Thaithong and Dimitrios Tsagdis

Introduction

In this chapter, Samui Island in Thailand is focused upon to illustrate the attempts of tourism stakeholders to adopt 'green' practices to address the serious environmental impacts resulting from mass tourism. Island destinations are particularly vulnerable due to their fragile ecology, peripherality (resulting in their geographic isolation, both from physical mainland and population centres), small size (both in terms of population and surface), and limited socio-economic opportunities (Wilkinson, 1989). Moreover, island tourism can create significant negative environmental and socio-cultural impacts if it is not managed and organized well. For instance, Scheyvens (2011) points out how, in the Maldives, tourism benefits only a minority, as 42 per cent of the population earn less than 2 dollars a day due to rampant corruption and a repressive policy environment. Similarly, in Caribbean islands, where the economy is dominated by the tourism industry, inequality has set in due to large-scale ecological degradation, resulting in the marginalization of the weakest segments of the population (Burke and Maidens, 2004). These problems are compounded by a lack of understanding of the variability of island environments, particularly at the level of global planning for climate change, and sustainable management of coastal environments (Nunn *et al.*, 1999).

Given the extreme fragility of the coastal environment, it is imperative for island destinations to embrace 'green' practices, and develop sustainable relationships with the coast and its resources. The significance and the need for a transition towards the 'Green Economy' is evident in the Green Economy Initiative[1] of the United Nations Environmental Programme (UNEP), which emphasizes low-carbon, resource-efficient, and socially inclusive development. There is growing research in favour of promoting the cultural and environmental amenities that complement the coastal holiday (Lise and Tol, 2002; Lanza *et al.*, 2005; Brau *et al.*, 2007). Onofri and Nunes (2013) draw attention to the significant role of the 'greens' who represent the segment of international travellers preferring the natural and environmental dimension of coastal tourism, e.g. in financing the conservation programmes and influencing the marketing practices of individual tour operators. Since the World Economic Forum in 2009, the concept of low-carbon tourism is being regarded as a new way to conceive sustainable development, which can obtain a higher quality of tourism experience with low-carbon emissions and less pollution in the process of transportation, accommodation, sightseeing, shopping, and entertainment (Cai and Wang, 2010).

However, the transition towards a green economy is fraught with difficulties. Previous research on sustainable tourism well illustrates the implementation intricacies that developing economies encounter due to a lack of skills, funds, and political will (Cater, 1993; Tosun, 2001; Yasarata et al., 2010). Moreover, several studies have pointed out that issues such as rampant corruption and political instability, resulting in diminished community participation in decision-making and the planning process, have contributed to an uncontrolled development of mass tourism, and an unequal distribution of tourism benefits (Ioannides, 1995; Yasarata et al., 2010). As a means to overcome these difficulties, studies argue in favour of collaborative approaches that can bring together multiple stakeholders in policy formulation and implementation, and sustain tourism as a vehicle for socio-cultural and viable economic development (Bramwell and Lane, 2000; Saxena, 2005; Tosun and Jenkins, 1998; Kimbu and Ngoasong, 2013). Yet collaboration is not easy to achieve in practice. For instance, Fyall and Garrod (2004) point out that jurisdictional boundaries can often inhibit the adoption and functioning of effective collaborative tourism initiatives. Additionally, the actors' self-interest, blinkered vision, and inability to move beyond their narrow interests inhibit the ability of partnerships to achieve their strategic orientation (Dredge, 2006).

Indeed, there is much merit in pooling resources together, especially for actors in peripheral island destinations, as their combined energies can engender the innovative approaches needed to compete successfully in the global tourism economy (Lichrou and O'Malley, 2006). Thus, conceptually, stakeholder theory, social networks, and cluster approaches are drawn upon to outline actor profiles, their interrelationships, and the manner in which their interface has caused the emergence of unique tourism clusters in Samui. The development of such a conceptual framework is followed by an overview of Samui Island, illustrating the structure and profile of tourism clusters therein. The chapter concludes with an outline of the green economy potential in Samui to sustain the long-term future not only of the tourism industry but also, crucially, of marine ecosystems and resources.

Conceptual framework

As introduced in the previous section, three approaches (stakeholder theory, social networks, and clusters) are employed as the analytical framework to examine tourism stakeholders' profile, their interconnections (structures) that influence their behaviour and practices, and bring about the spatial formation of tourism clusters.

Stakeholder theory is particularly useful in the identification of key actors and their involvement (or stake) in tourism provision, planning and development (Jamal and Getz,

2000; Sautter and Leisen, 1999). Freeman (1984) defines stakeholder to mean 'any group or individual who can affect or is affected by the achievement of the organization's objectives' (p. 46). Thus, tourism stakeholders are both individuals and groups (e.g. government bodies, tourism organizations, business owners, residents, experts, the voluntary sector, media and pressure groups) who have a stake in the industry. Previous tourism studies have demonstrated that stakeholders cast a powerful influence on the running of tourism organizations and destinations, and can both facilitate and prevent them from achieving their goals (Bramwell and Sharman, 1999; Dredge, 2006). Hence, all stakeholders' interests have intrinsic value and need to be accounted for while developing tourism policies as they '. . . have the [legitimate] right to be treated as an end and not as a means to an end' (Byrd, 2007, p. 7).

To analyse the content and nature of stakeholder relationships formulated on (mis)trust, formal/informal networks, reciprocity, strong/weak ties shaping their attitudes and practices as they perform different tasks and activities, the social networks approach is employed (Pavlovich, 2003; Saxena, 2005). In particular, the business routines/behaviours among actors, which can enhance an understanding of how firms develop their learning capacities are focused upon (Boggs and Rantisi, 2003). This combination of the two approaches (stakeholders and networks) is useful in grasping the configuration of cross-sectoral relationships between diverse individuals and organizations, and how resources and information flow through them (Bodin and Prell, 2011; Taplin, 2011). Yet, in capturing the geographical dimension and the spatial agglomeration of tourism providers, research on clusters provides an added insight into 'geographic concentrations of interconnected companies, specialised suppliers, service providers, firms in related industries, and associated institutions in particular fields that compete but also co-operate' (Porter, 1998, p. 77). Thus, the main premise of this study is that the *worldview* (expectations, beliefs, norms) of tourism stakeholders (individuals and groups from public, private and voluntary sectors) – including community members, government bodies, tourism businesses, experts, volunteers, media, and pressure groups – and their *relational networks* determine the conception, formation, growth and maturity phases of (un)sustainable tourism clusters (see Figure 19.1).

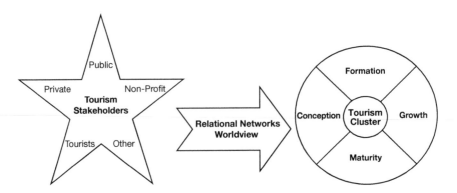

FIGURE 19.1 Conceptual framework
Source: Authors

Therefore, all three approaches appear necessary for identifying the interdependencies and complementarities existing within the tourism industry, as they allow conceptual means to analyse the profile of tourism stakeholders, their interface and the spatial spread of their activities and resources. The main contention is that stakeholder support or resistance to nature conservation, notwithstanding their differing interests and dynamic interface, can bring about the formation of (un)sustainable tourism clusters and 'establish a particular regime of resource and land use in a given territory' (Brenner and Job, 2012, p. 3). The aforementioned conceptual framework (Figure 19.1) is applied to chart the conflicting worldviews among tourism stakeholders in Samui. On the one hand, the stakeholders favour the capitalization of natural resources for the purposes of livelihood and profit, whereas on the other hand they are conservation-centred. This tension underpins much of the evolution and the gradual transition of Samui towards a green economy, and thus also manifests in the occurrence of 'green' goods and sustainable tourism practices. The findings are based on discourse analysis of policy documents, newspaper articles, tourists' travel blogs, and secondary research, highlighting specific collaborative programmes that state and non-state actors are engaged in at different spatial levels to bring about effective environmental governance. The chapter concludes by arguing in favour of a break from traditional forms of policy-making (i.e. that are cognizant of only a few specific forms of resource use and restricted to defined user groups) towards policy-making which is in tune with more socially complex and highly competitive multiple-use environments that Samui has become.

Samui Island

Samui is situated in the south-east of Thailand (see Figure 19.2), and occupies an area of 227 square kilometres making it the third largest after Phuket and Chang islands (Koh Samui Municipality, 2012). Administratively, Samui is divided into seven sub-districts (Ang Thong, Bo Phud, Lipa Noi, Meanum, Taling Ngam, Mared, and Na Muang), all of, which are rich in biodiversity, and culturally unique (Koh Samui Municipality, 2012). Unsurprisingly, this places tourism at the heart of the local economy, elevating it into a major income earner in the region, even though for the majority of the locals jobs remain low-paid (City Council of Koh Samui, cited in Soontayatron, 2010). In the 1980s, tourism in Samui was on a small scale, and either catered to the 'drifter tourist' market (i.e. the rave party avant-garde) or thrived on local art and craft enterprises that served a clientele with modest demands (Cohen, 1982; Malam, 2008). Today, featuring in New York Times' 'must-see list, 2012', Samui attracts over one million tourists who generate over 14,000 million baht[2] each year (Pakakrong, 2011).

The sub-districts of Samui are characterized by highly differentiated tourism clusters. For instance, the sub-districts of Meanum, Mared and Bo Phud are popular beach-based attractions with well-developed infrastructure and a preponderance of developers radically changing the local landscape, confirming that tourism spaces are constructed and crafted carefully by local elites (Urry, 1990; Kearns and Philo, 1993). While both the sub-districts of Ang Thong and Lipa Noi have ferry piers that transport tourists from the mainland to Samui, and have thriving clusters of (non)tourist businesses along with government offices and residential areas, Lipa Noi is the least urbanized of all the

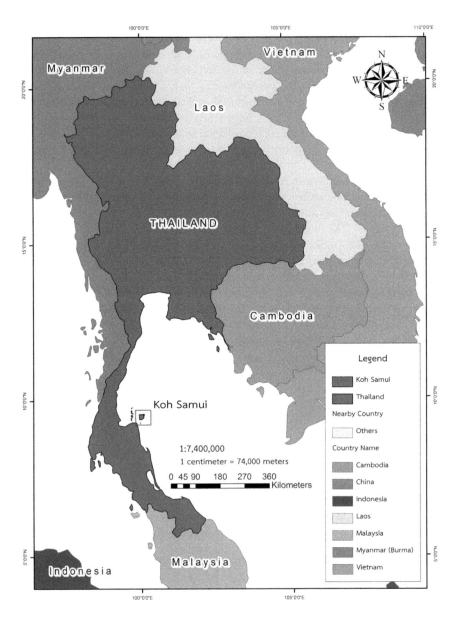

FIGURE 19.2 Map of Southeast Asia, showing location of Samui

Source: Department of Geography, Faculty of Arts, Silpakorn University

sub-districts due to its remoteness and mountainous terrain. Along with beach resorts that attract mass tourists, Samui is equally attractive to ecotourists who flock to the sub-districts of Na Muang and Taling Ngam that offer activities such as elephant trekking, mountain safaris, and wildlife tourism, providing valuable supplementary income to the island's hill tribes (Thaithong, 2013).

Irrespective of distinctive tourism clusters, Samui's sub-districts embody fragile ecosystems that warrant alternative pathways to push policy-makers and other stake-holders to consider more sustainable choices, and co-create benefits for natural resource management and livelihood improvement. However, the underlying vulnerability and trajectories of social inequality in the tourism-dependent coastal communities of Samui look set to become aggravated. For instance, the island's acclaimed emblem of greenness that drives the tourism industry is under threat from growing tourist demand for local foods, which is damaging rich tropical forests that are being cleared for farming (Thaithong, 2013). Further, a growth in the local population places immense pressure on the island's delicate ecology. According to the 2011 population census, there are 54,979 registered residents plus 300,000 non-registered[3] residents (Koh Samui Municipality, 2012).

As a result of overdevelopment, systemic corruption, and a questionable rule of law that has rather supported an unplanned growth of the tourism industry (see Howard, 2009), Samui's future appears precarious. Indeed, sub-districts are experiencing negative impacts from the industry such as waste accumulation, which is causing damage to coral reefs, degradation of vegetation, due to the rise in construction work, and encroachment of hotels and resorts into forested areas and mountains causing an increase in landslides and serious flooding (Pakakrong, 2011). A potent example of the tourism industry's brazen intrusion into the forest area has been the construction of the Conrad resort in Taling Ngam, owned by the Hilton chain of luxury hotels, which is sprawled across almost the whole mountain on the south-west tip of the island (see Figure 19.3).

Predictably, this resort has caused the degradation of the forest area. Unfortunately, it is not an isolated incident, as massive developments continue unabated. Fernquest (2013) reports in the Bangkok Post on the rapid progress of a substantial retail shopping complex coming up on 48,000 square metres of land in the beach area of Chaweng in Bo Phud sub-district. Further, the interests of the local population continue to remain sidelined, as is evident in their limited access to beaches, due to a proliferation of hotels and luxury resorts. These have developed in the form of what Smith (1992) refers to as 'ribbon development' (p. 28) – mainly impromptu, on the beachfront land replacing the natural tree cover and wetlands that have either been filled in or converted into open sewers, which pollute the sea and the beach, and damage coral reefs as a result of poorly treated waste-water. Many locals have sold their land at the beach-based resorts of Bo Phud, Meanum, and Mared to foreign investors and moved out, making them, as Thaithong (2013) points out, 'places for *farang* (foreigners)' who own most of the businesses, resulting in an inequitable distribution of benefits. Ironically, these are presented as ecotourism destinations, which authors decry as a mere marketing ploy to 'greenwash' customers with little appreciation of what conservation actually entails (Shepherd, 2002; Vivanco, 2002). Additionally, social impacts as a result of tourism and associated development, are manifest in the form of an increase in prostitution,

FIGURE 19.3 The Conrad Resort in Taling Ngam
Source: Authors

a plethora of bars, and drug-related crimes in Samui (Green, 2005). Overall, a lack of clear guidelines and repeated relaxation of 'no development zones' have resulted in an extensive increase in the number of accommodation businesses, which means that the notion of sustainable tourism has been adopted more in theory than in practice (Pongponrat, 2011). Against this backdrop, in the following section the transition towards a green economy in Samui is discussed; as shaped by macro-micro contexts that embody the potential of stemming the tide of unsustainable practices.

Samui's transition towards a green economy

A green economy can be defined as 'one that results in improved human well-being and social equity, while significantly reducing environmental risk and ecological scarcities' (UNEP, 2011a, p. 2). Thus, tourism in a green economy can be understood as comprising 'activities that can be maintained or sustained indefinitely in their social, economic, cultural, and environmental contexts' (UNEP, 2011b, p. 416).

In Thailand, there is political will to support the green economy, as evidenced by the Government's endorsement of the 1992 Rio Declaration on Environment and Development, and its subsequent adoption of regulatory policies aimed at reducing carbon emissions, waste accumulation and improving resource efficiency (Green, 2005). In fact, as a key tourism stakeholder, the Government has set the scene for a green, community-orientated tourism economy, evident in the Eleventh National Development Plan of Thailand (2012–16), emphasizing shared leadership, community well-being over individual profit, care towards and conservation of traditional culture, and responsible stewardship of the land (Wirudchawong, 2011). In a 1990s study, the maximum carrying capacity of Samui was set at 14,200 tourists per day, if the island was to maintain its identity (TISTR, 1995). Since then, this has been revised upwards several times in the island's action plan for development. Until now, in the light of increasing tourists and ensuing problems, the Ministry of Natural Resources and Environment (MNRE) has seriously considered implementing it with rigour. In fact, Wipatayotin (2013) reported in the Bangkok Post that several law enforcement agencies, such as the Department of Special Investigation, the National Police Office, the Internal Security Operations Command, public prosecutors, and the Sueb Nakhasathien Foundation (an eco-charity based in Samui) had joined hands with MNRE to oversee the demolition of illegal resorts and properties in national parks and forest reserves in the island from August 2013.

Further, at the national level, the Tourism Authority of Thailand (TAT), established in 1959, is advancing promotional campaigns and projects aimed at raising awareness about climate change and environmental preservation among public and private sector providers and travellers. In 2008, the Ministry of Tourism and Sports (MOTS) and TAT jointly planned and launched the 'Green Island Project' (2008–17) involving public and private sector organizations in Samui, the media, and the general public to define and agree guidelines on promoting sustainable tourism that uphold local culture and tradition, and most importantly, the Thai residents' aspirations from the industry (GIFT, 2012). TAT's recent initiative 'Seven Greens Concept'[4] aims to promote an understanding of sustainable tourism among tourists, businesses, Thai families, and especially the youth, in a bid to influence stakeholders' civic identity; urging them to care for the environment as consumers and providers (Thaithong, 2013).

At the regional level, business associations in Samui have taken a lead towards making Samui a green island, by pooling their energies in support of the 'Low Carbon Model Town project' (LCMT), launched in 2010 as part of the Asia-Pacific Economic Cooperation (APEC) 'Green Growth' venture to: reduce carbon dioxide emissions, reduce and reuse solid waste, and treat water for non-sanitary purposes (APEC, 2012). Yet, as Ockey (1998) states, political culture has developed at different rates in different places in Thailand, with Westernized notions of law and democracy much more established in Bangkok and urban areas than in peripheral localities such as Samui. Thus, in Samui, community groups, with support from non-State bodies such as international eco-charities (Green Leaf Foundation, Mangroves for the Future), and in partnership with the TAT, Samui municipality, Tourism Association of Samui (grouping of local businesses), Department of Marine and Coastal Resources, and MOTS, are actively developing their own version of conservation governance.

Re-earth, Samui's International Eco-festival, is one such innovative and collaborative event aimed at promoting awareness about sustainable coastal tourism through music, and is jointly organized by the: TAT, Swedish Environment Secretariat for Asia (SENSA), Music Television Asia, local musicians, and volunteers working on environmental projects in Samui (www.mangrovesforthefuture.org). The emphasis is on foregrounding the traditional wisdom of coastal communities in creating sustainable and attractive arts and crafts clusters in the middle of fishing villages, in contrast to the 'ecotourism sites' that have been systematically planned in locales that are pristine unspoilt natural landscapes, and discourage contact with locals (Thaithong, 2013). Music as a binding force has also been used by Walailak University students who organized 'The

Rhythm of Samui Sea' event (in June 2013) as part of their ongoing monitoring of corals they planted in 2012 in the Gulf of Thailand near Samui (Fernquest, 2013). Albeit with limited ability to influence – much less curtail – unsustainable development, these initiatives are proving to be assertive and complementary to traditional measures of law enforcement.

Undeniably, the advent of the 'politics of change' has gained ground due to support from the locals, and their growing impatience with the volume of tourists who, as Malam (2008) points out, are jokingly referred to as *sat anurat* (protected species). This term, she argues, is derogatory because *sat* is a classifier used for animals, not people. The current emphasis is on reconceptualizing the island as a showcase for local food, art and culture, evident in the core theme of the 2013 TAT Action Plan – 'Higher Revenue through Thainess . . . Thai Experience, Thai Way of Life, and Thai Culture' (TAT, 2012). Hence, through careful scripting and management of marketing messages, the idea is to target higher spending niche tourists interested in 'experiential travel', and provide them with good value for money, service excellence, fun, aesthetic appeal, and opportunities to learn something new or acquire a novel experience (Mathwick *et al.*, 2001). Kontogeorgopoulos and Chulikavit (2010) point out that as a result of increased political debate on the need to combat the ill-effects of the tourism industry in a timely fashion, the response from travel agents and tour operators in Thailand has been one of greater engagement with *gaan tong tieow cheung anoorak* (conservation tourism) and *gaan tong tieow cheung niwet* (ecological tourism), at least in theory.

Overall, Samui has real potential to transform itself into a green economy, if it involves diverse stakeholders in curtailing unplanned and rapid development of the coast, by increasing their awareness of the environmental impact of their activities. Indeed, in partnership with the sustainability consultancy Ricardo–AEA, Koh Samui Municipality is working on an environmental initiative focused upon improving air, transport, and water quality, while managing waste and chemical risk. Integrating tourism more explicitly into such initiatives can enhance the industry's input to conservation strategies, and enable it to better effect the change in the 'state' of the tourism system or destination, by fashioning completely new structures and networks (if necessary) required for the successful functioning of a green economy. However, Thaithong's (2014) research reveals that Samui's disparate stakeholders embodying diverse needs, nationalities, and ethnicities, and tourism aspirations are struggling to chart routes where their subgroups and social networks are able to gel together. Currently, information generated by tourism stakeholders, and disseminated through their networks is mostly commercial in nature, and rarely portrays aspects related to coastal safety, risk assessment, and care for the environment. Green economy strategists face some serious challenges in the region including, among others, insufficiency of funds, mutual mistrust, weak law-enforcement mechanisms, and negative attitudes (of the residents) towards the local government as a result of what they perceive to be the latter's inability to tackle problems of garbage accumulation and pollution (Thaithong, 2014). Thus, one of the key objectives of any Green Samui programme needs to be the delivery of a framework that can pull together different groups and sectors, enhancing their ability to transfer knowledge/skills and share resources for better shoreline management. This is imperative since the local government in Samui, like any other coastal region in a developing economy, is more concerned with issues of economic development, health, welfare, and education rather than environmental monitoring and/or conservation. Finally, the resources and scientific expertise are not readily available to undertake the vast amount of research required as Hall (2001) points out.

Conclusions

To conclude, the conceptual framework employed in this exploration provides an insightful analytical lens for understanding the island tourism configuration and its impacts at the micro-level. Combining stakeholder theory with social networks and cluster approaches enabled the consideration of the role of inter-relationships between tourism stakeholders, such as host communities, governmental bodies, the tourism industry, experts, the voluntary sector, media, and pressure groups, who can affect or are affected by tourism. Also, the notion of stakeholding was widened in this investigation to include the natural environment of Samui as a key player in sustaining its tourism industry and economy. Traditionally, in Samui, environmental protection has been seen as a cost to the economy; necessary, but to be minimized as much as possible. However, with the coastal environment teetering quite close to collapse, its strategic importance to the local economy and the tourism industry in Samui, has contributed to the reconfiguration of cross-sectoral networks, socio-political processes, and the formation of sustainable tourism clusters. For instance, resort owners have jointly agreed to include organic food in their menus, make the best use of sea breezes (as opposed to air conditioning) and co-produce tribal tourism videos and brochures to enable visitors to engage meaningfully with the natives (Sriburi, 2007). These small steps mark a gradual transition of Samui's tourism industry towards being in sync with local needs and circumstances. Independent think tanks, such as the Thailand Environment Institute, are providing guidelines for 'sound environmental management', which are translating into community-based projects in rural areas that foreground local wisdom and ways of valuing, using, owning, and approaching nature (Cohen, 2008).

An interesting and pertinent example of effective tourism marketing, that is in line with current trends, is the recent TAT campaign entitled 'The Little Big Project' designed to tap into a growing industry trend known as Volunteer Tourism, or *Voluntourism*, that gives travellers the opportunity to do little things such as preserving the environment, sharing their skills, or contributing to local communities and have a purposeful vacation (TAT, 2013). Moves towards achieving long-term and sustainable land use planning are also evident in the recent launch of low-carbon hotels following the low-carbon economy notion, exemplified by higher standards of living, with lower consumption of natural resources, minimal pollution, and more economic output (Can and Hongbing, 2011). Thus, the local resolve is to reform structures, activities (including tourist behaviour) and mutual exchange activities with each other (e.g. networks, clusters) to preserve the vital basis for the industry, that is, the environment.

Yet the task of reconciling nature conservation with economic development is not smooth. In fact, Kontogeorgopoulos (1999) points out that sustainable development in Thailand has been compromised for the sake of sustainable tourism, as the Thai government considers it as a mechanism for spurring environmental improvements to established sites, ultimately in order to both boost overall tourism growth, and shore up dwindling supplies of foreign exchange. Moreover, in Thailand, as in other developing economies, the influence of family ties and social networks at the local government level (including village headmen) often results in the misappropriation of funds for the benefit of family and friends of the local elites, who are able to secure approvals for infrastructure developments that contravene planning regulations (Larsen *et al.*, 2011). Although the notion that communities can manage natural resources and develop ecotourism fits well with neoliberal approaches to regulating, organizing, and implementing conservation; for the decentralized networks of 'stakeholders' to actually govern resources requires a radical reworking of actor worldviews, and subsequently a (re)shaping of their interface at all levels.

At the micro-level, in Thailand, the most significant agency is exerted by elite groups (e.g. local politicians and large investors well-connected to local, provincial and national levels of decision-making) who mobilize their resources and social networks to influence and shape government actions (Larsen *et al.*, 2011). Although the actions of the elite alliances mainly benefit their own interests, Sriburi (2007) argues that they also produce benefits for others, as well as for marginalized groups. Moreover, the family-orientated business model of most small and medium enterprises in Thailand has the potential to serve as the basis for the development and growth of sustainable business opportunities, and environmental conservation programmes (involving tourists) with continuous support and incentives from the government and community members (McCargo and Pathmanand, 2005). For instance, Ethic Tour, is a tour operator based in Bangkok that shares its profits with local schools and actively recruits/trains local youth as tour guides (Sriburi, 2007). REST (Responsible Ecological Social Tours project), established in 1994, is actively working with island communities in Thailand to help them develop community-based tourism, ensuring that they can maintain their cultures and ways of life, and direct their own futures by lessening the negative impacts tourism may have on their culture (www.responsibletravel.com). These are not just isolated incidents, as there is widespread stakeholder support from almost all sectors to reconfigure and redesign nature for sustainable consumption. However, the future viability of the green economy is not just a Samui issue. Thailand, as a whole, depends on the extent to which tourism stakeholders' social networks and clusters can chart out means for stringent conservation of undisturbed core zones, mitigation of conflicts concerning resource use within buffer and development zones, constant ecosystem evaluation and monitoring, as well as equitable sharing of benefits and burdens. To end on a positive note, it should perhaps be iterated that by acknowledging and incorporating, much more explicitly, the influence of stakeholders' agency, their social networks, and worldviews on (un)sustainable cluster formation, green economy strategists can innovatively frame and implement their responses to multiple challenges that fragile ecosystems such as Samui face.

Notes

1 UNEP in cooperation with the International Monetary Fund (IMF) is focusing on driving a green economy through fiscal policy reforms (*www.unep.org*).
2 In 2011 the exchange rate was approximately 49 baht to one pound.
3 Non-registered residents are those who are not local to the area (many are from other provinces) and are either students or migrant workers.

4   The main principles underlying the 'Seven Greens Concept' are: (1) Green heart – be conscious about nature and the environment when you visit any place; (2) Green activity – be responsible for the environment when you travel; (3) Green logistics – travel by green energy transportation; (4) Green community – enhance an awareness of communities' traditions and cultures to be part of tourism development; (5) Green service – service providers and enterprise owners should manage and operate in environment-friendly manner; (6) Green attraction – manage and develop attractions with awareness of environmental conservation; and (7) Green plus – take action for environmental preservation and development (Teiy, 2010).

References

APEC (2012) Samui Island low-carbon model-town project. APEC Energy Working Group – Energy Smart Communities Initiative. http://esci-ksp.org/?project=samui-island-low-carbon-model-town-project. Retrieved 6 January 2015.

Bodin, R. and Prell, C. (2011) *Social networks and natural resource management*. Cambridge University Press: Cambridge.

Boggs, J.S. and Rantisi, N.M. (2003) The relational turn in economic geography, *Journal of Economic Geography*, vol. 3, pp. 109–16.

Bramwell, B. and Sharman, A. (1999) Collaboration in local tourism policy-making, *Annals of Tourism Research*, vol. 26, no. 3, pp. 392–415.

Bramwell, B. and Lane, B. (2000) Collaboration and partnerships in tourism planning. In Bramwell, B. and Lane, B. (eds) *Tourism collaboration and partnerships: Politics, practice and sustainability* (pp. 1–19). Channel View: Clevedon, UK.

Brau, R., Lanza, A. and Pigliaru, F. (2007) How fast are small tourism countries growing? Evidence from the data for 1980–2003. *Tourism Economics*, vol. 13, pp. 603–13.

Brenner, L. and Job, H. (2012) Challenges to actor-oriented environmental governance: examples from three Mexican biosphere reserves, *Tijdschrift voor Economische en Sociale Geografie*, vol. 103, no. 1, pp. 1–19.

Burke, L. and Maidens, J. (2004) *Reefs at risk in the Caribbean*. World Resources Institute: Washington, DC.

Byrd, E.T. (2007) Stakeholders in sustainable tourism development and their roles: applying stakeholder theory to sustainable tourism development, *Tourism Review*, vol. 62, no. 2, pp. 6–13.

Cai, M. and Wang, Y.M. (2010) Low-carbon tourism: a new mode of tourism development, *Tourism Tribune* 1, pp. 3–17.

Can, H. and Hongbing, D. (2011) The model of developing low-carbon tourism in the context of leisure economy, *Energy Procedia*, vol. 5, pp. 1974–8.

Cater, E. (1993) Ecotourism in the third world: problems for sustainable tourism development, *Tourism Management*, vol. 14, no. 2, pp. 85–90.

Cohen, E. (1982) Marginal paradises: Bungalow tourism on the islands of Southern Thailand, *Annals of Tourism Research*, vol. 9, pp. 189–228.

Cohen, E. (2008) *Explorations in Thai tourism: Collected case studies*. Elsevier Science: Amsterdam.

Dredge, D. (2006) Policy networks and the local organization of tourism, *Tourism Management*, vol. 27, pp. 269–80.

Fernquest, J. (2013) Koh Samui tourism boom, *Bangkok Post*, 13 March 2013. www.bangkokpost.com. Retrieved 9 April 2015.

Fyall, A. and Garrod, B. (2004) *Tourism Marketing: A Collaborative Approach*. Channel View Publications: Clevedon.

Freeman, R.E. (1994) The politics of stakeholder theory, *Business Ethics Quarterly*, vol. 4, no. 4, pp. 409–21.

GIFT (2012) The green island project: a collaborative long term programme of projects and events for the sustainable protection of Koh Samui's natural environment, The Green Island Foundation Thailand (GIFT). www.globalislands.net/userfiles/thailand_5.pdf. Retrieved 25 July 2013.

Green, R. (2005) Community perceptions of environmental and social change and tourism development on the island of Koh Samui, Thailand, *Journal of Environmental Psychology*, vol. 25, pp. 37–56.

Hall, M. (2001) Trends in ocean and coastal tourism: the end of the last frontier? *Ocean & Coastal Management*, vol. 44, no. 9, pp. 601–18.

Howard, R. W. (2009) The migration of westerners to Thailand: An unusual flow from developed to developing world, *International Migration*, vol. 47, no. 2, pp. 193–225.

Ioannides, D. (1995) A flawed implementation of sustainable tourism: the experience of Akamas, Cyprus, *Tourism Management*, vol. 16, no. 8, pp. 583–92.

Jamal, T. and Getz, D. (2000) Community roundtables for tourism related conflicts: The dialectics of consensus and process structures. In Bramwell, B. and Lane, B. (eds) *Tourism collaboration and partnerships: Politics, practice and sustainability* (pp. 159–82). Channel View Publications: Clevedon, UK.

Kearns, G. and Philo, C. (eds) (1993) *Selling places: The city as cultural capital, past and present.* Pergamon: Oxford.

Kimbu, A.N. and Ngoasong, M.Z. (2013) Centralised decentralisation of tourism development: A network perspective, *Annals of Tourism Research*, vol. 40, pp. 235–59.

Koh Samui Municipality (2012) Tourism facts and figures. www.kohsamuicity.go.th/index.php?op=staticcontent&id=3744. Retrieved 16 May 2012.

Kontogeorgopoulos, N. (1999) Sustainable tourism or sustainable development? Financial crisis, ecotourism, and the 'Amazing Thailand' campaign, *Current Issues in Tourism*, vol. 2, no. 4, pp. 316–32.

Kontogeorgopoulos, N. and Chulikavit, K. (2010) Supply-side perspectives on ecotourism in Northern Thailand, *International Journal of Tourism Research*, vol. 12, pp. 627–41.

Lanza, A., Markandya, A. and Pigliaru, P. (2005) *The economics of tourism and sustainable developments.* Edward Elgar: Cheltenam, UK.

Larsen, R.K., Calgaro, E. and Thomalla, F. (2011) Governing resilience building in Thailand's tourism-dependent coastal communities: Conceptualising stakeholder agency in social–ecological systems, *Global Environmental Change*, vol. 21, pp. 481–91.

Lichrou, M. and O'Malley, L. (2006) Mining and tourism: Conflicts in the marketing of Milos Island as a tourism destination, *Tourism and Hospitality Planning & Development*, vol. 3, no. 1, pp. 35–46.

Lise, W. and Tol, R.S.J. (2002) Impact of climate on tourism demand. *Climatic Change*, vol. 55, no. 4, pp. 29–49.

McCargo, D. and Pathmanand, U. (2005) *The Thaksinisation of Thailand.* NIAS Press: Copenhagen.

Malam, L. (2008) Geographic imaginations: Exploring divergent notions of identity, power, and place meaning on Pha-ngan Island, Southern Thailand, *Asia Pacific Viewpoint*, vol. 49, no. 3, pp. 331–43.

Mathwick, C., Malhotra, N. and Rigdon, E. (2001) Experiential value: conceptualization, measurement and application in the catalog and internet shopping environment, *Journal of Retailing*, vol. 77, no. 1, pp. 39–56.

Nunn, P.D., Veitayaki, J., Ram-Bidesib, V. and Vuniseaa, A. (1999) Coastal issues for oceanic islands: implications for human futures, *Natural Resources Forum*, vol. 23, pp. 195–207.

Ockey, J. (1998) Crime, society, and politics in Thailand. In Trocki, C.A. (ed.) *Gangsters, democracy and the State in Southeast Asia* (pp. 39–53). Southeast Asia Program, Cornell University: Ithaca, NY.

Onofri, L. and Nunes, P. (2013) Beach 'lovers' and 'greens': A worldwide empirical analysis of coastal tourism, *Ecological Economics*, vol. 88, pp. 49–56.

Pakakrong (2011) Coconut tree growing to start again on Koh Samui. www.samuiindex.com/news/coconut-tree-growing-to-start-again-on-koh-samui-392.html. Retrieved 20 April 2012.

Pavlovich, K. (2003) The evolution and transformation of a tourism destination network: the Waitomo Caves, New Zealand, *Tourism Management*, vol. 24, pp. 203–16.

Pongponrat, K. (2011) Implement sustainable tourism practices before it is too late, *Contours*, vol. 21, no. 2, pp. 10–17.

Porter, M.E. (1998) Clusters and the new economics of competition, *Harvard Business Review*, pp. 77–90.

Sautter, E.T. and Leisen, B. (1999) Managing stakeholders: a tourism planning model, *Annals of Tourism Research*, vol. 26, no. 2, pp. 312–28.

Saxena, G. (2005) Relationships, networks and the learning regions: case evidence from the Peak District National Park, *Tourism Management*, vol. 26, no. 2, pp. 277–89.

Scheyvens, R. (2011) The challenge of sustainable tourism development in the Maldives: understanding the social and political dimensions of sustainability, *Asia Pacific Viewpoint*, vol. 52, no. 2, pp. 148–64.

Shepherd, N. (2002) How ecotourism can go wrong: the cases of SeaCanoe and Siam Safari, Thailand, *Current Issues in Tourism*, vol. 5, no. 3, pp. 309–18.

Smith, R.A. (1992) Coastal urbanisation: tourism development in the Asia Pacific, *Built Environment*, vol. 18, pp. 27–40.

Soontayatron, S. (2010) Socio-cultural changes in Thai beach resorts: a case study of Koh Samui Island, Thailand, PhD thesis. Bournemouth University, UK.

Sriburi, T. (2007) Meeting European standards for sustainable tourism management: capacity building of Thai enterprises and policy-makers, promotion of good practices in the Thai tourism sector. Environmental Research Institute, Chulalongkorn University, Thailand.

Taplin, I.M. (2011) Network structure and knowledge transfer in cluster evolution, *International Journal of Organizational Analysis*, vol. 19, no. 2, pp. 127–45.

TAT (2012) Highlights of the Tourism Authority of Thailand Action Plan, 2013, www.tatnews. org/highlights-of-the-tourism-authority-of-thailand-action-plan-2013/. Retrieved 9 April 2015.

TAT (2013) The Tourism Authority of Thailand TAT launches global digital marketing campaign to promote voluntourism, www.tatnews.org/the-tourism-authority-of-thailand-tat-has-launched-a-global-digital-marketing-campaign-to-promote-voluntourism/. Retrieved 9 April 2015.

Teiy (2010) 7 Greens Concept. www.teeteawthai.com/7- greens-concept. Retrieved 20 April 2012.

Thaithong, N. (2013) An investigation of tourism stakeholders' interrelationships affecting sustainability of tourism clusters in Samui Island (Unpublished) PhD Formal Assessment Report, The University of Hull, UK.

Thaithong, N. (2014) Preliminary case research findings from Samui, Unpublished PhD Thesis, The University of Hull, Kingston-upon-Hull.

TISTR (1995) *The revision of the action plan for tourism development of Ko Samui under its carrying capacity.* Executive Summary. Thailand Institute of Scientific and Technological Research: Bangkok.

Tosun, C. (2001) Challenges of sustainable tourism development in the developing world: the case of Turkey. *Tourism Management*, vol. 22, pp. 289–303.

Tosun, C. and Jenkins, C.L. (1998) The evolution of tourism planning in third-world countries: a critique, *Progress in Tourism and Hospitality Research*, vol. 4, pp. 101–4.

UNEP (2011a) Tourism: investing in energy and resource efficiency. www.unep.org/resource efficiency/Portals/24147/scp/business/tourism/greeneconomy tourism.pdf. Retrieved 26 July 2013.

UNEP (2011b) Towards a green economy: pathways to sustainable development and poverty eradication – A synthesis for policy makers. www.unep.org/greeneconomy. Retrieved 26 July 2013.

Urry, J. (1990) *The tourist gaze: Leisure and travel in contemporary societies.* Sage: London.

Vivanco, L. (2002) Escaping from reality, *Ecologist*, vol. 32, no. 2, pp. 26–31.

Wilkinson, P.F. (1989) Strategies for tourism in island microstates, *Annals of Tourism Research*, vol. 16, pp. 153–77.

Wipatayotin, A. (2013) Vichet vows to demolish illegal resorts, *Bangkok Post*, 17 July 2013. www.bangkokpost.com.

Wirudchawong, N. (2011) *Policy on community tourism development in Thailand.* Office of the Ombudsman: Thailand.

Yasarata, M., Altinay, L., Burns, P. and Okumus, F. (2010) Politics and sustainable tourism development: can they co-exist? Voices from North Cyprus, *Tourism Management*, vol. 31, no. 3, pp. 345–56.

20

GREENING THE HIGH-SPEND VISITOR

Implications for destination marketing

Emma Whittlesea, Victoria Hurth and Sheela Agarwal

Introduction

The growth of visitors and their associated travel needs and consumption patterns is creating one of the biggest tourism challenges for the future as an era of finite resources is entered, where reduced fossil-fuel dependency, low emissions and sustainable economic systems become paramount. The present economy is locked into high energy prices and a reliance on diminishing resources that are becoming fiercely fought over (Gössling *et al.*, 2010). This weakens the ability of countries across the globe to provide well-being for people and communities and threatens the ability of tourism to continue its upward trajectory of growth. If unrestrained, tourism is projected to grow to 43 million international tourist arrivals per year from 2010, amounting to a total of 1.8 billion arrivals by 2030 (UNWTO, 2011). However in the context of supply pressures on water (Postel, 2000), soil (Pimental and Kounang, 1998) and fossil fuels (Hirsch, 2005), it is inconceivable that these projections, and the associated value for people created by this level of tourism, can be achieved without drastic change to the current business model (Becken, 2007, Gössling *et al.*, 2010). Much has been made of the potential of a green tourism economy to help respond to these challenges, and achieving sustainable consumption and production is recognized as central to this (Pearce, 1989; Barbier, 2011; UNEP, 2011a, 2011b, 2012). In a resource-constrained and increasingly populated world, the sheer scale and continued growth of the sector raises serious questions about its viability and sustainability if a green economic model is *not* employed.

Most forms of tourism can be seen as a 'consumerist phenomenon', driven by capitalist tendencies and ideologies (Ioannides and Debbage, 1997) and nesting within an experience economy characterized by the creation of 'value' from memories and experiences that form the product (Pine and Gilmour, 1999). One approach to bring about a transition to a more sustainable green local economy involves tourism actors working to deliver the value, experiences and supporting products that satisfy tourists and yet fundamentally alter their associated impacts. In this vein, some commentators argue that eco-efficiency (maintaining existing provisions while reducing environmental impact) could enable sustainability without altering modes of consumption (DeSimone and Popoff, 2000); others call for a move to a circular economy, which transforms how products and services are created that moves beyond eco-efficiency (McDonough and Braungart, 2002). These 'supply side' approaches are critical, with Pomering *et al.* (2011) in particular, arguing this is the only way to enact change in tourism due to the limited demand for sustainable offerings and the inconsistencies of demand by those considered to be 'sustainable consumers'. Indeed, they state: 'short of global agreements that structurally force changes in tourist behaviour, the transformational consumer behaviour that sustainable tourism calls for will need to be driven by the supply side' (Pomering *et al.*, 2011, p. 965).

There is also recognition however, that sustainable consumption cannot be achieved without additionally altering the types of consumption people engage in (Heiskanen and Pantzar, 1997; Connolly and Prothero, 2003) combined with addressing the antecedents of such behaviour (Barr and Gilg, 2007). Indeed, the sustainable tourism literature has long recognized that the consumption patterns of tourists are unsustainable and that supply-side actions alone are unlikely to achieve the scale of change required (Gössling *et al.*, 2010; Mowforth and Munt, 2009). In particular, marketing has the potential to significantly influence sustainable tourist behaviour (Dinan and Sargeant 2000, Pomering *et al.*, 2011); guidance though, tends to be strategic, and practical advice on the mobilization of 'sustainable consumption' is often lacking. Thus, perhaps it is not solely the inability of tourists to engage in sustainable forms of tourism consumption as Pomering *et al.* (2011) suggest, but rather that marketing as a critical tool in creating this demand-side change has, to date, been inadequately applied.

It is in this context that this chapter is framed. It considers the role, contribution and potential of destination management organizations (DMOs) and their marketing activities to achieve a greener tourism economy. In particular, it identifies the scope and potential of marketing to effect a change in visitor consumption behaviours. Moreover, it investigates how DMOs could influence near-term and long-term sustainable consumption through their marketing activities and examines how this could be done for high-spend tourists that tend to have high environmental impact.

The chapter begins with a brief discussion of destinations, DMOs and the current role of marketing. This is followed by a review of the scope and application of contemporary marketing theory in order to create sustainable tourist behaviours, with a focus on high-spend market segments. The potential for practical application, product innovation and for an expanded interpretation and application of marketing at a destination level is explored and key priorities for DMOs are presented. It is hoped that this chapter will contribute to the theoretical discussions of the role of DMOs in mobilizing a 'greener' tourism economy at the macro and micro levels, and of the role of marketing as a strategic driver of sustainable tourist demand.

Destination management and marketing

The term 'destination' is nebulous, and a standard definition has proven difficult, but it can be argued that a destination is a geographical space in which a cluster of tourism resources exist (Pike, 2008). Similarly, DMOs are difficult to conceptualize as they can have a variety of forms and functions and there is no formally accepted model (VisitEngland, 2012, Pike 2004). Destination management can involve an array of activities and roles including: information provider, brand builder, convener and facilitator, catalyst, advocate, organizer, funding agent, community and network manager, and partnership coordinator (Wang and Pizam, 2011). Within a destination, the tourism product is a combination of goods and services that are produced and delivered by a range of participants and enterprises, each acting more or less autonomously, sometimes with little consideration for the needs and activities of other enterprises (Wang and Pizam, 2011). Due to the fragmented nature of the tourism industry, it is difficult for one single organization to have total and absolute control over a destination's production and marketing processes. However, managing the complexity of the tourism industry and working towards the achievement of valuable outcomes for all stakeholders is a role that destination management organizations (DMOs) are well placed to fulfil (Jamal and Watt, 2011). This means that in the absence of another body, it is critical that DMOs take responsibility and control over destination development and promotion, otherwise 'sustainable' tourism becomes a misnomer (Butler, 2010).

The concept of a 'greener' tourism economy has existed for decades, and despite intentions and efforts to integrate 'sustainable' or 'responsible' principles into tourism management practices, it appears to remain an 'add-on' or afterthought (Butler, 2010; Mowforth and Munt, 2009). This in part will be affected by the limited control of DMOs, but will also be exacerbated by the contested debates around the meaning and application of sustainability in tourism (e.g. Hunter, 1997; Sharpley, 2000; Mowforth and Munt, 2009), the lack of agreement on how it may best be achieved (Mowforth and Munt, 2009) and whether it is actually achievable (Sharpley, 2009). However, it has also been suggested that destinations are unaware of the opportunities and lack the skills or experience to integrate or apply sustainability into destination practice (UNEP, 2011a). There appears to be limited practical knowledge around the 'what can be done' to operationalize the concept, and to provide conceptual clarity that illustrates what a 'greener' tourism economic system could look like in practice. This includes the necessity for 'tourism promotion and marketing initiatives to emphasise sustainability as a primary option' (UNEP, 2011a, p. 442).

An analysis of destinations in England showed that, in reality, 98 per cent of destination strategies focus on marketing and promotion (Freezer, 2012). Moreover, all too often marketing is narrowly conceived as a tactical tool within destination management to increase visitor numbers and drive up spend (Dinan and Sargeant, 2000; Ritchie and Crouch, 2000; Richardson and Fluker, 2008; Butler, 2010; Freezer, 2012). Given this limited focus, arguably the potential for DMOs to make progress towards a green tourism economy is severely restricted. However, marketing in fact has the potential to enhance economic, social and environmental benefits if the activities encompassed within 'marketing' are broadened and strategically applied to drive sustainability. To realize this potential marketing must be used as a tool for deep change and not as a public relations tool or marketing ploy, as has happened in other areas where marketing has been ill-applied for sustainability in tourism (Mowforth and Munt, 2009; Lansing and DeVries, 2007). For marketing activities of DMOs to make a significant impact in delivering a green economy it first requires recognition that marketing's definition should be far broader than just *mass media* promotional advertising. Additionally, it requires the utilization of contemporary definitions of marketing which explicitly recognize the role of marketing in shaping the cultures, social norms and identities related to consumption, and through this, tourist behaviour. Finally, it requires the theoretical potential of marketing to be turned into tangible and practicable strategies and outcomes that enable physical and cultural leadership towards greener tourism products and services.

The potential of marketing for creating sustainable tourist behaviour

'Marketing' is a constantly evolving concept. The most recent definition of marketing proposed by the American Marketing Association (2007, p. 1) is 'the activity, set of institutions, and processes for creating, communicating, delivering, and exchanging offerings that have value for customers, clients, partners, and society at large'. This definition includes the social context of marketing while encompassing the 4Ps of price, promotion, place and product (McCarthy, 1960), which, despite criticisms (e.g. Grönroos, 1994), remain core to the field. In a tourism context Pomering *et al.* (2011) offer a useful agglomeration of 10Ps to create the Sustainability Tourism Marketing Model (STMM) to highlight possibilities for tourism businesses to develop more sustainability-orientated products and guest experiences. This comprises product, price, place, promotion, but also the three additional 'service' Ps of participants (people), process, physical evidence, offered by Booms and Bitner (1981), and the tourism Ps of partnerships, packaging and programming, as conceptualized by Morrison (2009). These are then cross-referenced against the three pillars of sustainability (triple bottom line) of people, planet and profit (Elkington, 1997) The benefit of such an approach is that it works to adjust the perception that marketing is the enemy of sustainability (Pomering *et al.*, 2011) by embedding it into the marketing process in the hope that it will lead to sustainable outcomes. The emphasis on a large range of Ps also helps to demonstrate that promotion is just one of the roles of marketing, with advertising being only one promotional tool, alongside others such as sales promotion and public relations.

Additionally, one of the clearest shifts within marketing over the past few decades has been a move from a 'make-and-sell' philosophy (where the aim was to persuade customers that what they really could do with buying was what the organization was producing) to a 'sense and respond' philosophy with an emphasis on business success through creating value for consumers (Kotler *et al.*, 2002, p. 25). Kotler *et al.* (2002) argue further that the digital landscape fundamentally advances this shift to a customer focus by placing power in the hands of consumers. This means that managing collaboration between different actors in order to maximize value-creation becomes the central role of marketing, and the 'relational capital' that is built through this collaboration is the core basis of competitive advantage. Related to this is the move away from marketing as part of a didactic process where value is exchanged with the customer at the point of sale or service, to one where value is built through the relationships created with customers at all levels of the organization across space and time (Grönroos, 1994). For DMOs this means that a coordinating and facilitating role becomes a vital marketing function in helping the various actors at a destination level to respond to customers in appropriate, innovative and sustainable ways. It also highlights the importance of DMOs entering into a distinct 'relationship' with the customer, where proactive innovation happens on behalf of, and with that customer, in order to maximize satisfaction levels and minimize environmental and social impacts. By taking this approach the risks of 'green marketing myopia' (Ottman *et al.*, 2006), are reduced so that, in the quest to improve sustainability, offers are not created, which are of reduced value or irrelevant for customers.

A further foundational change in marketing has come from a postmodern perspective to the marketing discipline (Firat *et al.*, 1995; Brown, 1998; Elliott and Wattanasuwan, 1998; Venkatesh, 1999). Two of the most significant advances that a postmodern perspective brings to marketing is first recognition that consumption is now primarily about the value gained from the symbolic services offered rather than any functional value (McCracken, 1990; Featherstone, 1991; Giddens, 1991; Bauman, 1998; Dittmar, 2008). Second, it has been observed that our identities are now primarily defined by what we consume rather than what we do for a living (Featherstone, 1991; Bauman, 1998; Baudrillard, 1998). It is not just how we fulfil identity, as one of our universal needs (Max-Neef, 1991), but how we fulfil all our universal basic needs beyond subsistence, which are heavily constructed, maintained and re-constructed by the symbolic connections between those needs and certain modes of consumption.

The symbolic connections between needs and consumption practices are negotiated in ongoing reciprocal relationships between the social, cultural and psychological realms and are therefore influenced by all actors in society (Wilk, 2002; Max-Neef, 1991). However, because marketing is situated at the heart of the consumption–consumer relationship and it engages in ongoing symbolic meaning-creation with large-scale impact, it is particularly influential. Marketing therefore has potential in negotiating and leading how different lifestyle groups normatively perceive how their needs are fulfilled and how value is determined by them (Firat *et al.*, 1995; Elliott and Wattanasuwan, 1998; Firat and Dholakia, 2006; Hurth, 2010; Hurth and Wells, 2007). As such, marketing is critical to shaping identities, lifestyles and cultures and therefore the values, attitudes and behaviours of future customers. As Firat *et al.* note: 'Marketing can no longer pretend to be an instrumental discipline that *affects* consumers and society but has to become reflexive and has to be studied as the sociocultural process that *defines* postmodern society' (1995, p. 21). For DMOs this means that how they market their destinations will shape not only which tourists arrive and what they decide to consume now, but what kind of expectations and behaviours they will display in the future. Marketing is therefore critical to creating the demand conditions of a green tourist economy. 'Sustainable marketing' is the term often used for the nexus of marketing and sustainability and can usefully be considered as both marketing sustainably (reducing the impact of products and services) and marketing sustainability (changing the behaviour of customers) (Martin and Schouten, 2011). Although marketing sustainably has a relatively long history, mainly within supply chain management, the notion that organizations, via their marketing, have the potential to shape customer behaviour in order to achieve sustainability is something that has only recently started to gain traction in both theory (Fuller, 1999; Dinan and Sargeant, 2000; Peattie and Peattie,

2009; Kotler, 2011; Martin and Schouten, 2011; Petersen, 2012) and more recently in practice (BITC, 2011).

Two of the most significant tools of sustainable marketing that can be used to change behaviour are social marketing and de-marketing (Dinan and Sargeant, 2000; Kotler, 2011; Pomering et al., 2011). De-marketing aims to apply marketing principles in reverse to reduce the demand of certain products and services (e.g. water) (Kotler, 2011) or in other words encouraging people 'not' to consume something. Meanwhile, social marketing attempts to effect behavioural change, which benefits individuals and society (Andreasen, 1994) and includes a focus on behaviour, segmentation targeting and positioning, and an emphasis on customer centricity. These principles help ensure that 'members of a target segment are given sufficient incentive to "activate" a new pattern of behaviour' (Dinan and Sargeant, 2000, p. 4). Social marketing has been successfully used to alter behaviour and the social/cultural antecedents of it in a range of contexts (see Dinan and Sargeant (2000) for a useful summary), including in a commercial context (Shewchuk, 1994; Maignan and Ferrell, 2004; BITC, 2011).

The advances within marketing theory and practice described above situate it as a fundamentally strategic, as well as a tactical, function and one which can shape, as well as respond, to demand patterns. However, the reality is that marketing practice has been out of step with such advances (Grönroos, 1994; Pomering et al., 2011). There is thus a real opportunity for DMOs to take advantage of these contemporary marketing developments in order to pursue a greener local economy agenda. This is because DMOs can provide a level of innovative leadership that is required to overcome the various challenges of sustainability. For example, ensuring economic viability by maintaining or increasing spend in destinations while at the same time drastically reducing the industry's negative environmental and social impacts. Or in other words, by taking advantage of the power of marketing to alter patterns of demand and supply, the chances of de-coupling spend from impact is maximized. However, to utilize marketing for these kinds of purposes requires an understanding of the ways different target market segments behave to currently fulfil their needs, and then designing marketing programmes that begin to shift how these needs are met. If a key aim is to de-couple spend from impact it makes sense to start by considering high-spend, high-impact tourist segments.

Reducing the impact of high-spend tourists through marketing

Evidence suggests that wealthier high-spend market segments are driving a large proportion of the unsustainability of tourism and there is a recognized link between income and a range of environmental impacts (Hurth and Wells, 2007). Research suggests that the rise in air travel is primarily through increased travel by affluent householders; it is therefore this group that should be the main focus of research and behavioural interventions (DEFRA, 2007). The UK Energy Research Centre (UKERC) has concluded that 'much of the recent expansion in flying has occurred because better off people are flying more often' (UKERC, 2006, p. 4), whereas the number of international leisure trips made from these airports by people with a household income of less than £29,000 p.a. actually fell (UKERC, 2006, p. 92). Furthermore, the UKERC predicts that much of future demand will also be from wealthier groups.

Currently destinations often use their marketing budget to pursue overseas and wealthy domestic visitors, based on the assumption that their spend will be high, which can increase the strength of local economies. This provides a challenge to the creation of a green economy because, as with flying, research shows that income and environmental impact are strongly linked across an array of consumption practices (Vringer and Blok, 1995; Schipper *et al.*, 1997; Lutzenhiser and Hackett, 1993; OECD, 2002; Moll *et al.*, 2005; Lenzen *et al.*, 2006; Hurth and Wells, 2007; Buchs and Schnepf, 2013). Therefore within current systems of production and demand, in general, the more people spend and consume, the higher the impact. This has been demonstrated in a tourism context where it has been shown that certain consumption patterns such as high visitor spend and/or spend on certain categories through choice and type of consumption, can equate to high environmental impact. For example certain visitor types or trips such as overseas tourists or 'weekend breaks' can have a significantly higher footprint than, say, domestic visitors or 'backpacking' (Whittlesea and Owen, 2012).

Data and evidence is critical to inform sustainable marketing approaches built on the usual variables such as spend levels and psycho-socio-demographic factors, however the process of pinpointing what action can be taken to effect positive results is enriched through additional data, performance measures and tools surrounding the social and environmental impacts and outcomes. Using REAP Tourism, a resource and environment accounting tool (Whittlesea and Owen, 2012), it is possible to explore the impact of different trips and to examine how different choices can affect the size and constitution of the environmental footprint. ArkLeisure provide the only values-based segmentation unique to the British travel consumer (ArkLeisure, 2011) and REAP Tourism is used here to examine the greenhouse gas footprint of two market segments and associated trips. The first is a Luxury Short Break (for two people away for two nights) that is likely to appeal to the Cosmopolitan segment, and the second a Family Holiday (for four people away for 7 nights), which is likely to be attractive to the High Street segment. Both segments are considered to be high spending and their characteristics are described in more detail in Table 20.1.

Table 20.2 details the spending and consumption assumptions on how long the visitors stay for, and what accommodation, travel, activity and spending choices they make on

TABLE 20.1 Characteristics of two ArkLeisure market segments

Cosmopolitans	*High Street*
• Independent and innovators	• Mass market
• Strong, active, confident and stylish	• Mainstream early adopters
• Style and brand is important but as an expression of their self-made identity	• Followers of high street fashion
• High spenders, justify buying expensive alternatives	• Care about what others think
• Looking for new challenges and experiences	• Happy to buy packaged options
	• Prepared to spend money on luxury that tends to mean more things

Source: Developed from the ArkLeisure website (2011)

TABLE 20.2 Data and assumptions for the REAP tourism analysis

Trip comparison	Cosmopolitan		High Street	
	Luxury break	'Greener' luxury break	Family holiday	'Greener' family holiday
Destination and length of stay	Bath for 3 days	Bath for 4 days	Torquay for 8 days	Torquay for 8 days, breaking the trip up with an additional 2 days at Exeter
Accommodation	2 nights in a luxury 5★ hotel	3 nights in a luxury 5★ GTBS accredited hotel	7 nights in a 3★ all inclusive resort	7 nights in a 3★ all inclusive resort in Torquay, 2 nights at a B&B in Exeter
Food	Eats out in high-end restaurants and cafes (assume spend of £10 on café food and £60 on restaurant food)	Eats out in restaurants and cafes that source 'local' food	Eats out in 'chain' restaurants and pubs (assume spend of £10 on pub food and £60 on restaurant food in total)	Eats out in a GTBS 'chain' restaurant and a pub that sources 'local' food
Travel	Flies to Bristol from Edinburgh and uses bus and train to get	First class train from Edinburgh to Bath and 'pedal carriage' to get around	Uses own car to travel to Torquay from Birmingham and travels on three 20km	Train travel from Birmingham to Torquay via Exeter and hire a car to travel on three 20km day

	to Bath and taxis to get around Bath (assume total domestic plane distance of 1,000km, local train distance of 20km and taxi distance of 5km)	Bath (assume total train distance of 1,020km and 'pedal carriage' distance of 5km)	day excursions (assume total car distance of 820km)	excursions (assume total train distance of 760km and hire car distance of 60km)
Shopping	Buys new jewellery and imported art (assume total spend of £300 on jewellery and £200 on art)	Buys antique jewellery and local art (assume total spend of £300 on jewellery and £200 on art)	Buys a surf board, some beach toys and goes shopping (assume total spend of £200 on large recreational items, £20 on toys and £100 on clothes)	Hires a surf board, buys locally produced toys and goes shopping in GTBS accredited shops (assume total spend of £40 on local toys and £100 on clothes)
Activities	Two sessions at the Spa	One session at a GTBS accredited spa and one walking trip along the canal	Days out to the beach	Days out to the beach
Attractions	Visits the Roman Baths and an art gallery	Visits the Roman Baths and a local art gallery	Visits a zoo, the Donkey Sanctuary and a Theme Park	Visits a zoo, and animal sanctuary and a historic property
Events	Goes to a comedy club	Goes to the night-time comedy walking tour around the city	Goes to the fair	Goes to see local live music

their trip. For both the Luxury Break and Family Holiday an alternative 'greener' trip option is provided should different choices be made by the consumer.

The data were entered into the REAP Tourism tool to estimate and compare the greenhouse gas footprint of each trip, and Figure 20.1 presents the results of the two trips alongside the 'greener' options with the highest total impact being the family holiday. The results of the 'greener' options are of particular interest because 'total' trip impact in terms of the Greenhouse Gas Footprint has been significantly reduced (58 per cent and 40 per cent) yet in both circumstances trip length and spend were increased.

To explore this further, the results of the greenhouse gas footprint are presented in relative terms on a per visitor day (pvd) basis to understand the proportional impact of the separate consumption categories as illustrated in Figure 20.2. Despite the family holiday having the highest 'total' trip footprint, it is unsurprising that the relative per visitor day footprint is considerably lower than the luxury break due to the number of nights they were away and double the number of people on the trip. The tourist on a luxury break has more than ten times the daily impact (an additional 569kg CO_2e) of a tourist on a family holiday with travel comprising the highest proportion of the luxury break footprint (37 per cent) and this would be almost double the size if the aviation component had been multiplied by 1.9 to account for radiative forcing, followed by shopping (31 per cent) and food (21 per cent). Despite the high daily impact associated with the luxury break, changes in consumption through 'greener' choices can reduce the daily footprint by 58 per cent, while at the same time increasing spend and length of stay. For example the travel component alone is reduced by 63 per cent from 234kg to 87kg CO_2e pvd by switching from air travel to the train.

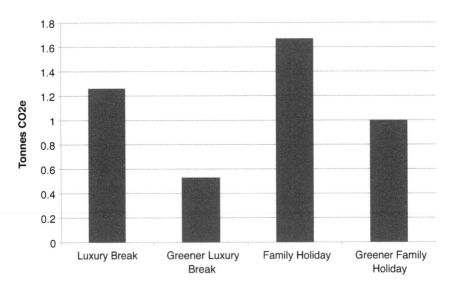

FIGURE 20.1 Total greenhouse gas footprint for the luxury break, family holiday and the 'greener' options

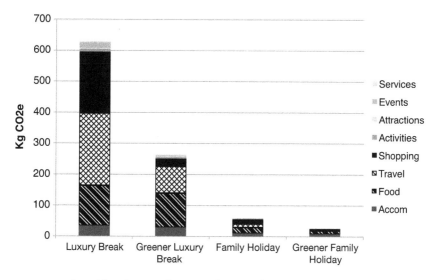

FIGURE 20.2 Per visitor day greenhouse gas footprint for the different trips

The compositions of the impact between the two different trips (Figure 20.2) are quite different, with the highest proportional impact of the family holiday tourist footprint being food (31 per cent), followed by shopping (26 per cent) and then travel (19 per cent). This type of visitor profiling activity can help to inform and prioritize the development of 'greener' tourism products, campaigns and target marketing to help drive a greener tourism economy. However, although it indicates what kinds of demand-side changes need to happen, actually enacting such change is the realm of marketing.

The high impact changes in behaviour that are required, as highlighted in Figure 20.2, are the mode of travel to the destination and the procurement choices for food and shopping, but accommodation and activities can also influence the size of the greenhouse gas footprint. By operationalizing the 10 Tourism Ps proposed by Pomering *et al.* (2011) and applying it to a matrix, which addresses the 'Cosmopolitan' consumer, some actions to effect such behaviour change are proposed (see Table 20.3).

The construction of this matrix was not without its difficulties, not least because of the overlap that exists between the 10 Ps and between the demand and supply side. However it does provide an important basis for innovation and demonstrates that opportunities do exist for DMOs to use marketing to help shape consumer demand, expand the interpretation and implementation of marketing activities and create the pull factor for 'greener' behaviours. Although this is not yet a case in practice, the process has potential and demonstrates how marketing can be used as a strategic tool for developing destination sustainability. To do this, DMOs would need to take the lead and proactively develop the consumer pull on sustainable tourism. Inevitably, such action requires DMOs to build a sound understanding of particular target groups but marketing theory suggests this will also require developing deeper relationships and a partnership

TABLE 20.3 Examples for driving 'greener' consumption from the 'Cosmopolitan' market segment

	Stay in green accredited accommodation	*Use the train 'to and from' the destination*	*Dine at restaurants that buy local food*
Product	Low 'negative' impact luxury accommodation that uses local produce and builds on the destination's quality green credentials	Train travel building on the destination's rail network, combining lower impact per km and quality relaxed 'guilt free' first class experience	Restaurants combining high quality service, contemporary design and locally produced sustainable food – building on a sense of place and the destination's quality local food and wine
Price	Relatively high price to signal quality and luxury	Demonstrate the ethical value to Cosmopolitan customers of the often high relative price of train over air, and/or to make the price comparable	Relatively high to demonstrate the connection between local sustainable food and quality/luxury
Promotion	Underground posters and on-board train magazine promoting luxury – stylish and contemporary green accredited accommodation, minimizing status symbols and maximizing collaborative non-materialistic values	Targeted e-banners for low impact luxury and price competitive rail travel highlighting benefits of slow travel and creating symbolic connections between luxury, style and low-impact experiences with train travel	Ensure destination's food and eating out guides highlight restaurants that utilize 'local' food and services and develop a 'locally produced' brand that creates symbolic connections between luxury, contemporary, ethical, quality taste and experiences
Place	Provide a search option for green accommodation and prioritize green accommodation on searches, working with other organizations to promote, incentivize and enable greener accreditation	Prioritize train travel and public transport in the listing of travel information and provide a normative context on reviews and quotes of the quality and feel-good factors of the experience	Prioritize restaurants and attractions that source and use 'local' and 'sustainable' food and services in restaurant guides and on destination websites
Participants	Facilitate training for staff in green accredited accommodation to maximize value and develop appropriate signage and symbols to encourage and not dissuade proactive green consumer behaviours	Facilitate training for staff, to promote to travellers and fellow staff, on public transport about luxury travel and the links to green high quality experiences.	Facilitate training for staff on the provenance and sustainable production of supplied food and how it enhances quality, taste and the experience. Share this information within the menus and in guest information

Process	Promote a green concierge service and free green chauffeur (only from the train station) and promote use of high-end sustainable innovations and technologies available	Promote and provide luxury waiting area and cafes at the destination station that sell 'local' and 'sustainable' products and food and utilize high-end sustainable innovations and technologies	Help ensure cosmopolitan customers have a high quality experience in restaurants serving 'local' and sustainable high end food e.g. short waiting times, ability to pay by card, automated online booking service etc.
Physical Evidence	Provide marketing guidance for appropriate green accommodation (e.g. décor, furniture, appliances, local procurement of quality biscuits and handmade bathroom products) that will ensure the tangibles of the green accommodation meet the stylish and contemporary expectations of the cosmopolitan consumer	Encourage train providers to procure high quality 'local' and 'sustainable' food that supports businesses along the route as part of the first class train experience. Provide evidence of the use of 'local', 'quality' and 'sustainable' services and supplies	Encourage restaurants to identify local produce and where it has been sourced on the menu aligning with the cosmopolitan identity. Integrate 'local' through every element of the experience, through the use of 'local' flowers on tables or the provision of locally produced organic chocolates or mints with the bill. Make the stories behind these artefacts clear where appropriate.
Partnership	Create partnerships with local employers to promote 'local' luxury green weekends to staff and to develop a network to promote and enhance 'local' luxury green products and services	Work with train and local taxi agents to provide green chauffeur pick-up and drop-off services to the train station and work with public transport operators to provide combined tickets that support, promote and encourage use of public transport 'within' the destination and to attractions	Work with 'local' sustainable food networks, accommodation providers and restaurants to provide clear, consistent, quality communications and labelling to recognize and identify providers who use local food and to increase the percentage per cent of local food supplied
Packaging/ Programming	Bundle vouchers for local high-end sustainable restaurants with 3-night stay in green accredited accommodation and offer tailored tours of the hotel to demonstrate 'sustainable management'	Encourage accommodation providers to offer a train booking service when booking accommodation and get a 'special' tour at a local sustainable experience relevant to a cosmopolitan customer if the train ticket is shown (e.g. vineyard)	Develop a 'golden green' reward card and offers e.g. a free bottle of quality 'local' wine if you have a three-course meal for two at a fine dining restaurant that sources 'local' food and services

approach with the relevant tourist segments to redefine value and need (Grönroos, 1994; Kotler *et al.*, 2002; Firat and Dholakia, 2006).

Conclusion

Developing a green tourism economy is not just desirable and arguably essential, but it is potentially feasible through the proactive management and marketing for the visitor type and pattern of tourism development desired (Pearce, 1992). If destination organizations are looking at the long-term competitiveness of their destination then they need to embrace sustainability. However, realizing the role of tourism in creating local green economies will require more than incremental changes to the efficiency of existing offers to existing segments, as a fundamental shift in the marketing approaches practised by DMOs is necessary. This is because current approaches to tourism marketing are often not embracing the full scope of marketing potential and also because the current marketing strategies tend to be incompatible with a 'green economy'; they often focus on 'quantity over quality' and attract tourists from market segments on the basis of economic criteria in isolation from their associated environmental and social impacts.

This chapter demonstrates that desirable higher spend visitors are an important yet challenging target group in the move to a green economy. Key challenges are related to their consumption behaviours, in particular around travel and shopping. Although alternative visitor segments and behaviours can be less impactful and therefore it may be tempting to shift the focus to these groups, it is demonstrated here that there is significant scope to reduce the impact per pound ($\pounds$) of high-spend consumers if they changed their behaviour and modes of consumption (demand). This is predicated on alternative 'greener' products and services that are appropriate to a segment being available and being supplied. Therefore the high-spend tourist is not necessarily the wrong type of tourist to attract, but their behaviour does require modifying to support and drive more sustainable and responsible tourism products and services. Through creating and delivering offers that are low impact and yet appropriately connected to underlying needs and a segment's current modes of satisfying them, the marketing that DMOs undertake is critical to achieving the deep changes in consumer demand patterns required. DMOs are also central to building and maintaining the relationships that are required between all tourism actors.

Thus, DMOs need to integrate sustainability into the delivery of marketing principles, planning and management in order to steer not only visitors, but also destinations, towards a greener tourism economy. In order to do this, it is imperative that such actions are neither reduced to 'greenwashing' nor fall into the trap of 'green marketing myopia' (Ottman *et al.*, 2006). Leadership and innovation will be required to drive such a paradigmatic change in the nature of tourism economies, with the necessity to alter both tourism production (how sustainably tourism services and products are delivered) and consumption (what kinds of service and products tourists derive value from). 'Truly' sustainable marketing at the destination level could be central to achieving this and could provide a strategic 'leadership' tool for destination management organizations (DMOs) in the drive to green the tourist economy.

References

American Marketing Association (2007) Definition of marketing. Available: www.marketing power.com/aboutama/pages/definitionofmarketing.aspx. Accessed 11 June 2013.

Andreasen, A.R. (1994) Social marketing: Its definition and domain, *Journal of Public Policy and Marketing*, vol. 13, no. 1, pp. 108–14.

ArkLeisure (2011) Introducing the ArkLeisure model. Available: www.arkleisure.co.uk/explore. Accessed 13 July 2013.

Barbier, E. (2011) The policy challenges for green economy and sustainable economic development, Natural Resources Forum, special issue: *Green Economy and Sustainable Development*, vol. 35, no. 3, pp. 233–45, August 2011.

Barr, S. and Gilg, A.W. (2007) A conceptual framework for understanding and analysing attitudes towards environmental behaviour, Geografiska Annaler: Series B, *Human Geography*, vol. 89, no. 4, pp. 361–79.

Baudrillard, J. (1998) *The Consumer Society. Myths and Structures.* Sage: London.

Baumann, Z. (1998) *Work, Consumerism and the New Poor.* Open University Press: Milton Keynes, UK.

Becken, S. (2007) Developing indicators for managing tourism in the face of peak oil, *Tourism Management*, vol. 29, (2008), pp. 695–705.

BITC (2011) Influencing consumer behaviour: A guide for sustainable marketing. Available: www.bitc.org.uk/our-resources/report/influencing-consumer-behaviour-guide-sustainable-marketing. Accessed 17 July 2013.

Booms, B.H. and Bitner, M.J. (1981) Marketing strategies and organizational structures for service firms. In Donnelly, J.H. and George, W.R. (eds) *Marketing of Services* (pp. 47–51). American Marketing Association: Chicago, IL.

Brown, S. (1998) *Postmodern marketing two: Telling tales.* International Thomson Business Press.

Büchs, M. and Schnepf, S.V. (2013) Who emits most? Associations between socio-economic factors and UK households' home energy, transport, indirect and total CO_2 emissions, *Ecological Economics*, vol. 90, pp. 114–23.

Butler, R. (2010) Sustainability or stagnation? Limits on development in tourist destinations. *European Journal of Tourism, Hospitality and Recreation*, vol. 1, no. 1, pp. 10–23.

Connolly, J. and Prothero, A. (2003) Sustainable consumption: consumption, consumers and the commodity discourse, *Consumption Markets and Culture*, vol. 6, no. 4.

DEFRA (2007) *Public understanding of sustainable leisure and tourism.* DEFRA: London.

DeSimone, L.D. and Popoff, F.P. (2000) *Eco-efficiency: The business link to sustainable development.* MIT Press: Cambridge, MA.

Dinan, C. and Sargeant, A. (2000) Social marketing and sustainable tourism – is there a match? *International Journal of Tourism Research*, vol. 2, no. 1, pp. 1–14.

Dittmar, H. (2008) *Consumer society, identity, and well-being: the search for the 'Good Life' and the 'Body Perfect'.* European Monographs in Social Psychology Series, Psychology Press: London and New York.

Elkington, J. (1997) *Cannibals with forks: the triple bottom line of twenty first century business.* Capstone: Mankato, MN.

Elliott, R. and Wattanasuwan, K. (1998) Brands as symbolic resources for the construction of identity, *International Journal of Advertising*, vol. 17, pp. 131–44.

Featherstone, M. (1991) *Consumer culture and postmodernism.* Sage: London.

Firat, A.F. and Dholakia, N. (2006) Theoretical and philosophical implications of postmodern debates: some challenges to modern marketing, *Marketing Theory*, vol. 6, no. 2, pp. 123–62.

Firat, F.A., Dholakia, N. and Venkatesh, A. (1995) Marketing in a postmodern world, *European Journal of Marketing*, vol. 29, no. 1, pp. 40–56.

Freezer, J. (2012) *Management or marketing? A study of destination organisation models in England*. Masters project in Responsible Tourism Management. Leeds Metropolitan University, UK.

Fuller, D.A. (1999) *Sustainable marketing: Managerial-ecological issues*, vol. 407. Sage: Thousand Oaks, CA.

Giddens, A. (1991) *Modernity and Self-Identity*. Polity Press: Cambridge.

Gössling, S., Hall, C.M., Peeters, P. and Scott, D. (2010) The future of tourism: can tourism growth and climate policy be reconciled? A mitigation perspective, *Tourism Recreation Research*, vol. 35, no. 2, pp. 119–30.

Grönroos, C. (1994) Marketing mix to relationship marketing, *Towards a paradigm shift in marketing management decision*, vol. 32, no. 2, pp. 4–20.

Heiskanen, E. and Pantzar, M. (1997) Toward sustainable consumption: two new perspectives, *Journal of Consumer Policy*, vol. 20, pp. 409–42.

Hirsch, R.L. (2005) The inevitable peaking of world oil production, *Bulletin of the Atlantic Council of the United States*, vol. VXI, no. 5, pp. 1–9.

Hunter, C. (1997) Sustainable tourism as an adaptive paradigm, *Annals of Tourism Research*, vol. 24, no. 4, pp. 850–67.

Hurth, V. (2010) Creating sustainable identities: the significance of the financially affluent self, *Sustainable Development*, vol. 18, no. 3, pp. 123–34.

Hurth, V. and Wells, P. (2007) Averting catastrophic climate change: Confronting wealth, *International Journal of Innovation and Sustainable Development*, vol. 2, no. 1, pp. 63–78.

Ioannides, D. and Debbage, K. (1997) Post-Fordism and flexibility: the travel industry polyglot, *Tourism Management*, vol. 18, no. 4, pp. 229–41.

Jamal, T. and Watt, E.M. (2011) Climate change pedagogy and performative action: toward community-based destination governance. *Journal of Sustainable Tourism*, vol. 19, no. 4–5, pp. 571–88.

Kotler, P. (2011) Reinventing marketing to manage the environmental imperative, *Journal of Marketing*, vol. 75, no. 4, pp. 132–5.

Kotler, P.J., Jain, D.C. and Suvit, M. (2002) *Marketing moves: A new approach to profits, growth, and renewal*. Harvard Business Press: Boston, MA.

Lansing, P. and de Vries, P. (2007) Sustainable tourism: Ethical alternative or marketing ploy? *Journal of Business Ethics*, vol. 72, no. 1, pp. 77–85.

Lenzen, M., Wier, M., Cohen, C., Hayami, H., Pachauri, S. and Schaeffer, R. (2006) A comparative multivariate analysis of household energy requirements in Australia, Brazil, Denmark, India and Japan, *Energy*, vol. 31, pp. 181–207.

Lutzenhiser, L. and Hackett, B. (1993) Social stratification and environmental degradation: understanding household CO_2 production, *Social Problems*, vol. 40, no. 1, pp. 50–73.

McCarthy, E.J. (1960) *Basic marketing*. Irwin: Homewood IL.

McCracken, G.D. (1990) *Culture and consumption*. Indiana University Press: Indianapolis, IN.

McDonough, W. and Braungart, M. (2002) *Cradle to cradle: Remaking the way we make things*. North Point Press: New York.

Maignan, I. and Ferrell, O.C. (2004) Corporate social responsibility and marketing: an integrative framework, *Journal of the Academy of Marketing Science*, vol. 32, no. 1, pp. 3–19.

Martin, D.M. and Schouten, J. (2011) *Sustainable marketing*. Pearson Prentice Hall: New York.

Max-Neef, M. (1991) *Human scale development*. Apex Press: New York.

Moll, H.C., Noorman, K.J., Kok, R., Engstrom, R., Throne-Holst, H. and Clark, C. (2005) Pursuing more sustainable consumption by analyzing household metabolism in European countries and cities, *Journal of Industrial Ecology*, vol. 9, no. 1–2, pp. 259–75.

Morrison, A. (2009) *Hospitality and travel marketing* (4th edn) Delmar Cengage Learning: Albany, NY.

Mowforth, M. and Munt, I. (2009) *Tourism and sustainability. Development, globalisation and new tourism in the Third World.* (3rd edn). Routledge: London.

OECD (2002) *Towards sustainable household consumption? Trends and policies in OECD countries.* Organisation for economic co-operation and development: Paris.

Ottman, J.A., Stafford, E.R. and Hartman, C.L. (2006) Avoiding green marketing myopia: ways to improve consumer appeal for environmentally preferable products. *Environment: Science and Policy for Sustainable Development*, vol. 48, no. 5, pp. 22–36.

Pearce, D.G. (1992) Alternative tourism: concepts, classifications, and questions. In Smith, V.L. and Eadington, W.R. (eds) *Tourism alternatives: Potentials and problems in the development of tourism* (pp. 13–30). University of Pennslyvania Press and the International Academy for the Study of Tourism: Philadelphia, PA.

Pearce, D.W. (1989) *Blueprint for a green economy: A report.* Earthscan: London.

Peattie, K. and Peattie, S. (2009) Social marketing: a pathway to consumption reduction, *Journal of Business Research*, vol. 62, no. 2, pp. 260–68.

Petersen, M. (2012) Envisioning and developing sustainable enterprise. A macromarketing approach, *Journal of Macromarketing*, vol. 32, no. 4, pp. 393–6.

Pike, D. (2008) *Destination marketing: An integrated marketing communication approach.* Butterworth-Heinemann: Burlington, MA.

Pike, S. (2004) *Destination marketing organisations.* Elsevier: Oxford.

Pimentel, D. and Kounang, N. (1998) Ecosystem ecology of soil erosion, *Ecosystems*, vol. 1, pp. 416–26.

Pine, B.J. and Gilmour, J.H. (1999) *The experience economy: work is theatre and every business a stage.* Harvard University Press: Cambridge, MA.

Pomering, A., Noble G. and Johnson, L.W. (2011) Conceptualising a contemporary marketing mix for sustainable tourism, *Journal of Sustainable Tourism*, vol. 19, no. 8, pp. 953–69.

Postel, S.L. (2000) Entering an era of water scarcity: the challenges ahead, *Ecological Applications*, vol. 10, no. 4, pp. 941–8.

Richardson, J. and Fluker, M. (2008) *Understanding and managing tourism.* (2nd edn). John Wiley & Sons: Brisbane.

Ritchie, J.R.B. and Crouch, G.I. (2000) The competitive destination: A sustainability perspective. *Tourism Management*, vol. 21, pp. 1–7.

Schipper, L., Ting, M., Khrushch, M. and Golove, W. (1997) The evolution of carbon dioxide emissions from energy use in industrialized countries: an end-use analysis, *Energy Policy*, vol. 25, no. 7–9, pp. 651–72.

Sharpley, R. (2000) Tourism and sustainable development: exploring the theoretical divide, *Journal of Sustainable Tourism*, vol. 8, no. 1, pp. 1–19.

Sharpley, R. (2009) The myth of sustainable tourism. Centre for Sustainable Development Working Paper Series 2009/2010, No. 4, University of Central Lancashire, UK.

Shewchuk, J. (1994) *Social marketing for organisations.* Available: www.omafra.gov.on.ca/english/rural/facts/92-097.htm. Accessed 18 July 2013.

UKERC (2006) *Predict and Decide. Aviation, climate change and UK policy.* United Kingdom Energy Research Centre: Oxford.

UNEP (2011a) *Towards a green economy: Pathways to sustainable development and poverty eradication.* Full report. Available: www.unep.org/greeneconomy. Accessed 18 July 2013.

UNEP (2011b) *Paving the way for sustainable consumption and production.* The Marrakech Process and Progress Report – Towards a 10 Year framework of programmes on sustainable consumption and production. Available: www.unep.fr/scp/marrakech/. Accessed 8 January 2014.

UNEP (2012) *Global outlook on SCP policies: taking action together.* Available: www.unep.fr/shared/publications/pdf/DTIx1498xPA-GlobalOutlookonSCPPolicies.pdf. Accessed 8 January 2014.

UNWTO (2011) *Tourism towards 2030: Global overview.* Advance edition presented at UNWTO 19th General Assembly.

Venkatesh, A. (1999) Postmodernism perspectives for macromarketing: an inquiry into the global information and sign economy. *Journal of Macromarketing*, vol. 19, no. 2, pp. 153–69.

VisitEngland (2012) *Principles for developing destination management plans.* VisitEngland.

Vringer, K. and Blok, K. (1995) The direct and indirect energy requirements of households in the Netherlands, *Energy Policy*, vol. 23, no. 10, pp. 893–910.

Wang, Y. and Pizam, A. (2011) *Destination marketing and management: Theories and applications.* CAB International.

Whittlesea, E.R. and Owen, A. (2012) Towards a low carbon future – the development and application of REAP Tourism, a destination footprint and scenario tool. *Journal of Sustainable Tourism*, vol. 20, no. 6, pp. 845–65.

Wilk, R. (2002) Consumption, human needs and global environmental change, *Global Environmental Change*, vol. 12, pp. 5–13.

21

STEPS TOWARDS A GREEN ECONOMY

Which factors contribute to the social inclusion and economic development of the locals in the Brazilian tourism industry?

Gilson Zehetmeyer Borda, Elimar Pinheiro do Nascimento, João Paulo Faria Tasso and Everson Cristiano de Abreu Meireles

Introduction

The Rio+20 conference highlighted the green economy as an important new approach to the traditional economic-centred view of dealings between people. The UNWTO (2012, p. 6) stated that 'sustainable tourism can boost the sector's contribution to economic growth, development and particularly job creation while also addressing major environmental challenges'. This creates a path where the tourism industry can be more inclusive and environmentally friendly, which is green economy based tourism (Sachs, 2009).

Reddy and Wilkes (2012, p. 15) highlight the challenges of the greening tourism process as a 'reduction of energy use in the travel and accommodation sector, water consumption, waste management, management of cultural heritage and growth of tourism from a global resource perspective'. Recent initiatives focusing on innovation in the use of natural resources, management of cultural heritage and the growth of tourism will be necessary to tackle these challenges.

In Brazil, during the last few years, several tourism-related research initiatives – short, medium and long-term – have been started in order to achieve this new goal. For example, the use of vegetable-origin energy (biomass) from sugar cane processing is being reviewed in bed and breakfast businesses and hotels, on the Alagoas State coast. The implementation and certification of sustainability programmes for small and medium hospitality companies in the hill region of Rio Grande do Sul State, south of Brazil – mainly in Gramado and Bento Gonçalves – has centered on the efficient use of hydric resources and solid waste recycling. In Rio de Janeiro State National Parks, there are initiatives for sustainable management of the areas. In Brotas and Socorro – the country area of São Paulo State – there are adventure tourism projects and hotels focusing on the inclusion of people with disabilities (Lohmann and Dredge, 2012; Borda *et al.*, 2013). This chapter focuses on social equity being at the heart of the green economy and sustainability. The central question discussed is 'which factors contribute to the social inclusion and economic development of the locals in the Brazilian tourism industry?'

The research was developed in three municipalities – Cavalcante, Jijoca de Jericoacoara and Barreirinhas – from two main regions of Brazil: Central West and Northeast Region. A total of 687 people were surveyed using 462 questionnaires (with locals), and 225 interviews were conducted with key people from the tourism industry (mainly employers in the sector). The research used bibliographical and documentary analysis of key documents from the selected municipalities as well as international research and practice literature about the green economy and social insertion through tourism (Ritchie *et al.*, 2005). This study was chosen to reflect a responsible tourism project prioritizing social inclusion, poverty reduction and a low impact on nature, in search of the ideal of sustainability, expanding on the research of Borda and Nascimento (2011).

Tourism towards a green economy in Brazil

The Rio+20 Conference declared (UN, 2012, p. 2) that 'we strive for a world that is just, equitable and inclusive, and we commit to work together to promote sustained and inclusive economic growth, social development and environmental protection and thereby to benefit all'. The Tourism Forum from People Summit (TFPS) at the same event searched for another model of tourism 'focused on questions such as social inclusion, responsibility and citizenship' (TFPS, 2012, p. 1).

The Brazilian Ministry of Tourism launched the International Task Force on Sustainable Tourism Development (ITF-STD) project – the Green Passport. The project defined simple responsible ways that make it possible for tourists to act sustainably. Its objective was to promote 'tourism that respects the environment and culture while triggering economic benefits and social development for the host communities' (ITF-STD, 2012, p. 1). Although the initial launch was in 2008,[1] this movement has been concerned with mega sports events happening in Brazil: the FIFA Confederations Cup in 2013, the 2014 FIFA World Cup and the forthcoming 2016 Olympic and Paralympic Games in Rio de Janeiro. It gives the travellers some tips, which include supporting community-based initiatives in the places visited, talking about their holidays and sharing their sustainable choices, writing to local embassies to report any incidents, and promoting a multiplier effect by 'kicking the CO_2 habit' from their holidays – actions that can reduce their carbon footprint.

The tourism industry has been called upon to participate at a national and local level[2] through committees composed of community leaders, local politicians and representatives of the region's tourism sectors to develop a responsible initiatives working plan focusing on the project, each at their own level contributing by their actions and developing communication materials.[3]

Beyond this, a project of social inclusion was launched in November 2012 – the Program of Accessible Tourism[4] – a nationwide programme with actions to encourage the Brazilian tourism industry to promote accessibility (Duarte and Borda, 2012). The UNWTO (2013, p. 1) outlined that 'the facilitation of tourist travel for persons with disabilities is a vital element of any responsible and sustainable tourism development policy'. Considering that, in Brazil, 23.9 per cent of the population (45.6 million people) have some impairment or disability (IBGE, 2011), this programme can increase social inclusion and economic insertion (MTUR, 2008a).

Nice Travel[5] is another Ministry of Tourism programme that has permeated the Brazilian tourism industry. It is a programme that helps the tourists to know their rights and avoid various travelling problems.

One programme to highlight is the Brazilian Tourism Volunteering Programme,[6] which was a capacitation programme developed by the Brazilian Ministry of Tourism for people who wanted to work as volunteers in forthcoming sporting events. This programme gave training and capacitation for more than 12,000 people – mainly youth – as an initial insertion into the Brazilian tourism industry (Planalto, 2013a).

Social inclusion and economic insertion through tourism – the Brazilian situation

Tourism has been seen as an economic activity that has two unique characteristics, a low impact on nature and a great capacity for social inclusion. On the first point, there is significant international debate, with assertions changing depending on whether the activities are restricted to the destination, or more broadly include displacement that is essential to tourism. In relation to social inclusion, there is considerable controversy in view of the fluidity of the concept.

The concept of inclusion started as a counterpoint to the modern phenomenon of social exclusion outlined by Rene Lenoir (1989) in 1972. Xiberras (1993) reviewed the social science literature to identify in the classics the way the social game of integration/exclusion has been embedded in the constitution of modern society, from its beginnings in the eighteenth century. However, drawing from its diverse configurations a state-of-the-art application was suggested by Paugam (1996) – preceded by critical works about the subject (Nasse et al., 1992; Bourdieu, 1993; Cohen, 1994) that had in the Chicago School their distant Anglo-Saxon antecedents (Jordan, 1996) and rich reflections in Brazil (Buarque, 1993; Nascimento, 1994; Leal, 2011).

However, all these works still did not settle the questions about the concepts of exclusion or social inclusion, with their excessive scope and tensions. To include is to take inside someone who is outside. However, modern society has no exteriority (Nascimento, 1997), and the exclusion is always relative to a circumscribed social space, and from the point of view of certain actors. This realization of the conceptual imprecision led to the pursuit of accuracy of the concept of socio-productive inclusion, meaning the moulding of a population contingent on certain economic activities. Thus, the concept does not imply exclusion, except in relation to the selected economic activity. Being excluded from one space does not mean that one is excluded from another. Thus, the fact that fishermen and farmers are not addressed in touristic activity, in a particular destination, does not mean that they are not part of a local or regional market. This situation was analysed in the study about tourism-related production in Lençois Maranhenses (Tasso and Nascimento, 2008).

The assumption of the concept of socio-productive insertion is that participation in tourist activity is seen from the economic and social point of view, which is a significant part of the social mobility of population contingents. First, because it means an effective increase in revenues, especially in areas of high social vulnerability such as the areas under investigation here. Second, because it implies an enrichment of social relationships, and thus of social capital with its consequence of recognition, particularly for women. Finally, it means increasing the economic and social security of the people addressed, although some studies, in the Costa Norte Pole in Brazil, have not shown the consistency of this proposition (Tasso *et al.*, 2012).

In Brazil, the flow of tourism has been increasing to around 5.7 million international tourists per year and 79.2 million domestic arrivals. It constitutes 3.4 per cent of GDP (Panrotas, 2013). The tourism industry was estimated to generate US$ 8.9 billion in international currencies and 2 million jobs by 2014 with international growth, but also domestically (Planalto, 2013b).

This growth has reverberated institutionally, and today Brazil has a National Tourism System (SISTUR) composed of the Ministry of Tourism (MTUR); the Brazilian Tourism Institute (Embratur); the National Tourism Council, and the National Forum of State Secretaries and Managers of Tourism. The MTUR, created in 2003, is the lead body in the system (MTUR, 2008b).

The country also has a National Tourism Plan, which is considered to be a pre-requisite for development, particularly of endogenous nature, citing among its objectives the reduction of social and economic disparities and ensuring the involvement of the host community in receiving the benefits derived from tourism activity (Planalto, 2013b).

Economic insertion in developing tourism destinations related to Brazilian protected areas through tourism

In the search for 'another tourism focused on questions such as social inclusion, responsibility and citizenship' (TFPS, 2012, p. 1), tourism related to protected areas is growing in importance. Brazil has 478 Federal and state strictly protected areas totalling 37,019,697 ha, and 436 sustainable-use areas totalling 74,592,691 ha (Rylands and Brandon, 2005). During recent years, the SNUC – the National System of Conservation Units[7] – has been changing its administration strategy for these areas. It has been increasing the Mosaic areas, a mix of strictly protected areas and areas where local communities can live and develop economic activities such as collecting fruit and nuts, subsistence agriculture and responsible/sustainable tourism activities (Delelis *et al.*, 2010). Economic insertion in tourism can increase revenues, establishing these populations on the land, helping to reduce poverty and slums in the big cities, and deforestation, while diminishing social exclusion and inequalities (Borda, 2009; Sharpley, 2009; Fischer *et al.*, 2010).

Central West Region: the case of Cavalcante, Goias State, Brazil

Cavalcante is one of the largest municipalities in Goias State (see Figure 21.1), approximately 7,000 km² in size, surpassing the Brazilian Federal District. The area has

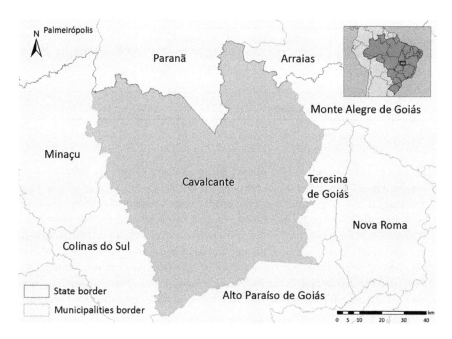

FIGURE 21.1 Location of the Municipality of Cavalcante
Source: IBGE (2013), prepared by Ana Ribeiro Pimenta

a high preservation rate of 90 per cent due to the establishment of protected areas, which include Chapada dos Veadeiros National Park (65 per cent), part of the APA (Environmental Protected Area) Pouso Alto and seven RPPNs (private reserve of natural heritage). The climate is tropically warm, characterized by a rainy summer, from October to April, and a dry winter, from May to mid-September (IBGE, 2013).

Currently, the area attracts nature and heritage-based tourists, mainly from Brasilia but also from the rest of the country. They come to the region attracted by the greenery, numerous mountains, wild animals, exotic plants, valleys, and rivers that form several waterfalls surrounding the city. Mining brought many black slaves to the region and those who managed to escape hid in the forests of the Cerrado (Brazilian savannah) forming a Quilombo. The Kalungas, African descendants, represent the largest remaining Quilombo (ex-slaves) community in Brazil. They are distributed in twenty groups, in the rural area (PMC, 2010).

In the local economy, handicrafts are predominantly decorative arrangements with regional plants. Mainly made with flowers, fruits and seeds and marketed under the name 'Flores do Cerrado' (flowers from savannah), these arrangements serve the domestic market and are exported.

Relative to the subject of economic insertion, there are several problems in the destination that prompted the development of the study. With a population of 9,394 people (4,747 live in urban areas and 4,647 in rural areas), the Gini coefficient is 0.63 showing great social inequality. The HDI (Human Development Index) is 0.62 (the

TABLE 21.1 FIRJAN Municipality Development Index (IFDM)/Cavalcante (2010)

Municipality	Total IFDM	Development areas		
		Education	Health	Employment and revenues
Cavalcante	0.5089	0.5505	0.6843	0.2920

Source: FIRJAN System (2013)

Brazilian national average is 0.77) and the poverty rate is 70.13 per cent, which is well above the national average of 32.75 per cent (IBGE, 2013).

Looking at the Municipality Development rates between the three analysed components, the lowest index is Employment and Revenues with 0.2920 points.

The numbers shown by these indexes are reflected in the results of the research at Cavalcante. The main factor of economic insertion in tourism highlighted both by employees and employers is 'professional training' (see Table 21.2). The education rate (0.5505) is lower than in most of the Brazilian counties[8] (the Cavalcante rate was normal in both education and total IFDM) and is reflected in the employment and revenues rate (rated low − less than 0.4).[9]

There were 462 semi-open questionnaires administered to the people of Cavalcante county − divided into two groups: people living in the city and people living in the countryside − from the ex-slave descendant (quilombo) community of Engenho II. Twenty-five interviews were conducted with people from the tourism industry (managers from hotels, restaurants, tourism local agencies, etc.).

The results presented in Table 21.2 show that both employees and employers highlighted 'professional training' − 51.2 per cent and 25.2 per cent, respectively − and 'indication from known people' − 12.5 per cent and 19.1 per cent, respectively − as the main factors. Regarding 'professional training', Dihman (2012) notes that the employers focused mainly on practical skills developed during the process of education. Regarding 'indication from known people', Borda (2007) notes that trust has an essential place in organizations and to recommend someone to the employer means putting trust in the person recommended and risking one's reputation with the employer (DiMaggio, 2001). At the same time, it is related to what Mauss (2012) calls 'social exchange'.

Employees stated that 'previous experience of the same activity' (12.5 per cent) and 'participation in cooperatives/associations' (4.2 per cent) were also significant. This item of collective association is related to social capital (Coleman, 1998; Swedberg, 2007) and trust (Simmel, 1992).

From the employers' point of view, the third factor in importance was 'responsibility/professionalism' (12.8 per cent) that was not mentioned by the employees. The fourth item in importance was 'previous experience of the same activity' (9.5 per cent) and fifth, at 3.2 per cent was 'good communication (sympathy/good humour/quality service to the tourist/attentive/extrovert)' 3.2 per cent.

Regarding the third and fifth items in the employers' list, Lin (2002) notes that professionalism, communication and adaptability related skills have the most influence on success in the job. Regarding the fourth factor 'previous experience of the same

TABLE 21.2 Factors identified in Cavalcante

Employees	Employers
1. Professional training = 51.2%	1. Professional training = 25.2%
2. Indication from known people = 12.5%	2. Indication from known people = 19.1%
3. Previous experience of the same activity = 12.5%	3. Responsibility/professionalism = 12.8%
4. Participation in cooperatives/ associations = 4.2%	4. Previous experience of the same activity = 9.5%
	5. Good communication (sympathy/good humour/quality service to the tourist/ attentive/extrovert) = 3.2%

activity', mentioned by both the employees and employers, previous experience can help the employee to engage faster in the job, but the employee still has to be trained because of the peculiarities of the new job (Huang and Lin, 2011).

Northeast Region: the case of Jijoca de Jericoacoara, Ceará State, Brazil

The municipality of Jijoca de Jericoacoara is located in the Brazilian Northeast Region (Figure 21.2), 295 km from the capital of Ceará State, Fortaleza. It has a territorial dimension of 204.793 km² and includes the National Park of Jericoacoara.

Rated by Travelers' Choice Destinations as the eighth most popular tourism destination in Brazil, Jijoca de Jericoacoara has 8,850 hectares of protected areas (O Povo, 2013). There are rocky formations surrounded by dunes, mangroves, temporary ponds, and a wide variety of beaches, with favourable wind conditions for practising water sports such as kitesurfing and windsurfing (ICMBio, 2013a).

Even so, it presents a difficult socio-economic context, regarding revenues and employment. With a population of 17,002 inhabitants, the town has 71.5 per cent of its economically active population (PEA) surviving with incomes below the minimum wage. The poverty incidence rate in the municipality is as high as 53.46 per cent (IBGE, 2013).

According to the Municipality Development Index, of the three components analysed (see Table 21.3), it is clear that 'Employment and Revenues' have the worst performance – ranked as low development – below 0.4 points.

The research technique used was to conduct interviews with two profiles of local actors: 'employers' and 'employees'.

Representing the 'employers' – semi-structured interviews were conducted with owners or managers from small, medium and large sized establishments of the municipality. Most of them were from the tourism industry – hotels, hostels, restaurants, resorts, receptive agencies etc.[10] In terms of the 'employees', locals were interviewed who worked in tourism industry establishments. The objective was to gain a better understanding of the factors that had, in their opinion, mainly contributed to their hiring.

FIGURE 21.2 Location of the Municipality of Jijoca de Jericoacoara
Source: IBGE (2013), prepared by Ana Ribeiro Pimenta

TABLE 21.3 FIRJAN Municipality Development Index (IFDM)/Jijoca de Jericoacoara (2010)

Municipality	Total IFDM	Development areas		
		Education	Health	Employment and revenues
Jijoca de Jericoacoara	0.6921	0.8174	0.8937	0.3652

Source: FIRJAN System (2013)

TABLE 21.4 Factors identified in Jijoca de Jericoacoara

Employees	Employers
1. Indication from known people = 42.5%	1. Good will (desire to learn/willingness/ proactive/unnecessary previous experience) = 12.1%
2. Professional training = 20.7%	2. Good appearance/personal hygiene = 11.1%
3. Previous experience of the same activity = 16.8%	3. Indication from known people = 9.0%

A total of 130 interviews were conducted, ninety-five with employees and thirty-five with employers. The results are presented in Table 21.4.

Among the employees, the main factor was 'indication from known people' with 42.5 per cent of respondents, followed by 'professional training', highlighted by 20.7 per cent, and the third, 'previous experience' with 16.8 per cent. These results show that relationships and trust can be rated higher than professional skills (Borda, 2009) and previous experience acquired by candidates, while recognizing the great importance of the latter.

From the point of view of the employers, 'indication from known people' ranked third, and while important (9.0 per cent), it was considered less important than the primary factors: 'good will' (12.1 per cent) and 'good appearance/personal hygiene' (11.1 per cent).

The results indicate that in order to work in the majority of establishments at Jijoca de Jericoacora, the candidate should have a predisposition for learning and performing various duties as requested (this was more relevant than professional training, education or previous experience). Beyond that, presenting a good appearance when searching for a job was emphasized as vital for being hired and maintaining the positionm, as well as always paying attention to personal hygiene (Huang and Lin, 2011).

Northeast Region: the case of Barreirinhas, Maranhão State

Located in the Brazilian Northeast Region (Figure 21.3), the municipality of Barreirinhas is 269 km from São Luis, the capital of Maranhão State. The county has a territorial dimension of 3,111,991 km^2 and a unique natural beauty, represented by Lençóis Maranhenses National Park.

Lençóis Maranhenses has been noted for integrating the 'Emotions Route', a tourism pathway composed of Jericoacoara (Ceara State), Delta do Parnaíba (Piauí State), and Lençóis Maranhenses (Maranhão State). It was commended by the Brazilian Ministry of Tourism in 2009 as the best tourism pathway of Brazil (Terra, 2013). Lençóis Maranhenses National Park covers an area of 155,000 hectares, characterized by free dunes, interdune ponds, sandbank areas and oceanic coast (ICMBio, 2013b).

FIGURE 21.3 Location of the Municipality of Barreirinhas
Source: IBGE (2013), prepared by Ana Ribeiro Pimenta

Barreirinhas clearly presents challenges in terms of its social and economic situation connected with revenues and employment. With 54,930 inhabitants, the city has a poverty incidence rate of 57.65 per cent, with 77.4 per cent of its economically active population (PEA) surviving on incomes below the minimum wage (IBGE, 2013).

The Municipality Development Rates also reflect the low development component 'employment and revenues' that is below 0.4 points, and can be considered the worst performer of all the components (see Table 21.5).

Looking at the same features described before, the study accessed 'employers' and 'employees' in the town. Altogether, seventy interviews were conducted: thirty-one with individuals working in any establishment of the tourism sector, and thirty-nine with owners, managers or people in charge of establishments in the local tourism industry (see Table 21.6).

TABLE 21.5 FIRJAN Municipality Development Index (IFDM)/Barreirinhas (2010)

Municipality	Total IFDM	Development areas		
		Education	Health	Employment and revenues
Barreirinhas	0.5466	0.5899	0.6583	0.3916

Source: FIRJAN System (2013)

TABLE 21.6 Factors identified in Barreirinhas

Employees	Employers
1. Indication from known people = 22.6%	1. Professional training = 18.1%
2. Professional training = 19.4%	2. Previous experience of the same activity = 10.3%
3. Responsibility and organization = 12.5%	3. Responsibility/professionalism = 10.3%
4. Previous experience of the same activity = 12.5%	4. Good communication (sympathy/good humour/quality service to the tourist/ attentive/extrovert) = 10.3%
	5. Indication from known people = 9.0%

The factor 'indication from known people' reflected a strong influence at the time of entry into the labour market, being the most recurrent among employees (22.6 per cent). 'Professional qualification' proved to have high importance, in second place (19.4 per cent). The factors 'responsibility and organization' and 'previous experience of the same activity' had the same evaluation – 12.5 per cent.

From the point of view of the employers of Barreirinhas, 'professional training' was highlighted as the most important factor (18.1 per cent of responses) when filling a vacancy. Three other factors followed: 'previous experience with the same activity', 'responsibility and professionalism' and 'good communication (sympathy, good humour, quality service to the tourist, attentive, extrovert)', each with 10.3 per cent of responses. Unlike in Jijoca de Jericoacoara, in Barreirinhas the item 'professional training' was considered the biggest contributing factor in the socio-economic inclusion of locals.

Reflections and comparisons between the three areas

The three study areas are located in two large Brazilian regions: the Northeast, comprising nine states, with a population of 53,081,950 inhabitants, and the Central West, comprising four units of the federation, including the Federal District (where the capital of the country is located), with 14,058,094 inhabitants (Figure 21.4).

FIGURE 21.4 Brazilian Map highlighting the locations of the municipalities studied
Source: IBGE (2013), prepared by Ana Ribeiro Pimenta

Interestingly, Barreirinhas is practically on the border of the Legal Amazon. Barreirinhas is the region where the process of occupation of Brazil by the Portuguese began in the sixteenth century. The Legal Amazon constituted the economic frontier of the years 1970/1980, with the 'March to the West', initiated by the military power, in order to 'integrate not dissever', that is, to occupy the interior of the country in order to prevent it being divided/split up.

There are many differences between the three municipalities in terms of area (ranging from 204 to 6,953 km_), population (ranging from 9,392 to 54,930 inhabitants) and social vulnerability (ranging from 36 per cent to 55 per cent poverty incidence rates). On the other hand, they have some similarities in terms of a clear improvement dynamic on social indicators. All the municipalities have increased per capita revenues, education,

TABLE 21.7 Characteristics of the researched municipalities and Brazil.

	Barreirinhas	Jijoca de Jericoacoara	Cavalcante	Brazil
Territorial area of the municipality (km²)	3,111.991	204.793	6,953.666	8,515,767.049
Total population	54,930	17,002	9,392	190,755,799
Per capita revenues (U$ dollars)	85.94	159.36	141.68	346.17
Life expectation at birth	70.11	68.35	73.47	73.94
Percentage of poor people	55.65	36.40	42.96	15.20
Illiteracy index (15 years or more)	25.37	23.51	26.82	9.61
Gini index	0.61	0.59	0.62	0.60

Source: IBGE (2013), PNUD (2013)

longevity and reduced illiteracy, infant mortality and poverty rates. Similarly, all have increased the Gini index. While the former movements are in compliance with the national dynamics, the increase in the Gini index represents a backward motion. Brazil has seen reduced poverty but also reduced inequality in a setting unique in the recent history of the country.

The recently published IDHM (Municipality Human Development Index) shows the movement of social vulnerability decreasing clearly in the last 20 years, in all three areas – in addition to the rest of Brazil (See Table 21.8).

The biggest change occurred in the dimension of 'education'. Cavalcante showed the lowest growth, with an increase of 0.243 between 2000 and 2010. In the same period Barreirinhas increased 0.307 points and Jijoca de Jericoacoara, 0.398. However, the education of the population is still very low. In 2010, only 15.19 per cent of the population of Barreirinhas 18 years or older had completed high school, while, in Cavalcante, this figure was 19.72 per cent and in Jijoca de Jericoacoara, 22.92 per cent.

Among employees in the two counties where tourism is already a success the 'indication from known people' is the main entry factor: Barreirinhas, 22.6 per cent and Jijoca de Jericoacora, 42.5 per cent. This is not the case in Cavalcante however (12.5 per cent), probably because the small size of its population makes the 'indication' less relevant: 'everybody knows everybody'.

Thus, professional training is more significant in this municipality, linked to a proactive attitude at work, which is probably due to the existence of higher competition among job seekers in tourism in this location (51.2 per cent), being ranked in second place in Jijoca de Jericoacoara (20.7 per cent) and in Barreirinhas (19.4 per cent). It should also be noted that the workforce in Cavalcante is far less qualified.

Finally, the last factor is 'previous experience of the same activity' that occupies an intermediary place from the point of view of the employers of the three study areas. It would appear that the differences between the municipalities in the hierarchy of factors can be attributed to the cycle of tourism activities and local specificities.

There has not yet been a detailed comparative study on the effects of tourism activity in the three areas. Research from the Laboratory for Tourism and Sustainability Studies

TABLE 21.8 Municipality Human Development Index and Gini Index from researched municipalities and Brazil

IDHM	Barreirinhas			Jijoca de Jericoacoara			Cavalcante			Brazil		
	1991	2000	2010	1991	2000	2010	1991	2000	2010	1991	2000	2010
TOTAL	0.251	0.361	0.570	0.189	0.422	0.652	0.285	0.396	0.584	0.493	0.612	0.727
Education	0.083	0.172	0.479	0.030	0.227	0.625	0.079	0.172	0.415	0.279	0.456	0.637
Revenues	0.358	0.435	0.515	0.421	0.506	0.614	0.458	0.509	0.595	0.647	0.692	0.739
Life expectation	0.531	0.627	0.752	0.535	0.653	0.723	0.640	0.710	0.808	0.662	0.727	0.816
GINI index	0.49	0.63	0.61	0.46	0.65	0.59	0.55	0.61	0.62	–	–	–

Source: PNUD (2013)

(LETS) at the University of Brasília in Brazil is still in progress and has not yet produced final conclusions. However, it draws attention to the fact that the dynamics of improvement in terms of social indicators are strongest in the area of Jijoca de Jericoacoara where tourism has been practised for a number of years and is more developed. The municipality had the highest HDI in 2010 (0.652), which was considered a medium level, but in 1991 it was the lowest among the three study areas (0.198). Likewise, Jijoca de Jericoacoara has the best performance in terms of per capita revenues, illiteracy rates and the Gini index. The largest improvement in social indicators, including HDI in Jijoca, has been due to the development of tourism. Could this be an indication of its ability in terms of socio-productive inclusion for the local population?

No doubt there is clear evidence. However, it is not possible to establish correlations as data on tourist flows in these municipalities is not currently available. For the time being, it remains as a substantive hypothesis to be worked on, hence, the relevance of the research on 'factors of insertion' identified in the three areas of study.

Conclusion

The green economy concept has been discussed widely in Brazil particularly since the Rio+20 conference. However, until now, the majority of people in decision-making positions in the government, industrial businesses and agribusinesses have not favoured the green economy, indicating that an economic–centred development mentality has dominated the future vision of many of these stakeholders.

However, there are some examples of governmental work with interesting projects in development: the International Relations Ministry has a centre of practical studies in sustainability – supported by PNUD – named 'Center Rio+'. The Ministry of Working Relations has a secretariat dedicated to Solidarity Economy stimulating recycling cooperatives related to socially vulnerable populations. The Ministry of the

Environment supports initiatives of vegetable extractive production as an economic alternative to keep the rain forest 'alive'. The Ministry of Tourism has stimulated and supported initiatives of responsible and sustainable tourism mainly in the Amazon Region (Lohmann and Dredge, 2012). In addition, the Ministry of Agricultural Development has several projects in the area of familiar organic agriculture.

Changing is always a challenge particularly when the new path, a green economy, stimulates technological innovation, which is a significant challenge for Brazil.

The study shows clearly that responsible tourism initiatives stimulated by public and private sectors have been growing consistently in Brazil. It strongly indicates that social inclusion and the economic development of local people in tourism destinations can foster steps in the direction of the green economy if sustained by adequate policies. The comparison between the three selected areas corroborates this perception. It seems to suggest that tourism activity is one of the activities that the green economy should prioritize. In this case, the positive results found could be applied to develop an integrated group of responsible tourism public policies focused on the most relevant factor for the socio-productive insertion of the local populations in tourism destinations: professional qualifications. It appears that this factor provides a better situation to compete with labour originating in other locations, enabling better internal circulation of the wealth produced in these places which can stimulate the key element of innovation.

These policies could construct a substantial basis for the development of 'another tourism' (TFPS, 2012; Borda *et al.*, 2013): tourism that can be an influential part of the future low-carbon socially inclusive sustainable growth. The Brazilian Responsible Tourism project could be beneficial in the move towards a green economy focusing on the economic development of the locals, with social inclusion of the excluded, and could contribute significantly to the eradication of poverty, thus representing another form of tourism that is walking the path to sustainable development, centring on the true focus of society – the people (Sachs, 2009; Borda and Nascimento, 2011; Costa, 2013).

To paraphrase Marcel Mauss (2012, p. 101) in *Essay sur Le Don* (*The Gift*) speaking about the inclusive system of King Arthur and The Round Table: the participants of the tourism industry will only find happiness when they sit as gentlemen around the wealth produced by a low-carbon socially inclusive form of developing tourism based on trust, reciprocity and mutual respect.

Notes

1 The campaign was launched jointly by UNEP's executive director, Achim Steiner, the French Minister of Ecology, Energy, Sustainable Development and Sea, the Brazilian Ministers of Environment and Tourism and other partners at the Berlin Tourism Fair in March 2008. The 'Green Passport' has already been established as a reference point for responsible travellers.

2 Paraty – a city in the Rio de Janeiro State, Brazil – was chosen to be the first tourism destination to implement the communication materials at the local level. It was selected due its natural and cultural features as well as the local commitment to sustainable tourism development.

3 The objectives of the Green Passport's working plan are to support the implementation of structured actions to improve the sustainability of the destination, strengthen the local agenda 21, promote capacity-building, environmental education, community-based ecotourism

initiatives and develop waste reduction schemes. The materials developed include radio and TV spots, an interactive website, postcards and posters (ITF-STD).

4 Accessible Tourism Programme (Portuguese), www.turismo.gov.br/turismo/o_ministerio/publicacoes/cadernos_publicacoes/17turismo_acessivel.html.
5 Nice Travel Programme (Portuguese), www.viajelegal.turismo.gov.br.
6 Brazilian Tourism Volunteering Programme, www.brasilvoluntario.gov.br/.
7 The manager of SNUC – National System of Conservation Units – is ICMBio – Chico Mendes Institute of Biodiversity – an organ of the Brazilian Ministry of Environment.
8 The FIRJAN Municipality Development rates are: low – less than 0.4; regular – 0.4 to 0.6; moderate – 0.6 to 0.8; and high development – superior to 0.8.
9 In Goias State, only 11.8 per cent of the counties have regular development (0.4 to 0.6), while 85.3 per cent are rated moderate development and 2.0 per cent have high development.
10 The purpose of the study was to recognize the recurrence of answers about the factors that the employers most take into consideration when filling a vacancy in their establishments. It is worth mentioning that the results presented here are preliminary, considering insertion primary factors, independent of the position held by the employee.

References

Borda, G.Z. (2007) Organizational social capital: Trust in superior educational institutions of Brasília [Portuguese]. PhD Thesis (Sociology), University of Brasília, Brasília.

Borda, G.Z. (2009) Trust relations adding value: social and environmental success cases [Portuguese]. In Félix, J.A.B. and Borda, G.Z. (eds). *Communication management and social and environmental responsibility: a new vision of marketing and communication for sustainable development* [Portuguese] (pp. 179–215). Editora Atlas: São Paulo.

Borda, G.Z. and Nascimento, E.P. (2011) Organizational social capital: Trust and social value [Portuguese], *Polêm!ca*, vol. 10, pp. 103–14.

Borda, G.Z., Duarte, D.C. and Serpa, A.B. (2013) Tourism for all: accessibility and social inclusion in Brazil – The case of Socorro (São Paulo State) tourism destination, International Critical Tourism Studies Conference V, Sarajevo, Bosnia & Herzegovina, 24–28 June 2013, pp. 1–17.

Bourdieu, P. (1993) *Les misères du monde*. Seuil: Paris.

Buarque, C. (1993) *O que é apartação?* Brasiliense: São Paulo.

Cohen, D. (1994) *Les infortunes de la prosperité*. Julliard: Paris.

Coleman, J.S. (1998) *Foundations of social theory*. Harvard University Press: Cambridge, MA.

Costa, H.A. (2013) *Destinos do Turismo: percursos para a sustentabilidade*. (1st edn) vol. 1, FGV: Rio de Janeiro.

Delelis, C.J., Rehder, T. and Mota, T.C. (2010) *Mosaïques d'aires protégées: réflexions et propositions de la coopération franco-brésilienne*. Ministère de l'Environnement du Brésil-MMA/Ambassade de France au Brésil/CDS-Centre pour le développement durable-Université de Brasilia: Brasilia.

Dihman, M.C. (2012) Employers' perceptions about tourism management employability skills, *Anatolia – An International Journal of Tourism and Hospitality Research*, vol. 23, no. 3, pp. 359–72.

DiMaggio, P.J. (2001) *The twenty-first-century firm: Changing economic organization in international perspective*. Princeton University Press: Princeton, NJ.

Duarte, D.C. and Borda, G.Z. (2012) Accessibility and sustainability: Challenges and opportunities in hospitality of Brasilia. In *RTD6–International Conference on Responsible Tourism 2012*, São Paulo.

FIRJAN System (2013) Índice FIRJAN de Desenvolvimento Municipal (IFDM). www.firjan.org.br/ifdm/consulta-ao-indice/, accessed 17 June 2013.

Fischer, R., Maginnis, S., Jackson, W., Barrow, E. and Jenarenaud, S. (2010) *Linking conservation and poverty reduction: landscapes, people and power*. Earthscan: London

Huang, Y. and Lin, C. (2011) Management trainee core competencies in the hospitality industry: Differences between managers and scholars, *Journal of Human Resources in Hospitality & Tourism*, vol. 10, no. 1, pp. 1–13.

IBGE (2011) Censo Demográfico 2010: resultados preliminares da Amostra. www.ibge.gov.br/home/estatistica/populacao/censo2010/resultados_preliminares_amostra/default_resultados_preliminares_amostra.shtm, accessed 18 June 2013.

IBGE (2013) Cidades. www.ibge.com.br/cidadesat/index.php, accessed 16 June 2013.

ICMBio (2013a) Parque Nacional de Jericoacoara, www.icmbio.gov.br/portal/o-que-fazemos/visitacao/ucs-abertas-a-visitacao/190-parque-nacional-de-jericoacoara.html, accessed 15 June 2013.

ICMBio (2013b) Parque Nacional dos Lençóis Maranhenses, www.icmbio.gov.br/portal/o-que-fazemos/visitacao/ucs-abertas-a-visitacao/191-parque-nacional-dos-lencois-maranhenses.html, accessed 15 June 2013.

ITF-STD (2012) Green Passport, www.unep.org/resourceefficiency/Portals/24147/scp/tourism/activities/taskforce/pdf/, accessed 8 June 2013.

Jordan, B. (1996) *A theory of poverty and social exclusion*. Polity Press: Cambridge.

Leal, G.F. (2011) *Exclusão social e ruptura dos laços sociais: Análise crítica do debate contemporâneo*. UFSC: Florianópolis.

Lenoir, R. (1989) *Les exclus: Um français sur dix* (4th edn). Seuil: Paris.

Lin, S. (2002) Exploring the relationship between hotel management courses and industry required competencies, *Journal of Teaching in Travel & Tourism*, vol. 2, no. 3/4, pp. 81–101.

Lohmann, G. and Dredge, D. (2012) (eds) *Tourism in Brazil: environment, management and segments*. Routledge: London.

Mauss, M. (2012) *Essai sur le don: forme et raison de l'échange dans les sociétés archaiques*. PUF: Paris.

MTUR (2008a) Accessible tourism: Introduction to an inclusive trip [Portuguese], www.turismo.gov.br, accessed 28 May 2013.

MTUR (2008b) Lei geral do turismo no. 11.771/08, de 17 de setembro de 2008, www.turismo.gov.br/, accessed 21 July 2013.

Nascimento, E.P. (1994) Hipóteses sobre a nova exclusão social: dos excluídos necessários aos excluídos desnecessários, *Cadernos do CRH*, no. 21, jul-dez.

Nascimento, E.P. (1997) Globalização e exclusão social: um novo fenômeno da crise da modernidade? In Dowbor *et al.* (eds), *Desafios da Globalização*. Vozes: Petrópolis.

Nasse, P., Strohl, H. and Xiberras, M. (1992) *Exclus et exclusions. Connaître les populations, comprendre les processus*. La documentation française: Paris.

OECD (2012) Green innovation in tourism can trigger major economic, social and environmental benefits, www.oecd.org/cfe/tourism/greeninnovationintourismcantriggermajoreconomic socialandenvironmentalbenefits.htm, accessed 12 June 2013.

O Povo (2013) Jericoacoara é o 8° destino turístico mais procurado do Brasil, www.opovo.com.br/app/fortaleza/2013/05/22/noticiafortaleza,3060920/jericoacoara-e-o-8-destino-turistico-mais-procurado-do-brasil.shtml, accessed 4 June 2013.

Panrotas (2013) Brazil received 5.7 million foreigners in 2012 [Portuguese], www.panrotas.com.br/noticia-turismo/mercado/brasil-recebeu-57-milhoes-de-estrangeiros-em-2012_87635.html, accessed 23 July 2013.

Paugam, S. (ed.) (1996) *L'exclusion: l'état des saviors*. La Découverte: Paris.

Planalto (2013a) Program recruits volunteers to help 12,000 spectators, tourists and media during the FIFA 2013 Cup of Confederations (Portuguese), www2.planalto.gov.br/imprensa/

noticias-de-governo/programa-...r-torcedores-turistas-e-imprensa-durante-a-copa-das-confederacoes, accessed 10 July 2013.

Planalto (2013b) National Tourism Plan 2013–2016 has goal to put Brazil among the world's largest tourism economies (Portuguese), www2.planalto.gov.br/imprensa/noticias-de-governo/plano-nac...eta-de-colocar-brasil-entre-maiores-economias-turisticas-do-mundo, accessed 18 July 2013.

PMC (2010) General data of the municipality of Cavalcante (Portuguese), www.cavalcante.go.gov.br/, accessed 6 June 2013.

PNUD (2013) Atlas do desenvolvimento humano: www.pnud.org.br/atlas/, accessed 20 July 2013.

Reddy, M.V. and Wilkes, K. (2012) *Tourism, climate change and sustainability*. Earthscan: London.

Ritchie, B.W., Burns, P. and Palmer, C. (2005) *Tourism research methods: Integrating theory with practice*. CABI: Oxford.

Rylands, A.B. and Brandon, K. (2005) Brazilian protected areas, *Conservation Biology*, vol. 19, no. 3, pp. 612–18.

Sachs, I. (2009) *The third edge: In search of ecodevelopment* [Portuguese], Companhia das Letras: São Paulo.

Sharpley, R. (2009) *Tourism development and the environment: beyond sustainability?* Earthscan: London.

Simmel, G. ([1908] 1992) *Soziologie: Untersuchungen über die Formen der Vergesellschaftung*, edited by O. Rammstedt, Frankfurt: Suhrkamp. Duncker & Humblot: Leipzig.

Swedberg, R. (2007) *Principles of economic sociology*. Princeton University Press: Princeton, NJ.

Tasso, J.P. and Nascimento, E.P. (2008) *Produção associada ao Turismo, Lençóis Maranhenses (MA)*. IABS/CDS-UnB/AECID: Brasília.

Tasso, J.P., Nascimento, E.P. and Costa, H.A. (2012) Factores de inserción socioeconómica en destinos turísticos emergentes: La búsqueda de inclusión en Barreirinhas (MA) – Brasil, *Estudios y Perspectivas en Turismo*, vol. 21, pp. 1075–93.

Terra (2013) Rota das Emoções reúne três destinos no Brasil e ganha prêmio. http://vidaeestilo.terra.com.br/turismo/brasil/rota-das-emocoes-reune-tres-destinos-no-brasil-e-ganha-premio,d1081675d4237310VgnCLD100000bbcceb0aRCRD.html, accessed 28 June 2013.

TFPS (2012) Declaration tourism, sustainability and future. http://turismoefuturo.webnode.com/sobre-nos/, accessed 14 February 2013.

UN (2012) The future we want. www.un.org/disabilities/documents/rio20_outcome_document_complete.pdf, accessed 18 February 2013.

UNWTO (2012) Destination wetlands: supporting sustainable tourism. Secretariat of the Ramsar Convention on Wetlands, Gland, Switzerland & World Tourism Organization: Madrid, Spain.

UNWTO (2013) Ethics and social dimensions of tourism, http://ethics.unwto.org/en/content/accessible-tourism, accessed 27 February 2013.

Xiberras, M. (1993) *Les théories de l'exclusion. Pour une construction de l'imaginaire de la deviance*. Merediens Klincksieck: Paris.

22

ECONOMIC GREENWASH

On the absurdity of tourism and green growth

C. Michael Hall

Introduction

Tourism's relationship to the environment has become increasingly problematic. Long held as an economic justification for conservation and use against competing industrial uses, it is becoming increasingly recognized that tourism leads to the short- and long-term decline of natural capital on local and global scales (Gössling and Hall, 2006). The continued growth in tourism-related emissions and contribution to biodiversity loss has occurred despite widespread reference to the concept of sustainable development in academic and policy circles (Hall, 2011a). The gap between concept use and empirical reality raises fundamental questions as to the prospects of achieving 'balance' between the economic, social and environmental goals entailed in sustainable development. 'Much tourism growth, as with much economic growth in general, is already uneconomic at the present margin as we currently measure it given that it is leading to a clear running down of natural capital' (Hall, 2010, p. 137). The promise of sustainable tourism has more recently been extended by the prospect of tourism in the 'green economy' and the promotion of 'green growth' (UNEP, 2011a). Yet, is it really possible to promote economic growth (and potentially visitor growth) over the long-term without damaging the stock of natural capital?

This chapter seeks to critique the notion of green growth and tourism's role within a so-called green economy. It does not deny the importance of a green economy that maintains or enhances natural capital, rather it suggests that such an economic paradigm needs a much broader understanding of the changes required to achieve these goals than appears to be the case. This chapter revisits the growth debate and links some of the discussions in tourism with respect to sustainability and long-standing concerns over the long-term feasibility and desirability of economic growth. It identifies some of the major weaknesses in the green growth/economy idea, particularly the belief in the value of technological change, innovation and efficiency in the absence of an appreciation of rebound effects and the need for sufficiency-based consumption. The chapter then concludes with some clues as to a possible genuinely green economic future for tourism that lie within the ideas of steady-state economics and economic degrowth. However, it is recognized that there are substantial political and academic barriers to the likelihood of such approaches being adopted.

Growth, environment, tourism: fiddling while Rome burns?

Although the current focus on green growth and concerns over the effects of global environmental change might suggest otherwise, critical examination of the relationship between growth and environment have existed since the 1960s. Figure 22.1 indicates some of the key works on growth and the environment in relation to humanity's global ecological footprint (GEF) from the 1960s through to the early 2000s. Some key tourism concepts related to reducing tourism's impacts are also noted. This is done, in part, because academic debates are connected to economic and biophysical realities.

Ecological Footprint is a measure of human demand on the biosphere. It measures the amount of biologically productive land and water area required to produce all the resources an individual, population, or activity consumes, and absorb the waste generated, given prevailing technology and resource management practices. This area is then compared with biological capacity (biocapacity), the amount of biologically productive land and water areas that are available to generate these resources and to absorb the waste, to identify a standard unit, the global hectare (gha), that quantifies the Earth's biocapacity in a given year (Ewing *et al.*, 2010).

In 2007, humanity's GEF was 18.0 billion global hectares (gha). With a world population at 6.7 billion people in 2007 the average person's footprint was 2.7 gha. Biocapacity was measured at 11.9 billion gha available or 1.8 gha per person. This overshoot of approximately 50 per cent means that in 2007 humanity used the equivalent of 1.5 Earths to support its consumption (Ewing *et al.*, 2010) leading to natural capital depletion and waste accumulation, such as greenhouse gas emissions. 'Half of the global footprint was attributable to just 10 countries in 2007. . . with the United States of America and China alone each respectively using 21 and 24 per cent of the Earth's biocapacity' (Ewing *et al.*, 2010, p. 18).

No assessment is available of the footprint of tourism on a global scale, although tourism's consumption of natural resources is recognized as being substantial (Gössling and Hall, 2006; Hall, 2011a). Patterson's (2005) study of biocapacity for Val di Mers, Italy, found that when arrival transport to and from the destination is included, the tourist equivalent resident Ecological Footprint increased from 5.36 to 38.15 gha/person. Marzouki *et al.* (2012) found that tourists to Tunisia had a footprint of the order of 0.53 gha per tourist for a length of stay of 5.1 days and those to the Seychelles, a footprint of the order of 1.85 gha per tourist for a length of stay of 10.4 days. The local results depend on inclusions into the assessment of biocapacity, with Patterson's (2005) study being the most detailed. If these results are converted to global tourism figures they lead to footprints of 254.4 million gha (Tunisian figure), 888 million gha (Seychelles figure) (0.075 times global biocapacity), and 18,312 million gha (Val di Mers' figure including transport) (1.54 times global biocapacity). The higher end figure indicates the critical role of transport's contribution to tourism's ecological footprint, an observation also reinforced by research on tourism's greenhouse gas emissions (Gössling *et al.*,

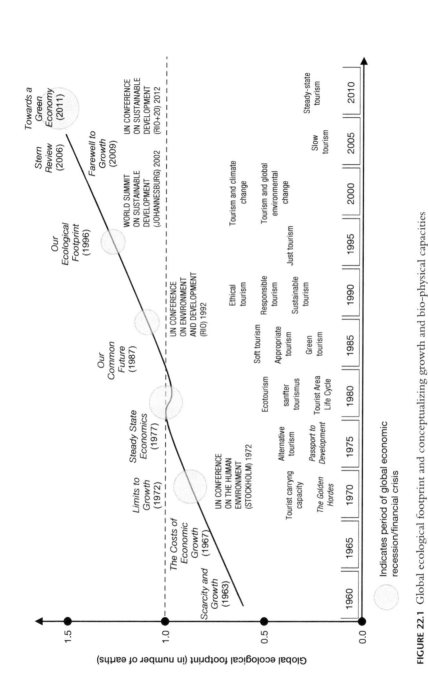

FIGURE 22.1 Global ecological footprint and conceptualizing growth and bio-physical capacities

Source: Hall (2013c)

2013), and reinforces the importance of understanding tourism's impacts throughout the entire tourism system rather than at just the destination (Hall and Lew, 2009).

The growth debate

The first challenges to economic growth emerged in the 1960s. This was also a time of increased awareness of environmental problems (Carson, 1962) and the threat of overpopulation (Ehrlich, 1968). In this intellectual climate the US think-tank Resources for the Future published *Scarcity and growth* (Barnett and Morse, 1963) which concluded, in a manner that presages present-day discussion, that technological innovation, resource substitution, recovery and discovery of new resources encouraged by the free market system would make Malthusian concerns obsolete. 'A limit may exist, but it can be neither defined nor specified in economic terms . . . Nature imposes particular scarcities, not an inescapable general scarcity' (Barnett and Morse, 1963, p. 11). Economic doubts about the feasibility or desirability of economic growth were initially few. However, by the end of the decade the work of Boulding (1966), on the economics of 'spaceship earth', and Mishan (1967), had started to open up spaces of critique that also contributed to works by Ayres and Kneese (1969) on externalities and Odum (1971) that led to the development of industrial ecology; Georgescu-Roegen's (1971) research on entropy, economic processes and energy/matter transformation that served as one of the foundations for ecological economics as well as concepts of degrowth, and Daly's work on the stationary state economy (Pigou, 1943) that developed into steady state economics (Daly, 1972, 1991). Nevertheless, broader awareness of such work was raised by the publication of the *Limits to growth* (LTG) report (Meadows *et al.*, 1972).

The benchmark LTG study examined the interaction of global population, industrial production, food production, pollution and natural resource systems. It assumed that population and industrial production were growing exponentially, in a world with absolute fixed available resources. In each of the scenarios that Meadows *et al.* (1972) ran, population collapsed during the twenty-first century due to ever-increasing pollution and food shortages along with other factors such as soil erosion. The study coincided with the hosting of the first United Nations Conference on the Human Environment held in Stockholm. However, LTG's main policy recommendation of stabilization similar to Daly's (1972) work on steady-state economics, was generally dismissed. In a foretaste of more recent debates over responsibilities for and limitations on carbon emissions, delegates at the Stockholm conference made it clear that they were not going to accept policies arising from resource limits that would hamper their future development (Beckerman, 1972). This is perhaps not surprising given the dismissal of LTG by the vast majority of mainstream economists. For example, Beckerman (1972) suggests,

> that the problem of environmental pollution is a simple matter of correcting a minor resource misallocation by means of pollution charges, and that most of the common objections to such a policy can be demolished with the aid of no more economics than that which is the stock-in-trade of any second year economics student. . . . [LTG] was such a brazen, impudent piece of nonsense that nobody could possibly take it seriously so that it would be a waste of time talking about it.
>
> (Beckerman, 1972, p. 327)

As Perez-Carmona (2012) notes, again anticipating much of the contemporary debate over response to climate change adaptation, 'The common argumentative line was that technological progress and the market mechanism could prevent scarcity and pollution from constituting a substantial limitation on long-term economic growth' (2012, p. 91). For example, Cole *et al.* (1973) reran the LTG model under different assumptions and suggested that an annual 2 per cent improvement in technological progress would postpone collapse indefinitely. To do this, the rates of improvement in available resources (through discovery and recycling) and pollution control 'must obviously be competitive with growth rates of population and consumption so that even if the overall growth is rapid, it is also "balanced"' (Cole *et al.*, 1973, p. 119). But, as Lecomber (1975, p. 42) warns, 'Everything hinges on the rate of technical progress and possibilities of substitution'.

LTG together with concerns over energy dependency and biodiversity loss helped contribute to the debates on sustainability in the late 1970s and early 1980s (Dryzek, 1997). For example, the 1980 *Global 2000 Report to the President* began by stating that

> If present trends continue, the world in 2000 will be more crowded, more polluted, less stable ecologically, and more vulnerable to disruption than the world we live in now. Serious stresses involving population, resources, and environment are clearly visible ahead. Despite greater material output, the world's people will be poorer in many ways than they are today.
>
> (Speth, 1980, p. 695)

The follow-up to the 1972 Stockholm Conference was the World Commission on Environment and Development (WCED) established in 1983. Although works on sustainable development had been published before its release, the WCED (1987) report, *Our common future* (often referred to by the name of its chairwoman, Gro Harlem Brundtland) undoubtedly set the benchmark for sustainable development discourse to the present-day. As has been discussed elsewhere, the concept of sustainable development has been extremely successful, including in tourism (Hall, 2011a). Dryzek (1997) suggests that the report was written in such a way as to ensure that it also received support from business interests. Although the WCED (1987, p. 44) noted that 'consumption standards within the bounds of the ecological possible and to which all can reasonably aspire' are required as part of achieving greater equity, they nevertheless suggested that although ultimate ecological limits exist, reaching them could be delayed by technological innovation. Importantly for the present discussion they also concluded that 'the international economy must speed up world growth while respecting the environmental constraints' (WCED, 1987, p. 89), primarily by encouraging qualitative economic growth that was less material/resource/energy (MRE) intensive and more equitable, i.e. more decarbonized and dematerialized–an approach that lies at the heart of much discussion of green growth to the present.

However, the WCED (1987) approach failed to recognize several significant implications of their strategy. First, while dematerialization may occur at a per unit level, overall industrial expansion continues. Second, becoming more efficient leads to an increase in throughput (input plus output), otherwise known as the 'Jevons paradox' or 'rebound effect' (Polimeni *et al.*, 2008) (discussed below). Third, being 'part of an interdependent world economy' (WCED, 1987, p. 51) provided a rationale not only for further liberalization of the global economy and the reduction of trade barriers by less developed countries (LDCs) but also for already wealthy countries to further pursue economic growth by increasing consumption so as encourage economic growth in the LDCs. Indeed, this last point has become one of the cornerstones of so-called 'pro-poor' tourism development. 'The alternative that poor countries could create their own markets' (Daly, 1991, p. 151), including with respect to tourism, is not one that has been greatly encouraged. However, the benefits of export-led growth as a means for poverty alleviation is moot (Zapata *et al.*, 2011; Perez-Carmona, 2012). As Simms (2008, p. 49) observes:

> During the 1980s, for every $100 added to the value of the global economy, around $2.20 found its way to those living below the World Bank's absolute poverty line. During the 1990s, that share shrank to just 60 cents. This inequity in income distribution – more like a flood up than a trickle down – means that for the poor to get slightly less poor, the rich have to get very much richer. It would take around $166 worth of global growth to generate $1 extra for people living on below $1 a day.

A further challenge to economic growth, and one that has become increasingly important in tourism, is climate change. The publication of the Stern Review (Stern, 2007) brought the relationship between economic growth and the environment back to the forefront of public policy, However, as Jackson (2009, p. 11) notes: 'it's telling that it took an economist commissioned by a government treasury to alert the world to things climate scientists – most notably the Intergovernmental Panel on Climate Change (IPCC) – had been saying for years'. Nevertheless, despite much of value in the report,

> When Stern published his review in 2006, the global economy already required almost 1.5 planets, yet a discussion on the causality's direction between economic growth and ecological obliteration . . . was completely absent in Stern's work. Economic growth was Stern's default assumption for the entire globe.
>
> (Perez-Carmona, 2012, p. 107)

Green growth and the green economy

The notion of a green economy is not new (Miles, 1985). For example, as a response to the WCED (1987), Pearce *et al.* (1989) provided a 'blueprint for a green economy' as part of an extension of the concept of sustainable development to the UK (see also Jacobs, 1991). A number of works have also used the term to describe 'green capitalism' or market-based approaches to environmental problems and/or the development of new green and ethical markets (Patridge, 1987; Henderson and Seth, 2006), although others have provided a more fundamental critique (Milani, 2001) or alternative economic structures (Galtung, 1990; Seyfang, 2009). However, current discourse has been stimulated by the inter-related responses of various NGOs, green parties and institutions to the unemployment and economic issues created by the global financial crisis from 2008 on. These can be broadly categorized as belonging to a 'green new deal' approach in that they are marked by substantial state intervention in environmental infrastructure and development as a means of kickstarting the economy in a manner reminiscent of the Great Depression New Deal.

Two think-tank reports are arguably seminal to contemporary green economy/ growth thinking; a July 2008 report published by the UK New Economics Foundation (Elliott *et al.*, 2008), and a September 2008 report sponsored by the Center for American Progress (Pollin *et al.*, 2008). Elliott *et al.* (2008) called for a Keynesian style 'new green deal' in order to respond to the 'triple crunch' (credit-fuelled financial crisis, accelerating climate change, and soaring energy prices underpinned by peak oil) that the world was facing. Two main initiatives were outlined; first, a re-regulation of national and international financial systems, and major changes to taxation systems, and second, a sustained investment and deployment programme in energy conservation and renewable energies, coupled with effective demand management.

The Center for American Progress report outlined a $100 billion 'green economic recovery' programme to stimulate the US economy 'and leave it in a better position for sustainable prosperity' (Pollin *et al.*, 2008, p. 1). The proposal was to invest in six green infrastructure investment areas (building retrofitting, mass transit/freight rail, smart grid, wind power, solar power, advanced biofuels) in order to transition to a low-carbon economy 'to create new green jobs – particularly in the struggling construction and manufacturing sectors' (Pollin *et al.*, 2008, p. 1), a proposal that it was claimed would promote 'sustainable economic growth'.

Both the Elliott *et al.* (2008) and Pollin *et al.* (2008) reports coincided with the economic zeitgeist in that many developed economies were seeking to come to terms with the global financial and economic crisis. In late 2008, UNEP (2008; Steiner and Sukhdev, 2010) launched an inquiry into how a 'green economy' model could be seeded at this critical time as part of a 'global green new deal' (GGND) in order to stimulate a sustainable recovery. Promoted as an 'initiative to get the global markets back to work' (UNEP, 2008), according to Pavan Sukdhev, a senior banker from Deutsche Bank seconded to UNEP,

> Investments will soon be pouring back into the global economy – the question is whether they go into the old, extractive, short-term economy of yesterday or a new green economy that will deal with multiple challenges while generating multiple economic opportunities for the poor and the well-off alike.
>
> (UNEP, 2008)

The six sectors initially identified by UNEP as likely to generate the biggest transition in terms of economic returns, environmental sustainability, and job creation were:

- clean energy and clean technologies including recycling;
- rural energy, including renewables and sustainable biomass;
- sustainable agriculture, including organic agriculture;
- ecosystem infrastructure;
- reduced emissions from deforestation and forest degradation (REDD);
- sustainable cities including planning, transportation and green building.

The publication of a UNEP policy brief in March 2009 provided further impetus to the development of the green economy concept, with the three broad objectives of a GGND being

1) Make a major contribution to reviving the world economy, saving and creating jobs, and protecting vulnerable groups;
2) Reduce carbon dependency and ecosystem degradation, putting economies on a path to clean and stable development; and
3) Further sustainable and inclusive growth, achievement of the MDGs, and end extreme poverty by 2015.

(UNEP, 2009a, p. 5)

However by April 2010, Edward Barbier, one of the architects of the GGND commented, 'most national recovery plans have missed this opportunity to invest in the planet while saving the economy' (Barbier, 2010, p. 832). This was in part because the G20 countries had not invested a recommended expenditure 1 per cent of GDP on green initiatives (only China and South Korea had exceeded this target), nor had they removed resource-depleting energy, agriculture and fishing subsidies, advanced far on the taxing and trading of carbon emissions, or substantially aided the world's poor (Barbier, 2010). Nevertheless, despite such setbacks the notion of a green economy has become firmly embedded in the discourse of sustainability, with the UNEP (2011a) *Green economy report* providing the new institutional orthodoxy of the significance of sustainable/ green growth that has already influenced tourism studies, if not the tourism industry.

According to UNEP (2011a, p. 16) the green economy is 'one that results in improved human well-being and social equity, while reducing environmental risks and ecological scarcities'. Such a definition is as broad as that of the WCED on sustainable development. However, like the concept of sustainable development the acceptability – and potential weakness – of the green economy probably lies in its generality. In contrast to the neoliberal policies that pervade global governance, including with respect to tourism (Hall, 2011b), UNEP (2011a) argue that market instruments alone cannot manage environmental externalities and that therefore substantial government intervention is warranted to both develop green technologies and regulate activities that harm the environment. The UNEP also suggest, 'The concept of a "green economy" does not *replace* sustainable development, but there is now a growing recognition that achieving sustainability rests almost entirely on getting the economy right '(UNEP, 2011b, p. 2), although it is interesting to note Khor's (2011, p. 6) warning that 'if the green economy concept gains prominence, while the sustainable development concept recedes, there may be a loss of the use of the holistic sustainable development approach'.

So what does getting the economy right mean? First, there remains a continued commitment to growth, albeit 'sustainable' and 'green'. Second, UNEP (2011a) maintains that while there are a variety of causes for several concurrent crises that have unfolded since 2000: climate, biodiversity, fuel, food, water, and the global financial system, 'at a fundamental level they all share a common feature: the gross misallocation of capital' (UNEP, 2011a, p. 14). However, the trajectories of socio-technical systems with a limited focus on more environmentally benign investment areas were set well before 2000. As Perez-Carmona (2012, p. 110) suggests, 'An alternative fundamental reason would be that ecological and related social problems exist because of the metabolism of the industrial economy, and the economic policy of perpetual economic growth largely driven by the search of profits and rents in a non-growing planet'. Third, for how long can improvements in MRE efficiency be sustained? Is it possible to have a completely, or even substantially, dematerialized economy in real terms? This is where the notion of green growth runs up against the 'Jevons paradox' (Polimeni et al., 2008; Santarius, 2012).

On the rebound

In *The coal question* (1865), William Stanley Jevons noted that, paradoxically, efficiency improvements in the use of coal result not in savings of coal but in increased coal consumption, because technical progress boosts the demand for energy. In contemporary studies of efficiency and productivity the paradox is referred to as a rebound effect that 'describes the increased demand that is caused or at least enabled by one or a number of productivity increases' (Santarius, 2012, p. 5). This means that *efficiency does not equal savings*. Such an observation has enormous issues for tourism given the emphasis on technological efficiencies in reducing emissions and energy consumption.

> Tourism in a green economy refers to tourism activities that can be maintained, or sustained, indefinitely in their social, economic, cultural, and environmental contexts: 'sustainable tourism'. Sustainable tourism . . . aspires to be more energy efficient and more 'climate sound' (e.g. by using renewable energy); consume less water; minimise waste.
>
> (UNEP, 2011a, p. 416)

There are several rebound effects that can potentially affect the potential of green growth to limit the decline of natural capital (Table 22.1). Three types of rebound effects are generally identified (Santarius, 2012). First, the direct rebound effect, indicated by increased demand for the same product or service. For example, the switch from a 6-litre to a 3-litre car may result in additional journeys being made in the 3-litre car. Second, indirect rebound effects, expressed in increased demand for different products or services: The savings made by the change from a 6-litre to a 3-litre car may be used for other consumption and may result in consumers taking more holidays by air. Third, structural or macroeconomic rebound effects: Because more consumers drive 3-litre cars, overall demand for petrol is lower, causing relative prices to fall and creating an incentive for increased demand for energy-using products in other sectors. The level of a rebound effect is generally defined as the percentage of an efficiency-boosting measure/technology that is offset by a rise in demand. According to Santarius (2012, p. 4),

> in the long term and on average, combined rebound effects of at least 50 per cent must be assumed . . . energy efficiency improvements in an economic system will on average yield half the theoretical savings potential of efficiency technologies and measures, and in some cases the saving that is achieved will be even less than this.

TABLE 22.1 Rebound effects

Financial rebound effects	Increases in energy efficiency result in an income gain and therefore encourage new consumption, e.g., the income effect may be triggered if petrol costs fall by 50 per cent when a driver switches from a 6-litre to a 3-litre car and releases money for increased energy use in other areas – whether for additional journeys or for other goods and services that also consumes energy.
Material rebound	The manufacture and use of more efficient technologies can be accompanied by increased use of energy, e.g. to produce efficient building insulation products or to develop new infrastructure and markets for energy-efficient products.
Psychological rebound	The shift to energy-efficient technologies can boost the symbolic meaning of these goods and services, e.g, increases in the driving distance of 'environmentally friendly' cars as compared with their previous vehicle.
Cross-factor rebound	Increasing the productivity of labour or capital can increase the demand for energy, e.g. through mechanization and automation that uses energy or if the use of energy-efficient technology leads to time savings.

Sources: Jenkins *et al.* (2011), Santarius (2012), Hall (2013a)

Rebound effects do not appear to have been considered in any forecasts of potential efficiency gains in the tourism industry with respect to either energy consumption or emissions (Jenkins *et al.*, 2011). No studies have been conducted on rebound effects specifically in relation to tourism, although Sorrell (2007) observed that increased consumption of air travel and tourism would potentially be driven by increases in macroeconomic efficiency gains, while Hall (2009, 2010) cautioned as to the impacts of an efficiency focus in relation to sustainable tourism consumption. Barker (2009) modelled the rebound effects resulting from the global energy efficiency measures incorporated into the IPCC's (2007a) Fourth Assessment Report and estimated that for transport there would be a worldwide direct rebound of 9.1 per cent in 2020 and 9.1 per cent in 2030, and a macroeconomic rebound of 26.9 per cent in 2020 and 43.1 per cent in 2030, thus leading to a total economy wide rebound of 36.0 per cent in 2020 and 52.2 per cent in 2030. This compares with an estimated rebound for all sectors of 31 per cent of the projected energy savings potential by 2020, rising to 52 per cent by 2030 (Barker, 2009). If this scale of rebound were applied to tourism then, even allowing for the estimated greater use of low-carbon fuels, the potential increase in tourism-related emissions would likely be over 200 per cent by 2030 (Hall *et al.*, 2013). This means that by 2030 the impacts of forecast energy-efficiencies on proposed tourism emissions reduction will potentially be more than halved and that the reduction in the potential gains in energy efficiencies over the period to 2035 (Table 22.2) are cut by more than 35 per cent (Gössling *et al.*, 2013).

Table 22.2 illustrates the enormous challenges facing the tourism industry with respect to emissions reduction and green growth. Forecasts suggest an increase in growth above any targeted or suggested increases in per passenger/tourist efficiency that are estimated at around 1.5–2 per cent per year (Hall, 2010, 2011a; Gössling *et al.*, 2013). For example, the UNWTO forecasts growth in international tourist arrivals 2010–30 of 3.3 per cent

TABLE 22.2 Tourism sector emissions and mitigation targets

Year	Emission estimates and BAU projections (CO_2)		Mitigation targets	
	UNWTO, UNEP, and WMO (2008)	WEF (2009)	WTTC (2009)[1]	5% allocation of CO_2 emissions from a 'below +2°C scenario' to tourism sector[2]
2005	1.304 Gt	1.476 Gt	–	
2020	2.181 Gt	2.319 Gt	0.978 Gt	1.254 Gt
2035	3.059 Gt	3.164 Gt	0.652 Gt	0.940 Gt

1 WTTC (2009) aspirational emission reduction targets are −25% in 2020 and −50% in 2035 (both from 2005 levels specified by UNWTO, UNEP and WMO (2008).

2 Pathway that limits global average temperature increases to below 2°C; assuming CO_2 continues to represent approximately 57%(IPCC, 2007b) of the median estimate of 44 Gt CO_2-e total GHG emissions in 2020 and 2035 (Rogelj et al., 2011) and the tourism sector continues to represent approximately 5% of global CO_2 emissions (UNWTO-UNEP, 2008; WEF, 2009) over the same timeframe (Gössling et al., 2013).

per year (central projection). These estimates are also consistent with those of aircraft producers, which project that the global fleet of aircraft will double between 2011–2031, with growth in revenue passenger kilometres increasing by 150 per cent (Airbus, 2012; Boeing, 2012). UNEP (2011a, p. 438) proposes that in a BAU scenario 2011–2050, tourism growth will imply increases in energy consumption (111 per cent), greenhouse gas emissions (105 per cent), water consumption (150 per cent), and solid waste disposal (252 per cent). Even in the optimistic greener investment scenario the tourism-related drawdown of natural capital still increases:

> the tourism sector can grow steadily in the coming decades (exceeding the BAU scenario by 7 per cent in terms of the sector GDP) while saving significant amounts of resources and enhancing its sustainability. The green investment scenario is expected to undercut the corresponding BAU scenario by 18 per cent for water consumption, 44 per cent for energy supply and demand, and 52 per cent for CO_2 emissions.
>
> (UNEP, 2011a, p. 438)

It is a cruel joke to describe a situation in which absolute growth in emissions and other impacts continue to expand as a result of tourism growth exceeding efficiency gains as 'green growth' or a 'green economy'. But this is what is being done. Are you laughing yet?

Significantly, the above UNEP (2011a) figures do not consider rebound effects although elsewhere, for example with respect to maritime and aviation emissions, the report notes, 'Aviation emissions are projected to increase exponentially in the next few decades, fuelled by income growth and reductions in the price of air travel' (UNEP,

2011a, p. 383). While behavioural responses and rebound effects are recognized (UNEP, 2011a, pp. 257, 267, 357, 360, 461, 474, 479, 481), together with fragmented governance, lack of affordability, investment, negative tradeoffs, consumer preference, vested interests, and risk aversion (UNEP 2011a, p. 473), as barriers to the green economy, UNEP (2011a), rather optimistically, appears to suggest that such savings can be put into further energy-saving consumption. However, in tourism the significance of the rebound effect, as well as some of the other barriers, remains generally unacknowledged.

The industry response to green economy issues, such as climate change, suggests that technical solutions that promote greater energy efficiency are the primary means to address emissions. However, as stressed above, absolute emission reductions are unlikely, as growth in transport volumes and infrastructure outweighs efficiency gains (Scott et al., 2010), and potentially large rebound effects (Santarius, 2012) have not been accounted for in the tourism sector. The IEA (2009) suggest that the technical capacity to reduce the energy intensity of new aircraft is equivalent to 0.6–1.0 per cent per year on average and that the annual historical rate of improvement in load factors (approximately 0.2 per cent per year) could reach close to its upper limit by 2025. The reliance on biofuel as a technological solution remains problematic because of uncertainties over full life-cycle emission benefits and land-use requirements that put energy and food crops in conflict (UNEP, 2009b; Vera-Morales and Schäfer, 2009).

Furthermore, even if new technologies and energy sources do become available, this does not mean that 'old' carbon-intensive energy sources stop being used. Instead, they will probably run in parallel as investment costs are paid off (Hoffmann, 2011; Hall et al., 2013). The optimism of a green growth paradigm based on MRE efficiency and major changes in the energy mix to renewables yet providing for continued increases in visitor numbers (Cabrini, 2012; UNEP, 2011a) is therefore extremely problematic given constraints of the arithmetic of growth and efficiency limits, governance and market limits, and systemic limits (Hoffmann, 2011) (Table 22.3). There are then significant limits of containment (Santarius, 2012): Efficiency standards harbour the greatest risk of evoking rebound effects. Real income gains and falls in market prices that arise from efficiency increases can theoretically be absorbed by ecotaxes. However, this would require a complex taxation scheme with sector and product-specific tax rates, which is difficult to implement (e.g. the EU travel tax). Finally, in theory rebound effects cannot arise if resource use is limited by caps that provide absolute upper limits on consumption/waste. However, unless caps are introduced globally, rebound effects can still occur via international trade and increased imports, including tourism.

Beyond green growth?

The concept of green growth raises the fundamental difference between sustainable growth and sustainable development. Growth refers to the quantitative increase in economic output, whereas development refers to an increase in the quality of output *without* an increase in MRE use (Hall, 2010, 2011a). Given the role of rebound effects and the interconnectedness of growth and MRE consumption, 'Energy-efficient technological improvements as the solution for the world's energy and environmental problems will not work. Rather energy-efficient technology improvements are counter-

TABLE 22.3 Key weaknesses of the green growth paradigm

Arithmetic of growth and efficiency limits

- Dominance of the prevailing growth paradigm in policy-making and advice
- Enhanced MRE efficiency will encourage 'rebound effects' (Jevons Paradox)
- Much of the MRE efficiency that has been gained in developed countries has been achieved by outsourcing very intense MRE production to developing countries
- Technically challenging to completely replace fossil fuel with renewables, especially as old and new technologies exist on parallel energy paths for considerable time periods
- The relative scarcity of conventional oil, which is especially important for transport, means that it is likely to experience increased prices but extreme price explosions are unlikely
- Continued absolute increase from tourism sector (as well as other sectors such as agriculture) at a rate exceeding efficiency gains
- Population growth, and hence consumption growth, including mobility consumption, are forecast to continue

Governance and market constraints

- Governance via market-based instruments has been problematic
- International governance regimes for the environment are incoherent
- Level of public debt complicates structural change
- Externalization of costs as fundamental part of the capitalist market economy
- Need for appropriate indicators
- Political willingness to use carrots, e.g. subsidies, but not sticks, e.g. increased regulation
- Colossal de-carbonization of the economy and society will only be achieved if current consumption patterns, methods and lifestyles are also subject to profound change

Systemic limits

- Bio-physical limits, including those entangled with growing emissions, pollution, and global environmental change
- The capitalist economic system is predicated upon growth, capitalism rests upon the perpetual search for surplus value (profit), and functions poorly in a contracting economy (with the exception of short-term cyclical crises)

Sources: Hoffmann (2011), Hall (2011a, 2013a, 2013b, 2014), Jenkins *et al.* (2011), Santarius (2012)

productive, promoting energy consumption. Yet energy efficiency improvements continue to be promoted as a panacea' (Polimeni *et al.*, 2008, p. 169). Yet this is not to suggest that MRE-efficient technologies should not be promoted. Rather it depends on their context and the overall nature of consumption, not only within tourism but the transfer of consumption between tourism and other aspects of what individuals consume within specific socio-technical systems. As Polimeni *et al.* (2008, p. 169) note, 'If individual energy consumption behaviours are significantly altered to reduce consumption and this behaviour is unwavering, then energy efficient technologies can further reduce energy consumption'.

So what is to be done? As Polimeni *et al.* (2008) argue, and what others have been suggesting in the debate over growth and the environment since the 1960s (Daly, 1991; Latouche, 2009), is that a sufficiency approach that looks to limit consumption patterns to bio-physical constraints is required. As long as economic growth is the goal, with green or not, 'technological progress will not result in biodiversity conservation; rather, an expansion of the human niche and the consumption of more natural resources will result' (Czech, 2006, p. 1653).

An alternative conceptualization of sustainable tourism development can be found in Figure 22.2. This is an approach grounded in ecological economics and suggests, for the reasons noted above with respect to efficiency-oriented green economy approaches, that sustainability also requires attention to sufficiency, i.e. that behaviour and system change are essential if tourism's contribution (or humanity's for that matter) to the drawdown of natural capital is to be attended to. This also means paying heed to those commentators who have focused on the problematic fixation with economic growth, what Georgescu-Roegen (1977) termed 'growth mania', including in tourism.

Daly's (1991) concept of an ontological steady state as:

> an economy with constant stocks of people and artefacts, maintained at some desired, sufficient levels by low rates of maintenance 'throughput', that is, by the lowest feasible flows of matter and energy from the first stage of production (depletion of low entropy materials from the environment) to the last stage of consumption (pollution of the environment with high entropy wastes and exotic materials)
>
> Daly (1991, p. 16)

provides the basis for defining steady state tourism as a tourism system that encourages qualitative development, with a focus on quality of life and social and ecological well-being measures, but not aggregate quantitative growth to the detriment of natural capital (Hall, 2009). The problem with tourism is that the larger something has grown, the greater, ceteris paribus, are its maintenance costs. More new production, more throughput, is required just to keep the larger stock constant (Daly, 1996, p. 68). Given the central role of service in contemporary economies it is significant to note that Daly (1991) emphasized the straightforward maxim that service is the ultimate benefit of economic activity and should be maximized while throughput is the ultimate cost of this service and should be minimised. Indeed, Latouche's (2009) recommendations for degrowth, or rightsizing the economy, of restructure, redistribute, reduce, reuse and recycle, are all entailed in Daly's (1991) stock-service throughput notion and are useful and stimulating keywords for implementing it (Kerschner, 2010).

Yet changing consumption and concomitant lifestyles is a socio-political issue, not just an economic and environmental one, factoring in equity within and between societies in particular (Khor, 2011). There can be no presumption that growth alone increases welfare, rather welfare is an issue of distribution of wealth. If progressive taxes and appropriate regulation and state intervention were necessary for the functioning of the welfare state as a response to the socio-economic shocks of the Second World War and the preceding depression, then similar socio-technical system change is surely required for the current environmental shock. This is particularly important because

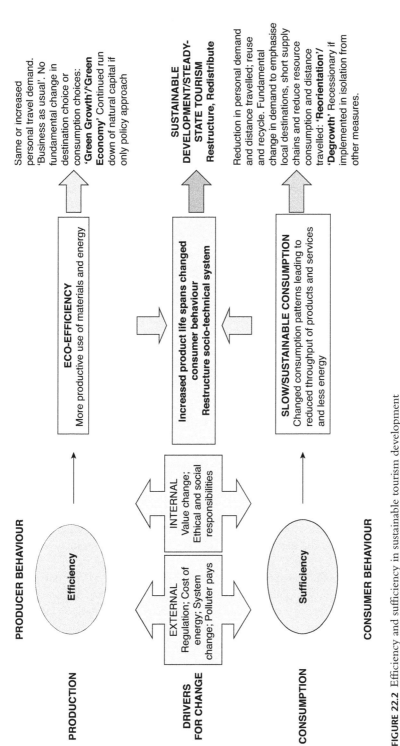

FIGURE 22.2 Efficiency and sufficiency in sustainable tourism development

Source: After Hall (2009)

of the limited capacities for changing individual behaviours via social marketing or nudging in the required time period to avoid disastrous climate change (Hall, 2013b; 2014). As Vermeulen (2009, p. 25) argues, the focus of responses to overconsumption needs to be on

> structures as a whole, rather than their individual actions. Short-term solutions may rely on improving efficiencies within existing modes of production and consumption (reformist changes). In the longer term, however, what is needed is a rethink of how and what we consume (transformist changes).

Green growth and the green economy is therefore mere reform of a socio-economic system unsustainably geared towards economic growth. It is not a major shift in policy paradigm (Hall, 2011a). It is not just a case of tourism getting more efficient. It is shifting consumption around spatially and temporally and reducing its overall emissions and MRE consumption. Tourism needs to adopt the 'polluter pays' principle, and shift to shorter trips and, in some cases, less frequent travel and longer stays (Peeters and Landré, 2011). This will mean that many destinations and sectors will actually benefit, the exception being aviation, which for too long has avoided the environmental costs of its activities. As Figure 22.1 indicated, there is a long legacy of alternative tourisms seeking to describe more sustainable forms of tourism. Perhaps some may think that to this we should now add another – Utopian tourism – for what is called for is a fundamental transformation not only of tourism mobility but the socio-technical system within which it resides. But what other choice is there?

Conclusion: Morality, Heisenberg and a final twist

If current trends continue and if no environmental tipping points are met, the GEF will have reached a factor of 2 by 2030, meaning that we would need two planets to sustain our population and consumption levels (Hoffmann, 2011). Any social system in its process of evolution has to decide how to become a different system, while maintaining its own individuality in this process (Funtowicz and Ravetz, 1990). This also applies to the tourism system. Choices with respect to sustainability are also a problem of reflexivity at both the individual and collective level – the willingness to change yourself in order to be able to co-evolve with other humans and the environment (Polimeni et al., 2008). This applies as much to the tourism academy as it does to the tourism industry and the wider community. Explicitly addressing 'the moral and cultural issues raised by the predominant emphasis in economic thinking on individual preferences, self-interest and competitive growth' (Ekins, 1993, p. 286) also means considering how tourism education (and research) promulgates growthism, over-consumption and industry orthodoxies as part of 'good [BAU] practice'. As Daly (1991) suggests steady-state economics is concerned as much with 'moral growth' as it is with biophysical equilibrium.

Nevertheless, a sting in the sustainable tale still awaits. A steady-state economy inevitably requires stabilization or degrowth of the number of humans. We cannot continue to expand the potential tourist market. Humanity's carrying capacity is defined by the maximum sustainable impact (I) of our society. Impact (I) in turn is given by the equation I = PAT: population size (P), times its affluence (consumption) (A), times the environmental damage (T) caused (Daily and Ehrlich, 1992). The reduction of (A) by sufficiency as well as that of (T) by sustainable behaviour and technological progress cannot proceed indefinitely (Polimeni *et al.*, 2008), so (I) will inevitably continue to grow if population is not stabilized or reduced (Kerschner, 2010).

Perhaps we may be lucky. Perhaps the Heisenberg principle may apply in that the act of observing and forecasting events can affect the outcome by stimulating an appropriate response. However, the embrace of green growth by many in tourism, including government, industry, academics and especially consultants suggests that this is unlikely. Green growth and many of the green economy measures will only provide real prosperity for some. Although major environmental and climate change-related disasters may roll back development gains, in particular when certain tipping points are reached (Hoffmann, 2011), we can sit back secure in the knowledge that under the conventional system of measuring economic growth, GDP may likely increase in response to such massive environmental and human loss.

References

Airbus (2012) *Global market forecast 2012–2031*, www.airbus.com/company/market/forecast/, accessed 23 November 2012.

Ayres, R.U. and Kneese, A.V. (1969) Production, consumption and externalities. *The American Economic Review*, vol. 59, pp. 282–97.

Barbier, E. (2010) How is the global green new deal going? *Nature*, 8 April, vol. 464, pp. 832–3.

Barker, T. (2009) The macroeconomic rebound effect and the world economy, *Energy Efficiency*, vol. 2, pp. 411–27.

Barnett, H. and Morse C. (1963) *Scarcity and growth: The economics of natural resource availability.* Johns Hopkins Press: Baltimore, MD.

Beckerman, W. (1972) Economists, scientists, and environmental catastrophe, *Oxford Economic Papers*, vol. 24, pp. 327–44.

Boeing (2012) *Current market outlook 2012–2031*, www.boeing.com/commercial/cmo, accessed 23 October 2012.

Boulding, K.E. (1966) The economics of the coming spaceship earth. In Jarrett, H. (ed.) *Environmental quality in a growing economy.* John Hopkins University and Resources for the Future: Baltimore, MD, pp. 3–14.

Cabrini, L. (2012) Tourism in the UN green economy report, in UNWTO High-level Regional Conference on Green Tourism, Chiang Mai, Thailand, 2012, asiapacific.unwto.org/sites/all/files/.../2012may_chiangmai_lc_0.pdf, accessed 14 November 2012.

Carson, R. (1962). *Silent spring.* Houghton Mifflin Harcourt: New York.

Cole, H.D.S., Freeman, C., Jahoda, M. and Pavitt, K.L.R. (eds) (1973) *Thinking about the future: A critique of the limits to growth.* Chatto & Windus: London.

Czech, B. (2006) If Rome is burning, why are we fiddling? *Conservation Biology*, vol. 20, pp. 1563–5.

Daly, H.E. (1972) In defense of a steady-state economy, *American Journal of Agricultural Economics*, vol. 54, pp. 9 45–54.

Daly, H.E. (1991) *Steady-state economics*, (2nd edn). Island Press: Washington, DC.

Daly, H.E. (1996) *Beyond growth*. Beacon Press: Boston, MA.

Daily, G.C. and Ehrlich, P.R. (1992) Population, sustainability, and earth's carrying capacity, *BioScience*, vol. 42, pp. 761–71.

Dryzek, J.S. (1997) *The politics of the earth*. Oxford University Press: New York.

Ehrlich, P. (1968) *The population bomb*. Ballantine Books: New York.

Ekins, P. (1993) 'Limits to growth' and 'sustainable development': Grappling with ecological realities, *Ecological Economics*, vol. 8, pp. 269–88.

Elliott, L., Hines, C., Juniper, T., Leggett, J., Lucas, C., Murphy, R., Pettifor, A., Secrett, C., and Simms, A. (2008) *Green New Deal. Joined-up policies to solve the triple crunch of the credit crisis, climate change and high oil prices*. The first report of the Green New Deal Group. New Economics Foundation: London.

Ewing, B., Moore, D., Goldfinger, S., Oursler, A., Reed, A. and Wackernagel, M. (2010) *The ecological footprint atlas 2010*. Global Footprint Network: Oakland, CA.

Funtowicz, S. and Ravetz, J. (1990) Post-normal science: A new science for new times, *Scientific European*, vol. 169, pp. 20–22.

Galtung, J. (1990) The green movement: A socio-historical explanation. In Albrow, M. and King, E. (eds) *Globalization, knowledge and society: Readings from international sociology*. Sage: London, pp. 235–50.

Georgescu-Roegen, N. (1971) *The entropy law and the economic process*. Cambridge Harvard University Press: Cambridge, MA.

Georgescu-Roegen, N. (1977) The steady state and ecological salvation: A thermodynamic analysis, *Bioscience*, vol. 27, pp. 266–70.

Gössling, S. and Hall, C.M. (eds) (2006) *Tourism and global environmental change*. Routledge: London.

Gössling, S., Scott, D. and Hall, C.M. (2013) Challenges of tourism in a low-carbon economy, *WIRES Climate Change*, vol. 4, pp. 525–38.

Hall, C.M. (2009) Degrowing tourism: décroissance, sustainable consumption and steady-state tourism, *Anatolia*, vol. 20, pp. 46–61.

Hall C.M. (2010) Changing paradigms and global change: From sustainable to steady-state tourism, *Tourism Recreation Research*, vol. 35, pp. 131–45.

Hall, C.M. (2011a) Policy learning and policy failure in sustainable tourism governance: From first and second to third order change? *Journal of Sustainable Tourism*, vol. 19, pp. 649–71.

Hall, C.M. (2011b) A typology of governance and its implications for tourism policy analysis, *Journal of Sustainable Tourism*, vol. 19, pp. 437–57.

Hall, C.M. (2013a) Green growth and tourism for a sustainable future: 'We just need to put the right policies in place', or, the lunatics have taken over the asylum, presented at *International Critical Tourism Studies Conference V*, Sarajevo, Bosnia & Herzegovina, 26 June.

Hall, C.M. (2013b) Framing behavioural approaches to understanding and governing sustainable tourism consumption: Beyond neoliberalism, 'nudging' and 'green growth'? *Journal of Sustainable Tourism*, vol. 21, pp. 1091–109.

Hall, C.M. (2013c) Environmental trends: Will tourism respond to environmental and energy pressures? 12th European Tourism Forum – a Force for Economic Growth, Social Change and Welfare 17–18 October, The Palace of the Grand Dukes of Lithuania, Vilnius, Lithuania.

Hall, C.M. (2014) *Tourism and social marketing*. Routledge: Abingdon.

Hall, C.M. and Lew, A. (2009) *Understanding and managing tourism impacts: An integrated approach*. Routledge: London.

Hall, C.M., Scott, D. and Gössling, S. (2013) The primacy of climate change for sustainable international tourism, *Sustainable Development*, vol. 21, no. 2, pp. 112–21.

Henderson, H. with Seth, S. (2006) *Ethical markets: Growing the green economy*. Chelsea Green Publishing: White River Junction.

Hoffmann, U. (2011) Some reflections on climate change, green growth illusions and development space, UNCTAD Discussion Paper 205. UNCTAD: Geneva.

IEA (2009) *Transport, Energy and CO₂: Moving towards sustainability*. IEA: Paris.

IPCC (2007a) *Climate change 2007: Impacts, adaptation and vulnerability*, Contribution of Working Group II to the Fourth Assessment Report. Cambridge University Press: Cambridge.

IPCC (2007b) *Climate change 2007: The physical science basis*, Contribution of Working Group I to the Fourth Assessment Report. Cambridge University Press: Cambridge.

Jackson, T. (2009) *Prosperity without growth*. Earthscan: London.

Jacobs, M. (1991) *The green economy: Environment, sustainable development and the politics of the future*. Pluto Press: London.

Jenkins, J., Nordhaus, T. and Shellenberger, M. (2011) *Energy emergence: Rebound and backfire as emergent phenomena*. Breakthrough Institute; Oakland, CA.

Kerschner, C. (2010) Economic de-growth vs steady-state economy, *Journal of Cleaner Production*, vol. 18, pp. 544–51.

Khor, M. (2011) Risks and uses of the green economy concept of sustainable development, poverty and equity. Research Paper No. 40, South Centre: Geneva.

Latouche, S. (2009) *Farewell to growth*. Polity Press: Cambridge.

Lecomber, R. (1975) *Economic growth versus the environment*. Macmillan: London.

Marzouki, M., Froger, G. and Ballet, J. (2012) Ecotourism versus mass tourism: A comparison of environmental impacts based on ecological footprint analysis, *Sustainability*, vol. 4, pp. 123–40.

Meadows, D.H., Meadows, D.L., Randers, J. and Behrens, W.W. (1972) *Limits to growth: A report for the Club of Rome's project on the predicament of mankind*. Universe Books: New York.

Milani, B. (2000) *Designing the green economy: The postindustrial alternative to corporate globalization*. Rowman & Littlefield: Lanham, MD.

Miles, I. (1985) The new post-industrial state, *Futures*, vol. 17, pp. 588–617.

Mishan, E.J. (1967) *The costs of economic growth*. Staples Press: London.

Odum, H.T. (1971) *Environment, power and society*. Wiley: New York.

Patridge, M. (1987) Building a sustainable green economy: Ethical investment, ethical work. In Hutton, A. (ed.) *Green politics in Australia*. Angus and Robertson: Sydney.

Patterson, T.M. (2005) The ecological economics of sustainable tourism: Local versus global ecological footprints in Val Di Merse, Italy, unpublished PhD, University of Maryland.

Pearce, D.W., Markandya, A. and Barbier, E.B. (eds) (1989) *Blueprint for a green economy*. Earthscan: London.

Peeters, P. and Landré, M. (2011) The emerging global tourism geography: An environmental sustainability perspective, *Sustainability*, vol. 4, pp. 42–71.

Perez-Carmona, A. (2012) Growth: A discussion of the margins of economic and ecological thought. In Meuleman, L. (ed.) *Transgovernance: Advancing sustainable governance*. Springer: Dortrecht, pp. 83–161.

Pigou, A.C. (1943) The classical stationary state, *The Economic Journal*, vol. 53, pp. 343–51.

Polimeni, J.M., Mayumi, K., Giampietro, M. and Alcott, B. (eds) (2008) *The Jevons Paradox and the myth of resource efficiency improvements*. Earthscan: London.

Pollin, R., Garrett-Peltier, H., Heintz, J. and Scharber, H. (2008) *Green recovery: A program to create good jobs and start building a low-carbon economy*. Prepared under commission with the Center for American Progress. Political Economy Research Institute, University of Massachusetts, Amherst, MA.

Rogelj, J., Hare, W., Lowe, J., van Vuuren, D.P., Riahi, K., Matthews, B., Hanaoka, T., Jiang, K. and Meinshausen, M. (2011) Emission pathways consistent with 2°C global temperature limit, *Nature Climate Change*, vol. 1, pp. 413–18.

Santarius, T. (2012) *Green growth unravelled: How rebound effects baffle sustainability targets when the economy keeps growing.* Wuppertal Institute for Climate, Environment and Energy: Berlin.

Scott, D., Peeters, P. and Gössling, S. (2010) Can tourism deliver its 'aspirational' emission reduction targets? *Journal of Sustainable Tourism,* vol. 18, pp. 393–408.

Seyfang, G. (2009) *The new economics of sustainable consumption: Seeds of change.* Palgrave Macmillan: London.

Simms, A. (2008) The poverty myth, *New Scientist,* 15 October, vol. 200 no. 2678, p. 49.

Sorrell, S. (2007) *The rebound effect: an assessment of the evidence for economy-wide energy savings from improved energy efficiency.* UK Energy Research Centre: London.

Speth, G. (1980) The Global 2000 Report to the President, *Boston College Environmental Affairs Law Review,* vol. 8, pp. 695–703.

Steiner, A. and Sukhdev, P. (2010) Foreword. In Barbier, E. *Global green new deal: Rethinking the economic recovery.* Cambridge University Press: Cambridge, pp. xiii–xv.

Stern, N. (2007) *The economics of climate change: The Stern review.* Cambridge University Press: Cambridge.

UNEP (2008) Global Green New Deal: Environmentally-focused investment historic opportunity for 21st century prosperity and job generation. UNEP launches green economy initiative to get the global markets back to work. London/Nairobi, 22 October, www.unep.org/Documents. Multilingual/Default.asp?DocumentID=548&ArticleID=5957, accessed 1 April 2013.

UNEP (2009a) *Global green new deal.* Policy brief. UNEP: Geneva.

UNEP (2009b) *Towards sustainable production and use of resources: Assessing biofuels.* UNEP: Paris.

UNEP (2011a) *Towards a green economy: Pathways to sustainable development and poverty eradication.* UNEP: Nairobi.

UNEP (2011b) *Towards a green economy: Pathways to sustainable development andpoverty eradication – a synthesis for policy makers.* UNEP: Nairobi.

UNWTO, UNEP and WMO (2008) *Climate change and tourism: Responding to global challenges.* UNWTO: Madrid.

Vera-Morales, M. and Schäfer, A. (2009) *Final report: Fuel-cycle assessment of alternative aviation fuels.* Institute for Aviation and the Environment: Cambridge.

Vermeulen, S.J. (2009) *Sustainable consumption: A fairer deal for poor consumers.* Environment and Poverty Times, No. 6, September. UNEP and GRID: Arendal, Norway.

WCED (1987) *Our common future* [The Brundtland Report]. Oxford University Press: Oxford.

WEF (2009) *Towards a low carbon travel & tourism sector.* World Economic Forum: Davos, Switzerland.

WTTC (2009) *Leading the Challenge,* www.wttc.org/bin/pdf/original.pdffile/climatechangefinal. pdf, accessed 1 July 2011.

Zapata, M.J, Hall, C.M., Lindo, P. and Vanderschaeghen, M. (2011) Can community-based tourism contribute to development and poverty alleviation? *Current Issues in Tourism,* vol. 14, pp. 725–49.

INDEX

Lightning Source UK Ltd.
Milton Keynes UK
UKHW02f0907110218
317666UK00002B/165/P